INTRODUCTION TO BUSINESS

2nd Edition

H. James Williams, Ph.D., C.P.A., C.M.A., J.D., L.L.M.
Seidman College of Business
Grand Valley State University
Grand Rapids, MI

Marvelle S. Colby, D.P.A.
Selig Alcon, M.B.A.

Contributing Editor
Kipling M. Pirkle, Ph.D.
Williams School of Commerce, Economics, and Politics
Washington and Lee University
Lexington, VA

Collins
An Imprint of HarperCollins*Publishers*

INTRODUCTION TO BUSINESS. Copyright © 1992, 2007 by HarperCollins Publishers.

All rights reserved. Printed in the United States. No part of this book may be used or reproduced in any manner whatsoever without written permission except in the case of brief quotations embodied in critical articles and reviews. For information, address HarperCollins Publishers, 10 East 53rd Street, New York, NY 10022.

An American BookWorks Corporation Production

HarperCollins books may be purchased for education, business, or sales promotional use. For information, please write: Special Markets Department, HarperCollins Publishers, 10 East 53rd Street, New York, NY 10022.

Library of Congress Cataloging-in-Publication Data

Williams, H. James.
Introduction to business / H. James Williams, Marvelle S. Colby, Selig Alcon ; contributing editor, Kipling M. Pirkle. – 2nd ed.
    p. cm. – (Collins college outlines)
Includes bibliographical references.
ISBN: 978-0-06-088149-8
ISBN-10: 0-06-088149-6
  1. Business. 2. Industrial management. I. Colby, Marvelle S. II. Alcon, Selig. III. Pirkle, Kipling M. IV. Title

HF1008.W55 2006
650—dc22   2006053088

---

07 08 09 10 11 CW 10 9 8 7 6 5 4 3 2 1

Contents

Preface iv

Part 1: The Foundations of Business in the Global Economy 1
Chapter 1 Understanding Basic Economics 3
Chapter 2 The Role of Government 17
Chapter 3 Business Law and Ethics 27
Chapter 4 Business Sustainability: Economic, Environmental, and Social Responsibilities 40
Chapter 5 The Global Marketplace 53

Part 2: Business Formation and Structure **65**
Chapter 6 The Legal Forms of Business 67
Chapter 7 Small Business, Entrepreneurship, and Franchising 79
Chapter 8 Organizational Structure 87
Chapter 9 Management Fundamentals 95

Part 3: Managing Personnel and Production **109**
Chapter 10 Human Resources Management 111
Chapter 11 Labor-Management Relations 120
Chapter 12 Producing Goods and Services 131

Part 4: Marketing Management **145**
Chapter 13 The Marketing Concept 147
Chapter 14 Product and Pricing Strategies 157
Chapter 15 Supply Chains, Channels of Distribution, and Logistics 171
Chapter 16 Promotional Strategy 186

Part 5: Management Tools **199**
Chapter 17 Management Information and Statistical Analysis 201
Chapter 18 Accounting and Financial Statements 213

Part 6: Financial Management **229**
Chapter 19 Money, Banking, and Credit 231
Chapter 20 Financial Strategies: Short- and Long-Term Financing 243
Chapter 21 Risk Management and Insurance 250
Chapter 22 The Securities Markets 262

Part 7: The Challenge of the Future **277**
Chapter 23 Business Careers 279

Glossary 291
Index 315

Part 1: The Foundations of Business in the Global Economy

CHAPTER 1

Understanding Basic Economics

Economics is the study of rational human behavior in trying to meet basic wants and needs. This is especially important because humans live in an environment of limited resources to fulfill those wants and needs. The better you understand economics the better you will be able to satisfy those basic wants and needs. In the final analysis, economics focuses on how individuals and nations make choices, in a world of limited resources, to meet basic wants and needs. Business is one important component of economics.

■ WHAT IS "BUSINESS"?

A business is an organized effort of individuals to produce and sell goods and services for a profit. Businesses vary in size, as measured by number of employees or by sales volume. Large companies such as ExxonMobil and General Motors count their employees in the hundred thousands and their sales revenues in the billions. But most (98 percent) of the businesses in the United States are small businesses—independently owned and operated and having fewer than twenty employees. The key people responsible for creating businesses, either as a result of their original ideas or willingness to bear the inherent risks—or both—are called entrepreneurs.

All businesses, whether they employ one person working at home, 100 working in a retail store, 10,000 working in a plant or factory, or 100,000 working in branch offices nationwide, share the same basic definition and are generally organized for the same primary purpose: to earn profits. Profit is the money that remains after the costs of a business (expenses and taxes) are subtracted from the revenue received from the sales of goods and services.

Goods and Services

The source of a business's revenues and, therefore, of its profits, is its goods and services. Goods are tangible items; that is, products such as automobiles, shoes, iPods, computers, and cellular phones. Services are intangible items, such as the professional advice and assistance provided by lawyers, doctors, electricians, accountants, and hairdressers. Consumers and businesses will buy only those goods and services they need or want. Therefore, to be successful, businesses must provide goods and services that satisfy consumers' and businesses' needs and wants. Consumers need shoes and will buy shoes. Consumers may not need expensive high-tech sports shoes, but they may purchase them if they want them. In the same way, businesses need manufacturing and other materials to produce goods and services.. Thus, identifying consumer and business needs and wants are key factors in business success.

Factors of Production

All goods and services are produced from five specific resources: land, labor, capital, information resources, and entrepreneurs. These resources, known as the factors of production, are the basic elements a business uses to produce goods and services.

Land

Land includes not only real estate but the resources associated with land—water, minerals, and timber.

Labor

Labor, sometimes called human resources, refers to the mental and physical skills and abilities of employees. Labor includes all the employees, from top-level executives to truck drivers, who produce and distribute the goods and services a business sells.

Capital

All businesses require capital (money) to operate. Businesses need capital to buy buildings, machinery, and tools, all of which are also considered capital. In addition, they need capital to hire labor, distribute finished products, and so on.

Information Resources

Information resources supply the facts, intelligence, and knowledge needed to manage and operate a business. Because information resources enable managers to control and to effectively use all other resources, its value as a factor of production has increased greatly in recent years. In fact, the era in which we find ourselves is often referred to as the Information Age, emphasizing the importance of information access, processing, and utilization.

Entrepreneurs

Entrepreneurs are the risk-takers who create businesses; the persons who assemble all the other factors of production in an effort to start and operate a business and to make a profit. Entrepreneurs have vision. Recognizing consumers' needs and wants for certain goods and services, they risk their time and financial resources, gather capital, and apply their information resources to create and manage a business enterprise.

■ AVAILABILITY OF RESOURCES

Economics is the study of how goods and services are produced, distributed, and consumed. In any society, the resources that are available are limited, and economics is concerned with (1) how one segment of society—that is, businesses—uses those limited resources to create and distribute goods and services; and (2) how the other segment of society—consumers, which includes individuals and other organizations, including other businesses—consume those goods and services.

Economics can be partitioned into two fields: macroeconomics and microeconomics. Macroeconomics addresses the broader, big picture of the behavior of the nation's economy. Microeconomics has a narrower focus; it studies the behavior of individual organizations or people in particular markets. Business is applied economics. Moreover, because resources are limited, businesses must consider factors related to resource limitations, including scarcity and opportunity cost.

Scarcity

All resources, those related to humans as well as those related to nature, are limited in some ways. Here are several examples: (1) skilled labor may not be plentiful in a particular location; (2) capital is not free; (3) some natural resources, such as timber, are renewable, but others, such as oil, are nonrenewable. The scarcity of resources forces society, including businesses, to make choices.

Opportunity Cost

Opportunity cost is the foregone value of the next best alternative use of a resource. For example, one important opportunity cost of your attending college is the money you could otherwise earn if attending college prevented you from working full-time. You cannot receive the wages or salary (e.g., $12,000) you could earn from the alternative use of selling your services to an employer if you were not in college. Consequently, the total cost of your education is the actual cost (tuition, fees, and room and board), plus the $12,000 opportunity cost. Similarly, if you spend your last $100 dollars on an outfit, you cannot spend that $100 on another desirable product, say a pair of $100 shoes. The opportunity cost of purchasing the outfit is the "value" (presumed to be at least $100) you would place on owning the pair of shoes. The total cost of purchasing the outfit is, then, $200 ($100 actual purchase price plus the $100 opportunity cost). Note that every decision includes an opportunity cost component, yet few decision-makers explicitly consider the opportunity cost when considering the total cost of a purchase.

A business that purchases, for instance, new production-line equipment instead of hiring additional employees, must consider the opportunity cost (i.e., the value of that alternative use for that particular resource). Consequently, either explicitly or implicitly, opportunity cost shapes every decision.

■ ECONOMIC SYSTEMS

Every society must answer these three economic questions.

1. **What will be produced?** What goods and services will be produced, and in what quantity will each be produced?
2. **How will these goods and services be produced?** Who will produce these goods and services, and which resources will be used to produce them?
3. **For whom will these goods and services be produced?** Who gets what?

How a society answers these economic questions determines its economic system—that is, its methods for distributing resources to meet the needs of its people. Keep in mind that an economic system includes the production and distribution of goods and services, while a political system, for example, comprises the organization of government, ideology, conduct of public affairs, and the pursuit of national interests.

Three economic systems worth noting are the market economy, the planned economy, and the mixed economy.

- In a **market economy**, individuals control all or most of the factors of production and make all or most of the production decisions. The market economy (capitalism) is also called the free-market or free-enterprise system.
- In a **planned economy** (e.g., a communist system), the government controls all or most of the factors of production and makes all or most production decisions.
- In a **mixed economy** (e.g., a socialist system), as its name suggests, the system shares some of the features of both the market and planned economies.

Most countries do not rigidly follow one economic system but, rather, tend to mix to varying degrees some features of communism, socialism, and capitalism. For example, Britain, France, India, and other free-enterprise societies incorporate a degree of socialism. Most of the remaining communist societies (e.g., China) have incorporated elements of free-enterprise systems into their economies.

Capitalism

Capitalism is a market economy. It relies on free markets, not on government, to determine what, how, and for whom goods and services will be produced. In a market economy, businesses are owned by individuals and are controlled by owners or by managers who are accountable to the owners. The profits flow to the owners and investors. Market economies place a high premium on entrepreneurship. The economy is driven by the profit motive, the desire to maximize profits.

Socialism

In a socialist economy, the government controls key industries such as transportation, communications, banking, utilities, and steel as well as major natural resources. Private ownership of businesses that are not in vital industries is permitted to varying degrees, depending on the country. The government establishes national goals for utilizing the country's resources. Socialist countries place a high priority on achieving an equitable distribution of income and on providing a high level of social and medical services. The public welfare programs underwritten by socialist countries such as Sweden are financed by high taxes. In the last twenty years many socialist countries have encouraged privatization, which is the selling of government-controlled industries to private investors.

Communism

Communism is both a political and an economic system based on the doctrines of Karl Marx, whose goal was to achieve a more equitable distribution of wealth than that found in capitalist systems. Communist governments control economic decisions through their centralized state planning committees, which set, for example, wages and prices. Communist economic systems emphasize producing capital goods such as machinery rather than consumer goods. Countries that remain communist today include China, North Korea, and Cuba.

■ ECONOMIC FORCES

A number of forces and conditions interact to determine the price of goods and services in the market. The theory of supply, demand, and equilibrium helps explain the interaction of these forces and their effects on the economy.

Supply

Economists define supply as the amount of output of a good or service that producers are willing and able to make available to the market at a given price at a given time. The law of supply states that producers are willing to produce and offer for sale more goods at a higher price than at a lower price.

Demand

Demand is the willingness of purchasers to buy specific quantities of a good or service at a given price at a given time. The law of demand states that people will buy more of a product at a lower price than at a higher price.

Equilibrium

According to the laws of supply and demand, the lower the price, the more consumers will want to buy, but the less producers will be willing to supply. If the price is so low that producers cannot make a sufficient profit, some suppliers will not produce, and the supply will drop. The satisfaction of both the buyer and the seller will balance at some point called the equilibrium. At the point of equilibrium, demand (the number of units buyers are willing to buy at a given price) equals supply (the number of units the producer is willing to produce at that price). The point of equilibrium, in theory, is the market price.

If the supply is greater than the demand, there is a surplus, and the price will fall. If the supply is less than the demand, there is a shortage, and the price will rise. It is important to note that supply and demand work simultaneously. As the price of a product goes up, suppliers produce more, and at the same time, consumers buy less. As the price goes down, suppliers produce less, and consumers then demand more.

■ COMPETITION

Competition describes the degree of rivalry among businesses for sales to potential customers. At the same time, it describes the constant effort on the part of a business to operate efficiently so as to keep its costs low, develop new and improved products, and make a profit. The intensity of competition varies from one industry to another. Economists identify four basic degrees of competition: pure competition, monopoly, monopolistic competition, and oligopoly.

Pure Competition

Pure competition describes a situation in which a large number of firms are producing identical, or nearly identical, products. Because consumers consider the product identical from company to company and because both consumers and producers know the price in the marketplace, no one firm has the power to affect the price. As a result, the price is set by supply and demand. In pure competition situations, producers can enter or leave the industry very easily. Except for the fact that it enjoys government price supports, the agricultural industry is a good example of pure competition. Corn from one farm is the same as corn from another farm, and both producers and buyers are aware of the market price.

Monopoly

A company has a pure monopoly when it is the only producer in a market, an industry, or an area. Because of its absolute control, the company can set prices as it wishes and prevent other companies from competing. The company's only constraint on pricing is how much consumer demand will fall as prices rise. Monopolies are discouraged by law with one exception: utility companies such as water and electric companies enjoy monopolies. However, such natural monopolies, as they are known, are regulated by the government to prevent exploitation of society.

Monopolistic Competition

Monopolistic competition exists when (1) there are many buyers and few sellers, and (2) the sellers' products appear at least slightly different from those of their competitors. In such situations, product differentiation and brand names give sellers some control over the price. The market for light bulbs is an example of monopolistic competition.

Oligopoly

In an oligopoly, a small number of very large firms has the power to influence the price of the firms' products. Would-be competitors are restricted from entering the market because doing so requires huge amounts of capital. The automobile, steel, and aircraft manufacturing industries are examples of oligopolies. The actions of one firm in an oligopoly are usually copied by the other firms. For example, when one steel company lowers its prices, the others are usually forced to lower their prices. As another example, when one automobile manufacturer offers a rebate program, the other automakers also offer rebate programs. Because substantial price reductions would adversely affect profits, the competition is usually based on product differentiation.

■THE FREE-ENTERPRISE SYSTEM

The American economy thrives on competition. It is based on a system of voluntary association and exchange and is called a free-enterprise or a free-market system. The voluntary nature of association and exchange in the marketplace depends on individuals having the freedom and power to make their own choices, both in what they produce and what they buy.

Basic Freedoms

The free-enterprise system, as its name implies, offers a number of freedoms, including the freedom of choice, the freedom to own property, the freedom to earn a profit, and the freedom to go out of business. Freedom of choice is every individual's right to choose his or her occupation and place of employment. Freedom to own property permits a business or an individual to buy or sell land, machines, or buildings and to use these assets to generate income. Freedom to earn a profit allows individuals (1) to decide what to make, how to make it, and how to sell it; and (2) to keep the profits that result from their risk-taking. The freedom to go out of business cannot be restricted by the government. If a business cannot make a profit, the government cannot prevent it from declaring bankruptcy. Thus, businesses have free exit from the market. Land and material resources earn rent. Labor earns wages. Capital earns interest. Entrepreneurs earn profits.

Entrepreneurs enjoy a special place in the business world. Although lenders receive interest and stockholders receive dividends, only entrepreneurs receive profits. Profit is the difference between the selling price of a good or service and the cost of producing and marketing that good or service. For example, if all the costs of producing and marketing a toy total $2.50 and the manufacturer sells that toy for $3.15, the profit is $0.65 for each toy. Profits are entrepreneurs' rewards for their risks, their work, and their investment of time and money—in other words, for their success in creating and operating a business.

■THE DEVELOPMENT OF THE AMERICAN ECONOMIC SYSTEM

Originally, America's economy was agricultural and land-based. Then, as a result of the Industrial Revolution, the American economy began to rely heavily on industry. In recent years, the American economy has changed once again; it is now a service-oriented, information-based economy. The origins of the American economic system help explain these transitions.

The Colonial Era

European kings financed the first settlements in America. Their goal was to harvest the raw materials of this vast new continent abounding with natural resources. But the settlers had goals of their own as well as their own views of how the raw materials around them should be put to use. Because many had fled oppressive governments, settlers resisted control and, instead, sought freedom, liberty, and independence in all things religious and political. The richness of their surroundings offered them great opportunities to achieve their goals.

Colonial Values

Almost all the early settlers lived on farms. Each family member contributed to the struggle for survival and shared in the tasks of obtaining food, shelter, and clothing. Their lifestyles reinforced the belief that hard work, resourcefulness, courage, independence, and self-reliance were the keys to success. These values form the foundation of the American free-enterprise system and still support that structure today.

Bartering

Colonists relied on bartering; that is, exchanging goods and services for others' goods and services, a system that did not require money. As colonial society expanded, colonial trade increased. Settlers began to open small individual enterprises—sole proprietorships (i.e., businesses owned by one person), and then small partnerships (i.e., businesses owned jointly by two or more persons). By the 1700s, the colonial business world included shipbuilding, fishing, lumber, fur trading, and rum production for export to Britain (with tax and tariff policies heavily favoring Britain). Some entrepreneurial colonists reaped profits from the "domestic system." Under this system, entrepreneurs (by definition, enterprising individuals) distributed raw materials to persons who worked in their homes to process the materials into finished goods, which the entrepreneurs then sold at a profit.

Politics and Economics

In 1776, the United States gained its independence. Its political system, developed by the Founding Fathers, was democratic, based on freedom from government oppression, private ownership of resources, and free enterprise. In 1776 in Scotland, Adam Smith published *The Wealth of Nations,* which set forth his theory of laissez-faire, an economic system that called for private ownership of property, free entry into markets, and an absence of government intervention. Clearly, America's political system and Smith's economic system were compatible and complementary, and their merging signaled the beginning of remarkable growth in the American economy.

The Growth of Trade

Beginning around the time of the Revolutionary War, domestic trade grew. Colonists began producing a wider variety of goods for domestic consumption and built roads to transport those goods. At the same time, export trade also flourished. While European countries were at war between 1793 and 1812, neutral America found ready markets for its exports. America's export trade to Europe thrived until near the end of this period. English and French trade restrictions, embargoes, and finally, America's war with England in 1812 all contributed to the decline of the export trade to Europe and the resulting emphasis on and growth of domestic trade.

The Industrial Revolution

The Industrial Revolution refers to a series of events and inventions that dramatically changed the way people worked, moved their workplace, improved their work efficiency, and raised their standards of living.

Key Events

The first key event occurred around 1750 in England as a result of Sir Richard Arkwright's development of a water-powered spinning machine to replace the hand-operated spinning wheel. In the United States, the effects were felt later, early in the nineteenth century, when textile mills began using Arkwright's invention to spin cotton.

As the new machinery gained in use, the workplace shifted from the home to the textile mills and factories where all the materials, machinery, and workers were assembled. At the same time, the factories began dividing manufacturing procedures into separate tasks, each task assigned to different workers. This division of labor, known as specialization, not only changed the way people worked, but also improved their productivity. Thus, the Industrial Revolution was characterized by these three key changes: (1) the replacement of human labor with newly invented machines (mechanization); (2) a shifting of the workplace from home to factory; and (3) the division of labor into smaller work tasks (specialization).

Many early factories were in New England, where labor, waterpower, and capital were available. The new principles worked so well that they spread from textiles to other products and from New England to other parts of the growing nation. More inventions followed, increasing the mechanization of work. Eli Whitney's cotton gin, Elias Howe's sewing machine, and John Deere's and Cyrus McCormick's farm machinery all increased the mechanization of work, widened the variety of American products, and contributed to economic expansion.

Economic Expansion

A number of key factors contributed to the growth and success of American industry. The push westward greatly expanded the market for American goods. During the mid-1800s, railroad systems grew dramatically, connecting markets throughout the country as they transported increasing amounts of factory-produced goods. The steam engine further opened river transportation by steamboat. Waves of immigrants provided a continuous source of hard-working, inexpensive labor and at the same time increased the number of consumers of the country's goods. Also contributing to the expansion were the inventions of Thomas Edison, Alexander Graham Bell, and others, along with the buildup of industrial empires by Andrew Carnegie (steel), John D. Rockefeller (oil), Gail Borden (dairy products), Frederick Weyerhaeuser (lumber), and the railroad barons.

Government Regulation

Until shortly after the Civil War, laissez-faire had consistently been the federal government's policy toward business. After the Civil War, for the first time the federal government departed from its laissez-faire attitude and enacted antitrust laws to curb the power of the trusts (the groups that controlled vast industrial empires) and to promote a free-market economy. Government regulation of business was born.

During the Great Depression (1929–1939), the government once again regulated economic affairs in an effort to help the nation rebound from a number of problems that affected its economy: bank failures, the stock market crash, business scandals, an extremely severe drought that turned Midwestern states into a dust bowl, and a worldwide economic crisis. As the situation worsened and continued over a longer period, the government and the people felt the need for government intervention.

After Franklin Roosevelt's election as president in 1932, and under his leadership, Congress enacted a number of laws regulating the securities markets, labor, banking, and business. Economic conditions improved. Then, in 1939, as the country was emerging from the depression, World War II began. In order to control, plan, and organize the war effort, every sector of the economy was subject to government controls.

Deregulation

From the first, reaction to government regulation has never been neutral. There are strong opponents to regulation, especially from the business community, and some presidents have taken steps toward deregulation. In 1977, for example, President Jimmy Carter began the deregulation of the transportation and banking industries. His successor, President Ronald Reagan, greatly accelerated and expanded the deregulation process. More recently, telecommunications and energy transmission have been deregulated. Deregulation has had a number of unintended consequences; for example, the collapse of the savings and loan industry. The debate on regulation versus deregulation continues.

The New Economy

Since the 1970s, the American economy has undergone a number of shocking changes. Smokestack industries—shipbuilding, coal, and steel—declined. Oil crises occurred. Inflation and a series of recessions followed. Foreign-made electronics and automobiles became increasingly competitive with American-made products, in some cases displacing them altogether. At the same time, American scientific and technological power combined to offset these economic shocks. Research in both product development and marketing techniques expanded, and two sectors grew rapidly: the service sector and the information sector.

The Service Sector

Businesses in the service sector do not produce goods; they provide intangible professional assistance, advice, and other forms of help. The service sector covers all the professions (doctors, lawyers, and accountants, for example), restaurants, banks, airlines, retailers, health care, education, and government. A growing number of persons are engaged in producing services rather than goods.

The Information Sector

The information sector is a specialized (and a very fast-growing) part of the service sector. The information sector includes persons employed in the computing and systems development areas. All businesses highly value any information that improves production and distribution and increases efficiency and profitability. Thus the accumulation, manipulation, and dissemination of customer credit histories, financial data, sales statistics, and similar information is essential to business, and these tasks fall to the information sector. The information sector now claims a substantial segment of the labor market.

Globalization

All businesses today, American and others, operate in a global economy. American trade with foreign countries has increased tremendously. American businesses have expanded their trade relations with traditional partners such as the United Kingdom and Japan; at the same time, American trade has spread to new partners, for example, the People's Republic of China, India, and Eastern European countries. The result is that American companies compete in foreign markets, trade regularly with foreign companies (often with critical foreign supply chains), and, in many instances, operate production facilities in foreign countries. And the reverse is also true: Foreign-based (for example, Japanese, German, and Korean) businesses actively compete in American markets with products such as automobiles, electronic goods, and services.

The growth of foreign markets and competition, most notably those in China and India, is having a tremendous impact on the manner in which companies conduct business all over the globe. In fact, the advent of outsourcing (the contracting out of previously inside activities and services to persons and companies outside the business to realize efficiencies and cost-savings) and off-shoring (the shifting of production to sites outside the United States), which helped place China and India on the economic map, have created quite a debate in the United States and abroad as to whether economic globalization is a good or an evil. Many, however, suggest that globalization is a good thing, and that outsourcing and off-shoring are simple manifestations of the economic theory of comparative advantage, which holds that everyone gains when each country specializes in what it does best (i.e., engages in those activities in which it has a comparative advantage over the rest of the world).

■ ECONOMIC GOALS AND PERFORMANCE

Several performance indicators provide key methods for measuring how well an economy has achieved its goals and how much it has grown.

Economic Goals

Nearly all economic systems share the same goals: stability, full employment, and growth.

Stability

Stability is a condition in which the relationship among money, goods and services, and labor remains relatively constant. A major threat to stability is inflation (especially when it manifests itself in rising prices). Other threats are recession, which decreases employment, income, and production, and depression, which is a severe, prolonged recession characterized by high unemployment.

Full Employment

Full employment, meaning that everyone who wishes to work has a job, is an ideal, but never a reality. Realistically, even in the best of times, some workers will be unemployed for a variety of reasons.

- **Frictional unemployment** describes workers who have left one job but have not yet found another.
- **Seasonal unemployment** includes all seasonal workers who are unemployed due to the seasonality of their work (e.g., those employed in agriculture and other seasonal industries).
- **Structural unemployment** identifies unemployment precipitated by the very makeup of the economy. Demand may be down across the economy for certain goods or services. Similarly, unemployed persons may not possess skills necessary for the existing economy.
- **Cyclical unemployment** includes workers who are temporarily unemployed due to a downturn in business activity.

Thus, the realistic goal is not full employment but minimal unemployment. Indeed, the phrase "full employment" now implies as much as 5 percent unemployment.

Measuring Growth

Growth is an increase in the amount of goods and services produced by the total economy in a given period, in comparison with another period. With specific measurement tools, businesspeople can evaluate economic performance. Among the most useful economic measurement tools are gross domestic product, productivity rate, the balance of trade, economic growth, inflation or deflation, and federal deficits. These are discussed in the following sections.

Gross Domestic Product

For more than 50 years (approximately 1941 though 1992), gross national product (GNP) was the preferred measure of the country's economic growth. However, due to economic globalization, goods and services as well as capital, labor, and information, flow much more easily and steadily across borders. As a result, gross domestic product (GDP) has now supplanted GNP as the measure of choice. The difference between the two is significant.

- GNP measures the total market value of all goods and services produced by U.S. companies, whether inside or outside the country. GDP, on the other hand, measures the total market value of all goods and services produced in the United States, irrespective of the source.
- GDP includes profits earned by foreign companies inside the United States, but excludes profits earned by U.S. companies abroad. Ultimately, then, the focus has turned to the economic activity that occurs within the borders of the United States.

Productivity Rate

The productivity rate measures efficiency by comparing how much is produced with the resources consumed in the process. For example, if Company A uses 2,000 pounds of raw materials to produce a certain product and Company B produces the same product with only 1,850 pounds of raw materials, Company B has a higher productivity rate. Total productivity includes all inputs necessary to produce a certain amount of products: Total productivity = Specified output/Total inputs.

Balance of Trade

Each country exports goods, for which it receives money, and imports goods, for which it pays money. The phrase "balance of trade" refers to a country's total exports minus its total imports. A positive balance of trade, or trade surplus, is favorable; it indicates a net flow of money into the country. A negative balance, or trade deficit, is not favorable; it indicates a net flow of money out of the country.

Inflation

Inflation is a rise in the general prices of goods and services. One cause of inflation is the relationship between productivity and wages. Productivity is the output per worker. When workers' wages increase faster than their productivity, consumers (which include workers) have more money available to buy goods, so the price of goods inches up. The most commonly quoted measurement of inflation is the consumer price index (CPI), which measures the effect of price increases and inflation on the buying power of a typical American household. The producer price index (PPI) measures inflation from the point of view of business wholesalers.

Deflation

Deflation is a general decline in the prices of goods and services. Since the Great Depression, deflation has not been a serious nationwide problem, but at times it has affected specific industries and specific regions. The collapse of oil prices in 1986, for example, had a profound impact on the domestic oil industry and the economy of Texas for a period of time.

Federal Deficits

The federal deficit is the measure of the excess of money spent over money received by the federal government. Federal deficits affect interest rates. The government finances its deficits by borrowing money (i.e., by issuing and selling treasury securities, primarily bonds). The more money the government borrows, the less money is available for businesses. To compete for these reduced funds, businesses must bid higher, raising the cost of credit and compounding the effects of interest rates. Higher rates, in turn, make it more difficult (and more expensive) for businesses to borrow money for new factories or machinery. Thus federal deficits provide an important means of measuring the economy and can affect business activity and productivity. Increasingly, foreign investors, including foreign governments (notably India and China) are purchasing federal government securities. That helps the federal government address its deficits, but raises nationalistic concerns and fears.

This chapter has presented the development of the business environment in the United States and described other economic systems. Basic economic principles, types of businesses, and resource utilization serve as stanchions as we continue to examine the foundations of business.

Selected Readings

Boone, Louis E., and David L. Kurtz. *Contemporary Business*. 2006.

Ben-Ner, Avner, and Louis G Putterman. *Economics, Values, and Organization*. 2000.

Chandler, Alfred D., Jr. *Strategy and Structure: Chapters in the History of American Industrial Enterprise*. 1962.

Freidman, Thomas L., *The World is Flat: A Brief History of the Twenty-First Century*. 2005.

Heilbroner, Robert L., and Lester C. Thurow. *Economics Explained*. 1987.

Madison, James, Alexander Hamilton, and John Jay; Isaac Kramnick, editor. *The Federalist Papers.* 1987.

Marx, Karl. *Capital: A Critique of Political Economy,* Volume 1. 1977.

Samuelson, Paul A., and William D. Nordhaus. *Economics.* 1989.

Schumpeter, Joseph A. *Capitalism, Socialism, and Democracy.* 1983.

Schumpeter, Joseph A. *Theory of Economic Development: An Inquiry into Profits, Capital, Credit, Interest, and the Business Cycle.* 1934.

Silk, Leonard. *Economics in Plain English.* Simon and Schuster. 1978.

Smith, Adam. *An Inquiry into the Nature and Causes of the Wealth of Nations.* Reproduction of 1776 edition.

Smith, Steven, and Subrata Ghatak. *Introduction to Development Economics.* 2003.

Sowall, Thomas. *Basic Economics: A Citizen's Guide to the Economy.* 2004.

Varian, Hal R., Joseph Farrell, and Carl Shapiro. *Economics of Information Technology: An Introduction.* 2004.

Test Yourself

1) What are the five factors of production?

2) Yvette can work an extra hour as a security guard and earn $10, or she can leave early and go to a free movie showing. What is the opportunity cost of seeing the movie?

3) What does the law of demand say will happen when demand decreases?

4) What are the four degrees of competition, what characterizes the products of each degree, and how prevalent is the degree in the U.S. economy?

5) Axio Corporation produces high-performance mufflers. What competition does it likely face? Can it set its own price?

6) We tend to think of monopolies as bad for consumers. When do monopolies make sense? Please provide an example.

7) Why will full unemployment never be a reality?

8) How do federal deficits impact business growth? Explain in terms of supply and demand.

Test Yourself Answers

1) Land, labor, capital, information resources, and entrepreneurs.

2) $10. Since the hour could have produced $10 of revenue, which she is giving up to see the movie, the opportunity cost is $10. Therefore, the total cost of going to the movies is $10, even though the movie is free.

3) Price will decrease, and supply will follow.

4) Pure competition reflects many firms producing the same product in a manner that precludes any one firm from affecting the price of the product. A monopoly, on the other hand, occurs when only one firm produces a distinct product, with no competition, thus allowing it free reign in determining price. Monopolistic competition occurs when many firms compete in the same product space but with slightly different products, resulting in no firm's being able to significantly affect the price of the product. An oligopoly occurs when a few firms produce the same product and, thus, one firm can significantly affect the price of the product.

5) It probably faces monopolistic competition, since its mufflers are probably somewhat different from other mufflers, but there are many similar products. Axio can set its own price, since its product is probably differentiated, but as it increases its price, the demand will decrease because of the competition of similar products.

6) Monopolies make sense when a large amount of capital needs to be invested and maintained in a specific area in order to provide a good or service, and only enough demand exists to support one company at a profitable level. A monopoly on water services makes sense, since lots of piping must be laid throughout the city and duplicating the pipes for a second provider would be inefficient.

7) Some workers will always be between jobs, creating frictional unemployment. Some workers will be in off-season or seasonal unemployment. Some workers will not have the skills needed for the jobs available (structural unemployment). Some industries will be experiencing down periods, resulting in cyclical unemployment.

8) Government deficits cause the government to borrow money from investors to conduct government business. Businesses also borrow money from investors to conduct their activities including, for financing new projects and for growth. Together, these two forces increase the demand for money. Higher deficits increase the government's dependence on the investor market. This increases the price of money (i.e., the interest rate). Businesses must compete for the investors' money by paying higher interest rates. Although the higher interest rates will attract additional supply (i.e., investors willing to invest), which will minimize the impact, generally, federal deficits can hinder business growth.

CHAPTER 2
The Role of Government

In the free-market economy of the United States, the role of government in business affairs is extremely complex. Basically, the government—that is, federal, state, and local governments—serves three key roles: regulator, consumer, and business supporter.

■ GOVERNMENT IN A FREE-MARKET SYSTEM

A free-market system is one in which the providing and securing of goods and services are unregulated. In a free-market system government plays an important role of assuring that the playing field is relatively level without tipping the balance of power toward either providers or purchasers of goods and services; government does not, however, determine either supply, demand, or price. In a controlled market system, on the other hand, government determines the basic components of the economy.

The Role of Regulator

In its role of regulator, the government attempts to provide a balance among all the forces in the economy, a stable environment, and a level playing field. Toward this end, government does the following.

- Supervises and enforces a vast network of laws and regulations enacted to encourage some, and to limit other, business activities and policies
- Provides a legal foundation that defines and enforces laws and contracts and establishes environmental and safety regulations
- Defines property rights
- Encourages competition, while limiting unfair practices
- Establishes fiscal and monetary policies that profoundly affect business

The Role of Consumer

Another key role government plays is that of consumer. Although the government provides a number of important social services, it is not a major producer of general consumer goods or services; it generally does not compete with commercial enterprises. On the other hand, the U.S. government is the largest consumer of goods and services in the world. Indeed, much of its spending serves as a catalyst to the U.S. economy.

Using revenues raised through taxation, government re-channels money by injecting vast amounts back into the economy through its spending. It purchases a wide range of goods, from paper clips to the most powerful computer networks available. It pays for the building and maintenance of dams, roads, and harbors. It also makes direct payments to the aged, to veterans, and to welfare recipients, among others. In addition, the government funds and supports a wide range of research at colleges and universities, in industry, and at government installations.

The Role of Business Supporter

In its role of business supporter, the government provides direct support (for example, through farm subsidies) and indirect support (by levying tariffs, for example). The government collects vast amounts of information, much of which it then makes available to businesses at little or no cost. One example is the Census Bureau's demographic data, which offers businesses a wealth of marketing information. Government weather reports are invaluable to the farming, entertainment, transportation, and construction industries in planning business activities. Perhaps government's greatest support role is that of encouraging and protecting competition.

■ GOVERNMENT REGULATION

Over the years, a substantial body of laws and regulations has been enacted to guard against monopolies, price fixing, and other restraints of competition. These laws protect consumers by giving them freedom of choice in the marketplace, and they protect business by giving companies the freedom to compete.

The need for these laws emerged in the late 1800s when a number of industries were dominated by individual businesses or trusts (i.e., cartels). A monopoly exists when one firm obtains control of an industry. A trust of firms or corporations that combine for the purpose of reducing competition and controlling prices throughout a business or an industry can effect the same kind of monopoly. For example, John D. Rockefeller's Standard Oil Companies, as a trust, controlled over 80 percent of the oil industry, enabling Standard Oil to destroy competing companies and charge whatever prices the cartel of Standard Oil companies chose. In response to public outcry and to encourage competition, the first piece of antitrust legislation was passed: the Sherman Antitrust Act of 1890.

Antitrust Legislation

In its efforts to control the abuses of the trusts, the government enacted the following six key pieces of antitrust legislation, each discussed in the following sections.

The Sherman Antitrust Act of 1890

The Sherman Antitrust Act of 1890 made it illegal (1) to monopolize or attempt to monopolize an industry; and (2) to conspire, contract, or combine in restraint of trade. Although enacted to limit abuses in the 1880s, this legislation remains equally useful in today's business environment.

In 1960, General Electric, Westinghouse, and other companies were convicted of rigging bids for contractual work from the government and other customers. Heavy fines and several jail sentences resulted.

In 2002, a federal judge approved a settlement between Microsoft and a group of states because of antitrust claims. The judgment required Microsoft, among other things, to allow competitors and customers to remove icons for some of its software and to release enough technical data to allow software developers to write programs for its Windows software that work as well as its products do.

The Clayton Act of 1914

The Clayton Act of 1914 expanded and strengthened the earlier Sherman Act. It recognized that company size alone is not the problem, but that business practices must also be addressed. The Clayton Act prohibits a number of practices that are considered in restraint of competition, including price discrimination, tying contracts, and interlocking directorates.

- **Price discrimination:** Practices, for example, that charge larger firms less, thereby giving larger firms a competitive edge are prohibited. However, the Clayton Act does not prohibit volume discounts.
- **Tying contracts:** A practice that forces a buyer to purchase other, perhaps unwanted, goods in order to obtain the desired merchandise is also outlawed by the Clayton Act.
- **Interlocking directorates:** The naming of one or more persons to sit on the board of two or more competing companies is also prohibited by the Clayton Act.

The Federal Trade Commission Act of 1914

In spite of the Sherman and Clayton Acts, abuses continued. In a further effort to control those abuses, the Federal Trade Commission Act of 1914 established the Federal Trade Commission, known popularly as the FTC. The act, which states that "unfair methods of competition in commerce are hereby declared unlawful," gives the FTC power to police the marketplace and act against unfair competition, including behavior that falls short of violation of the earlier acts.

As shortcomings in the Clayton Act became evident, amendments strengthening the act were passed into law.

The Robinson-Patman Act of 1936

The Robinson-Patman Act of 1936 amended the Clayton Act by making unfair pricing practices illegal where the result was to reduce competition. For example, a seller cannot charge two stores different prices for the same product. Also, the seller must make available to both stores the same advertising and promotional assistance.

The Celler-Kefauver Act of 1950

The Celler-Kefauver Act of 1950 amended the Clayton Act to prohibit (1) the merger of one company with a direct competitor, and (2) the purchase of assets by a direct competitor. As a result, corporations prevented from buying companies in their own fields instead acquired firms in unrelated fields, leading to the growth of conglomerates (i.e., corporations operating in widely diverse fields). This act is enforced by both the FTC and the Justice Department. The government has continued to update antitrust legislation and regulation. The Antitrust Improvements Act of 1976 strengthened previous legislation and gives additional time to the FTC and the Justice Department to evaluate proposed mergers. In fact, antitrust cases may run for years, as did the ten-year-long suit that led to the breakup of AT&T. The changing attitudes of the courts, which must interpret the laws, and of the political climate have affected enforcement. Pressure for change also comes from the increase in competition due to foreign trade and economic globalization.

Regulation of Monopolies

The government considers natural monopolies legal, even desirable. A natural monopoly—a public utility, for example—is considered "in the public interest" and is, therefore, a desirable monopoly. The reason is that public utility companies require huge investments of capital. Duplicating facilities would be wasteful and, therefore, work against the public interest.

Table 2.1: Federal Regulatory Agencies

Agency	Jurisdiction
Federal Energy Regulatory Commission (FERC)	Regulates rates of electrical power sales and pipeline rates for oil and natural gas in interstate trade.
Nuclear Regulatory Commission (NRC)	Licenses and regulates nuclear power plants.
Interstate Trade Commission (ICC)	Regulates rates, service, safety, and other aspects of railroads, common carriers, and water transportation.
Federal Railroad Commission (FRC)	Prescribes safety regulation for all railroads (wider safety jurisdiction than ICC).
Federal Aviation Administration (FAA)	Supervises certification of aircraft for flight, the licensing of personnel, and the development of airports.
Federal Communications Commission (FCC)	Regulates rates and services for interstate communications by wire. Establishes charges for international cable and radio messages, satellite communication, and cable television. Allocates television channels and radio frequencies.

In addition to public utilities, the government once acknowledged other natural monopolies: the communications and the transportation industries. Recent technological advances, among other factors, led to the much deregulation in both of these industries. Still, since they are involved in both interstate and intrastate commerce they remain regulated by both federal and state agencies. In fact, a number of federal regulatory agencies/commissions have been established to exercise jurisdiction over these areas, as shown in Table 2.1.

Another kind of natural monopoly is also legal. Imagine an industry in which all competitors except one go out of business—for example, banjo manufacturers. That one remaining company would have a natural monopoly, and it would be legal because the company did not merge with or buy the assets of its competitors or in any other way violate antitrust laws.

Deregulation

Beginning in the 1970s, a trend toward deregulation has developed and gained strength. The objectives of deregulation are multiple.

- One is to reduce both the complexity of regulations and the high cost of complying with them.
- A second goal is to reduce the size and cost of government. In this and subsequent chapters of this book, many agencies are listed. As the number of regulatory agencies has grown, so has the government expense of operating those agencies.
- Another goal is to increase competition. Many persons, both in business and in government, believe that market forces will more effectively spur competition than will government intervention. Nonetheless, deregulation has caused unforeseen problems in some areas. When the Civil Aeronautics Board stopped setting fares and allocating routes, new airlines entered heavily traveled routes, and established airlines dropped less-profitable routes, resulting in price wars. As a result, many cities were left without service, and major airlines were faced with operating losses. Today, a handful of carriers control most of the market and are raising fares while cutting service. As another example, the savings and loan collapse can be traced, in large part, to the deregulation of the banking industry.

Many politicians and consumers believe that further deregulation will lead to a reduction of worker safety, inferior products, and greater pollution. Both the private and public sectors are evaluating the goals, costs, and effectiveness of government regulation.

The Role of Lobbyists and PACs

The most effective way to create or amend laws that affect business and the public is to communicate with legislators, the elected representatives of the people. Influencing legislators is, therefore, a key method of achieving goals of business or of the public. Legislators hear the voices of the public and the voices of business mainly through lobbyists and political action committees (PACs).

Lobbyists

Lobbyists represent specific groups—called special-interest groups—and attempt to influence legislators to approve legislation favorable to the group and oppose legislation that is not. The groups may be private-interest groups—that is, representing private businesses or industries—or they may be public-interest groups—which represent the general public. For example, a public-interest group might lobby for stronger auto safety and stronger antipollution laws, while a private-interest group representing the auto manufacturing industry may lobby for fewer safety and antipollution features.

Political Action Committees (PACs)

Campaign laws limit the amount that business can directly contribute to political campaigns. However, a company can solicit donations from its employees and funnel these funds to Political Action Committees (PACs), which in turn, pass the funds on to the campaigns of politicians who favor the company's views. Many companies work through trade-association PACs.

■ GOVERNMENT AND TAXATION

Government fiscal policy determines how tax money is raised, how much is raised, and how those funds are used. Tax laws serve two purposes in the United States. The first is to raise revenue to pay for the costs of government. Local, state, and federal taxes pay for all government services, including maintaining schools and the military, grants for medical research, business regulation, social services (e.g., welfare), and interest payments on the national debt.

A second purpose is to supply incentives or disincentives. A tax reduction for the interest paid on a mortgage loan provides an incentive to encourage home ownership. A cigarette tax is an example of a disincentive; it serves not only to raise funds, but also to discourage smoking.

The taxes that most affect business are of two types: (1) taxes assessed to raise revenue (such as personal and corporate income taxes, and property, sales, and value-added taxes); and (2) taxes assessed to regulate and control certain business activities (such as customs duties and excise taxes).

Major Taxes

The principal taxes paid by business and by individuals are discussed in the following sections.

Personal Income Tax

Individuals must pay personal income tax to the federal government's Internal Revenue Service (IRS). Most state governments also assess personal income taxes. But personal income tax also affects corporations. First, corporations are required to withhold estimated taxes from employee wages, and the expense of such recordkeeping and administration is considerable. In addition, personal income tax decreases the amount of money individuals have to spend on goods and services and to invest in stocks, bonds, securities, and savings, thereby further affecting businesses.

Corporate Income Tax

Corporations pay income tax on profits, just as individuals pay tax on their income. For the year 2005, the minimum corporation tax was 15 percent, and the maximum rate was 38 percent.

Many state and local governments also impose corporate income taxes. Corporate decisions to move or build often depend on whether a state has a corporate tax and, if so, the rate of that tax. When corporations conduct business in other countries and are taxed by the other countries, the United States allows a tax credit for taxes paid in those foreign countries.

Property Tax

Property tax is the major source of revenue for local governments. Local assessors determine the assessed value of property, both land and buildings (if any). From this assessed value, property tax is then determined according to the applicable tax rate. Commercial property is frequently taxed at a higher rate than residences and farms. As a result, businesses often pay a larger portion of local property taxes.

Sales Tax

Some states, cities, and counties charge a sales tax on purchases of retail merchandise. Retail businesses are required to collect the tax at the point of sale and forward the receipts to the government. Merchandise that a business buys for resale is generally not taxable.

Excise Tax

An excise tax is a tax on the manufacture or sale of a particular product. Revenues from excise taxes are used to offset the expense of government services provided in connection with that particular product or in some cases to limit the use of the product.

The excise tax on gasoline is used to offset the expense of building and maintaining highways. Excise taxes on alcohol and tobacco are intended to discourage their use by raising the price.

Customs Duties

Customs duties and tariffs are imposed for the specific purpose of raising the price of imported goods and, as a result, protecting American-made products that compete with those goods. Customs duties are selective; they vary, depending on the product and the country of origin. Essentially, customs duties are an instrument of foreign policy: Favored nations are taxed at lower rates than others.

Value-Added Tax (VAT)

The United States has not yet used value-added taxes (VATs), though they have been considered periodically. The VAT is the main type of tax on goods and services in the European Economic Union. VATs are assessed at each level in the chain of distribution: the raw material, the manufacturing, the wholesale, and the retail levels. At each level, the value of the goods and services is determined at the beginning and at the end of that level, and a tax is levied on the difference in that value.

Other Taxes

In addition to the taxes discussed in the preceding section, the government also collects a variety of other taxes.

Social Security Tax

The Social Security tax, collected under the Federal Insurance Contribution Act (FICA), is a tax on personal wages and is paid by both the employee and the employer. The revenues collected are used to provide retirement, disability, hospitalization, and death benefits for contributing employees. The employer withholds the tax from the employee's wages or salary and sends it, along with the employer's contribution, to the government.

Unemployment Tax

Unemployment tax is paid by employers under the Federal Unemployment Tax Act (FUTA). The proceeds of this tax are used to fund benefits for unemployed workers.

Estate and Gift Taxes

Estate and gift taxes are levied on estates and gifts over a specified dollar value. A base amount of value is allowed tax-free; the value over and above this base amount is taxed. State versions of the taxes vary from state to state.

The Federal Deficit

Each year, the government spends vast amounts of money on human services, national defense, employee salaries, supplies, equipment, operating expenses, and interest on the national debt. Each year, it also collects enormous amounts of money through taxes. However, in most years since 1960, government expenditures exceeded revenues (this is known as deficit spending). As the government borrows funds to finance these excess expenditures, these shortfalls, over time, have created a national debt exceeding $8 trillion ($8,000,000,000,000.00).

As a result of concern over the continuing budget deficits, in 1985, Congress enacted the Emergency Deficit Control Act, commonly known as the Gramm-Rudman-Hollings Act, after its sponsors. The purpose of the act is to balance the budget to bring spending into line with revenues over a period of years and to limit deficit spending. This act mandates an arbitrary across-the-board cut in spending if this goal is not achieved voluntarily through reduced spending, a tax increase, or a combination of both.

Selected Readings

Bernstein, Marver H. *Regulating Business by Independent Commission.* 1955.

Featherstone, Liza. *Selling Women Short: The Landmark Battle for Workers' Rights at Wal-Mart.* 2004.

Fremont-Smith, Marion R. *Governing Nonprofit Organizations: Federal and State Law and Regulation.* 2004.

Goehiert, Robert, and Nels Gunderson. *Government Regulation of Business: An Information Sourcebook.* 1987.

Hurst, James Williard. *The Legitimacy of the Business Corporation in the Law of the United States: 1780–1970.* 1970.

Jurik, Nancy C. *Bootstrap Dreams: U.S. Microenterprise Development in an Era of Welfare Reform.* 2005.

Keijzers, Gerald. *Business, Government and Sustainable Development.* 2004.

Kohn, Stephen M., Michael D. Kohn, and David K. Colapinto. *Whistleblower Law: A Guide to Legal Protections for Corporate Employees.* 2004.

Liebhafsky, H. H. *American Government and Business.* 1971.

Lodge, George C. *Perestroika for America: Restructuring the U.S. Business-Government Relations for Competitiveness in the World Economy.* 1990.

McCraw, Thomas K. *Prophets of Regulation.* 1984.

Magaziner, Ira C., and Robert B. Reich. *Minding America's Business.* 1983.

Scholes, Myron S., Mark A. Wolfson, Merle M. Erickson, and Edward L. Maydew. *Taxes and Business Strategy: A Planning Approach.* 2004.

Steiner, George A., and John F. Steiner. *Business, Government and Society.* 1988.

Tolchin, Susan T., and Martin Tolchin. *Dismantling America: The Rush to Deregulate.* 1983.

Weidenbaum, Murray. *Business and Government in the Global Marketplace,* Seventh Edition. 2003.

Test Yourself

1) In a free-market economy, what are the three major roles the government plays?

2) The government plays an important role in a free-market system. In its role as regulator, what does the government do to attempt to provide a balance among the forces in the economy, create a stable business environment, and develop and maintain a level playing field?

3) The government's consumer role is an important one. Explain how the government plays its role of consumer.

4) What six key pieces of government legislation seek to control the abuses of monopolies and trusts?

5) What is a natural monopoly and why is it not prohibited by law?

6) What role do lobbyists play in the effective interaction of government and business?

7) Government fiscal policy determines how tax money is raised, how much is raised, and how those funds are used. What are the two major purposes taxes serve?

8) Recently, much discussion focuses on the viability of the Social Security system. Describe the Social Security tax, including who pays it, how it is collected, and how it is used by the government?

9) Who pays the unemployment tax? How is it used?

10) Distinguish between the federal deficit and the federal debt.

Test Yourself Answers

1) The government serves three major roles: (1) regulator, (2) consumer, and (3) business supporter.

2) In its regulator's role, the government does the following: (1) supervises and enforces a vast network of laws and regulations; (2) provides a legal foundation that defines and enforces laws and contracts; (3) establishes environmental and safety regulations; (4) defines property rights; (5) encourages competition while limiting unfair practices; and (6) establishes fiscal and monetary policies that profoundly affect business.

3) First, the government generally does not compete against commercial enterprises. On the other hand, it consumes tremendous amounts of goods and services provided by commercial enterprises; in fact, it is the largest single consumer of goods and services in the world. The government uses tax revenues to purchase goods and services (from paper clips to computers), pay for the building and maintenance of roads, and make direct payments to the aged, veterans, and other citizens.

4) The government passed the following six pieces of anti-trust legislation: (1) The Sherman Antitrust Act of 1890, which makes it illegal to monopolize (or attempt to monopolize) an industry or to conspire, contract, or combine in restraint of trade; (2) The Clayton Act of 1914, which expanded the Sherman Act by prohibiting a number of practices that are considered in restraint of trade, including price discrimination, tying contracts, interlocking directorates; (3) The Federal Trade Commission Act of 1914, which established the Federal Trade Commission (FTC), giving it power to police the marketplace and to act against unfair competition; (4) The Robinson-Patman Act of 1936, which makes unfair pricing practices illegal where the result is to reduce competition; and (5) The Celler-Kefauver Act of 1950, which prohibits the merger of one company with a direct competitor and the purchase of assets by a direct competitor; (6) The Antitrust Improvements Act of 1976, which strengthened earlier legislation and granted additional time to evaluate proposed mergers.

5) A natural monopoly (e.g., a public utility) is "in the public interest" and is considered a desirable monopoly. These types of operations require huge investments of capital, the duplication of which would be wasteful to society.

6) Lobbyists represent special-interest groups and attempt to influence legislators to approve legislation favorable to the group and oppose legislation that is not. The groups may be private-interest or public-interest groups.

7) Taxes serve as revenues used to pay for the costs of government, including all government services. Taxes also serve to either supply incentives or disincentives; a cigarette tax is an example of a disincentive.

8) The Social Security tax is a tax on personal wages. It is paid by the individual employee and by the employer. The employer collects the individual's tax (withholding it from the employee's pay) and pays it to the government, along with its own matching share. The government uses the proceeds to provide retirement, disability, hospitalization, and death benefits for contributing employees.

9) Employers pay the unemployment tax, in accordance with the Federal Unemployment Tax Act (FUTA). The proceeds of this tax are used to fund benefits for unemployed workers.

10) The deficit is the excess of federal spending over federal revenues in a particular year; to fund the spending that exceeds revenues, the federal government borrows monies, either from other governmental agencies or from outside parties. The total net borrowing over the years equals the federal debt.

CHAPTER 3
Business Law and Ethics

Governments promulgate laws specifically designed to facilitate business transactions and to allow for a level playing field for individuals and businesses and buyers and sellers of goods and services. Individuals and businesses engaging in commerce must either adhere to these federal, state, and local laws or face monetary penalties or imprisonment. Moreover, society develops another set of expectations—moral standards—for business decision-making and activities. Individuals and businesses that fail to adhere to these standards face the prospects of losing the trust and support of the marketplace and their existing and potential business partners and customers.

■ SOURCES OF THE LAW

Law is a body of principles, rules of behavior, and standards used to settle disputes in an orderly way. Simply put, law is what makes civilization civil. Every individual is subject to the law, and every business or organization is subject to special laws that apply to businesses. Understanding business law requires a brief overview of the categories of law and the judicial system.

Categories of Law

Laws in the United States fall into three broad categories, based on their origin. These categories are statutory, common, and regulatory.

Statutory Law

Statutory law includes all statutes—that is, all laws enacted by federal, state, or local legislatures under their constitutions. Article I of the Constitution empowers Congress to "lay and collect taxes . . . regulate commerce . . . define and punish piracy and felonies on the high seas . . . make rules for government . . . [and] make all laws which shall be necessary and proper for carrying into execution the foregoing powers." With this mandate, Congress has enacted laws under which we live and function.

The various state and municipal legislatures and councils also pass laws affecting individuals and business on the state and local level. These local laws cover taxes, zoning, the environment, and a host of other laws that concern business and industry. These laws, too, are part of the body of statutory law.

Common Law

The early settlers brought to the New World a body of unwritten principles and regulations that had been used for centuries to govern their communities in England. The settlers adopted these principles, called common law, for use in their new communities. As the early courts recognized and enforced these laws, their decisions established precedents for future court cases.

Common law reflects legal opinions and decisions of courts based on statutory laws over the years and may serve as the basis for statutory law in further legislation.

Regulatory Law

Regulatory law, also known as administrative law, is a body of law formed by the decrees, the regulations, of government agencies. Regulatory law began with the establishment of the regulatory or administrative agencies such as the Federal Trade Commission and the Environmental Protection Agency. As federal agencies issued regulatory directives with the force of law, this body of law has grown vastly. Through deregulation, Congress is trying to reduce the burden of reporting and compliance that results from regulatory laws.

Public Law and Private Law

Laws can also be categorized as public or private, depending on their intent. Public law deals with relations between individuals or businesses with society. Violations of public law are called crimes.

Private law deals with the relationships between two or more individuals or businesses. The legal term that defines a violation of another's rights is *tort,* derived from the French word for "wrong." In most cases involving torts, the remedy is monetary damages to compensate the injured party or punish the person committing the tort.

■ THE JUDICIAL SYSTEM

The U.S. judicial system has three levels: federal, state, and local. Laws exist only on paper until and unless they are enforced. Much of the responsibility of enforcement of the judicial system lies with the court system. The highest court is the U.S. Supreme Court. Figure 3.1 shows how the U.S. Supreme Court heads the nation's judicial system.

Federal Courts

The federal court system was established by the U.S. Constitution. Federal courts hear cases involving questions of constitutional law, maritime law, postal law, bankruptcy, patent and copyright law, tax law, and violations of federal statutes.

U. S. Supreme Court

U.S. Appellate courts	State Supreme court
Federal Trial courts	State Trial courts
Federal Special courts	State Special courts
Federal Administrative courts	State Administrative agencies
Federal agencies	Local courts

Figure 3.1: The Federal and State Courts System

State and Local Courts

State and local courts hear cases involving state and local laws, not federal laws. State courts include specialized lower courts, called inferior courts, such as probate, criminal, family, traffic, and special agency courts.

Appellate Courts

Basic to the U.S. judicial system is the right to appeal a decision to the next higher level court. As Figure 3.1 shows, both the federal and the state courts have appellate courts specifically for the purpose of hearing appeals. Appellate courts reconsider evidence and review the lower courts' interpretations of law. Appellate courts have the power to affirm or reverse the decision or to order a retrial. The ultimate authority for all appeals is the U.S. Supreme Court, the highest court in the land.

Other Courts

At the lowest level of both federal and state courts are the trial courts, special courts, and administrative agencies. These courts hear all cases that are not assigned specifically to another court, such as tax cases, international disputes, and claims against the government.

Most legal issues faced by businesses fall into one of these basic areas: contracts, property, commerce, torts agency, and bankruptcy.

■ CONTRACT LAW

A contract is a legally enforceable agreement between two or more parties. The key words here are legally enforceable.

Requirements of Contracts

A contract must meet a number of requirements to make it legally enforceable. The key six requirements are discussed in the following sections.

Agreement

The basis of any contract is agreement. For agreement to exist, one party must communicate a serious offer, and a second party must accept, or agree to that offer.

Key to agreement is that the offer is serious: "I'd give a hundred dollars for a hamburger right now" does not constitute a serious offer.

Real Consent

Even if both parties agree, there must be real consent for a contract to be legally enforceable. Real consent is lacking in the presence of an honest mistake, fraud, or duress. If one party makes an honest mistake in arithmetic, the contract is not enforceable in court. If one party intentionally deceives (for example, by claiming a gold-plated ring is solid gold), that party commits fraud and the contract is not enforceable. If one party threatens the other (for example, if a supplier threatens to damage property unless the other party buys goods), the contract is not enforceable.

Capacity

Capacity, the mental competence needed for individuals to manage their own affairs, is necessary to enter into a contract. A person under the influence of alcohol or drugs might not be considered competent. A person not of legal age, which varies from state to state, is not considered competent to execute a contract.

Consideration

For a contract to be legally binding, each party must receive consideration; that is, something of value. The value is not limited to money; goods and services may also be exchanged. In addition, the exchange need not be "rational" or a "good deal" for both sides in order for the contract to be enforceable.

Lawful Purpose

A contract must be for a lawful purpose—that is, it must comply with federal, state, and local laws, as well as with any licensing regulations. A contract between two companies to fix prices of products is illegal and, therefore, unenforceable. Likewise, contracts to buy or sell narcotics and contracts involving usury (exorbitant, illegal interest rates) are not legal or enforceable.

Proper Form

A contract must be in proper form. That "form" may be written, oral, or implied. A contract must be in writing under certain conditions, for example, if the agreement (1) involves goods worth over $500 or the sale of land, (2) requires more than one year to fulfill, or (3) concerns assuming someone else's financial obligations. A written contract must contain the names and signatures of the parties involved and the purpose of the contract and all the agreed conditions.

Even when not required, a written contract is preferred. A written contract minimizes mistakes, misunderstandings, confusion, and disputes.

Breach of Contract

When all obligations of all parties to a contract are fulfilled, the contract is terminated by performance. Under certain conditions, contracts are terminated before performance, for example, in the event of death, disability, bankruptcy, or by mutual agreement. All these terminations are legal.

However, if one party fails to fulfill the terms of the contract without a legal reason, a breach of contract exists. Injured parties in a breach of contract may pursue several courses of action. In such cases, they may cancel the contract by not fulfilling their end of the agreement or they may sue. They may sue (1) for monetary damages to repay the cost of having a third party complete the contract, or (2) for specific performance—that is, to force the other party to fulfill his or her contractual requirements. Courts will require specific performance in cases of a unique service or product that cannot be obtained from some other source—for example, the appearance of a certain celebrity or performer or the sale of a rare antique.

■ PROPERTY LAW

Property defines anything that can be owned. The law classifies property as either real or personal.

Real Property

Real property includes land and anything permanently attached to it, such as a house with all its built-in appliances or a factory with all its machinery.

Tangible Personal Property

Tangible personal property includes all movable items that can be bought, sold, owned, or leased, for example, automobiles, clothes, and jewelry.

Intangible Personal Property

Intangible personal property includes insurance policies, stocks, bonds, bank accounts, receivables, trade secrets, and other property that can be documented in writing but cannot be seen. Intangible personal property also includes patents, copyrights, and trademarks.

Patents

A patent grants exclusive rights to the owner for a machine, process, or other useful invention for a period of twenty years. Holders of patents can sell or license the use of their creations within the period of exclusivity.

Copyright

A copyright grants to the owner exclusive rights to publish, perform, or sell an original book, article, design, illustration, computer program, film, or other creation for a period ending seventy years after the creator's death. Holders of copyrights can sell or license the use of their creations within the period of exclusivity.

Trademarks

Trademarks, brands registered with the U.S. Patent and Trademark Office, can be renewed indefinitely. Examples of trademarks are Kleenex brand tissues and Perdue Farms brand chickens.

Transfer of Real Property

The contract concerning the sale of real property must be in writing. Deeds are used to transfer real property on a permanent basis; leases are used to transfer property on a temporary basis.

Deeds

The document transferring ownership of real property is called a deed. The deed must contain the names of both the previous owner and the new owner, along with a legally acceptable description of the property. Listing the price of the property or anything of value given in exchange is not required, but a deed is necessary even when the exchange is a gift.

Property rights are not absolute. Owners of waterfront property may have to permit fishermen or others to cross property to reach a river, lake, or ocean. Mineral rights to land may be owned by someone other than the landowner, and utility companies can run wires over or under one's property.

Leases

A lease is an agreement for the temporary transfer or use of property from owner to tenant. A lease usually specifies the period of time and the amount of rent. Lease renewals may be negotiated, but when the lease is terminated, the property reverts to the owner.

Transfer of Personal Property

A buyer who purchases a pair of shoes has, in effect, executed a contract. Ownership passes immediately to the buyer. If the buyer charges the shoes or makes a partial payment, the buyer has in effect made a legally enforceable promise to pay, even though title passes to the buyer at the time of sale.

In place of what would be the deed for real property, most businesses supply a sales slip or a bill of sale to transfer title.

COD

Goods are often purchased and shipped on a COD basis. COD means "collect on delivery." In such cases, title or ownership of the goods passes to the buyer when the goods are delivered from the supplier to the carrier, the shipping company.

FOB Point of Origin (or Shipping Point)

When goods are shipped FOB ("free on board") point of origin, the buyer is responsible for shipment, and title passes to the buyer when the goods are delivered to the carrier.

In both COD and FOB point of origin, title passes to the buyer upon delivery to the carrier. Thus if the goods are damaged in shipment, the buyer is responsible for collecting damages from the carrier.

FOB Destination Basis

If the goods are shipped FOB destination basis, title does not pass to the buyer until delivery is made. In this case, if the goods are damaged, the seller, not the buyer, must sue the carrier.

■ COMMERCIAL LAW: THE UNIFORM COMMERCIAL CODE

As commerce spread throughout the United States, individuals and businesses engaged in interstate commerce found that laws varied widely from state to state. To achieve a degree of uniformity in all state laws governing business, in 1952, the National Conference of Commissioners on Uniform State Laws and the American Law Institute drew up the Uniform Commercial Code (UCC). Adopted by all states except Louisiana, the UCC describes the rights of buyers and sellers in business transactions.

Under the UCC, sellers who feel that buyers have not performed can cancel the contract and (1) not deliver the merchandise; or (2) if the merchandise has been delivered, either sue for the purchase price or repossess the goods. Buyers who feel that sellers have not performed can cancel the contract, refuse delivery, and demand the return of any deposit. Further, buyers may buy the same merchandise elsewhere and sue for the additional cost, if any. The UCC also covers warranties and negotiable instruments.

Warranties

A warranty is a seller's promise to stand by his or her products after the sale—for example, to replace or repair the product or to give a full or partial refund under certain conditions. Warranties can be express or implied.

Express Warranty

An express warranty describes a warranty that is specifically stated by the seller. Express warranties may be limited to a certain period of time (say, ninety days) or to certain components (for example, the motor of an appliance), depending on the product and the manufacturer.

Implied Warranty

The terms of an implied warranty are dictated by law—they are not necessarily stated by the manufacturer. For example, that a product is as advertised or as described by the seller and will work properly are implied warranties. Likewise, the purity and safety of food products are implied. The seller does not need to state such warranties. Warranties can be limited, disclaimed, or waived by the seller, forcing dissatisfied customers to seek remedies by suing under tort law.

Negotiable Instruments

A negotiable instrument is any form of business paper used instead of cash—for example, checks, bank drafts, certificates of deposit, and promissory notes. In order to be negotiable, an instrument must meet four requirements: (1) it must be in writing and signed; (2) it must contain an unconditional order or promise to pay a stated sum of money; (3) it must be payable on demand (meaning whenever it is presented for payment) or at a specified future date; and (4) it must be payable to a specific person or firm, called the payee, or to the bearer.

Endorsement

To transfer a negotiable instrument, the payee must sign or endorse it. This signature is called an endorsement.

Blank Endorsement

A blank endorsement consists of only the payee's signature; it includes no other instructions. Therefore, a blank endorsement makes the instrument payable to anyone who has possession of it, legally or otherwise.

Restrictive Endorsement

Restrictive or special endorsements protect the negotiable instrument in case it is lost or stolen. A restrictive endorsement states a specific purpose for which the instrument can be used and, therefore, restricts its potential uses. For example, if a check includes an endorsement (signature) and "For deposit only to account #456934," then the check is restricted to that use; it can only be deposited to that specific account.

Special Endorsement

A special endorsement further limits the potential use of the instrument. For example, "pay to the order of S. Smith" means that only S. Smith may deposit or negotiate the check.

■ TORT LAW

A crime is a violation of law, and the state must bring action when a crime has been committed. On the other hand, a tort is not a crime. It is not a violation of law; it is a civil injury—that is, a non-criminal and non-contractual injury to people, to their property, or to their reputation.

A tort may be intentional, or it may arise out of negligence. Whatever the cause, the injured party is entitled to compensation. To receive compensation, the injured party may bring suit in a court of law.

Intentional Tort

An intentional tort, as its name clearly tells, results from a deliberate action. Deliberately failing to rectify a dangerous error in a product is an intentional tort. Sexual harassment in the workplace is an intentional tort.

Negligence

Negligence, failure to exercise reasonable care and caution can be the basis for a tort suit. For example, failure to properly mark an excavation would be grounds for a negligence action.

Product Liability

Product liability holds a company responsible for harm caused by a product it makes or markets, whether the oversight is intentional or the result of negligence.

Strict product liability holds a company liable for harm caused by a defect in its product even if there is no intentional tort or negligence involved. Because plaintiffs in strict liability suits do not have to prove intention or negligence—only that harm resulted—they are often successful.

■ THE LAW OF AGENCY

The agency-principal relationship is rich in potential problems, many of which can be avoided by executing a written contract that specifies the conditions and limitations of the agency. The relationship between agent and principal varies, depending on the specific situation.

Agents

An agent is a person who acts for, and in the name of, a second person, who is known as the principal. Sales representatives, representatives of performers or athletes, brokers, and attorneys often act as agents. Loosely interpreted, all business partners, corporate officers, and directors, and in some cases, employees, are agents of that business.

Agents should be compensated for their work and for expenses incurred, warned of any dangers, and have limits of authority clearly stated. Agents owe their principals loyalty. This loyalty requires that they should turn profit opportunities over to the principals, preserve confidentiality of trade secrets and internal company information, and keep and render accurate accounts.

Principals

The principal is liable for acts committed by his or her agents. However, if an agent performs an unauthorized act, the principal, although still liable, may sue that agent for damages. Many tort cases succeed because the courts often consider employees as agents.

■ BANKRUPTCY

At one time, those who could not pay their debts went to debtor's prison. Today, individuals or companies who cannot pay their debts may seek relief by filing for bankruptcy.

Bankruptcy is court-granted permission not to pay some or all of an individual's (or a company's) outstanding debts. Bankruptcy serves two purposes: (1) it assures fair treatment of creditors, those who are owed money; and (2) it permits the debtors, those who owe, to make a fresh start. Bankruptcy can be voluntary or involuntary.

Voluntary Bankruptcy

Voluntary bankruptcy can be initiated by businesses or individuals that can no longer meet their financial obligations and that have debts of at least $1,000 more than the total value of their assets.

Involuntary Bankruptcy

Bankruptcy is not always initiated by the person or business having financial problems. Bankruptcy—involuntary bankruptcy—can be initiated by creditors. In such cases, creditors must prove that the person or business has debts in excess of $5,000 and cannot pay these debts as they come due.

Methods of Resolving Bankruptcy

Bankruptcy may be resolved by one of three methods under the Bankruptcy Reform Act of 1978 and the Bankruptcy Abuse Prevention and Consumer Protection Act of 2005.

Liquidation

To liquidate means to sell. In bankruptcy cases, liquidation (Chapter 7 of the act) means selling the assets of the individual or business. As money is received from the sale of assets, debtors are paid—but debtors' claims are paid following a specific order, as stated by law.

The order in which payments are made follows: (1) debtors with secured claims (they are permitted to repossess the collateral pledged as security); (2) costs involved in the bankruptcy court case; (3) claims that arose from business activity after commencement of the bankruptcy case; (4) wages, salaries, and commissions due, up to $2,000 per claimant; (5) benefit plans; and (6) federal and state taxes. Anything left after these payments have been made is divided among creditors with unsecured claims and paid to them in proportion to their claims.

Reorganization

Chapter 11 of the act covers reorganization, a process that allows the business firm to continue to operate under the supervision of the court. Reorganization is especially effective for firms that are able to make some operating profits, though they are not yet able to cover longer-term debt. Creditors hope that reorganization, allowing the business to continue to function, will realize a greater return than liquidation.

Repayment

Chapter 13 of the act covers repayment, an option available only to individuals in bankruptcy, not to businesses. To file under Chapter 13, individuals must have regular income, owe less than $100,000 in unsecured debts, and owe less than $350,000 in secured debts. The individual files a plan with the court for repaying specific debts. For the plan to be accepted, creditors must receive at least as much under a Chapter 13 repayment as they would receive under Chapter 7 liquidation described above.

Bankruptcy Abuse Prevention and Consumer Protection Act

The Bankruptcy Abuse Prevention and Consumer Protection Act of 2005 makes some sweeping changes to the former bankruptcy law. It was codified to check perceived abuses of the Bankruptcy Reform Act of 1978, in the face of U.S. consumers' skyrocketing debt. In fact, the number of Americans filing for bankruptcy has also skyrocketed, with more than $40 billion in debt being forgiven annually.

The act requires consumers to demonstrate the necessity for filing for Chapter 7 relief, which generally discharges unsecured debts. Moreover, the act makes it easier for either the trustee or any creditor to bring a motion to dismiss a Chapter 7 bankruptcy, in favor of Chapter 13 bankruptcy, if the debtor's income is greater than the state median income.

Student Loans

Generally, regardless of the nature of the lender, student loans cannot be discharged. This includes loans from nongovernmental and for-profit organizations.

Luxury Goods and Cash Advances

Debts owed for luxury goods incurred within 90 days of filing and cash advances taken within 70 days, generally, can no longer be discharged.

Filing Limit

The Bankruptcy Abuse Prevention and Consumer Protection Act of 2005 limits consumer's filing for Chapter 7 to only once every eight years.

Financial Counseling

The act includes two provisions requiring financial counseling and education, before consumers may file for bankruptcy. Consumer must also receive information on alternatives to bankruptcy. Finally, as a measure to avoid future financial problems, prior to receiving a bankruptcy discharge, a debtor must now complete a personal financial management course.

■ BUSINESS ETHICS

Closely related to law is the study of right and wrong, of the morality of individual choices as judged by some standard of behavior. Business ethics is the application of moral standards to business decisions and actions.

Unfortunately, there are all too many examples of unethical actions of individuals and companies, including Wall Street insider-trading scandals, overcharging and bid-rigging by defense contractors, the savings-and-loan collapse, and the earth-shattering Enron financial fraud that virtually destroyed the lives of so many employees and related parties. Newspapers provide examples almost daily, pointing up the need to review business ethics and prompting business schools to offer courses in ethics.

Business ethics involves all relationships among the people involved in a business, both inside and outside—employees, investors, customers, creditors, competitors, and so on. Each group has a responsibility in its dealings with the firm. In an effort to remind employees of their specific responsibilities, many companies have developed for distribution to their employees a written corporate code of ethics to encourage ethical behavior in all business dealings. Government and trade associations, too, have established ethics guidelines.

But businesspeople often do, when they wish, justify unethical behavior. For example, businesspeople involved in international trade may find different ethical standards in other countries; if bribery and payoffs are common in a particular country, individuals may fall into the trap of excusing such practices because "everyone does it." Or the businessperson who works long hours may justify receiving and keeping an expensive gift from a supplier because of his or her efforts. In the final analysis, corporate ethics is likely to reflect the personal ethics of the employees and management of the corporation.

In 2002, in response to a number of high profile cases of unethical business activity, Congress passed the Sarbanes-Oxley Act. This act imposes a number of legally required checks and balances against unethical behavior in publicly held companies. The act also created an oversight board to govern accountants as they discharge their responsibilities to the public in auditing ethically as well as in accordance with generally accepted auditing standards (GAAS).

Selected Readings

Baumer, David L., J.C. Poindexter, and Evan Sheffel. *Legal Environment of Business in the Information Age*. 2003.

Bowie, Norman E., editor. *The Blackwell Guide to Business Ethics*. 2002.

Brown, William D. *The Ethics of Legal Ethics*. 1995.

Caroselli, Marlene. *The Business Ethics Activity Book: 50 Exercises for Promoting Integrity at Work*. 2003.

Chen, Morris L., and Robert C. Berring. *How to Find the Law*. 1983.

Clark, Lawrence S., and Peter D. Kinder. *Law and Business*. 1987.

Corley, Robert N., and Peter J. Shedd. *Fundamentals of Business Law.* 1990.
Dixit, Avinash K. *Lawlessness and Economics: Alternative Modes of Governance.* 2004.
Donaldson, Thomas. *Ethics of International Business.* 1991.
Eichenwald, Kurt. *Conspiracy of Fools: A True Story.* 2005.
Etzioni, Amitai. *The Moral Dimension.* 1988.
Freeman, R. Edward, editor. *Business Ethics: The State of the Art,* Volume 1. 1990.
Garner, Ryan A., editor. *Black's Law Dictionary,* Eighth Edition. 2006.
Hagen, Willis. *Digest of Business Law.* 1986.
Henszey, Benjamin M. *Introduction to Basic Legal Principles.* 1994.
Hoffman, W. Michael, and Jennifer M. Moore. *Business Ethics: Readings and Cases in Corporate Morality.* 1990.
Jacobstein, Myron, and Roy Mersky. *Fundamentals of Legal Research.* 1986.
Kohn, Stephen M., Michael D. Kohn, and David K. Colapinto. *Whistleblower Law: A Guide to Legal Protections for Corporate Employees.* 2004.
Mann, Richard A., and Barry S. Roberts. *Business Law and the Regulation of Business.* 2004.
Maxwell, John D. *There's No Such Thing as "Business" Ethics: There's Only One Rule for Making Decisions.* 2003.
Peterson, Robert A. *Business Ethics: New Challenges for Business Schools and Corporate Leaders.* 2004.
Posner, William M. and Richard A. *The Economic Structure of Tort Law.* 1987.
Rice, Michael Downey. *Prentice-Hall Dictionary of Business, Finance and Law.* 1983.
Stelzer, Irwin M. *Selected Antitrust Cases.* 1976.
Stone, Bradford. *Uniform Commercial Code.* 1975.
Toffler, Barbara L. *Tough Choices: Managers Talk Ethics.* 1986.

Test Yourself

1) What are the three broad categories of laws in the United States?

2) True or false: The ultimate authority for all appeals in the United States are the State Supreme courts.

3) List the six key requirements to make a contract enforceable.

4) Ordinarily, may a person not of legal age enter into an enforceable contract?

5) What is an intangible personal property? Please provide three examples.

6) How long does a copyright grant the creator exclusive rights to publish, perform, or sell an original book, article, design, illustration, computer program, or other creation?

7) What is a warranty?

8) What requirements must an instrument meet to be classified as negotiable?

9) What is a tort?

10) Describe the basic concept of bankruptcy. What purpose does it serve? What are the two basic types of bankruptcy for an individual?

Test Yourself Answers

1) The three broad categories are statutory law, common law, and regulatory law.

2) False. The U.S. Supreme Court is the ultimate authority for all appeals in the United States.

3) The six key requirements are agreement, real consent, capacity, consideration, lawful purpose, and proper form.

4) No. Ordinarily, the person must be of legal age to enter into an enforceable contract.

5) Intangible personal property cannot be seen or handled. It includes bank accounts, receivables, stocks, bonds, patents, copyrights, trademarks, and other items that can be documented in writing but cannot be seen.

6) A copyright provides protection for seventy years after the creator's death.

7) A warranty is a seller's promise to stand by his or her product after the sale. Warranties can be express or implied.

8) The instrument must be in writing and signed, must contain an unconditional promise to pay a stated sum of money, must be payable on demand or at a specified future date, and must be payable to a specific persons or to the bearer of the instrument.

9) A tort is not a crime. It is a civil injury to a person, to his or her property, or to his or her reputation. A tort may be intentional or unintentional (arising out of negligence).

10) Bankruptcy is a court-granted permission not to pay either some or all of an individual's or a corporation's outstanding debts. Bankruptcy has two major purposes: It assures fair treatment of creditors (those who are owed money) and permits debtors (those who owe money) to make a fresh start. Individuals may file either for Chapter 7 bankruptcy, which requires the debtor to sell all assets to pay off the debts, or a Chapter 13 bankruptcy, which focuses on repayment, without a selling off of all assets.

CHAPTER 4

Business Sustainability: Economic, Environmental, and Social Responsibilities

Business survival depends on how well it reacts to change, and the 21st century will continue to bring great economic, social, technical, and political changes that will challenge the business world. Many business organizations are beginning to recognize the importance of being responsive to all these stakeholder groups by focusing on the evolving concept of sustainability, which is a focus on the triple bottom line: economic viability, environmental integrity, and social equity.

■ THE CHANGING BUSINESS ENVIRONMENT

Companies do not exist in a vacuum. They exist within many environments—for example, political, social, and natural environments. These environments exert pressures on business to change, and at the same time, business exerts pressure on these environments to change. The result is a complicated interaction of business and society, and the key to understanding this interaction is the systems theory.

The Systems Theory

A system is a group of elements acting as one. The elements in the systems theory are inputs, processes, outputs, and feedback. Inputs are resources that a business takes from the environment. Inputs include the factors of production—the material, human, financial, and information resources. These inputs are transformed into outputs as a result of technological or managerial processes. Outputs are the products or services that a business sells to generate a profit. As consumers react to the outputs—that is, as they buy or use the output products or services—they provide feedback, information that reenters the system as input. This process can be diagrammed as shown in Figure 4.1.

Open versus Closed Systems

Systems are of two types: open and closed.

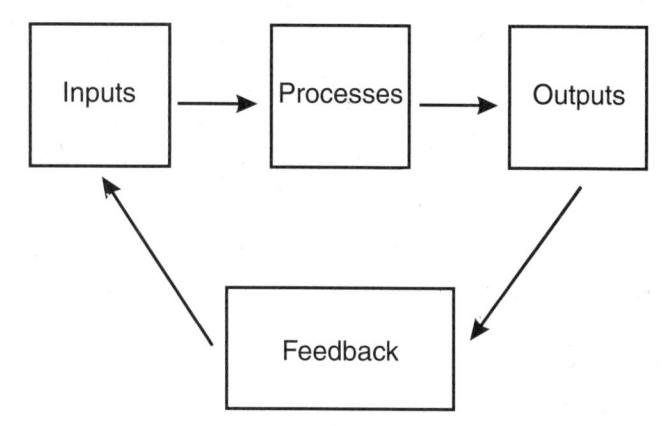

Figure 4.1: Systems Theory

Open Systems

A system is open when the business interacts with its environments. Examples of interaction include government legislation leading a company to change its hiring practices, technological advances convincing a company to change its manufacturing processes, and changes in consumer tastes telling a company to alter its marketing strategies. Interaction provides feedback, and feedback provides businesses with information that is critical to its future. A business that does not interact with its environments fails to do so at its peril. Disregarding feedback has led to the demise of many once-powerful companies. In the 1980s, Chrysler, for example, neglected to respond to environmental demands for smaller, fuel-efficient automobiles, and its neglect brought Chrysler to the brink of bankruptcy. For business, the lesson is clear: Feedback helps to evaluate the input/process/output cycle. Consumer feedback informs the business as to whether its products or services are acceptable.

Closed Systems

A system is described as closed if it does not interact with the environment. In closed systems, most of the factors influencing the organization are internal and, therefore, controllable. In theory, the standardized procedures, specialization, and proper controls of closed systems lead to success. Changes in the external environment—that is, social, economic, political, and technological changes—do not significantly affect the business's internal operations.

The Need for Balance

The ultimate survival of an organization and, therefore, its success, depends on its ability to adapt to the demands of its environment. To survive, a business must achieve a balance between inputs, processes, and outputs. Achieving a balance requires business executives to be sensitive to all the elements in their particular environment and to understand how those elements influence the business.

Elements of the Business Environment

The elements of a business environment include employees, stockholders, directors, suppliers, government officials at all levels, managers of competitors, customers, clients, and the "general public." Because all these people have an interest or stake in the organization, they are collectively known as stakeholders. A stakeholder is anyone who wants the organization to behave in a way that will benefit him or her, and satisfy his or her wants and needs for goods, services, or profits. The wants and needs are different, of course, for each group of stakeholders; they are not necessarily compatible. For example, employees want higher wages, but shareholders want a higher return on their investment. Customers want lower prices, but businesses want higher profits.

Internal Stakeholders

Internal stakeholders are people inside the business—shareholders, directors, managers, and employees, for example.

External Stakeholders

External stakeholders include customers; clients; suppliers; vendors; special interest groups (such as consumer advocates or environmentalists); the media; labor unions; financial institutions; competitors; and federal, state, and local governments.

Forces of Change

The major external forces or variables that influence the way businesses function are economic, social, technological, and political. Businesses cannot control these variables, which make up the ever-changing environment within which business decisions have to be made.

Economic Variables

Economic variables are (1) the economic conditions and trends that affect the cost of producing goods and services, and (2) the market conditions under which they are sold. Economic variables include raw material costs, sales, and government fiscal policy. Economic changes greatly affect the profitability of industries and of individual business firms; economic change is constant. The difficulty lies in distinguishing between cyclical changes and structural changes.

Cyclical Changes

Cyclical changes are periodic swings upward or downward in the general level of economic activity. Cyclical changes affect interest rates, inflation, and housing starts, for example.

Structural Changes

Structural changes are major alterations, permanent or temporary, in the relationships among different sectors of the economy. The shift from an industrial to a service economy and the rise in energy costs relative to the cost of raw materials are examples of structural changes.

Social Variables

The three social variables are demographics, lifestyles, and social values.

Demographics

Demography, the statistical study of the characteristics of human populations, offers valuable business information, such as general population increase or decrease, specific segments that are most affected by the increase or decrease, changes in the makeup of specific age groups, and geographic shifts within the total population.

For example, demographic studies show the following: (1) the population of the United States will reach 310 million by the year 2010; (2) the fastest growing population segments are Hispanic and Asian-American groups; (3) in the next fifty years, the number of people age 65 or over will more than double;

and (4) the Sun Belt (Western and Southern states) is gaining in population more rapidly than the Midwest and Northeast.

Thus, demographic studies offer businesses a wealth of information about their customers.

Lifestyle

Lifestyle, an individual's way of living, affects the composition, location, and expectations of business's labor supply and of its customers. Americans' lifestyles are changing in many ways. People are showing an increased emphasis on electronic interactions. A greater percentage of Americans have attended and have graduated from college than ever before. The proportion of so-called traditional families is shrinking. Fewer households are now made up of married couples. Instead, more households are comprised of single adults and one-parent families.

Businesses "read" such information to analyze their products and services and to determine how well they fit the needs of the marketplace.

Social Values

Social values reflect the attitudes and beliefs of a society, and these values are also subject to change. For example, as people became more and more concerned about environmental issues, their attitudes toward companies that abuse the environment have impacted many businesses. Growing fears about globalization have led to certain consumers only choosing fair-trade produced products. In this way, then, social values also make up the ever-changing business environment.

Technological Variables

Technological variables include new developments and advances in science and manufacturing, all of which affect business activities. The level of technology in a society or in a particular industry determines to a large extent which goods or services will be produced, what equipment will be used, where and how many people will be employed, and at what tasks these people will be utilized. The first step in technological advancement is research and development (R&D).

Basic Research

Basic research is aimed at discovering new knowledge. This is research purely for the sake of learning. Although the results of basic research may lead to the improvement of products or processes, the original objective is pure research.

Applied Research

Applied research is aimed at discovering new knowledge that has some specific potential use.

Development

Development is aimed at putting new or existing knowledge to use in producing goods or services. Technological advances are responsible for vast changes in the proportion of our population now working in the service sector. Specifically, fewer people are now employed in manufacturing and more people are employed in service jobs. In 1900, for example, 72 percent of the workforce was found in manufacturing and 28 percent in service jobs. By 1950, the service sector accounted for 40 percent of the overall population and 83 percent by 2005. Technology is also responsible for changing the tasks performed and the skills needed in service positions. Traditional service positions were found in restaurants, hotels, and repair businesses. Technological advancements have brought about a shift to service industries that provide customer technical support or that connect people in unique ways.

Political Variables

The political process and the political climate are two variables that influence business. The political process involves competition among interest groups seeking to advance their own values and goals. Thus, consumer safety advocates battle automobile manufacturers, conservationists fight the lumber and oil industries, and public health advocates clash with the tobacco industry. The political climate toward business depends on the administration in power and, of course, the point of view of the observer. In 1925, President Calvin Coolidge said, "The chief business of America is business." Today, even pro-business administrations adopt a much milder stance.

■ SOCIAL RESPONSIBILITY

Every business has an obligation to make a profit for its shareholders. Clearly, it also has an obligation to operate within the law. Although there is widespread agreement on these two business obligations, a third, social responsibility, is subject to debate. Social responsibility refers to a business's obligations to society. Many businesses recognize that their activities and decisions impact on their employees, on the environment, on minority groups, and on their local communities. As a result, they feel a responsibility to contribute positively by adopting policies that go beyond their own narrow concerns of making a profit and growing. But although being socially responsible is admirable, it is also costly. Opponents to the idea that business has a social responsibility abound. Economist Milton Friedman, winner of the Nobel Prize, summarized the opposition's viewpoint: "There is one and only one social responsibility of business—to use its resources and engage in activities designed to increase its profits so long as it stays within the rules of the game, which is to say, engages in open and free competition without deception and fraud." Understanding the evolution of social responsibility will shed some light on both views.

The Evolution of Social Responsibility

Through the 1920s, business owners were extremely powerful. For one thing, the government's laissez-faire policy offered minimal interference. For workers nationwide, wages, working conditions, and working hours were generally deplorable. Vacations, health insurance, and overtime pay were unknown. For consumers, the policy of caveat emptor, meaning "let the buyer beware," was in full force and summed up the attitude toward consumers. The only protection consumers could rely on was their own common sense and shrewdness in dealing with all businesses. There was little recourse.

True, a few government regulations had been enacted to protect consumers, such as the following.

- The Interstate Commerce Act (1887)
- The Sherman Antitrust Act (1890)
- The Pure Food and Drug Act (1906)
- The Clayton Act (1914)

In addition to legislation, the Federal Trade Commission had been established in 1914. But all were designed to encourage competition, not to correct abuses. And abuses were commonplace. Unfortunately, things would get worse before they got better. With the Great Depression of 1929, conditions did indeed deteriorate. As production and employment fell, and economic and social conditions worsened, public pressure increased for the government to take action. After his inauguration in 1933, President Franklin D. Roosevelt set into motion the New Deal, a series of programs and legislation that established minimum wages, the 40-hour work week, and Social Security, and that regulated financial services, energy, and transportation. Business was now subject to standards of performance set by the government. The door to social responsibility had been opened and would remain opened for decades to come.

For example, in the 1960s, the civil rights movement gained a stronghold. By the 1970s, consumer-advocacy groups proliferated, as did consumer-protection regulations and environmental legislation from government agencies such as the Federal Election Commission, the Occupational Safety and Health Administration (OSHA), and the Consumer Products Safety Commission. Today, government legislation on behalf of the consumer continues, but whether there is too much or too little legislation depends on one's point of view. Regardless of their degree of commitment, large companies, and certainly all corporations with nationwide reputations, have well developed strategies for dealing with their social responsibilities.

Strategies Concerning Social Responsibility

Companies adopt different strategies to meet, or to limit, their social responsibilities, depending on their policies. Some of the most common management strategies are discussed below.

Denial Strategy

A denial strategy claims that the problem does not exist. Tobacco companies, for example, adopted a denial strategy when they tried to refute the irrefutable evidence that smoking is a health hazard.

Reaction Strategy

When a company adopts a reaction strategy, it offers a deliberate response to a perceived problem. The liquor industry's reaction strategy to public opinion toward alcohol is to develop designated-driver campaigns.

Defense Strategy

A defense strategy, often utilized by trade associations, attempts to use legal maneuvering or public relations to avoid additional obligations. The automobile industry's attitude toward mandating costly safety features is a defense strategy.

Accommodation Strategy

An accommodation strategy is often a company's response to pressure or lawsuit threats, as when a company tries to accommodate or placate its employees or the government, for example. When one of its ships, the Exxon *Valdez,* spilled vast amounts of oil in Alaska in 1989, Exxon adopted an accommodation strategy to deal with the public outcry. The company, which merged with Mobil in 1991 to become ExxonMobil, then paid a record $1 billion fine for the cleanup.

Proactive Strategy

A proactive strategy is prompted by internal desires within the company, not by external pressures or threats of any kind. A proactive strategy indicates a company's voluntary commitment to social responsibility. Examples of proactive strategies are (1) Apple Computers' donation of laptops and iPods to schools, (2) the "adoption" by corporations of inner-city schools, and (3) Johnson & Johnson's voluntary withdrawal of unsealed medicines that might have been tampered with by outside sources.

Areas of Responsibility

A business's social responsibility spans environmental, consumer, and employee issues.

Environmental Issues

Concern for the environment is receiving global attention, and so are the companies that meet (or flaunt) their responsibility to maintain the environment. Pollution, toxic waste, the ozone layer, climatic changes, the depletion of natural resources, and global warming all are of growing concern worldwide.

Pollution—that is, the contamination of water, air, or land—now threatens human, animal, and plant life around the globe. In response to the concerns of individuals, organizations, and governments worldwide, pollution has become a major business issue. As a result, many laws have been enacted to protect the environment, as shown in Table 4.1.

Table 4.1: Laws Protecting the Environment

Legislation	Effect
National Environmental Policy Act of 1970	Established the Environmental Protection Agency (EPA) to enforce federal laws involving the environment
Clean Air Amendment of 1970	Set automotive-, aircraft-, and factory-emission standards
Water Quality Improvement Act of 1970	Strengthened existing water-pollution regulations and set fines for violators
Resource Recovery Act of 1970	Expanded the solid-waste disposal program and gave the EPA the power to enforce regulations
Water Pollution Control Act Amendment of 1972	Set standards for cleaning navigable inland waterways, lakes, and streams
Noise Control Act of 1972	Established standards for noise abatement that covers the aviation industry, among others
Clean Air Amendment of 1977	Established new deadlines for cleaning up polluted areas and required reviews of existing air-quality standards
Comprehensive Environmental Response, Compensation, and Liability Act (or Superfund) of 1980	This law imposed a tax on the chemical and petroleum industries and conveyed broad Federal authority to address releases or threatened releases of hazardous substances that may endanger public health or the environment.
Resource Conservation and Recovery Act of 1984	Amended the 1976 solid-waste laws and established federal regulations for dangerous solid-waste disposal
The Superfund Amendments and Reauthorization Act of 1986	Made several important changes and additions to the complex Superfund program, based on the program's first six years of experience
The Emergency Planning & Community Right-to-Know Act of 1986	Enacted by Congress as the national legislation on community safety, this law helps local communities protect public health, safety, and the environment from chemical hazards.
The Oil Pollution Act of 1990	Streamlined and strengthened the EPA's ability to prevent and respond to catastrophic oil spills
The Pollution Prevention Act of 1990	Focused industry, government, and public attention on reducing the amount of pollution through cost-effective changes in production, operation, and raw materials usage
Food Quality Protection Act of 1996	Amended the Federal Insecticide, Fungicide, and Rodenticide Act (FIFRA) and the Federal Food Drug, and Cosmetic Act (FFDCA) by fundamentally changing the way EPA regulates pesticides
Chemical Safety Information, Site Security, and Fuels Regulatory Relief Act of 1999	Amended the Clean Air Act, to remove flammable fuels from the list of reportable items and for other purposes

Although these laws address past damages and try to prevent further damage, they do not address the costs of repair and prevention, and more to the point, who should pay those costs.

For environmentalists, the answer is clear: Corporations should pay. Environmentalists claim that proper treatment and disposal of industrial wastes are part of the expense of doing business. For business leaders, the answer is tax money. They argue that business is not the sole source of pollution and that tax money, therefore, should be used to pay for cleaning up the environment and preventing further damage. In either case, whether through higher prices or higher taxes, the public will indirectly bear the burden of the costs.

Consumer Issues

Consumerism identifies all activities intended to protect consumers in their dealings with business. Consumerism emerged as a force in the 1960s with President John F. Kennedy's consumer bill of rights, which underscored consumers' rights to safety, to be informed, to choose, and to be heard.

The Right to Safety

The right to safety states that consumer products must be safe for their intended use. Manufacturers must provide complete directions for product use and must test products to ensure quality and reliability.

The Right to Be Informed

The right to be informed gives consumers complete information about a product. Food packaging must itemize ingredients, clothing labels must reveal fabric content and laundering instructions, and credit agreements must detail all financing costs.

The Right to Choose

The right to choose, which gives consumers the privilege of choosing from among different products, is intended to increase competition. Antitrust legislation contributes to consumers' right to choose by increasing choices and reducing prices.

The Right to Be Heard

The right to be heard means that consumers' complaints should be heard, and that appropriate action should be taken as a result of consumer complaints. Most businesses value consumers' comments and actively solicit their responses to products and services. Many companies have Consumer Relations Departments for the specific purpose of listening to consumers' comments and satisfying their needs; doing so can provide a competitive edge. The Better Business Bureau, a private organization, helps consumers be heard. In support of these consumers' rights, legislation since 1960 has resulted in major advances in consumer protection, as shown in Table 4.2.

As a result of consumer legislation, business has, understandably, become increasingly sensitive to consumer issues.

Employee Issues

As awareness of social issues and of consumer issues grew, advances were achieved. Likewise, in the area of employment issues, awareness preceded advances. Title VII of the Civil Rights Act of 1964 forbids discrimination on the basis of race, color, religion, or national origin in hiring, compensation, terms of employment, working conditions, and any other privileges of employment. The Equal Employment Opportunity Act of 1972 was passed as an amendment to Title VII. This act established the Equal Employment Opportunity Commission (EEOC), a government agency that has the right to file suit against

Table 4.2: Laws Protecting the Consumer

Federal Hazardous Substances Labeling Act of 1960	Required manufacturers to place warning labels on toxic household chemicals
Color Additives Amendment of 1960	Required full disclosure concerning the addition of any food colorings to edible products
Kefauver-Harris Drug Amendments of 1962	Established drug-testing practices and requires pharmaceuticals to be labeled by their generic names
Cigarette Labeling Act of 1965	Required warning labels on cigarette packages
Fair Packaging and Labeling Act of 1966	Required that packaging of products sold interstate include net weight, ingredients, and the manufacturer's name and address
Motor Vehicle Safety Act of 1966	Established standards for safer cars
Wholesome Meat Act of 1967	Required state inspection of meat (not poultry) sold within a state
Flammable Fabrics Act of 1967	Strengthened the standards of flammability of children's sleepwear
Truth in Lending Act of 1968	Required lenders and credit merchants to disclose the full cost of finance charges in both dollars and percentage
Land Sales Disclosure Act of 1968	Provided consumer protection in interstate land sales
Child Protection and Toy Act of 1969	Banned toys with mechanical or electrical defects from interstate commerce
Credit Card Liability Act of 1970	Limited a cardholder's liability to $50 and prohibited the issuance of unsolicited cards
Fair Credit Reporting Act of 1971	Required credit bureaus to provide reports to consumers regarding their individual credit files and to correct errors, if any
Consumer Product Safety Commission Act of 1972	Established the Consumer Product Safety Commission
Trade Regulation Rule of 1972	Established the 72-hour cooling-off period for door-to-door sales, essentially giving consumers the right to cancel any door-to-door purchase within a three-day period of signing the agreement
Fair Credit Billing Act of 1974	Amended the Truth in Lending Act to permit consumers to challenge billing errors
Equal Credit Opportunity Act of 1974	Provided equal credit opportunities for males and females, and for married and single individuals
Magnuson-Moss Warranty-Federal Trade Commission Act of 1975	Provided for minimum disclosure standards for written warranties for products costing over $15
Amendment to Equal Credit Opportunity Act of 1976	Prohibited discrimination based on race, creed, color, religion, age, and income when granting credit
Fair Debt Collection Practices Act of 1977	Outlawed abusive collection practices by third parties
Drug Price Competition and Patent Restoration Act of 1984	Abbreviated procedures for registering generic drugs
Orphan Drug Act of 1985	Amended the 1983 Act and extended tax incentives to encourage development of drugs for rare diseases
Fair Credit Reporting Act of 2001	Required credit-reporting agencies to provide free annual reports

Table 4.3: Laws Protecting the Employee

Fair Labor Standards Act (FLSA) of 1938	Prohibited employment of persons under the age of 18 and established a minimum wage, time-and-one-half pay for overtime, and a forty-hour work week
Equal Pay Act of 1963	Called for equal pay for men and women for jobs requiring equal skill, effort, responsibility, and working conditions
Civil Rights Act of 1964, Title VII	Prohibited employment decisions that discriminate on the basis of race, sex, religion, color, or national origin
Executive Order 11246 (1965)	Required federal contractors underutilizing minorities to specify goals and timetables to affirmatively recruit, train, and promote minority individuals
Age Discrimination in Employment Act of 1967	Prohibited (1) discrimination in employment based on age and (2) mandatory retirement before the age of 70
Occupational Safety and Health Act (OSHA) of 1970	Requireed employers to provide working conditions that will not harm employees
Vocational Rehabilitation Act of 1973	Required federal contractors to develop programs to employ handicapped persons

employers if an acceptable resolution of job discrimination charges against them cannot be obtained within a reasonable time period. In essence, the equal opportunity legislation protects the rights of citizens to work and get a fair wage rate based on merit and performance.

Government Legislation

Among the laws and executive orders intended to combat discrimination and protect the rights and safety of employees are those shown in Table 4.3.

Selected Readings

Carroll, Archie B. *Social Responsibility of Management.* 1984.
Case, John. *Understanding Inflation.* 1981.
Churchman, C. West. *The Systems Approach.* 1968.
Council of Economic Priorities. *Rating America's Corporate Conscience.* 1986.
Drucker, Peter F. *The New Realities.* 1990.
Dunphy, Dexter, Suzanne Ben, and Andrew Griffiths. *Organizational Change for Corporate Sustainability: Understanding Organizational Change.* 2002.
Friedman, Milton. *Capitalism and Freedom.* 1962.
Friedman, Thomas. *The World is Flat: A Brief History of the Twenty-First Century* 2005.
Fuchs, Victor R. *How We Live: An Economic Perspective on Americans from Birth to Death.* 1984.
Fullan, Michael. *Leadership and Sustainability: System Thinkers in Action.* 2004.
Galea, Chris, editor. *Teaching Business Sustainability: From Theory to Practice.* 2004.
Hart, Stuart L. *Capitalism at the Crossroads.* 2005.
Jacoby, Neil H. *Corporate Power and Responsibility.* 1973.
Janeway, Eliot. *The Economics of Chaos.* 1989.

Krugman, Paul. *The Age of Diminished Expectations: U.S. Economic Policy in the 1990s,* Third Edition. 1997.

Levien, Roy, and Marco Iansiti. *The Keystone Advantage: What the New Dynamics of Business Ecosystems Mean for Strategy, Innovation, and Sustainability.* 2004.

Manley, Walter W., and William A. Shrode. *Critical Issues in Business Conduct: Legal, Ethical, and Social Challenges for the 1990s.* 1990.

Millstein, Ira M., and Salem M. Katsh. *The Limits of Corporate Power: Existing Constraints on the Exercise of Corporate Discretion.* 1981.

Nader, Ralph. *Unsafe at Any Speed.* 1972.

Peters, Tom. *Thriving on Chaos.* 1987.

Pfeffer, Jeffrey, and Gerald Salancik. *The External Control of Organizations: A Resource Dependence Perspective.* 1978.

Prahalad, C.K. *The Fortune at the Base of the Pyramid.* 2005.

Rawls, John. *A Theory of Justice.* 1971.

Rostow, Walt W. *Stages of Economic Growth.* 1973.

Stern, Alisa J., and Tim Hicks. *The Process of Business/Environmental Collaborations: Partnering for Sustainability.* 2000.

Stone, Christopher D. *Where the Law Ends: The Social Control of Corporate Behavior.* 1975.

Toffler, Alvin. *The Third Wave.* 1984.

Von Hippel, E. *The Sources of Innovation.* 1988.

Test Yourself

1) Which element in an automobile manufacturing system would the following items be: a finished automobile, steering column assembly, increased automobile sales, and sheet metal?

2) List five stakeholders for a coal-mining company.

3) True or false: Companies are less active in attempting to affect public policy than they were 100 years ago.

4) List four consumer rights.

5) True or false: The Civil Rights Act of 1964 prohibits age discrimination in the workplace.

6) What are the external forces or variables that influence the way businesses function?

7) Companies adopt different strategies to meet, or to limit, their social responsibilities, depending upon their policies. Name some of the more common strategies they adopt.

8) The Fair Labor Standards Act of 1938 limits the employment of persons under the age of 18. Name three other important provisions of the act.

9) What does the Fair Credit Reporting Act of 2001 require?

10) What is the significance of the Trade Regulation Rule of 1972?

Test Yourself Answers

1) The elements, respectively, would be output, process, feedback, and input.

2) Potential stakeholders include miners, shareholders, local community, country, government, managers, customers, suppliers.

3) False. Companies face much greater government regulation and intervention, and so are more involved in minimizing the intervention.

4) The four consumer rights are the right to safety, the right to be informed, the right to choose, and the right to be heard.

5) False. This act prohibits discrimination based upon race, sex, religion, color, or national origin. It took a second act, the Age Discrimination in Employment Act, to prohibit age discrimination.

6) The forces are economic, social, technological, and political.

7) Common strategies include denial strategy, reaction strategy, defense strategy, accommodation strategy, and proactive strategy.

8) The act also established a minimum wage, time-and-one-half pay for overtime, and a forty-hour work week.

9) The act requires credit-reporting agencies to provide free annual reports.

10) The rule established a 72-hour cooling-off period for door-to-door sales, giving consumers the right to cancel the sale within three days of entering the agreement.

CHAPTER 5
The Global Marketplace

In the earliest days of society, trade was carried on within a village. Then it expanded to neighboring villages. As states and countries emerged, this expansion process included larger and larger areas of trade. Today, trade crosses all borders and oceans.

■ THE FOUNDATIONS OF INTERNATIONAL TRADE

International trade—that is, trading between countries—has been long established. But the globalization of business, multinational businesses operating worldwide, is a newer, important factor in international trade, and globalization will grow even more important in the years immediately ahead. About half of the total revenues of ExxonMobil, Texaco, IBM, Citicorp, Dow Chemical, and many others already come from operations outside the United States.

The key factors in international business are discussed in the following sections.

Specialization

Natural resources, populations, climate, and navigable waterways are not evenly distributed throughout our planet. As a result, a country that is better equipped to produce certain goods or services than other countries has an opportunity to specialize in that good or service. Specialization may give that country an absolute advantage or a comparative advantage.

Absolute Advantage

Two countries that provide excellent examples of specialization because of their huge reserves of valuable natural resources are Saudi Arabia (oil) and South Africa (diamonds). In the United States, California and Florida have a climate that is perfect for growing citrus fruit, while Maine and Idaho have a climate perfect for producing potatoes. Each country or region has an absolute advantage regarding that specific product, allowing it to produce that product more efficiently than any other region.

Comparative Advantage

A country has a comparative advantage when it can produce a specific product more efficiently than other countries can produce the product.

Exporting and Importing

For a number of reasons, in today's world, no country is self-sufficient. Because of the demands of contemporary lifestyles and other key factors, a country buys goods—that is, imports goods—from countries that have a comparative advantage in the production of those goods. In turn, the importing country sells goods—that is, exports goods—in which it has a comparative advantage to other countries. This exchange between countries forms the basis of importing and exporting. For each international transaction there is an importer and exporter.

- **Importing** consists of purchasing goods, raw materials, or services from other countries and bringing the goods into the home country.
- **Exporting** consists of selling and shipping goods, raw materials, or services from the home country to another country.

Balance of Trade

The difference between a country's total imports and its total exports (both measured in dollar value) over a given period is its balance of trade.

- A **trade deficit**, or an unfavorable balance of trade, exists when the value of the imports exceeds the value of exports.
- A **trade surplus**, or a favorable balance of trade, results when the value of exports is greater than the value of imports.

Balance of Payments

Another measure, the balance of payments, is much broader than the balance of trade. The balance of payments includes not only the imports and exports that make up the balance of trade but also money invested by foreigners, money spent by foreign tourists, foreign investments by Americans, and money spent overseas by American tourists. The balance of payments also includes payments from foreign governments, aid given to foreign governments, and any other international payments and receipts. In the last decade, the United States has had an increasingly unfavorable balance of payments.

Exchange Rates

In international trade, the value of any currency, or money, is expressed in terms of another currency, and this value is its exchange rate. The United States trade deficit has resulted in a less-favorable exchange rate for the U.S. dollar.

Exchange rates respond to the law of supply and demand. For example, since the early 1980s, the United States has bought Japanese products in far larger amounts than it has sold U.S. goods to Japan, increasing the supply of U.S. dollars in Japan. In turn, the value of the dollar in relation to the Japanese yen has fallen steadily, until very recently.

Exchange rates vary from day to day. For example, on October 11, 2005, one U.S. dollar could be exchanged on the world market for the currencies noted in Table 5.1.

Table 5.1: Currency Exchange Rates

Currency	Currency Per U.S. Dollar
British pound	0.57270
Canadian dollar	1.1765
Euro	0.83390
Japanese yen	114.55
Swiss franc	1.2898

Until 1971, the world economy operated on a fixed rate of exchange set by each country. For example, one U.S. dollar always equaled .3571 British pounds. In 1971, most countries abandoned the fixed rates because fixed rates no longer reflected economic reality. Instead, the exchange rate was allowed to fluctuate (that is, float). Today, China stands as the one superpower that continues to maintain a fixed exchange rate, pegged to a basket of world currencies.

Adjusting Currency Values

A continuing imbalance of trade will cause the value of one currency to decline and the other to rise. There are two artificial solutions to the problem: devaluation and revaluation.

- **Devaluation** is an arbitrary downward adjustment of one country's currency in terms of another country's currency.
- **Revaluation** is an arbitrary upward adjustment of one country's currency in terms of another country's currency.

Balancing Payments

To attain a desired balance of payments, the former Soviet Union set a fixed rate of exchange and enforced the rate by law. The free-market solution is to increase exports from the nation with the unfavorable balance to its trading partner with the favorable balance. For example, to reduce its trade deficit with Japan and bring payments back into balance, the United States tries to sell more of the goods and services in which it has a comparative advantage to Japan. The free market, however, is not completely unrestricted.

■ RESTRICTIONS ON TRADE

In 1776, in *The Wealth of Nations,* Adam Smith argued that specialization and free trade with no artificial barriers would eliminate trade imbalances. His theory has been tested ever since. Although over 200 years have passed, Smith's ideal of a free market has yet to be realized. Among the obstacles has been protectionism.

Protectionism describes the creation of artificial barriers to free international trade. These barriers are designed to protect domestic industries and jobs or to equalize the balance of payments.

Protectionism can take many forms. Proponents of protectionism are found among labor unions, business managers in certain industries, farmers, and others who feel threatened by foreign competition. There are a number of barriers to protectionism, discussed in the following sections.

Tariffs

Nations have historically used tariffs to protect their industries and their balance of payments.

Protective Tariffs

Protective tariffs are taxes imposed on imported goods. By making the goods more expensive, protective tariffs limit the sales of the imported goods and, therefore, protect domestic industries. For example, a tariff on imported shoes attempts to protect the domestic shoe industry by raising the price of imported shoes as compared to shoes produced domestically.

Revenue Tariffs

Revenue tariffs are imposed solely to generate income for the government.

Import Quotas

Import quotas limit the quantity of a particular good that can be brought into a country during a specified period of time. In recent years, the United States imposed an import quota on the number of Japanese cars entering the country. However, the Japanese responded by exporting fewer but more-expensive automobiles to the United States. Thus, they were able to continue to increase their dollar volume and profit while still meeting the demands of the import quotas.

Embargoes

An embargo is a government law or regulation forbidding either the importing or the exporting of certain specified goods. An embargo is designed to protect technology or to punish another nation, not to protect domestic business and industry. As a national defense measure, for example, the United States embargoes the export of nuclear-related technology. As a punishment, the United States has embargoed the import of Cuban goods since 1961, and exports to Iraq from before the first Gulf War (1991) through the ousting of Saddam Hussein in the second Gulf War (2003 to present).

Bureaucratic Red Tape

Bureaucratic red tape, the colorful name given to describe the complicated web of government regulations and procedures, is perhaps the most widely used and most effective trade barrier. Either deliberately (as a result of policies) or accidentally, in many countries, the regulations and paperwork involved in import-export transactions produce delays, confusion, and frustration. Among the international barriers encountered are laws that require permits, licenses, and item-by-item inspections as well as business-practice laws that, in some cases, make the payment of bribes legal and permit cartels to control prices.

Foreign-Exchange Control

Foreign-exchange control restricts the amount of a particular foreign currency that can be bought or sold, in effect limiting the amount of goods an importer can purchase with that currency. Critics of foreign-exchange controls point out that the cost of these restrictions can be considerable, that these costs are passed on to the consumer in the form of artificially higher prices, and that controls restrict consumer choice, causing resources to be misallocated.

■ INTERNATIONAL TRADE AGREEMENTS

In spite of the protectionist barriers cited above, there has been a strong movement toward encouraging international trade. Virtually every country has trade agreements with other countries or groups of countries for the specific purpose of encouraging international trade.

General Agreement on Tariffs and Trade (GATT)

The General Agreement on Tariffs and Trade (GATT), signed by ninety-two countries shortly after the end of World War II, is both a treaty and an organization (based in Geneva, Switzerland) to administer the treaty. GATT offers a forum for settling international trade disputes and for negotiating tariffs. GATT has sponsored a number of international meetings, called rounds, intended to reduce trade restrictions. The Kennedy Round (begun in 1964) and the Tokyo Round (begun in 1973) succeeded in reducing a number of both tariff and non-tariff barriers. One of GATT's aims was to reduce import taxes to 5 percent worldwide; however, this aim has been ignored by most signatories.

United Nations Agencies

Two agencies of the United Nations help finance international trade, although they are not involved in either reducing tariffs or pricing goods. They are the International Monetary Fund and the World Bank.

The International Monetary Fund (IMF)

The International Monetary Fund (IMF) uses contributions from UN member nations to make loans to nations with balance-of-trade problems. The IMF ties certain economic changes to loan approvals, often including, for example, cuts in social programs designed to reduce inflation; as a result, some countries are unwilling to accept IMF loans.

The World Bank

The World Bank makes loans to less-developed countries in order to help them improve their production capacity.

■ INTERNATIONAL ECONOMIC COMMUNITIES

The aim of GATT is to remove barriers on a global scale. On a more modest scale, several groups of countries have joined to promote common economic policies and free movement of products and resources among their members. The major organizations are listed in the following sections.

The European Union (EU)

The European Union (EU) group of nations came together to advance its common interest. It was formed in January, 1958. However, since that time, membership has increased significantly, and the scope of activities and concerns has expanded tremendously.

The EU currently consists of 25 member countries, with five more scheduled to join in the near future (see Table 5.2).

Table 5.2: European Union Member Countries

Member Countries		Candidate Countries
Austria	Latvia	Bulgaria
Belgium	Lithuania	Croatia
Cyprus	Luxemburg	Romania
Czech Republic	Malta	Turkey
Denmark	The Netherlands	Former Yugoslav Republic of Macedonia
Estonia	Poland	
Finland	Portugal	
France	Slovakia	
Germany	Slovenia	
Greece	Spain	
Hungary	Sweden	
Ireland	United Kingdom	
Italy		

As of January 1, 2003, the EU has had its own currency, which replaced the currencies of a number of the member countries. Moreover, the currency has proven to be very strong.

The European Free Trade Association (EFTA)

The European Free Trade Association (EFTA), formed in 1960 in response to the formation of the EU, has eliminated many trade restrictions among its members and has developed some common policies for trade among its members and the 25 members of the European Union. Currently, the EFTA includes four nations: Iceland, Liechtenstein, Norway, and Switzerland.

A number of former members of the EFTA withdrew to join the EU. However, the EFTA now has a working relationship with the EU, including a free-trade agreement.

The Latin American Integration Association (LAIA)

The Latin American Integration Association (LAIA), successor to an earlier Latin American Free Trade Association, includes the following member countries.

- Argentina
- Bolivia
- Brazil
- Chile
- Colombia
- Ecuador
- Mexico
- Paraguay
- Peru
- Uruguay
- Venezuela

To date, the LAIA has achieved only limited economic integration.

The North American Free Trade Agreement (NAFTA)

In January 1994, Canada, the United States, and Mexico signed the North American Free Trade Agreement (NAFTA), forming the world's largest free-trade area. At least arguably, the agreement has had a significant impact on the economic interactions among the three countries. However, in the United States, the agreement is both applauded as a resounding success and blasted as a resounding bust.

The U.S./Canada Free Trade Agreement

The U.S./Canada Free Trade Agreement between the world's largest trading partners went into effect in 1989. When fully implemented, and after a gradual removal of all trade barriers, the result will be a North American marketplace resembling that of the current European Union, in terms of a more integrated marketplace.

The Organization of Petroleum Exporting Countries (OPEC)

The Organization of Petroleum Exporting Countries (OPEC) is an international economic organization of a different kind. OPEC was formed in 1960 not to reduce trade barriers but to control and regulate the price and production of crude oil. The membership has changed over its life. The OPEC's member nations as of March 2007, include the following.

- Algeria
- Angola
- Indonesia
- Iran
- Iraq
- Kuwait
- Libya
- Nigeria
- Qatar
- Saudi Arabia
- United Arab Emirates
- Venezuela

Although members do not always fully cooperate, OPEC has succeeded in raising and maintaining the price of crude oil well above pre-OPEC levels.

■ LEVELS OF INVOLVEMENT IN INTERNATIONAL TRADE

Businesses that decide to enter the international trade arena must decide on their level of involvement. Several approaches, discussed in the following sections, are available to companies.

Licensing

Licensing, a basic level of entering international trade, is a contractual agreement in which one firm permits another to produce and market its product or to use its brand name in return for a royalty or other compensation. Licensing permits a company to expand into a foreign market with little investment; however, since the licensee is in charge of the operations, the licensing firm gains no firsthand foreign marketing experience. Another disadvantage is the risk that the licensee may not maintain quality levels, thereby damaging the product's image.

Exporting

A higher level of involvement is needed when a firm decides to export manufactured products for sale in foreign markets. The exporting firm may use its own sales force. Or it may sell its products to an import/export merchant firm, a merchant wholesaler that assumes all the risks of product ownership, distribution, and sales. The import/export firm may even purchase the goods in the manufacturer's home country and take all responsibility for export.

As an alternative, an exporting firm may use an import/export agent, who is a resident of the foreign country and represents the firm's products in that country. Import/export agents have the necessary market knowledge, sales knowledge, and contacts in that particular environment. Agents are paid on the basis of their sales and represent a low-cost entry into exporting.

The reputation of the agent is an important consideration. Since the manufacturing firm has no office in the foreign country, the agent is the only recourse for customers who have problems with product quality or defects or with service.

Joint Venture

Under an international joint venture, a domestic firm forms a partnership with a foreign company in order to produce and/or market the domestic firm's product abroad. Unlike a licensing arrangement, both parties put resources and capital into the new venture, and both parties share in the profits.

Joint ventures have become an increasingly popular way to move into international trade. In some countries, joint ventures are almost the only way to start an international business, because many countries have laws requiring that firms making an investment in the country have a local joint-venture partner. Although an international joint venture supplies a partner with local knowledge and expertise, it also removes some of the domestic company's control.

Direct Investment

Many major corporations and some smaller ones have chosen to make direct investments overseas by establishing plants or other facilities or buying an existing firm in a foreign country. A substantial portion of the total assets of companies such as ExxonMobil, IBM, General Motors, and Dow Chemical is represented by direct investment overseas. The decision on the part of Japan's Honda to build automobiles in the United States is another example.

Although direct investment requires higher costs, it makes the company a part of the business life of the foreign country. Benefits include access to information; tax advantages; and exemption from import duties, regulations, and laws governing outside firms. Because of the size of the investment involved, errors concerning the marketability of the product can be costly. In addition to the economic risks of direct investment, there can be political risks in some countries—for example, the risk of nationalization: seizure of the company's assets by the foreign country.

International Firms

An international firm does business overseas by selling goods designed and manufactured domestically. It may have plants overseas, but its headquarters are domestic. Domestic marketing and manufacturing are the company's main concerns.

Multinational Firms

A multinational firm designs, produces, and markets products in many countries. It operates on a worldwide scale, without ties to any specific nation. It does not have a domestic division and an international division, for example, but instead gears its planning and decision-making to one international level regardless of where its headquarters may be. Unilever, Royal Dutch Shell, Nestlé, Ford, IBM, ExxonMobil—all are truly multinational firms. Ford, for example, with plants in several countries, plans and builds models in the United States, some of which are not sold overseas; at the same time Ford plans and builds other models overseas, some of which are not sold in the United States.

There are many advantages to multinationalism, including local management, the ability to buy raw materials locally, local R&D, and some protection from international currency fluctuations. Overseas operations for multinational firms are important independent enterprises.

This chapter has addressed the globalization of business, a new but important factor in international trade—and growing more important every year. Each day, meetings at many levels are underway for the specific purpose of trying to reduce or limit trade barriers, to find ways to finance international trade, and to move toward a free-market economy. Governments worldwide are increasingly involved with commercial diplomacy, encouraging and promoting international trade and a world economy.

Selected Readings

Ball, Donald A., editor. *International Business: The Challenge of Global Competition.* 2005.

Barlett, Christopher A. *Managing Across Borders.* 2002.

Chandler, Alfred D., Jr. *Scale and Scope: The Dynamics of Industrial Capitalism.* 1990.

Chen, Ming-Jer. *Inside Chinese Business: A Guide for Managers Worldwide.* 2003.

Davies, Paul. *What's This India Business: Offshoring, Outsourcing, and the Global Services Revolution.* 2004.

Dicken, Peter. *Global Shift: Reshaping the Global Economic Map in the 21st Century.* 2003.

Dun & Bradstreet's *Principals of International Businesses.* Annual, 1974–.

Harris, Philip R., Robert T. Moran, and Sarah V. Moran. *Managing Cultural Differences: Global Leadership Strategies for the 21st Century.* 2004.

Hart, Stuart L. *Capitalism at the Crossroads.* 2005.

Johannson, Hano, and G. Terry Page, editors. *International Dictionary of Business.* 1986.

Marber, Peter. *Money Changes Everything: How Global Prosperity Is Reshaping Our Needs, Values, and Lifestyles.* 2003.

Nelson, Carl A. *Global Success: International Business Tactics for the 1990s.* 1990.

Ohmae, Kenichi. *Beyond National Borders.* 1987.

Porter, Michael E. *The Competitive Advantage of Nations.* 1990.

Prahalad, C.K. *The Fortune at the Bottom of the Pyramid.* 2005.
Rostow, W.W. *Theorists of Economic Growth from David Hume to the Present: With a Perspective on the New Century.* 1990.
Servan-Schreiber, Jean-Jacques. *The American Challenge.* 1968.
Thomas, David C., and Kerr Inkson. *Cultural Intelligence: People Skills for Global Business.* 2004.
Walter, Ingo and Tracy Murray, editors. *Handbook of International Business.* 1982.
Wilkens, Mira. *The Emergence of Multinational Enterprise.* 1970.

Test Yourself

1) Define both imports and exports, and explain their impacts on the balance of trade.

2) Distinguish the balance of trade from the balance of payments.

3) Define protectionism and provide examples.

4) What is the European Union and how many member countries are members?

5) Distinguish an international firm from a multinational firm.

6) What is the Organization of Petroleum Exporting Countries (OPEC)?

7) What is the General Agreement on Tariffs and Trade (GATT)?

8) Two entities of the United Nations help finance international trade. What are they?

Test Yourself Answers

1) Imports are the purchasing of goods or raw materials from other countries, while exports consist of the selling of goods or raw materials from the home country to another country. When the value of imports exceeds the value of exports, a trade deficit results. On the other hand, when the value of exports is greater than the value of imports, a trade surplus results.

2) The balance of trade represents a country's total imports and its total exports over a given period of time. The balance of payments is much broader than the balance of trade; it includes not only the imports and exports, but also money invested by foreigners, money spent by foreign tourists, foreign investments by Americans, and money spent overseas by American tourists. The balance of payments also includes payments to and from foreign governments and any other international payments and receipts.

3) Protectionism is the creation of artificial barriers to free international trade, designed to protect domestic industries and jobs or to equalize the balance of payments. Protective tariffs are taxes imposed on imports. Import quotas limit the quantity of a particular good that can be brought into a country during a specified period of time. An embargo is a government law or regulation forbidding either the importing or the exporting of certain specified goods. Bureaucratic red tape—government regulations and procedures (e.g., required permits, licenses, and item-by-item inspections)—is perhaps the most widely effective trade barrier. Finally, foreign-exchange control restricts the amount of a particular foreign currency that can be bought or sold, in effect limiting the amount of goods an importer can purchase with that currency.

4) The European Union was formed in January 1958 to encourage free commerce among its member countries. Since then, the group of countries has grown to its current size of 25 members and five candidates.

5) An international firm does business overseas by selling goods designed and manufactured domestically. Its headquarters are domestic. A multinational business, on the other hand, designs, produces, and markets products in many countries. It operates on a worldwide basis.

6) OPEC is an international economic organization, formed in 1960, to control and regulate the price and production of crude oil.

7) The GATT is both an agreement and an organization. It was signed by ninety-two countries shortly after World War II. It is primarily aimed at providing a form for settling international trade disputes and for negotiating tariffs.

8) The International Monetary Fund (IMF) uses contributions from UN member nations to make loans to nations with balance-of-trade problems. The World Bank makes loans to less-developed countries to help them improve their production capacity.

Part 2: Business Formation and Structure

CHAPTER 6
The Legal Forms of Business

A business is a legal entity, and as legal entities, businesses can be organized in a variety of legal forms. In the United States, the three most common types of business organizations are sole proprietorship, partnership (including the limited liability partnership), and corporation (including the limited liability corporation) (see Figure 6.1). Each of these three forms of business ownership has advantages and disadvantages that business owners must consider at the time the business is organized. These advantages and disadvantages, as well as the features of these different forms of organization, are detailed in the following sections.

■ SOLE PROPRIETORSHIPS

Sole proprietorships are by far the most widely used business form in the world. Nearly 72 percent of all businesses in the United States are sole proprietorships; in fact, many of the largest companies in the country began as sole proprietorships. Although owned and managed by one person, the proprietorship may have many employees. Many local neighborhood businesses are sole proprietorships—retail, gift, floral, and shoe repair shops, for example—and are, therefore, owned by people who are self-employed.

Advantages of Sole Proprietorships

One advantage of a sole proprietorship is the ease of starting the business. Unless the business requires a license, as some professions (doctors and lawyers) and trades (plumbers and electricians) do, sole proprietorships can usually be established simply by opening the door and doing business. Other advantages are the cost of organization, tax considerations, and the ease of dissolution (i.e., the cessation of business).

Ease and Cost of Organization

Again, sole proprietorships are the easiest and least expensive forms of business to start. They demand no legal or organizational expenses. Frequently, the main investment is the labor and ability of the sole proprietor himself or herself. As long as the proposed activity is legal, anyone can start a sole proprietorship.

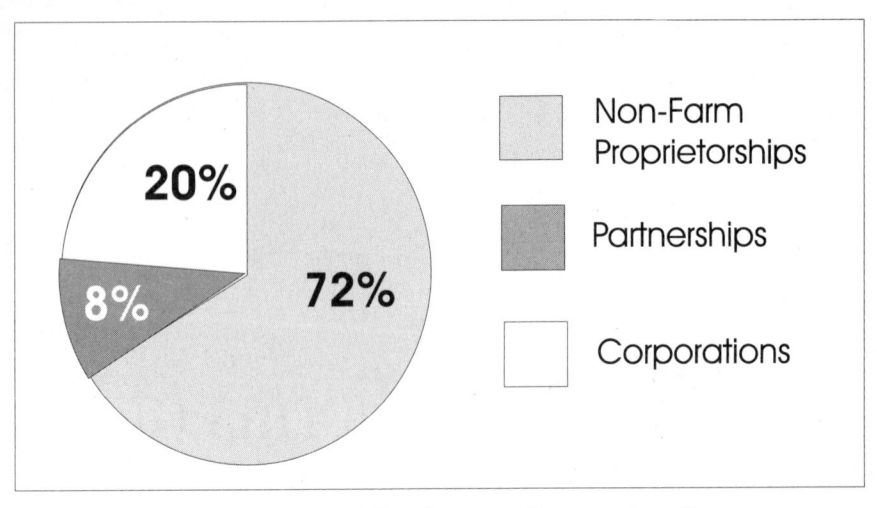

Percentage of Business Organizations

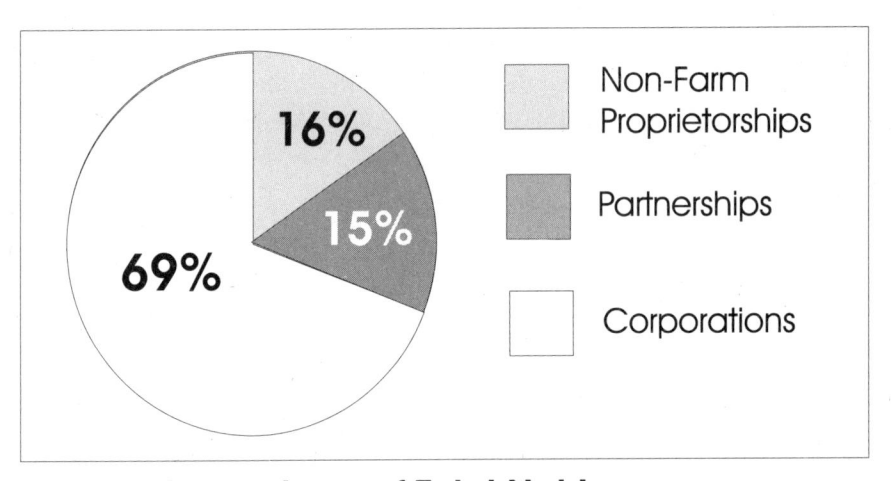

- Non-Farm Proprietorships: 72%
- Partnerships: 8%
- Corporations: 20%

Percentage of Total Net Income

- Non-Farm Proprietorships: 16%
- Partnerships: 15%
- Corporations: 69%

Figure 6.1: Relative Percentages of Types of Business Organizations

Tax Considerations

The sole proprietor directly receives any profits the business makes and absorbs any loss that the business may experience. The business pays no taxes, but all of the income from the business is considered the owner's personal income and is taxed accordingly. Thus, the owner has no obligation to reveal financial information to anyone other than the IRS. He or she can make all business decisions independently.

Ease of Dissolution

To dissolve a sole proprietorship, the owner can sell the business (remember that it is his or her personal property) or simply close the doors and stop doing business.

Disadvantages of Sole Proprietorships

The disadvantages of owning a sole proprietorship are several-fold. First, the owner has complete liability for the business. The owner of a sole proprietorship has limited ability to borrow. Also ownership does not continue automatically to others; there is a lack of continuity of ownership. And finally, sole proprietorships offer fewer career opportunities to employees and place greater demands on management.

Liability of Ownership

A sole proprietor has unlimited personal liability. His or her personal assets—home, automobile, personal savings, and so on—are considered part of the business. Therefore, the owner's personal assets are not protected from creditors.

Limited Ability to Borrow

When sole proprietors borrow money, they do so as individuals, using their own personal assets to finance personal loans. Borrowing power, therefore, is directly dependent on the credit standing of the proprietor. Thus, the owner of a successful business may not be able to borrow money for business expansion if he or she, for example, has large personal debts from a home mortgage or college tuition expenses.

Continuity of Ownership

The sole proprietorship has a limited life—namely, the life of the sole proprietor. With the death of the owner, the sole proprietorship ceases to exist.

Fewer Career Opportunities

Since the business is generally small, and career advancement is limited, recruiting and retaining good personnel can be difficult.

Demands on Management

Because a sole proprietorship is usually owned by a single individual, that person must have a multitude of abilities, skills, and experience in management, bookkeeping, sales, marketing, production skills, and so on.

■ PARTNERSHIPS

Partners are described in the legal definition of the Uniform Partnership Act as "co-owners of a business for profit." The partners agree to carry on a business and to share the profits and losses. Partnerships are easy to organize—a written or an oral agreement is all that is required. Partnerships can be small, with just two people, or large, with hundreds of partners (as in a very large law firm). Yet despite several positive features, the partnership is the least used of the three common forms of business ownership.

The partners need not be "equal"—that is, each partner's share of the ownership may vary, depending on the agreement among the partners.

Types of Partnerships

The individuals who participate in partnerships can be classified as general partners or limited partners.

A general partner bears full liability and is active in managing the business. Law and accounting firms are often made up of many general partners.

The liability of a limited partner, as the name suggests, is narrower—specifically, it is limited to the amount of the investment she or he made in the firm. Unlike general partners, limited partners usually are not actively involved in managing the firm. For liability purposes, a limited partnership is a hybrid, having some of the features of a partnership and some of a corporation. Limited partnerships are typically found in ventures in theatrical production, real estate, oil and gas, and professional athletic teams.

Advantages of Partnerships

Because a partnership is like joining two or more sole proprietorships, a partnership shares some of the advantages of a proprietorship, as discussed in the following sections.

Ease and Cost of Organization

The formation of a partnership does not require complicated or expensive organization. The major element is the partnership agreement, which an attorney can easily develop.

Tax Considerations

A partnership is neither singled out for government regulation nor subject to special taxes. The partnership's profits are not taxed, but treated instead as personal income of the partners, whether or not the profits are distributed to them.

Ability to Borrow

Because more than one person owns the business, the financial resources of the partners is increased—and with it, borrowing capacity.

Continuity of Ownership

When a partner wishes to leave the partnership or dies, that partner's share of the business can be sold to the remaining partner(s). An alternative solution is to sell the partner's share to an outside person, someone who is acceptable to the remaining partners. In this way, partnerships have continuity.

Fewer Demands on Management

Because there are at least two partners, in theory the partnership has greater management skills and other business talents available to it. Frequently, in fact, partnerships are formed by people of complementary skills, for example, a sales expert who works outside, bringing in business, and an operational professional who works inside, managing and supervising the day-to-day operation of the enterprise.

Career Opportunities for Employees

Partnerships have an added incentive for job applicants and talented employees alike—the opportunity to become a partner.

Disadvantages of Partnerships

The disadvantages of partnerships include the liability of ownership, potential for disagreement among partners, and the difficulty of dissolution.

Liability of Ownership

The major disadvantage is the degree of liability of the partners. Each general partner is liable for the full debts of the partnership.

Potential for Disagreement

Managerial difficulties may arise when two or more partners cannot agree. And even when there is agreement, control is divided, making operations very difficult.

Difficulty of Dissolution

It is easy to enter into partnerships, but often difficult to withdraw with the full original investment. It is not easy to sell one's share of a partnership. A partnership is dissolved every time a new member is added or an existing member ceases to be a partner either through withdrawal or by death.

The Limited Liability Partnership (LLP)

A Limited Liability Partnership (or LLP) operates much like a ordinary partnership; however, it allows the members of the LLP to engage actively in the management of the business of the partnership without becoming personally liable for others' acts, except to the extent of their investment in the LLP. The partners remain unlimitedly liable (i.e., to the extent of their personal assets) for their own transgressions. Many law and accounting firms now operate as LLPs.

■ CORPORATIONS

The corporation is clearly the dominant element in the American economy in terms of total sales, profits, and number of employees. Corporations employ millions of people and are owned by millions of investors. United States Chief Justice John Marshall, in a famous 1819 decision, wrote that a corporation "is an artificial being, invisible, intangible, and existing only in the contemplation of the law." Although it is not a real person, a corporation can conduct business, own and sell property, borrow money, and sue and be sued. In fact, most laws that apply to people also apply to corporations.

A corporation must be chartered. A charter is the official agreement that establishes and describes the corporation. When selecting the state in which to charter the corporation, the incorporators must consider where the corporation will conduct most of its business, what charter restrictions may be imposed in that particular state, and which taxes and fees must be paid to the state. Each state specifies the minimum amount of capital required to start the corporation and imposes both an annual fee for the privilege of doing business as a corporation and an incorporation fee.

Forming a Corporation

A corporation comes into being when a state, in response to an application by the incorporators, issues a certificate of incorporation or corporate charter authorizing the corporation to do business. The corporate charter, also called the articles of incorporation, provides information such as the purpose of the corporation, its name and address, the names and addresses of its officers and board of directors, the number of shares of stock, the classes of stock (common, preferred), and the rights of each class of stockholder.

Domestic, Foreign, and Alien Corporations

A corporation is considered a domestic corporation in the state in which it is incorporated. In other states, it is considered a foreign corporation. An American corporation that does business in a foreign country is known as an alien corporation. American Express, for example, is incorporated in Delaware, and in Delaware it is a domestic corporation. In Illinois, American Express is a foreign corporation and in England, an alien corporation.

Differences between Corporations and Other Forms of Business

Corporations are different from sole proprietorships and partnerships in several ways. Corporations must meet formal legal requirements before they are formed. Ownership (that is, the shareholders) and management are separated; the shareholders do not directly manage the corporation. Corporate owners have limited financial liability. Finally, corporations have unlimited life.

Each of the forms of business organization has its own set of advantages and disadvantages. The choice of the best form for any given enterprise is not always clear and must be carefully considered. Many businesses start as sole proprietorships or partnerships. As they grow and both financial and management needs increase, they may choose to incorporate to increase their ability to secure funds. As a corporation, additional funds for purchasing new equipment or developing new products can be obtained by selling additional shares of stock.

Corporate Framework

The corporation has a clearly defined framework, consisting of shareholders, a board of directors, and management.

Shareholders

Each share of stock represents ownership in the corporation. Thus, the owners of stock are called shareholders. Each share of common stock carries with it the right to cast one vote in electing members of the board of directors. The number of directors is established in the corporate charter.

Shareholders also vote on any changes in the corporate charter and on the appointment of a certified public accountant (CPA) to audit the firm's books. When shareholders cannot attend the corporation's annual meeting, they vote by proxy. A proxy is a statement that authorizes someone else to vote for the shareholder.

Board of Directors

The board of directors represents the shareholders, sets corporate policy, and distributes dividends. It has the final authority for all corporate actions. The board of directors meets regularly and is required to hold an annual meeting, which is open to all shareholders. Within the board of directors there are committees that deal with company audits, compensation of the chief executive officer (CEO), long-range strategy, and other issues. An inside director is an employee of the corporation, someone engaged in its day-to-day operations. Usually, the president of the corporation serves as an inside director on the board. An outside director is not an employee, but someone outside the corporation, frequently a banker, a supplier, or someone representing a group of stockholders.

Management

The board of directors selects and hires the corporation's senior managers in charge of day-to-day operations, such as the president and chief executive officer.

Types of Corporations

There are a number of types of corporations. The type of corporation is determined by the purpose specified in its charter.

Public Corporations

A public corporation is one set up by Congress or a state legislature for a specific public service. Examples are the Federal Deposit Insurance Corporation (FDIC) and the Student Loan Marketing Association.

Quasi-Public Corporations

A quasi-public corporation is a corporation to which the government has granted a monopoly in an effort to provide certain services to the public. Public utility companies, supplying gas or electricity, and regional telephone companies are examples of quasi-public corporations.

Private Corporations

Most corporations are private corporations, formed by private individuals or companies and chartered for some purpose other than providing a public utility service. There are several types of private corporations.

A nonprofit corporation is one set up for charitable, educational, or fraternal purposes. Examples include the Multiple Sclerosis Society, the Girl Scouts of the USA, and all private colleges. A nonprofit corporation, despite its name, may make a profit, but profits cannot be distributed to owners; the use of profits is clearly stipulated in the corporate charter.

A for-profit corporation is formed to make profits for its owners, who receive these profits in the form of dividends. Most corporations are for-profit corporations. In fact, there are millions of for-profit corporations, and most are privately owned.

For-profit corporations may be privately owned, or they may be publicly traded. The distinction is that privately owned corporations do not allow outside investors to buy shares, as publicly traded corporations do. Relatively few corporations are publicly traded, but most of the very largest corporations are, including all those listed on the various stock exchanges where stocks are bought and sold. However, some very large companies—Mars Candy and Revlon Cosmetics among them—are privately owned.

There are three additional varieties of privately owned for-profit corporations.

- A **professional corporation (PC)** is one whose shareholders are professionals offering medical, legal, or engineering services.
- A **closely held corporation** cannot have more than fifty shareholders. Some states allow closely held corporations to dispense with a board of directors.
- A **subchapter S corporation** takes its name from a certain section of the Internal Revenue Code that describes corporations treated, for federal tax purposes, essentially as partnerships. A subchapter S corporation can have no more than 35 shareholders.

Other Types of Corporations

Other types of corporations are created by combinations or associations of several corporations.

A holding company is a corporation organized to own stock in and manage another company or companies. Holding companies are frequently found in banking or public utilities.

A joint venture is a separate corporation owned by two or more corporations. The corporations form the joint venture to work on a specific project or in specific markets. They agree to share the profits and losses in proportion to their contribution. The joint venture is limited to that one project.

A subsidiary is a corporation that is (1) owned by another corporation (50 percent or more of its stock is owned by that other corporation), and (2) operated as a separate entity.

A syndicate is a group of firms operating together, usually on a large project. For instance, a syndicate developed the Alaska pipeline. Although the companies in a syndicate work together, they retain their separate identities.

A cooperative is a nonprofit corporation owned collectively by its members to supply services for the distribution, marketing, or purchasing of goods. Its profits are divided among its members. Cooperatives are common in the agricultural industry. Land O' Lakes, the Minnesota dairy cooperative, and Sunkist Growers are two well-known examples.

Advantages of Corporations

The main advantages of the corporate form are in these areas: liability of ownership, the ability to borrow, continuity of ownership, and career opportunity for employees.

Liability of Ownership

A major advantage of the corporate form is that corporations have limited liability. Owners of the corporation (shareholders) are not personally liable for the acts or the debts of the corporation. Owners' losses are limited to their individual investments in the shares they own.

Ability to Borrow

When a corporation is formed, it raises capital by selling shares in the business to individuals, who then become shareholders. At its formation, a corporation's shares may sell for pennies, enabling virtually everyone to invest and to own a tiny portion of ownership.

Once formed, a corporation can then raise money in two basic ways: (1) by issuing more shares of stock, a process that increases ownership in the corporation; or (2) by issuing bonds, a process that increases the indebtedness of the corporation.

Continuity of Ownership

A corporation has an unlimited life. Its existence is not dependent on the life of any individual or any group. The owners are the shareholders, and as shares are bought and sold, ownership changes and continues into the future.

Career Opportunities for Employees

Employees generally have a wider range of opportunities in a corporation, especially if the corporation is large. Employees can benefit from the potential for growth and promotion that corporations offer, perhaps even share in ownership.

Disadvantages of Corporations

The disadvantages of the corporate form include the expense and complication of organizing a corporation, legal restrictions, tax considerations, and disclosure problems.

Expense and Complications of Incorporating

Compared to proprietorships or partnerships, corporations are more expensive and complex to form and to operate. Corporations must pay legal and filing fees and must file numerous federal, state, and local tax and regulatory reports.

Legal Restrictions

Corporate activities are limited to the purposes stated in the corporate charter as well as by laws that specifically cover the corporate form.

Tax Considerations

Corporate income is subject to double taxation. First, the corporation's income is taxed. Then the income distributed to the stockholders (through dividends) is also taxed.

Disclosure Problems

Corporations are required to submit detailed reports to government agencies and stockholders, which include details of the corporation's financial operations. Because these reports are public, they are available to all, including competitors.

Mergers, Acquisitions, and Takeovers

Corporations grow in a variety of ways, among them, by merging with, acquiring, or taking over other corporations.

Mergers

Combining two companies in related industries is called a merger. Often, a new corporation is formed as a result of the merger. For example, Time Inc. merged with Warner Brothers to form a new corporation, Time Warner Inc.

Horizontal Merger

A merger is horizontal when the acquired company is a direct competitor. If one newspaper acquired another, or if two tire manufacturers merged, each would be an example of a horizontal merger.

Vertical Merger

A merger is vertical if the acquired company is in the same chain of supply—for example, if a tire manufacturer acquired a rubber company that supplies it with raw material or if it acquired a retail chain that sells tires.

Acquisitions

An acquisition is the purchase of a controlling share in a corporation by another corporation. The acquired company might still be managed separately.

Conglomerate

When a company acquires another company in an unrelated business to increase its size or profits, or because it feels the acquired company is undervalued and a bargain, the new company is called a conglomerate.

Hostile Takeovers

Most mergers and acquisitions are friendly, but hostile takeovers are not. Because of the frequency of hostile takeovers, businesses have developed strategies to avoid an unwanted takeover. The four main defenses have colorful names: greenmail, the poison pill, the white knight, and the leveraged buyout (LBO).

Greenmail

Greenmail is the term used for the process in which the target company purchases its outstanding stock to prevent a hostile takeover—either from its existing shareholders or from the company seeking to effect the hostile takeover. Generally, the target must pay a price significantly higher than the market value of the stock.

Poison Pill
The poison pill describes a situation in which the target company grants stock options to its existing shareholders that allow them to purchase additional shares at severely discounted prices, if another companies makes a takeover bid. This results in many more shares being outstanding for the purchasing company to buy. This could make the total price too high.

White Knight
A third defense is to find a white knight, a friendly purchaser who will buy the company and rescue it, much as medieval white knights rescued people in distress. A friendly takeover avoids the cost of a prolonged battle and leaves the company, along with its management, intact.

Leveraged Buyout
In a leveraged buyout, LBO for short, the management of the target company borrows money, using the company itself as collateral. The management then purchases the company. This defense is also known as going private.

The Limited Liability Corporation (LLC)
A limited liability company (LLC) is a business structure that falls between the partnership and the corporation. As do partners, LLC owners report business profits and losses on their personal income tax returns. On the other hand, similar to a corporation, all LLC owners enjoy the protection of limited liability. Creditors normally cannot reach the personal assets of the owners.

The LLC combines the best features of the partnership and corporate forms of business organization. Most states preclude lawyers, accountants, and other professionals from operating in the form of a LLC; in those instances, the LLP remains a viable option.

Selected Readings
Clifford, Denis, and Ralph Warner. *The Partnership Book: How You and a Friend Can Legally Start Your Own Business.* 1987.

Goldstein, Arnold. *Starting Your Subchapter "S" Corporation.* 1988.

McQuown, Judith H. *Inc. Yourself: How to Profit by Setting Up Your Own Corporation.* 1988.

Mancuso, Anthony, and Beth Lawrence. *Form Your Own Limited Liability Company.* 2002.

Rohrlich, Chester. *Organizing Corporate and Other Business Enterprises.* 1975.

Siper, Robert M. *ESOPs in the 1980s: The Cutting Edge of Corporate Buyouts.* 1988.

Steingold, Fred. *Legal Forms for Starting & Running a Small Business.* 2004.

U.S. Small Business Administration. *Selecting the Legal Structure for Your Firm.* 1985.

Test Yourself

1) What are the three basic types of business organization in the United States?
2) List the three major advantages of the sole proprietorship form of business organization.
3) What are the major disadvantages of the sole proprietorship form of business organization?
4) Why is the partnership the least used form of business organization in the United States?
5) In the corporate form of organization, what is the role of the board of directors?
6) List and distinguish the three basic types of corporations.
7) What are some major advantages of the corporate form of organization?
8) Distinguish between a horizontal and a vertical merger.
9) What is a conglomerate?
10) What are four defensive mechanisms utilized to defend against a hostile takeover?

Test Yourself Answers

1) The three types are the sole proprietorship, the partnership, and the corporation.

2) The three major advantages are ease and cost of organization, tax considerations, and ease of dissolution (i.e., the cessation of business).

3) They are the liability of ownership, a limited ability to borrow, continuity of ownership, fewer career opportunities for employees, and the significant demands on the management.

4) Partnerships are not popular because of the unlimited liability of ownership, the potential for disagreement in managing the business, and the difficulty of dissolution.

5) The board of directors represents the shareholders, sets corporate policy, and distributes dividends. It has the final authority for all corporate actions.

6) Public corporations are established by either Congress or a state legislature to provide a specific public good or service. Quasi-public corporations are those to whom the government has granted monopoly rights to provide certain services to the public (e.g., utility companies). Most corporations are privately established and can be either nonprofit or for-profit.

7) The owners of corporations have limited liability, the corporation has a greater ability to borrow, it has continuity of ownership, and can generally provide more career opportunities for its employees.

8) The horizontal merger involves the combining of two companies that were competitors in the same industry, while the vertical merger occurs between two companies that are in the same supply chain (e.g., a tire manufacturer purchases a rubber company that supplies it with raw materials).

9) A conglomerate results when a company purchases another company in a different business or industry from itself.

10) The four defensive mechanisms are greenmail, the poison pill, the white knight, and the leveraged buyout.

CHAPTER 7

Small Business, Entrepreneurship, and Franchising

Small businesses have long constituted the predominant type of business organization in the United States and abroad, accounting for approximately 50 percent of gross domestic product since the early 1970s. Entrepreneurship is the process of starting new businesses, usually as small businesses, first. Over the past fifteen years it has become a major focus of federal, state, and local governments, as a way to jump-start stagnant economies. Finally, franchising, the using of another company's products, services, and/or name, is alternative way to become an entrepreneur and to start a small business. This chapter addresses each, in turn.

■ AN OVERVIEW OF SMALL BUSINESS

Small business serves many roles in the American economy, including the roles of employer, supplier, purchaser of goods and services, and taxpayer. In just one of its roles, that of employer, small business makes a huge contribution to the American economy: More than 99 percent of American businesses employ fewer than 100 people, yet they account for 56 percent of the total workforce. But the contributions of small business to the economy do not end there. Even large corporations benefit greatly from small business, because most of the products made by large corporations are distributed to and sold by small business. They also are major suppliers of parts and components to large manufacturers.

Small-business owners, who are independent, unencumbered by corporate bureaucracy, and free to make quick decisions, aggressively seek new opportunities and technologies, and as a result, they are responsible for many major innovations and breakthroughs. Small business can more easily fill the needs of niche markets not covered by others. Many products with small initial demand not suited for mass production or for specialized markets would never be available were it not for small business.

■ WHAT IS A SMALL BUSINESS?

In the last two decades, small business has experienced a major revival, fueled mainly by the influx of immigrants, the entry of women into the workforce, the restructuring of business during the late 1980s, and ease of entry. Small business is, indeed, a major force in the American economy. But what is a "small" business?

Definitions vary. According to the U.S. Department of Commerce, a small business has fewer than 500 employees. The Small Business Administration (SBA), a government agency created to assist, counsel, and protect the interests of small business, defines a small business as one that is independently owned and operated for profit and is not dominant in its field. The SBA also uses annual sales and/or number of employees to measure small business, and does so for specific industries. The SBA established the following qualifications for a small business: A retailing and service business must have annual sales of no more than $2 million to $7 million; a wholesaler must have annual sales of no more than $9 million to $22 million; and a manufacturer must have 1,500 or fewer employees.

Advantages of a Small Business

Almost every list of advantages for small business begins with the opportunity to be one's own boss. The independence, creative freedom, and challenges of managing a small business are appealing to people who enjoy innovating, adapting to change, and making and executing decisions quickly. Small business owners take risks but keep the profits. They develop close relationships with customers and employees. They can control the work environment; for many, this means working at home. They can often keep overhead (rent, utilities, and other expenses) low, making more capital available for productive purposes and raising profitability.

Disadvantages of a Small Business

The small-business owner cannot always afford to hire others to perform tasks. Thus, he or she is often sales manager, production manager, chief financial officer, and secretary; and as a result, usually puts in long hours and works hard. Also, because raising capital is difficult for small business, the owner must put his or her personal resources at risk.

Types of Small Business

Most small businesses are independently owned and are local operations, not part of another business. There are several types of small business; most fall into the categories of lifestyle, high-growth venture, niche, and cottage businesses.

Lifestyle Business

Lifestyle businesses describe modest operations with little growth potential, such as neighborhood groceries, restaurants, and small retail stores. They are intended to provide the owners with a comfortable living. Lifestyle businesses are sometimes called mom-and-pop businesses.

High-Growth Venture Business

High-growth ventures try to introduce new products or services; thus, their goal is to grow and become large companies, and they have great potential success. High-growth ventures may require considerable capital. Many large, major companies in the computer industry started as small high-growth ventures.

Niche Business

A niche business is a business that fills a small need in the marketplace, a need or niche not addressed by other companies. A company that sells only salsa dresses and Latin dancewear and a company that organizes cooking classes for foreign guests are examples of niche businesses.

Cottage Business

Cottage business is the term used to describe an individual who works in his or her home (thus "cottage"). Many computer-related jobs can be performed just as well in the home, because electronic technology permits data transmission via cable and wireless networks, allowing more and more people to work at home or anywhere. Among the obvious benefits are no commuting, flexible hours, and the ability for parents to work while they mind their children.

Entrepreneurs—The People Behind the Business

An *entrepreneur* (the word is derived from a French word meaning "to undertake") is that person who undertakes the responsibility to bring together the idea, the money, the organization, the materials, and any other resources required to start a business. Entrepreneurs are, then, the business owners we have been discussing.

The phrase "entrepreneurial spirit" is reserved for those businesspeople, whether they literally own a business or not, who exemplify the characteristics common among entrepreneurs: the desire to create a new business; the freedom to determine one's own destiny; the need for independence; and the willingness to meet a challenge. Entrepreneurs are highly motivated and have great determination and perseverance. No wonder they form the back-bone of small business.

Entrepreneurs generally continue to manage the businesses they create. They tend to choose risks over certainty, hard work over a life of ease, all in an effort to make money. For some, the independence that owning and operating their own businesses affords far outweighs the financial return. Thus, they will continue in their businesses even if they might earn more by working for someone else.

Popular Industries

With the exception of industries that require extensive resources (for example, the steel and the automobile industries), small business thrives in every industry and in every business segment. Some industries, however, have a greater concentration of small businesses.

Service Business

The fastest-growing area of small business is the service business. The reason? Most service businesses do not require extensive financial investment and huge resources. The range of service businesses is enormous, including dog walking, beauty shops, house painting, garden services, interior decorating, and management consulting. The list seems endless. Service businesses are frequently based on the owner's special interest, knowledge, or skills.

Retail Business

Another very popular industry group is retail business. Because of the enormous range of merchandise sold to consumers, the variety of retail businesses is very broad. Many are limited-inventory specialty shops selling a narrow range of merchandise, permitting the owners to focus on their areas of expertise and to limit their investments.

Wholesale Business

Wholesaling is one of the few sectors of the economy dominated by small business. Wholesaling consists of buying products in bulk from the manufacturer and storing them in quantities and locations convenient for the retailers. Most small wholesalers enter the business with some experience in the industry, since success is based on relationships with both manufacturers and retailers.

Manufacturing Business

The manufacturing industry is dominated by big business, partly because of the economies of scale and the high investment needed for manufacturing equipment and raw materials. However, small business thrives in industries where innovation is important, such as construction, electronics, toys, and computer software. Apple Computers, Microsoft, and Google, once small, are now well-known large businesses. Such success stories are common in the computer industry.

■ GOVERNMENT AND SMALL BUSINESS

Recognizing the far-reaching impact of small business on the American economy, the government tries to support small business in a number of ways. Some are discussed in the following sections.

The Small Business Administration (SBA)

The Small Business Administration (SBA) was established by the government in 1953 in recognition of the importance of small business. The SBA offers a number of services designed to help small businesses get started and grow, including management advice, financial aid, and information about getting government contracts and cutting through bureaucratic regulations and red tape.

SBA Loans

The SBA offers a variety of loan plans for businesses that meet SBA guidelines. Among the SBA loans available to small businesses are direct loans, guaranteed loans, and participation loans.

Direct Loans

A small business that meets SBA guidelines may be eligible for a direct loan of up to $150,000 if the owner's loan application has already been rejected by two banks. Most direct loans are limited to Vietnam veterans, disabled veterans, and handicapped individuals.

Guaranteed Loans

In order to help business owners get loan approval from banks, the SBA participates in a substantial guaranteed-loan program. The program guarantees a private sector loan for either $500,000 or 85 percent of the loan, whichever is less. Guaranteed loans make up the major part of SBA loans.

Participation Loans

Participation loans are jointly granted by the SBA and a private financial institution. The SBA's share is limited to $350,000 or 75 percent of the loan, whichever is less. Most participation loans are limited to women and minorities.

Small Business Investment Corporation Loans

The SBA also sponsors private venture-capital companies called small business investment corporations—SBICs for short. SBICs can make loans only to small businesses, using funds raised from private investors.

Other SBA Programs

The SBA distributes many publications and pamphlets designed to help small business and offer other forms of nonfinancial assistance.

Small Business Development Centers (SBDCs)

Funded by the SBA, Small Business Development Centers (SBDCs) are generally set up on college campuses to supply counseling and training.

Service Corps of Retired Executives (SCORE) and Active Core of Executives (ACE)

The Service Corps of Retired Executives (SCORE) and the Active Corps of Executives (ACE) are agencies funded by the SBA to provide advice to small business. Through these agencies, retired executives from industry, professional fields, and education volunteer their management-consulting service to small businesses. Thus, small-business owners benefit from talent and experience that would not otherwise be affordable.

■ FRANCHISING

Franchising, a growing and popular route to establishing a small business, presents an alternative way to start a new business or buy an existing one. A franchise is a license to sell another company's products or to use another company's name or both. A franchisor is the company that sells a franchise—that is, the company that sells the license to use its name or products. The franchisee is the person who buys the franchise and with it acquires the rights to a name, a logo, methods of operation, national advertising, products, and other elements of the franchisor's business. The appeal of franchising includes the expertise and training that franchisors provide, helping franchises avoid many of the start-up pitfalls and risks of starting a new business.

Franchise agreements vary from one franchisor to another. Generally, the terms require the franchisee to pay a flat fee initially plus a monthly or an annual percentage of sales or profits. The amount of the initial fee (which depends on the type of franchise, the success of the franchisor, and other factors) can vary from a few thousand dollars to over $1 million.

Franchises are most commonly found in retail services. Among the best known are Starbucks, McDonald's, Burger King, Holiday Inn, and Hertz. Nearly all automobile dealerships are franchises.

Advantages of Franchising

There are a number of advantages to franchising, including the name recognition of the product, marketing plan, management assistance and training, the economies of central purchasing and quality control, and others.

Name Recognition

Most franchises have national recognition among consumers, thanks to each franchisor's advertising and promotion. As a result, a franchisee who purchases a Domino's Pizza, Midas Muffler, or Radio Shack franchise has a recognized name on the first day of business.

Management Assistance and Training

Some franchisors operate elaborate training programs and facilities for their franchisees, providing management training, established business systems and procedures, and operation plans. They also assist in location selection, store layout, and employee training.

Central Purchasing and Quality Control

Many franchisors supply almost everything needed to do business. The advantage of large-scale purchasing is passed on to the franchisee, and uniformity of product quality throughout the system is passed on to the consumer. The customer who buys a Burger King hamburger in Maine knows it will taste the same as one bought in Texas.

Disadvantages of Franchising

The initial high cost of buying a quality franchise is a disadvantage; on the other hand, however, it also prevents the common pitfall of trying to start a business with insufficient capital. In addition, profits must be shared with the franchisor, who may already be making a generous profit on the supplies sold to the franchisee. A franchise limits the owner's independence and control of what to buy, from whom, how to operate, and so on. Also, each badly operated franchise reflects on the acceptance of all other franchisees. But the major potential disadvantage is that success or failure depends so strongly on the franchisor—that is, on product quality, on quality and quantity of advertising, and other factors controlled by the franchisor.

Selected Readings

Acs, Joltan J., and David B. Audretsch. *Handbook of Entrepreneurship Research: An Interdisciplinary Survey and Introduction.* 2003.

Association of Small Business Development Center. *Franchising 101: The Complete Guide to Evaluating, Buying and Growing Your Franchise Business.* 1998.

Basic Books. *The Ultimate Small Business Guide: A Resource for Startups and Growing Businesses.* 2004.

Bond, Robert S. *The Source Book of Franchise Opportunities.* 1988.

Bradach, Jeffrey L. *Franchise Organizations.* 1998.

Bridge, Simon, Stan Cromie, and Ken O'Neill. *Understanding Enterprise, Entrepreneurship, and Small Business.* 2003.

Brown, Deaver. *The Entrepreneur's Guide.* 1986.

Constable, George, and Bob Somerville. *A Century of Innovation: The Engineering That Transformed Our Lives.* 2003.

Drucker, Peter F. *Innovation and Entrepreneurship.* 1986.

Farson, Richard Evans, and Ralph Keyes. *The Innovation Paradox: The Success of Failure, the Failure of Success.* 2003.

Frisch, Carlienne. *Careers in Starting and Building Franchises.* 1998.

Harper, David A. *Foundations of Entrepreneurship and Economic Development.* 2003.

Ireland, R. Duane, S. Michael Camp, and Donald L. Sexton. *Strategic Entrepreneurship: Creating a New Mindset.* 2002.

Kowalski, Gary M. *The Franchise Ratings Guide: 3000 Franchisees Expose the Best & Worst Franchise Opportunities.* 2006.

Lasser, Jacob K. *How To Run A Small Business.* 1988.

Longenecker, Justin G., and Carlos W. Moore. *Small Business Management.* 1987.

McClelland, David C. *The Achieving Society.* 1961.

McDaniel, Bruce A. *Entrepreneurship and Innovation: An Economic Approach.* 2002.

Maul, Lyle R., and Dianne C. Mayfield. *The Entrepreneur's Road Map.* 1990.

Parker, Simon. *The Economics of Self-Employment and Entrepreneurship.* 2004.

Stonecipher, John E. *Getting the Money: How to Successfully Borrow the Cash Your Business Needs.* 1990.

Vesper, Karl M. *Entrepreneurship and Public Policy.* 1983.

Wilken, Paul H. *Entrepreneurship: A Comparative and Historical Study.* 1979.

Wylie, Irwin C. *The Self-Made Man in America: The Myth of Rags to Riches.* 1966.

Test Yourself

1) Small businesses play many roles in the American economy; what are they?
2) What is the definition of a small business?
3) What are four basic types of small businesses?
4) Which industries reflect a greater concentration of small businesses?
5) What is the Small Business Administration (SBA) and what is its prime purpose?
6) SBA offers a number of loan programs; name four such loan programs.
7) What are Small Business Development Centers (SBDCs) and what are their major goals?
8) What is a franchise?
9) What are some of the advantages of franchising?
10) What are the major disadvantages of franchising?

Test Yourself Answers

1) Small businesses serve the roles of employer, supplier, purchaser of goods and services, and taxpayer.

2) No universal definition exists. According to the U.S. Department of Commerce, a small business employs fewer than 500 persons. The Small Business Administration (SBA) defines a small business as one that is independently owned and operated for profit and is not dominant in its field. The SBA also defines a retailing and service business as one having annual sales of no more than $2 million to $7 million; a wholesaler must have annual sale of no more than $9 million to $22 million. Finally, a manufacturer must employ 1,500 or fewer employees to qualify as a small business.

3) Small businesses generally fall into the categories of lifestyle, high-growth venture, niche, and cottage businesses.

4) The service, retail, and wholesale businesses include greater concentrations of small businesses than other industries.

5) The SBA was established in 1953, with the primary purpose of supporting the creation and growth of small businesses.

6) SBA provides direct loans, guaranteed loans, participation loans, and small business investment corporation loans.

7) SBDCs are funded by the SBA and are generally set up on college campuses, with the major goal of providing training and counseling for small businesses.

8) A franchise is a license to sell another company's products or to use another company's name, or both, to conduct business.

9) Name recognition, management assistance and training, and central purchasing and quality control are major advantages of franchising.

10) Franchises can be quite costly. In addition, profits must be shared with the franchisor. The franchise limits the owner's independence and control of how to conduct business. The major disadvantage is that success or failure of a franchise depends so strongly on the franchisor.

CHAPTER 8
Organizational Structure

After organizational goals are established and strategies for meeting them have been planned, organizational structure indicates the way work is arranged and the manner in which people and other resources are allocated. It delineates the jobs and reporting relationships to accomplish the work.

■ AN OVERVIEW OF ORGANIZATIONAL STRUCTURE

The actual structure of organizations differs widely, depending on the industry and the particular company as well as on the company's mission, size, technology needs, and other factors. Most employees work within an organizational structure they did not create. In order to work well within that organization and that structure, employees must understand the organizational structure and how the organization functions, where the authority lies, what the tasks are, and how the work is accomplished.

The Components of an Organization

A company may have, for example, sales, production, design, shipping, human resources, advertising, public relations, and finance departments. Each department is one component, one part of the whole organization. Each component has its own specific purpose and its own set of goals, yet each component must fit in with all the other components so that "the company" works as one.

■ THE ORGANIZATION CHART

The organization chart is a blueprint of the company's structure, a map showing all the components or departments of the organization. Through a series of connecting lines, the chart positions all components to show the relationship of every department in the company, the chain of command, and where employees fit into the firm's operations.

An organization chart may be simple or complex, depending on the size of the corporation. Solid lines show the direct chain of command or the lines of authority in the company; that is, the reporting relationships or line positions (see Figure 8.1). Dotted lines show staff or advisory positions, not line positions. Line positions and staff positions are discussed later in this chapter (see "Line Management" and "Staff Management" on page 89).

■ SPECIALIZATION AND DEPARTMENTALIZATION WITHIN AN ORGANIZATION

The organization of any business answers two basic questions:

- Who will perform each of the functions needed?
- How will the employees who perform these functions be grouped together?

Specialization

Specialization, also called division of labor, describes the use of individuals with specialized skills to perform specialized tasks. For instance, a person who owns his or her own business and works alone must perform all tasks. As the business grows, each new person may become responsible for one specialized area. The first person hired may be a sales representative; the next person, a production supervisor; then an accountant; an advertising manager; and so on. Each additional employee takes over a specialization.

Departmentalization

Departmentalization describes the grouping together of jobs into manageable work units, or departments, usually based on function, geography, product or service, customer, process, matrix, or a mixture or combination of these.

Function

When employee groupings are based on functions, all positions that are related to the same functional activity are brought together in one department. For example, everyone who handles accounting and bookkeeping, including related clerical positions, might be grouped into the accounting department. Other functions are finance, production, marketing, and human resource management.

Geography

Some firms are divided not by function but by region. The regional units may be large (continent or country, for example) or small (a police precinct or a district). Within a region, the unit may be organized by function, but the region itself represents a geographical unit of the parent organization.

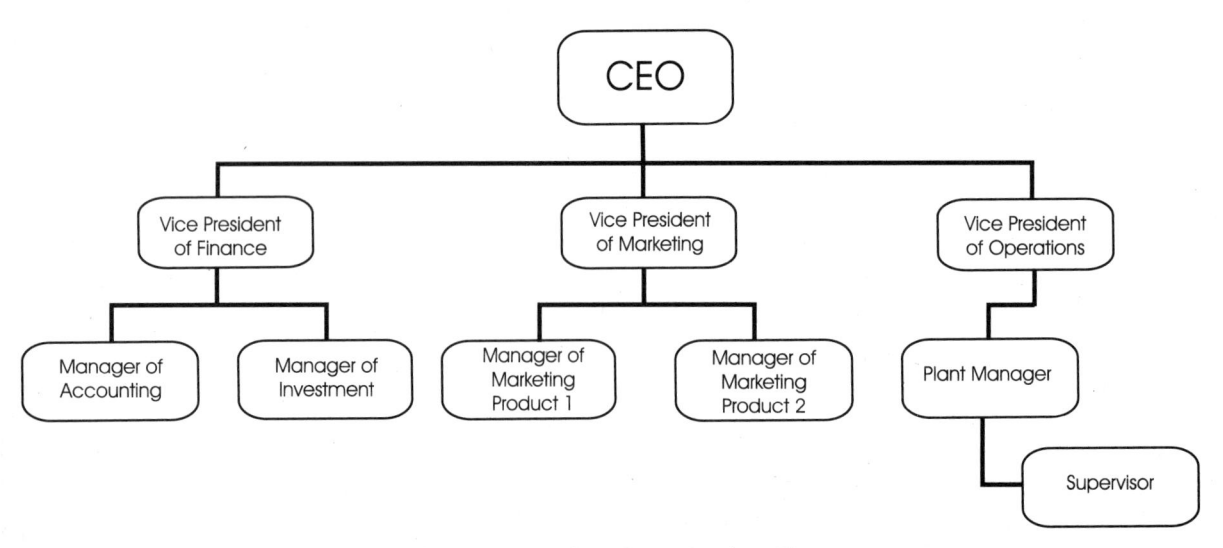

Figure 8.1: A Typical Organization Chart

Product or Service

A firm may establish departments based on their products or service. For example, a clothing manufacturer might have separate men's and women's divisions. The women's division might have its own departments for formal, casual, athletic, and other products. And the men's division will have its own departments.

Customer

In some firms, departments are organized by customer. A telephone company, for example, may have a separate department for residential customers and another for business customers. Service organizations such as banks and travel agencies often separate corporate clients from individual clients. In such cases, the product or service itself might be the same for all customers, but the separate departments allow the firm to target its marketing, advertising, and other functions more effectively.

Process

Departmentalization by process is most common in manufacturing companies, where divisions may be machining, assembly, painting, and finishing, for example.

Matrix Organization

Matrix organization, an organizational form pioneered by the National Aeronautical and Space Administration (NASA), consists of a matrix in which people are brought together from different functional departments as a task force for a specific project. The assigned people have two distinct reporting lines, one to the task-force leader and the other to their supervisors.

One disadvantage of this sharing of command is that, according to Fayol's classical management organization theory (see Chapter 9), an employee should have only one boss. Another is that the matrix is temporary; it is dissolved when its task is completed.

Mixed

Companies—especially large firms—need not follow one type of organizational form from top to bottom. Instead, they mix and combine forms. A company might organize its top level by function, the next level by geographic region, and the lowest level by product.

■ LINE AND STAFF MANAGEMENT

The management structure of an organization consists of two types of management, line and staff management.

Line Management

Line management represents that part of the chain of command that has direct responsibility for achieving the goals of the organization. Line managers have direct authority and responsibility for producing and selling the goods or services produced by the company.

Staff Management

Staff management supplies advice, support, and expertise to line management, but staff managers have no direct authority or responsibility for producing and selling goods and services. Staff managers advise; they do not order. Lawyers, accountants, and human resource personnel are some examples of staff positions.

Smaller organizations can function without staff positions. But as size and complexity increase, the need for staff functions also increases.

■ CENTRALIZED VERSUS DECENTRALIZED STRUCTURES

Organizational structures can be described as centralized or decentralized.

- **Centralized** describes organizations in which most of the decision-making authority is retained by upper-level management working out of a central location.
- **Decentralized** describes organizations in which much of the decision-making authority is delegated—that is, assigned—to lower management. Multinational organizations and firms in which major divisions are separated by geographic boundaries or impediments often have decentralized decision making.

Small businesses start with authority centralized, often in one individual. But as the business grows and the number of decisions increases, the firm may move toward greater decentralization.

■ THE ROLE OF DELEGATION

Delegation plays a key role in understanding the concepts of centralization and decentralization. *To delegate* means "to assign to someone." Delegation is the assignment of a task by a manager to a subordinate. Successful delegation requires managers to balance responsibility, accountability, and authority.

- **Responsibility:** Responsibility originates at the time an individual accepts a task. Once that individual accepts an assignment, he or she has an obligation, a responsibility, to accomplish or perform the assigned task.
- **Accountability:** Accountability, the acceptance of credit for success or blame for failure, accompanies responsibility. The lowest organizational level that has sufficient ability and information to carry out a task competently is accountable for that task.
- **Authority:** Authority is the power to make decisions, to give commands or orders, and to control the resources necessary to accomplish the assigned task.

If a manager delegates to an employee the task of checking time cards, for example, and the employee accepts that task, the employee becomes responsible for completing that task. However, to complete that task effectively, the employee must have the authority to complete the task—that is, whatever power is needed to accomplish that task. Then the employee has both the responsibility and the necessary authority and, therefore, can be held accountable for accomplishing the task assigned. In all cases, however, the ultimate responsibility always remains with the manager.

■ SPAN OF MANAGEMENT AND ORGANIZATIONAL HEIGHT

The span of management, also called span of control, is the number of people that one manager is responsible for supervising. A wide span exists when there are a large number of subordinates reporting to one manager. A narrow span exists when a manager has only a few subordinates.

Organizational height refers to the number of levels of management in a firm. Organizational height is described as tall or flat, references that are more understandable if you picture an organization chart.

- **Tall:** A tall organization has many levels of management (the chart would also be "tall"). A good example of a tall organization is the United States Army. Consider privates as workers, and all the

corporals, sergeants, lieutenants, captains, majors, colonels, and generals as managers or supervisors. Tall organizations are costly because more managers are required, and the flow of information both upward and downward is slowed.
- **Flat:** The opposite of a tall organization is a flat one. A flat organization has few levels of management (its chart would look "flat"). Law firms, even very large law firms, have comparatively few partners supervising the associates and are, therefore, very flat organizations. The wider the span of an organization's management, the more likely it is to be flat. Flat organizations more closely fit the description "lean and mean."

The design of organizational structures is a dynamic process influenced by changes in an organization's size, product, market, and competition. The fact that structure impacts employees' job performance and job satisfaction is rooted in Herzberg's motivation-hygiene theory.

Herzberg's Motivation-Hygiene Theory

Frederick Herzberg's theory holds that the degree of satisfaction and the degree of dissatisfaction felt by workers as a result of performing a job are two different variables and are determined by two different elements. Herzberg calls the dissatisfaction factors hygiene factors and the satisfaction factors motivation factors—see Table 8.1.

Hygiene Factors

These are sometimes called dissatisfiers. Working conditions, pay, and company policy must be present to an acceptable degree in order for employees not to be dissatisfied with their jobs. Improving these factors, although reducing dissatisfaction, will not lead employees to work harder. As for salary, an across-the-board or cost-of-living raise would be a hygiene factor, whereas a merit raise would be a motivation factor.

Motivation Factors

Motivation factors must be present in an acceptable degree for an employee to be satisfied, and, if increased, they will lead employees to work harder. They are sometimes called satisfiers. The greater the chance for promotion, for example, the more likely it is that people will work harder.

Herzberg's theory is utilized when designing the jobs that employees perform—i.e., how tasks are combined as job enlargement or job enrichment. In job enlargement, the employee is given more things to do within the same job. Job enrichment provides the worker with more tasks to do and greater control of how they are done. By blending more planning and decision-making into jobs, employees' sense of responsibility, motivation, and opportunities for growth are increased.

Table 8.1: Herzberg's Factors

Hygiene (Dissatisfiers) Factors	Motivation (Satisfiers) Factors
Company policies	Responsibility
Salary	Recognition
Supervision	Achievement
Social interaction	Growth
Working conditions	Challenge

■ THE ORGANIZATION WITHIN THE ORGANIZATION

Every business has its formal organization, the organization established by the management as outlined on an organization chart. Within every business there is also an informal organization, groupings of people based on interactions and friendships, a network unrelated to the relationships shown on the company's organization chart. Employees, acting on their own needs, establish the organization within the organization.

The rapid pace of change in business has led companies to rely more heavily on informal organization. The informal relationships that develop in an organization not only help satisfy social needs of employees, but also assist in getting things done. Although the formal structure has defined channels that delay information gathering and decision-making, the informal network can cut through the formal obstacles and contribute to the information-gathering and decision-making processes.

Selected Readings

Ashkenas, Ron, Dave Ulrich, Todd Jick, and Steve Kerr. *The Boundaryless Organization: Breaking the Chains of Organizational Structure.* 1995.

Burns, Tom, and G. M. Stalker. *The Management of Innovation.* 1968.

Cleland, David I., editor. *Matrix Management Systems Handbook.* 1984.

Collins, Jim. *Good to Great.* 2003.

Jones, Gareth R., and Jennifer M. George. *Contemporary Management.* 2006.

Kanter, Rosabeth Moss. *When Giants Learn to Dance.* 1989.

Katz, Daniel, and Robert L. Kahn. *The Social Psychology of Organizations.* 1966.

Kilmann, R. H. *Corporate Transformation: Revitalizing Organizations for a Competitive World.* 1988.

Lawrence, Paul R., and Jay W. Lorsch. *Organization and Environment: Managing Differentiation and Integration.* 1967.

Mall, Richard M. *Organizations: Structures, Processes & Outcomes.* 1987.

March, J. G., and M. A. Simon. *Organizations.* 1947.

Pfeffer, Jeffrey. *Power in Organizations.* 1981.

Price, Alan. *Human Resource Management in a Business Context.* 2004.

Schlesinger, Leonard, editor. *Managing Behavior in Organizations: Texts, Cases, Readings.* (1983).

Steers, R. M. *Organizational Effectiveness: A Behavioral View.* 1976.

Townsend, Robert. *Up The Organization.* 1970.

Weber, Max. *The Theory of Social and Economic Organization.* 1947.

Test Yourself

1) What is an organization chart?

2) What are the different bases upon which a company may group its jobs?

3) Distinguish between line management and staff management.

4) If the organization's top-level management insists on retaining all decision-making authority, is it said to have a decentralized structure? Why or why not?

5) Delegation is the assignment of a task by a manger to a subordinate. What are the essential ingredients of a successful delegation?

6) "Span of control" is an important management phrase. What does it mean?

7) What is organizational height and what is its significance?

8) Describe Herzberg's motivation-hygiene theory.

9) According to Herzberg's theory, what are some of the motivation factors management might use to motivate employees to work harder?

10) What is meant by the "organization within the organization?"

Test Yourself Answers

1) An organization chart is blueprint of the company's structure, showing all the departments of the company, the chain of command, and where employees fit into the firm's operations.

2) A company may group its jobs based on function, geography, product or service, customer, process, matrix, or a mixture or combination of these.

3) Line managers represent that part of the chain of command with direct responsibility for achieving the goals of the company. They have direct authority and responsibility for producing and selling goods or services provided by the company. Staff managers (e.g., lawyers, accountants, and human resource personnel), on the other hand, supply advice, support, and expertise to line management. These managers have no direct authority or responsibility for producing and selling goods and services.

4) No; it is said to have a centralized structure. A decentralized structure is one in which much of the decision-making authority is delegated to lower management. On the other hand, a centralized structure is one in which top management retains most of the decision-making authority, operating from a central location.

5) Successful delegation requires managers to balance responsibility, authority, and accountability.

6) Span of control is the number of persons that one manager is responsible for supervising. A wide span exists when a large number of employees report to a supervisor. A narrow span exists when a manager is responsible for only a small number of subordinates.

7) Organizational height refers to the number of levels of management in an organization. A tall organization has many levels of management, while a flat organization has only a few levels. Taller organizations are more costly and usually are slower to respond to changing circumstances. Flatter organizations tend to be less costly and can respond more quickly to changing situations because there are fewer levels of management to get to the top.

8) This theory holds that the degrees of satisfaction and dissatisfaction are determined by two different elements. The dissatisfaction factors—hygiene factors—do not motivate employees to work harder, even though reducing them can reduce the level of dissatisfaction. Satisfaction factors—motivation factors—can increase satisfaction and motivate employees to work harder.

9) Some motivation factors include responsibility, recognition, achievement, growth, and challenge.

10) Within every organization an informal organization exists, based on interactions and friendships. It is a network unrelated to the company's organization chart.

CHAPTER 9
Management Fundamentals

This chapter addresses the fundamentals of management, including the definition, the basic functions, and different management theories. It also addresses the issues of management skills and how to evaluate or assess management's success or productivity. Finally, the chapter addresses the issue of leadership, in the context of management.

■WHAT IS MANAGEMENT?

Management can be defined as "working with and through people and other organizational resources to achieve the organization's goals and objectives." Basically, management involves all business decisions—what to do, how to do it, who is to do it, where to do it, when to do it, and perhaps most important of all, whether to do it. The principles and processes can be applied to all organizations, even to managing our homes.

To begin, let's look at the basic functions and activities that all managers perform: planning, organizing, directing/leading, and controlling.

- **Planning** involves deciding what has to be done and determining the goals to be met.
- **Organizing** involves deciding how to utilize the organization's resources—land, labor, and capital—and determining which people will do the work that has been planned.
- **Directing/leading** involves putting the plans into action by motivating people to do the work.
- **Controlling** involves monitoring the people and the work to ensure what has been planned is being done.

■THEORIES OF MANAGEMENT

Management theories first emerged during the early 1900s. Knowing some of the classical theories is both interesting and helpful.

Scientific Management

Frederick W. Taylor is considered the founder of scientific management, an approach that studied jobs and broke them down into smaller tasks, determining the "one right way" of accomplishing those tasks. Taylor pioneered the piece-rate system, whereby each worker received the same wage for each piece produced.

Other contributors to the theory of scientific management were Frank and Lillian Gilbreth, who further refined time-motion studies to improve worker productivity through job simplification. Henry Gantt, an associate of Taylor's, is best known for the Gantt chart, a chart that made significant contributions to scheduling and controlling work and improving productivity (see Chapter 12). Gantt also developed the concept of a production bonus for producing above the daily quota.

Scientific management, despite its name, was concerned with worker and production efficiency, not with management.

Classical Organization Theory

Henri Fayol and Max Weber were two key contributors to classical organization theory.

Henri Fayol

Guidelines for managing complex organizations, such as factories, originated in France with Henri Fayol, founder of the classical management school, who attempted to identify principles and skills that underlie effective management.

Fayol made four major contributions to management theory.

- He distinguished between managers and supervisors at the operating level of organizations.
- He defined the five functions of management: planning, organizing, commanding, coordinating, and controlling.
- He developed his Fourteen Principles of Management, which include division of labor, unity of command, chain of command, mechanisms to ensure communications, and specialized groups.
- He maintained that flexibility was needed in applying his principles and, further, that managers could learn to manage.

We now take Fayol's total organization approach for granted, but Fayol's work on the subject, which was not translated into English until 1945, was considered revolutionary at the time.

Max Weber

Max Weber, a German sociologist, addressed the issue of organizational administration from a different perspective. His ideal organization, a bureaucracy, emphasized order, system, rationality, uniformity, and consistency, thus ensuring equitable treatment of employees by management. According to Weber, technical competence should be emphasized and performance evaluation made entirely on the basis of merit.

The Behavioral School

The classical approach focused on the work, not the worker. The worker was considered the economic man, driven by rational economic motives. In the 1920s, managers experienced difficulties and frustrations because people did not follow predicted or expected patterns of behavior. The behavioral school was developed by management scholars trained in social sciences, scholars who used their knowledge of social science and applied it to understanding and improving organization management.

Elton Mayo and his associates, through their Hawthorne studies, established the field of human relations. They found that work productivity was related to psychological and social variables, and as a result, they introduced the concept of the social man, motivated by the desire to form relationships with others. Thus behavioral scientists—sociologists, anthropologists, and psychologists (such as Abraham Maslow)—shifted the focus from the workplace to the worker.

Management Science

A quantitative approach to management, called operations research (OR), was developed in Great Britain at the beginning of World War II. OR brought together teams of mathematicians, physicists, and other scientists to use mathematical models to simulate management problems and generate potential solutions to the problems. With the development of the computer, OR procedures were formalized into what became known as management science.

The Systems Approach

The quantitative approach of management science neglected the behavioral side of an enterprise. The systems approach views the organization as one unified, directed system of interrelated parts.

Contingency Approach

According to the contingency approach, a manager's task is to identify which technique will best contribute to the attainment of management goals in a particular situation, under particular circumstances, and at a particular time. This approach is sometimes called situational and is characterized by the phrase, "it all depends."

■ MANAGEMENT RESOURCES

To achieve its goals, management must utilize the organization's resources. These resources are the organization's assets, the factors of production that are available to produce the company's products or services. Land includes buildings, raw materials, and equipment; labor includes the people, the human resources who work for the company; capital is the funds needed to operate the enterprise. Managers assemble these resources and use them to create goods or services, and they are evaluated by how well they do so. Two criteria for judging managers are effectiveness and efficiency.

- **Effectiveness** measures the manager's ability to accomplish the company's goals.
- **Efficiency** measures the manager's ability to minimize the use of resources—to get the most output with the least input.

A good manager must be both effective (do the right things) and efficient (do things right).

■ LEVELS OF MANAGEMENT

Every organization has several levels of management. The responsibility of each manager depends on his or her level in the organization. The chief financial officer and the supervisor of the purchasing department are both managers, but their duties and responsibilities are quite different.

Authority versus Responsibility

Authority is the power to command, and authority can be delegated. A manager can assign a task to another person and delegate the authority needed to accomplish it. Responsibility, on the other hand, is the obligation to perform, and the manager's responsibility cannot be delegated. The ultimate responsibility always remains with the manager.

One way to categorize managers is to separate them into three levels: top, middle, and first-line managers. In any organization, there is a small number of top managers, a larger number of middle managers, and the largest group of first-line managers. Top management has the most authority, first-line management the least, and the middle management's authority lies between the two groups. The CEO, or chief executive officer, has the most authority and, of course, the most responsibility (see Figure 9.1).

```
        Top
    Management

      Middle
    Management

  First-Line Management
```

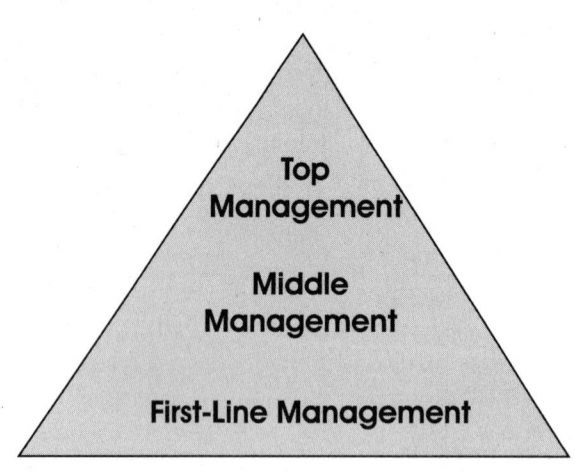

Figure 9.1: Levels of Management.

Top Management

Top management, the relatively small group at the top of the pyramid, is made up of the president, chief executive officer, and senior executives and is responsible for the overall management of the organization. They are general managers in that they are responsible for all activities, or for an entire company or subsidiary. They set the corporate objectives, policies, and strategies. They also deal with government relations and the external economic environment.

Middle Management

Middle management is made up of the managers who are not top management or first-level managers. They act as liaison between top management and lower, first-level management, whom they supervise. They are charged with coordinating and carrying out the policies set by top management. They are often functional managers, managers responsible for a single function, such as sales, marketing, or production.

First-Line Management

Supervisors, department managers, and team leaders at the base of the pyramid make up first-line management, the largest management group in an organization and the group responsible for getting the work done.

First-line managers supervise only non-management personnel, who report directly to the first-line managers. They oversee the scheduling of work, maintenance of equipment, and work routines on a day-to-day basis. They have considerable responsibility for seeing that tasks are accomplished.

■ MANAGEMENT SKILLS

The successful manager requires basic technical, people, and conceptual skills. Although the "mix" of these skills will vary from one level of management to another, every manager must be skilled in all three areas.

Technical Skill

Technical skill is the ability to use specialized knowledge about the mechanics of a job, such as tools, procedures, and techniques. A manager does not have to be the most proficient person in the production process, but he or she must know the process well enough to perform his or her responsibilities and make decisions.

People Skill

People skill is the ability to work with and motivate people, utilizing one's personal and interpersonal skills. Personal skills involve self-awareness, knowledge of how one is perceived by others, time management, and stress management. Interpersonal skills involve interaction with others—communicating, listening, leading, motivating, and resolving conflict among people.

Conceptual Skill

Conceptual skill is the ability to see how parts function as a whole. A manager must see how different departments and divisions of an organization are interrelated, how they work together. A manager must recognize that and see how a change in one element affects other elements.

Measuring these skills in terms of importance or the degree to which each is needed by specific managers is nearly impossible and, in any case, varies depending on the level of management. In general, however, all managers at all levels need people skills because, by definition, managers get things done through people. Because first-line managers are closest to the process, they generally spend more time using technical skill, and their technical skill will more greatly determine their success. Top-level managers must have keen conceptual skills because they are responsible for company planning. Middle-level managers will need a mixture of all three skills (human, technical, and conceptual).

■THE MANAGEMENT PROCESS

The management process can be discussed by function. A manager frequently performs more than one function at any given moment. These functions are planning, organizing, leading, and controlling.

Planning

Planning is the process of establishing objectives, and then setting policies, procedures, and a course of action to accomplish these objectives. It is a complex process and consists of the several steps discussed in the following sections.

Purpose

Planning begins with a purpose, a reason for establishing the organization. The purpose may be to make a profit for the owners. In the case of a university, it may be to develop and transmit knowledge, or in the case of a hospital, to provide health care.

Mission

Once an organization establishes its purpose, it states how it will accomplish this purpose; that is, it states its mission. A company's mission describes the path it will take to achieve its goals. General Motors' purpose is to make a profit; its mission is to manufacture automobiles. Within the automobile industry, other firms may adopt variations of the same mission. Ferrari, for example, may have as its mission to manufacture high-performance sports cars.

Goals

The next planning step is to develop goals, statements, of how the organization plans to achieve its mission. Goals are generally translated into more specific terms and provide a definite time frame.

Although a business will have a singular purpose and a singular mission, it will usually have several goals.

Goals are usually translated into measurable objectives, steps that provide guides to help accomplish the goals (examples include specific sales revenues, growth rates, and profits).

Broad goals must be converted to specific actions, usually stated in terms of an action plan. An action plan may be classified as either strategic or tactical.

Strategic Plan

A strategic plan describes the goals, objectives, and actions of a company over a long-term period, frequently three to five years—in other words, it describes a long-term strategy. Strategic plans are prepared by the top level of management and approved by the board of directors.

Tactical Plan

A tactical plan is specific, detailed, and current, focusing on present operations. Tactical plans, which typically cover a one-year period, are prepared by middle management and implemented by first-line management.

Planning Tools

Managers use three planning tools: rules, policies, and budgets.

Rules

A rule is a planning tool that precisely designates a specific required action. It indicates what an organization member should or should not do. "All employees must begin work by 9 o'clock" is an example of a rule.

Policies

Whereas a rule is specific, a policy is general. A policy furnishes broad guidelines for making decisions and taking action. A policy gives, in general terms, the kinds of actions needed to achieve goals. Wal-Mart's policies include being polite and considerate to customers and employees.

Budgets

A budget is a financial plan that covers a specific period of time. It details how funds will be obtained and how the factors of production will be allocated. In addition to showing how money will be spent, a budget sets limits on how much will be spent for each expense.

Organizing

Once objectives and plans have been established, the organizing function comes into play. Management must design and staff the organization to carry out its purpose; it must specify the people, the process, the equipment, the time, and the material. Management must establish clear lines of authority and communication. Specifically how the company will be organized depends on its objective. For example, in an automobile plant, management will organize the personnel of the assembly line differently from the personnel in the engineering department. And in a retail store, management will organize its personnel differently, too. Organization is discussed more fully in Chapter 8.

Leading or Directing

Key to management success is the process of influencing people so that they are motivated to behave in ways that meet the firm's objectives. This process, whether it is called leading, directing, or motivating, always involves influencing people. For the purpose of this discussion, we will use the words *leading* and *leadership*.

Leading is guiding the actions of organization members toward the attainment of the organization's goals and objectives. Managers have the authority, the formal right, to request and require performance and hold people responsible, but the most effective leaders get employees to perform tasks willingly. It is possible to be a manager without being a leader, and it is possible to be a leader without being a manager. If management is "the art of getting things done through people," then we may call leadership "the art of getting people to perform."

■ LEADERSHIP STRATEGIES FOR MOTIVATION

If leadership is the art of getting people to perform, managers must identify and implement effective strategies to motivate employees. The following sections of this chapter focus on the manager's ability to control the organization and to motivate employees.

Controlling

Controlling is the process of evaluating the organization's performance and taking corrective action as necessary to keep the firm on track. The controlling function ensures that the organization is performing according to the company's goals and is meeting those goals, as identified in its plan. Controlling and planning are inseparable functions.

After establishing performance standards, the controlling process consists of four steps: (1) measuring the performance; (2) comparing the performance to the established standards and the objectives of the plan; (3) identifying deviations from the plan and their causes; and (4) taking corrective action.

The management tools for this process are described in Part 5, Chapters 17 through 18.

Aspects of Leadership

Management must also determine how best to provide leadership. Indeed, a manager must decide on the leadership style to adopt, the leadership behavior most appropriate, and how best to motivate employees.

Leadership Styles

Although there is a wide range of leadership styles, they all stem from three basic approaches: autocratic, participative, and laissez-faire. Managers may adopt and use one style consistently, or they may use different styles in different situations; that is, they may employ situational leadership.

Autocratic Leaders

Autocratic describes leaders who make decisions without consulting employees, and then announce their decisions and expect (perhaps demand) compliance.

Participative Leaders

Participative describes leaders who share the decision-making process with others. They may gather information from others and make their own decision based on the information. In group situations, they may allow the groups they are leading to make the decisions.

Laissez-Faire Leaders

Laissez-faire describes leaders who allow employees to make decisions. Their attitude is based on the idea that the people performing the job are best qualified to make decisions that concern aspects of their jobs. Laissez-faire leadership tends to be most popular in situations where employees have greater technical knowledge than their managers.

Situational Leaders

Situational leadership recognizes that leadership success requires using a style that is appropriate to the specific situation and to the specific kinds of people involved in that situation. Situational leaders do not limit themselves to one style. As changes occur, they adopt the appropriate leadership style.

Leadership Behavior

Two aspects of leadership are job-centered and employee-centered behavior.

- **Job-centered behavior:** Job-centered leaders practice close supervision so that performance can be strictly monitored and controlled. Their primary interest is in production and in meeting production goals.
- **Employee-centered behavior:** Employee-centered behavior demonstrates concern for the well-being of employees. The leader who practices employee-centered behavior is interested in developing a cohesive work group and ensuring that employees are satisfied with their jobs.

Leadership and Motivation

Effective leadership depends strongly on a manager's ability to motivate employees to perform tasks to the best of their ability, and do so willingly. Thus, motivation is the stimulation and energizing of an individual to take those actions necessary to accomplish a desired goal or task. Motivational issues require a manager to be concerned with keeping workers challenged and productive and using their capabilities fully. Many of the same theories detailed earlier in this chapter pertain to motivation, especially Taylor's view of workers as concerned with the economic necessities of working and the behaviorists' view of workers as motivated by the social aspects of work. The theories directly related to encouraging high performance from employees are grounded in the work of Abraham Maslow.

Maslow's Hierarchy of Needs

Early theories claimed that needs were the basis of motivation, but no one formally classified those needs until 1943, when Abraham Maslow, a psychologist, published his theory of motivation based on a hierarchy of human needs.

Maslow organized human needs into five different levels. In Maslow's theory, the prime source of motivation is unfulfilled needs. The needs at any level do not have to be fully satisfied before the needs at the next level come into play.

- **Physiological:** The lower-level needs, according to Maslow's hierarchy (illustrated in Figure 9.2), are the most basic needs, our physiological needs, such as our requirements for food, water, shelter, and sleep. In a business environment, these needs are usually met by adequate wages.
- **Safety:** The next level is safety needs, which include physical and emotional security. These needs are met by health insurance, pension plans, safe working conditions, and job security.
- **Social:** Next up the hierarchy are social needs, such as the need for friendship and companionship and the need to belong. Friends, relatives, and coworkers help satisfy these needs.
- **Esteem:** On the next level are esteem needs, our need for status, recognition, and self-respect, which are satisfied by awards, promotions, and job titles.
- **Self-actualization:** The highest level of needs include our need to grow and develop and to realize our full potential, to become all we are capable of being.

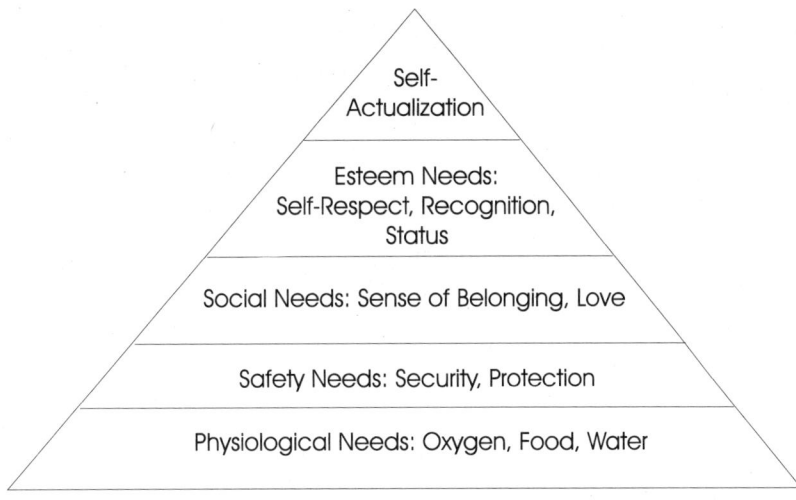

```
                    Self-
                 Actualization
              ─────────────────
              Esteem Needs:
           Self-Respect, Recognition,
                   Status
           ──────────────────────
          Social Needs: Sense of Belonging, Love
          ──────────────────────────────
          Safety Needs: Security, Protection
      ──────────────────────────────────────
      Physiological Needs: Oxygen, Food, Water
```

Figure 9.2: Maslow's Hierarchy of Needs.

Maslow's theory is, simply put, that ordinarily humans will try to satisfy a particular level of needs only when needs on the level below have first been satisfied. Thus, according to Maslow, the primary source of motivation is unfulfilled needs. Maslow's hierarchy has had a profound effect on various areas of motivation, management, and communication theory.

Theory X and Theory Y

Douglas McGregor, a psychologist, presented an approach to understanding motivation called Theory X, based on sets of assumptions that underlie management's attitudes and beliefs regarding worker behavior, which adopted a rather pessimistic view of employees as people who can be motivated only by fear (of job loss, for example). He also postulated a more-optimistic approach called Theory Y, which offered a humanistic approach. According to Theory Y, workers could be motivated by better challenges, personal growth, and improved work performance and productivity.

Knowing the theories on what motivates workers is not sufficient. The skills to put them into practice, to apply them, are necessary. One of the best programs to accomplish this is management by objectives.

Management by Objectives (MBO)

Management by objectives (MBO)—first described by Peter F. Drucker in his 1954 book *The Practice of Management*—is a set of procedures that starts with setting performance targets and continues through to performance review. It features involvement at every level of management and staff who set goals and clearly define every individual's areas of responsibility in terms of expected results or objectives, with periodic reviews and performance appraisals. MBO programs can vary greatly, but most contain the elements discussed in the following sections.

Commitment to the Program

Time, effort, and commitment at every level are required in setting objectives and reviewing results for an MBO program to be effective.

Top-Level Goal-Setting

The process begins with top mangers setting measurable preliminary objectives, such as "47 percent increase in sales next quarter." This furnishes managers and employees a clear idea of what it is hoped will be accomplished.

Individual Goals

Each manager and employee needs to have a clearly defined responsibility and objective, or goal. The objectives for each individual are set collaboratively between the individual and his or her superior.

Participation

The extent of employees' participation in setting objectives varies widely. As a general rule, the greater the participation of both managers and employees, the more likely realistic goals will be set and met. Individual goals linked to organization goals need to be worked out cooperatively, not assigned.

Autonomy in Implementation of Plans

Once the objectives have been set and agreed upon, the individuals need to be free to choose the means of accomplishing the objectives and implementing the program.

Review of Performance

Managers and employees meet periodically to review progress made toward the objective. This review reveals any problems that exist and zeros in on what can be done to resolve them, and allows for modification of goals if necessary. It is important that the review and feedback be based on measurable performance rather than subjective criteria.

MBO has proved to be an effective motivation tool, enhancing communication and understanding in many companies. In order for it to be effective, the process must begin at the top level of the firm and include all levels. Disadvantages are that it is time-consuming and can involve a considerable amount of paperwork and meetings.

■ DECISION-MAKING

Managers are continuously involved in decision-making, and they are evaluated by their organizations on the basis of the quality of their decisions. Managers' decisions range from minor and relatively unimportant to major and potentially life-threatening to the organization. They decide whether to buy another company, which overnight delivery service to use, how to price the company's goods and services, and so on.

Information-gathering is an integral and continuing part of the decision-making process. Successful decision-making utilizes this information effectively. Decision-making goes beyond choosing among options; it is based on a number of clearly defined steps, which are discussed in the following sections.

Define the Problem

The first step in decision making is to define the problem. Many managers skip this step because they assume they know what the problem is or because they mistakenly conclude that the symptom is the problem. For instance, a high level of rejects in a manufacturing process is a symptom, but the problem may stem from a variety of factors.

Identify Alternatives

Business problems seldom have just one solution. It is the manager's role to identify a range of creative solutions, a complete list of potential alternatives.

Evaluate All Alternatives and Choose One

Managers use several methods to screen and choose from among alternatives. One method is to eliminate, in a series of evaluations, the less-satisfactory alternatives until only one or two alternatives remain. Another method is to evaluate and score each alternative, much as a teacher grades papers, and then choose from the top-scoring alternatives.

Implement the Decision

The decision process does not end with making the decision. There are two more steps, the next of which is to implement the decision. After managers have selected the most effective solution to the problem, they must implement their decision—they must take the necessary actions to carry out their decision.

Monitor Decision Outcomes

The final step in decision-making is to monitor and control the outcome of the implemented decision. Evaluation performed after implementation is part of management control, and may call for corrective action and follow-up. Are the steps being implemented working according to plan? Does the plan need to be adjusted or altered? Should another alternative be considered and, if so, what other alternatives are available?

Selected Readings

Anthony, Robert N. *The Management Control Function.* 1988.
Atkinson, John W., and David Burch. *An Introduction to Motivation.* 1978.
Bass, Bernard M. *Stodgill's Handbook of Leadership: A Survey of Theory and Research.* 1981.
Bennis, Warren. *On Becoming a Leader.* 1990.
Chandler, Alfred D., Jr. *The Visible Hand.* 1977.
Cleveland, Harlan. *The Knowledge Executive: Leadership in an Information Society.* 1985.
Collins, Jim. *Good To Great.* 2003.
Drucker, Peter F. *Adventures of a Bystander.* 1978.
Druskat, Vanessa U., Fabio Sala, and Gerald Mount. *Linking Emotional Intelligence and Performance at Work.* 2006.
Jones, Gareth R., and Jennifer M. George. *Contemporary Management.* 2006.
Kempin, Frederick G., Jr. *Legal Aspects of the Management Process: Cases and Materials.* 1990.
Kotter, John P. *A Force for Change.* 1990.
Krajewski, Lee J., and Larry Ritzman. *Operations Management: Processes and Value Chains.* 2005.
McCormack, Mark M. *What They Don't Teach You at Harvard Business School.* 1986.
McGregor, Douglas. *The Human Side of Business.* 1985.
Machiavelli, Niccolo. *The Prince.* 1952.
Mintzberg, Henry. *The Nature of Managerial Work.* 1973.
Mintzberg, Henry. *Managers Not MBAs: A Hard Look at the Soft Practice of Managing and Management Development.* 2004.
Nelson, Debra L., and James C. Quick. *Organizational Behavior: Fundamentals, Realities, and Challenges.* 2003.
Odiorne, George S. *How Managers Make Things Happen.* 1982.
Peters, Thomas J., and Robert H. Waterman, Jr. *In Search of Excellence.* 1982.
Porter, Michael E. *Competitive Strategy: Techniques for Analyzing Industries and Competitors.* 1980.
Robbins, Stephen P., and Mary Coulter. *Management,* Eighth Edition. 2005.
Roethlisberger, Fritz J. *Management and Morale.* 1941.

Schein, Edgar H. *Organizational Culture and Leadership.* 1985.
Simon, Herbert A. *Administrative Behavior.* 1976.
Steers, Richard M., and Lyman W. Porter. *Motivation and Work Behavior.* 1979.
Stevenson, William J. *Operations Management.* 2004.
Stewart, Rosemary. *Managers and Their Jobs.* 1967.
Stoner, James A. F., and R. Edward Freeman. *Management.* 1989.
Taylor, Frederick W. *The Principles of Scientific Management.* 1911.
Vroom, Victor H., and Philip W. Yetton. *Leadership and Decision Making.* 1973.
White, William Foote. *Money and Motivation.* 1955.
Williams, Chuck. *Effective Management.* 2005.

Test Yourself

1) What are the four functions and activities that all managers perform?
2) What was the major focus of scientific management?
3) How did the Hawthorne studies affect the development of management theory?
4) What is another name for management science and what is its focus?
5) What are the three major levels of management and what are their major roles?
6) What are the three basic types of skills that all successful managers must possess?
7) Define and distinguish the four leadership styles discussed in the text.
8) Distinguish between job-centered and employee-centered leadership behavior.
9) Describe Maslow's hierarchy of needs.
10) Identify the steps inherent in successful, informed decision-making.

Test Yourself Answers

1) Managers plan, organize, direct/lead, and control.

2) Scientific management focused on the worker and worker efficiency, not management.

3) The Hawthorne studies found that worker productivity is related to psychological and social variables and that the worker is motivated by the desire to form relationships with others.

4) Management science is also referred to as operations research. Its focus is using mathematics and science to simulate management problems and generate potential solutions.

5) Top management is comprised of the president, chief executive officer (CEO), and a relatively small group of senior executives responsible for the overall management of the organization. This level of management sets company policies. First-line management includes supervisors, department managers, and team leaders. This level of management supervises only non-management workers, overseeing the day-to-day business activity and assuring that appropriate tasks are accomplished. Middle management is made up of those managers who are neither top management nor first-line management; they act as liaisons between top management and first-line management. They are charged with coordinating and operationalizing the policies set by top management.

6) The three basic types of skills that all successful managers must possess are human skill, technical skill, and conceptual skill.

7) The autocratic style involves a leader's making decisions without input from employees. The participative style of management entails a manager's sharing decision-making with others; the manager usually gathers information from others, and then makes decisions based on that information. A manager who utilizes the laissez-faire style of leadership allows employees to make the decisions, based on the idea that the persons performing the jobs are best qualified to make the related decisions. The situational leadership style recognizes that the appropriate leadership style to utilize depends upon the specific situation and the specific kinds of persons involved.

8) Job-centered leaders practice close supervision, strictly monitoring and controlling employee performance. On the other hand, employee-centered leaders are more interested in developing a cohesive work group, ensuring that employees are satisfied with their roles.

9) Maslow's theory holds that the main source of motivation for workers is the fulfillment of unmet human needs. His theory organizes human needs into five different levels. The lower-level needs are the most basic, physiological needs, including requirements for food, water, shelter, and sleep. The next level includes safety needs, both physical and emotional. Next up the ladder of needs is social needs, such as the need for friendship, companionship, and the need to belong. On the fourth rung of the hierarchy are the esteem needs (e.g., status, recognition, and self-respect). The highest and most sophisticated need in the hierarchy is the person's self-actualization—the need to grow and develop and to realize his or her full potential.

10) Effective decision-making requires the defining of the problem, the identifying of viable alternatives, the evaluation of the alternatives, the choosing of an alternative, and the monitoring of the implemented decision.

Part 3: Managing Personnel and Production

CHAPTER 10

Human Resources Management

A firm's human resources are all of its employees. Human resources management (HRM for short) was once called personnel management. The newer term reflects the most recent attitudes toward employees as "resources," not just "personnel."

■ AN OVERVIEW OF HUMAN RESOURCES MANAGEMENT (HRM)

Human resources management (HRM) involves every aspect of dealing with employees as a resource: planning, staffing (that is, recruiting and hiring), training and development, performance appraisal, and compensation.

■ PLANNING

Just as business must plan for its financial needs and equipment needs, it must also plan for its personnel needs. The first step of HRM planning is to forecast future human resources demand, and the second step is to forecast future human resources supply. Together, forecasts of supply and demand inform management of potential problems and, therefore, allow management to prepare for and possibly avoid future shortages in the labor supply.

Forecasting Human Resource Demand

A company forecasts its human resources demand based on the firm's strategic plans for new business ventures, new products, expansion or contraction of existing product lines, and economic trends. To forecast demand accurately requires information on job analysis, job description, and job specifications.

- A **job analysis** is a detailed study of the tasks to be performed and the skills required by the individual to accomplish the work. The job description and job specifications are developed from this analysis.
- A **job description** details all key tasks and responsibilities of each position, as well as the relationship of one job to another.
- A **job specification** addresses the knowledge, skills, education, and experience required to perform a job. With this information, HRM can forecast how many people will be needed for what jobs, and what the qualifications are for each position.

Forecasting Human Resources Supply

A company forecasts human resources supply by considering (1) its present workforce, and (2) any future changes or expected movement that may occur within its workforce. Many firms conduct a human resources audit on a regular basis and use the information gathered in the audit to establish a human resources information system, which is essentially an inventory of people and their skills, education, and training. The supply forecast begins with this inventory of present number of employees and their skills. Then it takes into account normal attrition—that is, all the usual reasons why employees leave: to take another job, to relocate to other areas, to retire, and so on. And, finally, the company determines whether it will need additional or fewer employees in the future.

If the company's strategic planning calls for downsizing—that is, a future decrease in the number of employees—the smaller future supply after attrition may be sufficient, depending on the skills of the remaining staff. If the strategic plan estimates organization growth, new people will have to be found and hired to staff the new positions and to replace those lost through normal attrition.

Matching Supply and Demand of Human Resources

Once forecasts for both supply and demand have been completed, HRM planners can establish a course of action to match supply and demand. They consider not only the number of people, but also the skills needed. Then, if the forecast shows that the demand will be greater than the supply, the HRM managers develop a plan for recruiting and selecting new employees. Timing is important: It is not efficient to hire workers before they are needed.

If the forecast shows that the supply will be greater than the demand, HRM managers will develop a plan to reduce the workforce. The most humane course is to allow a reduction through normal attrition, but attrition is a slow process. The company will not replace employees who leave, allowing the workforce to eventually shrink to the point where supply equals demand. To hasten the process, a firm may offer early retirement to workers near retirement age, giving them additional benefits in return for leaving. Together, these methods may bring supply and demand into alignment; when they do not, the company will release surplus workers.

■ STAFFING

Staffing involves all aspects of supplying the organization with the human resources it needs. Staffing, therefore, involves four activities: recruiting, selection, hiring, and providing orientation.

Recruiting

Recruiting is the process of finding and attracting sufficient qualified job applicants for the available jobs. Failure to attract sufficient applicants limits the choice. On the other hand, attracting too many applicants makes the evaluation process cumbersome and difficult.

Internal Recruiting

Many firms adopt the policy to promote from within the company, a basic internal recruiting strategy. The purpose of this policy is to motivate employees and retain quality personnel.

External Recruiting

External recruiting attempts to find and attract qualified applicants from outside the company through newspaper and magazine advertisements, employment agencies and college campuses, and Internet sites, for example. Although it is more expensive, external recruiting, by definition, brings to the company people with new opinions, ideas, perspectives, and skills.

Selection

Selection is the process of gathering information about applicants and using that information to choose the most appropriate applicant. The object of selection is also to eliminate inappropriate candidates.

Applicants' Qualifications

The proper applicant is the one whose qualifications are most appropriate for the job, not necessarily the applicant with the most qualifications. The information is drawn from application forms, résumés, references, interviews, and company-administered skill and aptitude tests—nondiscriminatory tests that are valid predictors of performance.

Job Requirements

The principle of job-relatedness states that all human resources decisions, policies, and programs should be based on job requirements. Indeed, the objectives of HRM selection policies are always to match applicants' qualifications with job requirements and to develop employees' skills to meet job requirements.

For example, an airline's decision to hire only female flight attendants violates the principle of job-relatedness because being female is not essential to performing that work. On the other hand, a clothing designer's policy to hire only women to model dresses is in keeping with the principle of job-relatedness.

Hiring

Hiring is the process that takes place after a selection has been made and the job has been offered and accepted.

Orientation

Orientation is the process of acquainting new employees with the company's policies and procedures and with the personnel with whom the new employees will work.

■ TRAINING AND DEVELOPMENT

HRM's responsibility does not end with hiring new personnel and providing them with an orientation. HRM is also responsible for training and development, providing employees with the skills they need to perform effectively on the job and grow.

Training Programs

There are many ways in which employees can develop their skills, including seminars and workshops of all kinds—available, for example, from the company's training department, taken at a local community college, or sponsored by a vendor. Programs may be designed for new employees, for managers only, for sales people, and so on. They may be aimed at developing specific skills, at correcting problems, at expanding broad business knowledge, or at offering opportunities for promotion. Training may be offered on the job, or off the job.

On-the-Job Training

As the name suggests, on-the-job training is offered at work. The trainee learns by working under a supervisor or the supervision of an experienced employee.

Off-the-Job Training

Off-the-job training may take place in a classroom at the work location or at some location away from the work site.

Management Development

Management development is a specialized form of training, designed to improve the skills and talents of present managers or to prepare potential managers. Management-development programs build conceptual, analytical, and problem-solving skills, rather than the technical skills of training programs. Some programs are offered by in-house personnel—by other managers or training specialists, for example. Such programs are tailored to the needs of that particular organization. Other programs are conducted at management-training centers, university campuses, hotels, conference centers, vendors' and suppliers' offices, trade associations, and other locations.

Evaluating the Effectiveness of Training and Development

Training and management-development programs are expensive. In order to be cost effective, they must improve the performance of the company. The most common test of effectiveness is to measure how well people perform both before and after training. For example, if the goal of a safety-training program is to decrease the number of accidents in a factory, the number of accidents per day or per week or per month would be measured and compared both before and after employees completed the safety-training program.

■ PERFORMANCE APPRAISAL

Performance appraisal is a formal program comparing employees' actual performance with expected performance. Performance appraisal is an effort to see how well employees are doing their jobs and to evaluate their contribution to the organization. It is used in making decisions about the training, promotion, compensation, and termination of employees.

Ideally, this annual process begins with both the supervisor and the employee establishing—and agreeing to—clear, reasonable, measurable goals for the year to come. Then, during the year, the supervisor and the employee meet to discuss progress toward achieving each goal and discussing any reasons why the goals should be changed for any reason (for example, a change in priorities set by the company or by the supervisor).

A less-objective method is to judge or rate the employee. Using a scale (say, from one to ten) the supervisor rates the employee on qualities such as safety habits, output, initiative, and punctuality.

Whatever appraisal method is used, the supervisor should always discuss the results with the employee, explaining the basis of the evaluation, praising or rewarding good evaluations, and specifying how the employee can improve. During the discussion, the supervisor must be sure to offer the employee the opportunity for any rebuttal. Well-defined and well-implemented appraisal procedures can improve productivity and employee morale and protect a company from lawsuits alleging discrimination or unfair treatment.

Separation

Separation describes both voluntary and involuntary departure of a person from an organization. There are various types of separations or conditions under which employees leave an organization.

Resignation

Resignation is voluntary; an employee resigns to take a position with another company, to relocate to another part of the country, or to pursue another career interest. For management, resignations are generally the easiest type of separation to manage.

Retirement

Retirement, either voluntary or mandatory, can be planned for in advance since age establishes the date of retirement. An employee may elect voluntary retirement after a certain number of years of service or attaining a specified age. Early retirement is sometimes offered employees as a method of reducing the workforce. Some companies establish an age threshold at which retirement is required, but legislation has barred mandatory retirement based solely on age before the age of seventy.

Layoff

A layoff is a temporary involuntary separation made with the expectation of recall at a later date.

Reduction in Force (RIF)

A reduction in force (RIF) is a permanent separation that results from a company reorganization that reduces the number of positions or from a retrenchment in the workforce because of poor business.

Termination

Terminating, or firing, an employee is a permanent, involuntary separation. The reasons for dismissal must be business-related and should be documented. Managers should keep careful records of past performance reviews, formal warnings to the employee, documentation of any breach of work rules or policy, and poor performance.

At one time, the doctrine of "employment at will" gave an employer the right to terminate an employee at any time with or without any reason. Union contracts make terminations subject to review under grievance procedures, and under present law, firing even nonunion workers is open to legal challenge.

■ COMPENSATION

Compensation is the monetary payment employees receive in return for their labor. Workers are compensated in various ways.

Forms of Compensation

- **Wages** describe compensation based on the number of hours worked or units produced.
- **Salary** describes the compensation paid in return for doing a job, regardless of time worked or output.

Incentive Compensation

Businesses offer several types of incentive compensation.

- **Commissions** are payments based on a percentage of sales revenues.
- **Bonuses** are extra rewards, compensation in addition to wages, salary, and commissions. Bonuses may be distributed to all employees or only to those who are deemed eligible for special rewards for having exceeded specific goals.

- **Profit sharing** is the distribution of a percentage of a firm's profits among its employees.
- **Stock options** are rights to purchase shares of the employer's stock at a specified price, irrespective of the market value of the stock, based on performance.

Measuring Wages

Labor is a major cost of business. An effective compensation system, therefore, is important not only to control costs but also to attract and retain employees. Most firms establish careful policies and strategies for establishing compensation levels.

Wage Level

Wage level compares the wages paid in one firm to the level paid by comparable firms. Most firms attempt to set levels at or near the average of prevailing wage rates within an industry or geographic area, or both.

Wage Structure

Wage structure refers to the relative pay level for all the positions within a firm. Businesspeople agree that the office manager should earn more than the custodian—but how much more? Job evaluations help determine the relative worth of each job within a company.

Individual Wages

Individual wages must be determined within the wage structure for a particular firm. Each position usually has a range of compensation. For example, for secretaries, the hourly rate may range from $9.00 to $19.00 in one company, depending on skill, experience, seniority, and performance.

Comparable Worth

The Equal Pay Act of 1973 requires that workers doing the same job receive the same pay. Comparable worth specifically addresses the disparity between men's and women's earnings. Comparable worth seeks equal pay for jobs requiring about the same level of education, training, and skills as well as for jobs that are of equal value to the company.

As more and more women entered the workforce in the 1970s, 1980s, and 1990s, comparable worth became more and more of an issue. The federal government enacted the Equal Pay Act of 1973, while several states enacted laws requiring equal pay for comparable work in government positions.

Employee Benefits

Employee benefits, although nonmonetary, are still a form of compensation. In fact, benefits may account for as much as one-third to one-half of a firm's compensation budget. Benefits are given in addition to wages or salary. Some benefits—for example, workers' compensation, unemployment insurance, and Social Security—are mandated by law. Vacation time, sick leave, and holidays are also employer-paid benefits.

Health, dental, or life insurance, and pension and retirement plans may be funded by the employer fully, or the cost may be partially paid by the employee. Some companies also offer tuition reimbursement, child care, credit unions, recreational facilities, or subsidized lunchrooms. As the range of benefits has grown, so have benefit costs and concern over those costs.

One approach to paying for benefits is the cafeteria approach. Under this plan, the employee is allocated a certain lump sum for benefits; the employee is free to choose how that sum will be allocated by selecting the benefits he or she wants from a "cafeteria" selection. This approach is designed to increase employee satisfaction and motivation as well as limit costs.

■ THE IMPACT OF FEDERAL LEGISLATION ON HRM

Federal legislation has had a tremendous impact on HRM practices and programs. In addition, every state also has fair-employment statutes. The major laws include Title VII of the Civil Rights Act of 1964, which forbids discrimination in hiring, firing, and compensation on the basis of sex, race, color, religion, or national origin, and the Age Discrimination in Employment Act of 1967, amended in 1978, which outlaws discrimination against people aged 40 through 69, and prohibits forced retirement before the age of 70. The Fair Labor Standards Act sets minimum wages, and the Occupational Safety and Health Act (OSHA) establishes safety and health standards in the workplace.

People are the most important resource in a successful business. Human resources management plays a vital role in an organization's success. How managers recruit and select applicants and how they train and develop employees determines the managerial talent at all levels of the organization.

Selected Readings

Effron, Marc, Robert Gandossy, and Marshall Goldsmith. *Human Resources in the 21st Century.* 2003.

Falcone, Paul. *101 Sample Write-Ups for Documenting Employee Performance Problems.* 1999.

Falcone, Paul, and Adrienne Hickey. *96 Great Interview Questions to Ask Before You Hire.* 1997.

Hackman, J. R., and G. R. Oldham. *Work Redesign.* 1980.

Handy, Charles. *The Future of Work.* 1984.

Herzberg, Frederick. *Work and the Nature of Man.* 1966.

Huselid, Mark, Brian Becker, and Dave Ulrich. *The HR Scorecard: Linking People, Strategy, and Performance.* 2001.

Levering, Robert. *A Great Place to Work.* 1988.

Mintzberg, Henry. *Managers Not MBAs.* 2004.

Peter, Lawrence J., and Raymond Hull. *The Peter Principle.* 1969.

Phillips, Jack J., Ron Stone, and Patricia Phillips. *The Human Resources Scorecard: Measuring the Return on Investment.* 2001.

Schein, Edgar, editor. *The Art of Managing Human Resources.* 1987.

Schuler, Randall S., Stuart A. Youngblood, and Vandra L. Huber, editors. *Readings in Personnel and Human Resource Management.* 1987.

Smith, Shawn A., and Rebecca Mazin. *The HR Answer Book: An Indispensable Guide for Managers and Human Resources Professionals.* 2004.

Swanson, Richard A., and Elwood F. Holton. *Foundations of Human Resource Development.* 2001.

Tichy, Noel. *Human Resource Management in the Multinational Corporation.* 1988.

Twomey, David P. *A Concise Guide to Employment Law.* 1986.

U.S. Department of Labor. *Occupational Outlook Handbook, 2004–2005: Bulletin 2570.* 2004.

Weiler, Paul C. *Governing the Workplace: The Future of Labor and Employment Law.* 1990.

Weiss, W. H. *Supervisor's Standard Reference Handbook.* 1988.

Yoder, Dale, and Herbert J. Heneman, Jr., editors. *ASPA Handbook of Personnel and Industrial Relations.* 1979; supplement, 1983.

Test Yourself

1) Human resources management (HRM) involves every aspect of dealing with employees as a resource. What are these aspects?

2) What are the major components of planning for HRM?

3) Why might a company establish a policy of internal recruiting to fill vacant positions, rather than external recruiting?

4) What is a management development program?

5) What is the euphemism *separation*, in the context of personnel management?

6) What is meant by compensation, in the context of human resources management?

7) Federal legislation has had a significant impact on human resources management? Describe some of this legislation.

8) Statistics continue to bear out a pay discrepancy between men and women in the same job titles; consistently, men earn more than women. What legislation was enacted in 1973 to combat apparent inequity?

Test Yourself Answers

1) HRM includes planning, staffing (i.e., recruiting and hiring), training and development, performance appraisal, and compensation.

2) The planning function entails forecasting the company's human resource demand, forecasting the company's human resource supply, and matching the supply and demand to determine whether to increase or decrease the company's human resources.

3) Internal recruiting provides incentive and motivates employees to work more diligently, and, in some instances, to remain with the company.

4) Management development is a specialized form of training, designed either to improve the skills and talents of present managers or to prepare potential managers.

5) Separation describes both voluntary departure (e.g., resignations and retirements) and involuntary departure (e.g., reductions in force and terminations) of a person from employment in an organization.

6) Compensation is generally thought of as including the monetary payment (including wages for hourly employees and salaries for nonhourly employees) employees receive in return for their labor. More and more, however, persons are beginning to realize and appreciate that employee benefits are also a very valuable form of compensation, sometimes accounting for as much as one-third to one-half of a company's compensation budget.

7) Title VII of the Civil Rights Act of 1964 forbids discrimination in hiring, firing, and compensation on the basis of sex, race, color, religious, or national origin. The Age Discrimination in Employment Act of 1967 prohibits discrimination against persons aged 40 through 69, and prohibits forced retirement before the age of 70. The Fair Labor Standards Act sets minimum wages. The Occupational Safety and Health Act (OSHA) establishes safety and health standards in the workplace.

8) The Equal Pay Act of 1973 requires that workers doing the same job receive the same pay. Jobs requiring the same level of education, training, and skills should pay the same.

CHAPTER 11
Labor-Management Relations

A union's main concerns, according to Samuel Gompers, an early labor leader, are bread-and-butter issues such as wages, hours, and working conditions. Management's concerns, on the other hand, are controlling costs, operations, and profits. Through the years, in the struggle for power, the pendulum has swung back and forth between labor and management.

■ THE EVOLUTION OF ORGANIZED LABOR

A labor union is an organization of employees formed to achieve common goals in the areas of wages, hours, and working conditions. An industrial union is made up of workers in a particular industry, regardless of skills or jobs.

The first organizations of American workers appeared shortly after the Revolutionary War. These early unions were craft unions modeled after the medieval European craft guilds; like the guilds, craft unions were made up of skilled craftsmen in one locality who strove for better pay and working conditions. The Industrial Revolution and the growth of manufacturing in the 1800s led to large-scale production and drew large numbers of industrial workers to factories, where management paid little heed to comfort or safety and created fertile ground for unions to take root. Among the early trade organizations formed were the National Typographers Union (1852), the United Cigarmakers (1856), and the Iron Molders (1859). The first national union was the Knights of Labor (1869).

The Knights of Labor

The Knights of Labor (1869) started as a craft union, but expanded to include all workers. In addition to wage and working conditions, which traditionally motivated unions, the Knights also had social goals such as ownership of factories by workers and free land to those who wished to farm. Membership grew to about 700,000 by the mid-1880s.

In 1886, at a rally called in Chicago's Haymarket square to demand a reduction in the workday from ten to eight hours, violence erupted. A bomb exploded and several police officers and civilians were killed or wounded. The Haymarket Riot, as it became known, killed in more ways than one. Although direct responsibility was never established, the riot triggered a wave of anti-unionism that led to the dissolution of the Knights of Labor in 1900.

The American Federation of Labor (AFL)

The American Federation of Labor (AFL) was founded in 1886 by a number of disenchanted Knights led by Samuel Gompers. Made up of craft unions, the AFL abandoned social and moral programs to concentrate on improving wages, hours, and conditions through collective bargaining. Unlike the Knights, the AFL believed that the strike, a temporary work stoppage by employees, was an effective labor weapon.

The Industrial Workers of the World (IWW)

The Industrial Workers of the World (IWW) was formed in 1905. A radical alternative to the AFL, the IWW had among its goals to overthrow capitalism. Its radical stance diverted the attention of anti-labor forces away from the AFL and focused it fully on the IWW.

The Congress of Industrial Unions (CIO)

The Congress of Industrial Unions (CIO) was formed in 1955. With the growth of mass production, the number of unskilled workers had grown, but the AFL remained open only to skilled craftsmen due to its craft union heritage. Unskilled workers in the automobile, steel, and mining industries were denied membership.

Dissident leaders like John L. Lewis of the United Mine Workers pressed the AFL to admit industrial unions—that is, unions that represented workers in a particular industry regardless of their skills or jobs. Instead, the AFL expelled thirty-two national unions, and those unions formed the CIO. In the next few years, the CIO organized the auto, steel, meatpacking, mining, paper, textile, and electrical industries, representing almost half of the 10 million unionized workers by the 1940s.

The AFL-CIO

The AFL and CIO were competitors until they merged in 1955, and a new era in labor history began. Before the merger, the AFL and the CIO competed for size and influence. For example, in an effort to gain members, the AFL began to accept industrial workers. Frequent bitter clashes erupted over which union had the right to organize and represent particular groups of employees. When the unions staged a series of highly visible strikes, public sentiment turned against the unions, and the government began enacting labor legislation. These experiences pointed up the negative effects of inter-union competition and paved the way for the merger of the AFL and the CIO into the new AFL-CIO.

The newly formed AFL-CIO represented about 16 million workers, or almost 90 percent of unionized workers. George Meaney, a plumber by trade, who had been president of the AFL, became the first president of the AFL-CIO, and Walter Reuther, an automotive toolmaker by trade and head of the United Auto Workers (UAW), became vice president.

But conflicts and problems still remained after the merger. In 1957, the Teamsters (International Brotherhood of Teamsters) one of the largest labor unions in the United States, were expelled from the AFL-CIO for alleged corrupt practices. In 1968, as a result of policy and personality differences, the UAW withdrew from the AFL-CIO. The UAW and the Teamsters, the two largest unions in the country, formed the Alliance for Labor Action (ALA). The ALA was later disbanded, and in 1981, the UAW rejoined the AFL-CIO, followed by the Teamsters in 1985. In 2005, however, the Teamsters disaffiliated itself from the AFL-CIO, in favor of another coalition, Change to Win.

■ ORGANIZED LABOR TODAY

Labor's power and its ability to negotiate effectively with management is based on two specific strengths: union membership and pro-labor legislation.

Union Membership

The more workers the union represents, the greater its strength and the stronger its bargaining position. Union membership currently accounts for less than one-quarter of the workforce and is concentrated in relatively few industries, or job categories. But in those few areas, unions wield considerable power. The AFL-CIO, with about 13 million members, is clearly the largest union. While it remains a member of the Change to Win coalition, the Teamsters is the largest independent union, with 1.4 million members.

Although the size of the workforce has increased, union membership relative to the workforce has declined. In 1983, union membership reached its high point of 20 million members, representing nearly 20.1 percent of the workforce (down from the 1955 high of 30 percent). In 2004, only 12.5 percent of the wage and salary employees called themselves union members (down from 12.9 percent in 2003). In an effort to counter this trend, unions have tried to organize any recognizable group, such as teachers and municipal workers. In fact, of the 12.5 percent, 36.4 percent of the union members were public sector employees (although that is down from the 37.1 percent rate of 2003). The rate for private industry workers, at 7.9 percent in 2004, is about half of what it was during 1983. The largest numbers of union members lived in California (2.4 million) and New York (2.0 million). Moreover, about half (7.8 million) of the 15.5 million union members in the United States in 2004 lived in six states (California, New York, Michigan, Illinois, Pennsylvania, and Ohio).

Whatever the outcome of unions' organizing efforts, they will remain a powerful force in certain industries.

Pro-Labor Legislation

For America's first 150 years, workers had little legal backing. Business, frequently aided by court injunctions, police, local militia, or the army, resisted the early efforts of labor to organize. But all that has changed.

Early Legislation

Today, legislation plays a key part in the balance of power between labor and management, leaning first one way then another, as discussed in the following sections.

Norris-LaGuardia Act of 1932

The first major legislation to secure rights for unions was the Norris-LaGuardia Act of 1932. It restricted the right of courts to issue injunctions prohibiting strikes, pickets, and union-membership drives. It also outlawed yellow dog contracts; that is, contracts that included, as conditions of being hired, statements that workers were not union members and would not join a union while employed at the firm.

The National Labor Relations Act of 1935

The National Labor Relations Act of 1935, also called the Wagner Act, gave workers the right to organize, to bargain, and to strike, and it forbade unfair labor practices such as discrimination in hiring, firing, or promoting union members. The Wagner Act established procedures for employees to decide whether they wish to be represented by a union, and it established the National Labor Relations Board (NRLB) to enforce its provisions.

The two main functions of the NRLB are to oversee elections in which employees vote to decide whether they wish to join and be represented by a union, and to investigate complaints of unions or employers.

The Fair Labor Standards Act of 1938
The Fair Labor Standards Act of 1938 established a minimum wage ($0.25 an hour at that time) and barred child labor. The act also mandated overtime pay for work beyond a forty-hour workweek.

Legislation after World War II
With the aid of the Norris-LaGuardia Act, the Wagner Act, and the Fair Labor Standards Act, organized labor grew in size and strength, and became a formidable economic and political force. Then, in the years immediately after World War II, a series of disruptive coal, steel, and trucking strikes turned public opinion against the unions, and Congress responded by passing a series of amendments to the Wagner Act.

The Labor-Management Relations Act of 1947
The Labor-Management Relations Act of 1947, popularly known as the Taft-Hartley Act, was enacted over the veto of President Harry Truman. The Taft-Hartley Act, which amended the Wagner Act, was intended to provide a balance between union and management power by forbidding unions to use certain unfair practices. The Taft-Hartley act forbid harassment and coercion of nonunion workers, it barred the closed shop (which required an employee to be a member of the union as a condition of employment), and it prohibited not bargaining "in good faith."

The Taft-Hartley Act opened the door for states to pass right-to-work laws to promote open shops, shops where union membership had no effect on hiring or firing. Right-to-work laws were passed in twenty states, mostly in the South, prohibiting union and agency shops.

- A **union shop** is a workplace that requires an employee to join the union within a certain period of being hired.
- An **agency shop** is a workplace that requires workers to pay union dues whether or not they are members.

Taft-Hartley also established procedures for resolving strikes that pose a national emergency. The president may request an injunction requiring a sixty-day, no-strike cooling-off period during which labor and management must attempt to resolve their differences. If the dispute is still unresolved after sixty days, the injunction can be extended another twenty days, and the workers must vote in a secret-ballot election whether to accept the latest management offer. If the offer is accepted, the strike ends. If it is not accepted, the president and Congress can force the workers to return to work under the threat of criminal action, or the workers can be fired and replaced by nonunion personnel.

The Landrum-Griffin Act of 1959
The Landrum-Griffin Act of 1959 further amended the Wagner Act as a result of congressional hearings that revealed unethical, illegal, and undemocratic union practices and corruption within unions. The act required unions to issue financial reports, and regulated internal union practices and elections.

The Postal Reorganization Act of 1970
The Postal Reorganization Act of 1970 gave postal workers the right to form unions and to bargain collectively, but not to strike.

The Federal Service Labor-Management Relations Statute of 1978

The Federal Service Labor-Management Relations Statute of 1978 (Title VII of the Civil Service Reform Act of 1978) gave other federal employees the right to organize and to bargain, but disallowed bargaining over economic items and strikes. It was under the provisions of this law that President Ronald Reagan discharged striking air-traffic controllers in 1981.

■ THE FORMATION OF UNIONS

The National Labor Relations Board (NLRB) establishes the rules for, and oversees, the formation of a union. Throughout the process, the NLRB closely monitors and regulates the actions of both labor and management.

The first step in forming a union is the organizing campaign, which attempts to develop widespread interest among employees in having a union. The organizing campaign may be instituted by the national union, or the employees themselves may decide they want a union. The employees must indicate their support in writing, by signing authorization cards.

If at least 30 percent of eligible employees sign authorization cards, the union can request that the firm recognize the union. The firm almost always rejects this request, and a formal election is held within forty-five days to determine whether to have a union. The election is held by the NLRB using a secret ballot and is decided by a simple majority of eligible employees. If the union gains a majority, it becomes the bargaining agent for the workers. Both sides have five days to challenge the election. If the union loses, the NLRB will not allow another election for one year.

■ UNION AND MANAGEMENT NEGOTIATIONS

The methods and procedures used by unions and management to negotiate contracts are many. Once a union is certified by the NLRB, the union will choose officers and representatives, and a negotiating committee will be appointed to begin collective bargaining.

Collective Bargaining

Collective bargaining is the process of negotiating a contract between labor and management. The union is represented by the negotiating committee, which includes a representative from the national union office. The management negotiating team is made up of people from the company's industrial relations, HRM, and legal departments. Each side is required by law to negotiate in good faith.

The union usually presents its demands first, and management then answers with its counterproposal. After a number of give-and-take meetings, a first contract is developed. If both sides cannot reach agreement, the union may strike, but strikes rarely occur during negotiations for the first contract. The final step in a first contract is ratification—that is, approval—by the union membership.

Later contracts are much more difficult to negotiate. After the first contract negotiations fail, both sides may have reconsidered their positions on certain issues. They may have recognized potential problems or difficulties, and as a result they may approach the negotiations with new demands. Later contracts may also carry the additional pressure of the current contract's expiration date.

Contract Issues

Many different issues are negotiated by labor and management and become part of the labor contract. These issues will vary from firm to firm, or from time to time, but certain issues are almost always present money: working hours and job security, for example.

Money

Money is central in union-management relations, and the issues concerning money have several aspects. Direct compensation is a straightforward issue: What wage or salary will the employees receive for specific work? Benefits are receiving increasing attention as the costs of benefit packages have grown. Cost-of-living adjustments, called COLAs, give employees automatic wage increases to keep pace with inflation.

Working Hours and Overtime

Federal legislation sets minimum standards for hours worked (forty) and for overtime pay rates (one and one-half times normal hourly pay), but unions try to negotiate higher standards—for example, fewer hours in the standard workweek, a higher rate for certain shifts, a choice of shifts and starting times for employees, a greater overtime rate for holidays and weekends, and longer lunch or coffee breaks.

Job Security

Job security is a serious concern for both the individual union member and for the union itself. For the individual, job security provides protection against unemployment. A union member's job security is generally based on his or her seniority, which ensures that the last person hired will be the first to be fired. For the union, job security of members directly affects union strength: The greater the membership, the greater the union's power. The Taft-Hartley Act prohibited closed shops, but union shops and agency shops (described in the "The Labor-Management Relations Act of 1947" section earlier in this chapter) are legal, and unions will try to negotiate these advantages.

Management Rights

Management tries to retain as much control as possible over all work issues—personnel, work schedules, discipline, and so on. Unions want control over these same issues and have made headway in gaining a voice in such so-called management matters, in some cases by winning seats on the board of directors. One of the first was Douglas Fraser, a UAW official who sat on Chrysler's board when Chrysler was faced with bankruptcy.

Grievance Procedures

Grievance procedures are part of almost every contract. A grievance procedure is a formally established course of action for resolving complaints of employees against management. An employee who feels he or she has been treated unfairly in violation of the contract may file a grievance.

To start the process, the employee brings the complaint to the shop steward, the person elected by the union members to be their representative in this particular work location. The shop steward and the employee discuss the grievance with the employee's immediate supervisor. Both the grievance and the supervisor's response are put in writing. If the problem cannot be resolved at this level, further discussions are held with a member of the union's grievance committee and a member of the company's industrial relations department. If the grievance is still not resolved, the group is expanded to include the full grievance committee and senior company executives.

When all parties cannot reach agreement, the final step is arbitration; whereby a neutral third party hears both sides of the dispute and renders a decision. That decision is binding, which means that all parties must adhere to the arbitrator's decision. The arbitrator's decision cannot add to, subtract from, or modify the contract in any way.

Union Weapons

Unions have several weapons that they can use, including strikes, slowdowns, and boycotts.

Strikes

The most extreme weapon unions have in their arsenal is the strike. A strike is simply a work stoppage. Workers do not report for work, but instead picket the company, marching in front of their workplace with signs notifying the public that a strike is in progress. The purpose of picketing is to enlist public sympathy for the striking workers, discourage people from patronizing the firm, prevent nonstriking workers from going to work, and encourage other unions not to cross the picket line.

Strikes are expensive. The firm loses business and profits during the strike, and the strikers lose their pay. Unions help by creating a strike fund, using union dues to supply financial support to striking workers.

Most contracts contain a clause that prohibits strikes during the life of the contract. *Note:* A wildcat strike is a strike that is not approved by the union.

Slowdowns

Workers may also engage in slowdowns. During a slowdown, workers do report to work, but they deliberately work at a slower pace than normal in an effort to put financial pressure on the firm.

Boycotts

A boycott is a refusal to do business with a particular firm. Unions urge their members and the public to refrain from doing business with the firm. Primary boycotts are directed against the firm with which the union has a dispute. Secondary boycotts, now prohibited by the Taft-Hartley Act, were directed against firms doing business with the employer.

Management Weapons

Management, too, has weapons at its disposal, including lockouts, strikebreakers, and other support.

Lockouts

The lockout, a firm's refusal to allow workers to enter the workplace, is the most extreme of management's weapons. The purpose is to stop production in time to avoid spoilage or damage of raw materials or finished goods.

Strikebreakers

Management may also employ strikebreakers, nonunion workers hired to replace striking workers. Strikebreaking has often led to violence as striking workers attempt to prevent strikebreakers from entering the workplace. Sometimes the management staff will assume the jobs of striking workers, as Bell Telephone did on more than one occasion.

Other Support

In many industries, managements are organized into associations such as the National Association of Manufacturers (NAM) or the National Dairy Association. Such associations help present a united front for the group represented and work to the group's advantage—for example, by lobbying for favorable legislation. Management may attempt to obtain a court injunction against striking or picketing workers.

■ MEDIATION AND ARBITRATION

Certain weapons are available to both labor and management. For example, both will try to utilize publicity to advance their particular point of view, gain public support, and if possible, enlist political support. In addition, both labor and management may try to use mediation and arbitration.

Mediation

Mediation is the use of a neutral third party to assist management and labor during negotiations. The mediator attempts to improve communication, promote compromise, and keep negotiations moving in a positive direction. Mediation is intended to aid, not force, both parties to reach a compromise.

Arbitration

Arbitration can also be utilized in contract negotiations. In such cases, the decision of the arbitrator is binding only if both parties agree to be bound in advance.

If both mediation and arbitration fail, the president of the United States (under provisions of the Taft-Hartley Act) may obtain an injunction to prevent or stop a strike if the strike jeopardizes national health or security.

■ THE FUTURE OF THE UNIONS

Union membership has suffered over the past few years, due in part to the shrinking number of industrial workers. As this trend continues, it is likely that union membership in the United States will not increase appreciably.

The strength of labor unions has always been tied to economic conditions. Like other products, labor is a commodity, and as such it has a fair market price. When the marketplace experiences hard times, the price of labor tends to fall, reflecting the changing economic conditions. The recent globalization of the economy poses a threat to unions and union membership in light of the pressures on wages from places such as China and India.

Although we still see occasions of labor-management confrontations, the inclusion of labor in management decisions and the acceptance of human relation principles has brought labor and management closer together.

Selected Readings

Atleson, James B. *Labor and the Wartime State: Labor Relations and Law During World War II.* 1998.

Chandler, Margaret K. *Management Rights and Union Interests.* 1964.

Dunlop, John, editor. *Labor in the Twentieth Century.* 1978.

Dunlop, John T. *The Management of Labor Unions: Decision Making with Historical Restraints.* 1989.

Elkouri, F., and E. A. Elkouri. *How Arbitration Works.* 1985.

Estey, Marten. *The Unions: Structure, Development and Management.* 1981.

Gifford, C. D., editor. *Directory of U.S. Labor Organizations.* 1988.

Gould, William B., IV. *A Primer on American Labor Law.* 1986.

Kerr, Clark. *Industrialism and Industrial Man.* 1964.

Lewin, D., and R. B. Peterson. *The Modern Grievance Procedure in the American Economy: A Theoretical and Empirical Analysis.* 1986.

Lichtenstein, Nelson. *State of the Union: A Century of American Labor.* 2003.

Marx, Karl, and Frederick Engels. *Marx and Engels on the Trade Unions.* 1990.

Millikan, William. *Union Against Unions: The Minneapolis Citizens Alliance and Its Fight Against Organized Labor.* 2004.

Mills, D. Quinn. *Labor-Management Relations.* 1988.

Nissen, Bruce. *Unions in a Globalized Environment: Changing Borders, Organizational Boundaries, and Social Roles.* 2002.

Olson, Mancur, Jr. *The Logic of Collective Action.* 1971.

Siegel, Abraham J., and David B. Lipsky, editors. *Unfinished Business: An Agenda for Labor, Management, and the Public.* 1978.

Stepan-Norris, Judith, and Maurice Zeitlin. *Left Out: Reds and America's Industrial Unions.* 2002.

Tillman, Ray M. *The Transformation of U.S. Unions: Voices, Visions, and Strategies from the Grassroots.* 1999.

Test Yourself

1) What is a labor union?

2) What is it about a union that provides it the power to negotiate effectively with the management of a company?

3) True or false: The Norris-LaGuardia Act of 1932 restricts the rights of courts to issue injunctions prohibiting strikes, pickets, and union membership drives.

4) Why is the National Labor Relations Act of 1935 important to labor-management relations?

5) The Taft-Hartley Act was written to establish more of a balance between unions and managements. What are some of the major features of the act?

6) What is a union shop and how, if at all, does it differ from an agency shop?

7) True or false: The Landrum-Griffin Act of 1959 amended the Wagner Act to allow unions more flexibility to conduct business.

8) As a result of an air-traffic controller strike during 1981, then-president Ronald Reagan discharged the striking employees. What legislation provided the power for President Reagan to discharge the unionized workers?

9) Describe how a union is formed.

10) What are some of the tools unions and management use to bolster their negotiating positions?

Test Yourself Answers

1) A labor union is an organization of employees formed to achieve common goals in the areas of wages, hours, and working conditions.

2) First, the union membership itself provides a compelling source of power; the larger the membership the more power the union wields. Moreover, the significant pro-labor legislation exists to buttress the power secured by union membership.

3) True. In fact, the Norris-LaGuardia Act of 1932 was the first act to secure the rights of unions.

4) The National Labor Relations Act of 1935 gives workers the right to organize, to bargain, and to strike. Moreover, it forbids unfair labor practices, such as discriminating in hiring, firing, or promoting union members. It also promulgated the mechanism that allows employees to decide whether they want union representation in the workplace. Finally, it created the National Labor Relations Board to enforce its provisions.

5) The Taft-Hartley Act forbids harassment and coercion of nonunion workers, bars the closed shop (which requires a worker to be a member of the union to be employed), and requires management and the union to bargain in good faith.

6) A union shop is a workplace that requires new employees to join the union as a condition of employment. An agency shop, on the other hand, requires all employees to pay union dues, irrespective of whether they are union members. These kinds of arrangements remain lawful, except in states (mostly Southern) that specifically prohibit them.

7) False. The Landrum-Griffith Act did amend the Wagner Act, but by requiring unions to issue financial reports and by regulating internal union practices and elections.

8) The Federal Service Labor-Management Relations Statute of 1978 gave federal employees (other than postal workers, who are covered under a separate statute) the right to organize and to bargain, but not the right to strike.

9) Ordinarily, an organizing campaign occurs, spearheaded by union representatives, which seeks to create widespread interest among employees. Interested employees must indicate their desire to unionize by signing authorization cards. If at least 30 percent of eligible employees sign the authorization cards, the union can request the firm to recognize the union. If the firm rejects the request (as is usually the case) it must hold a formal election within 45 days to determine whether to have a union. The National Labor Relations Board (NLRB) conducts the election, using a secret ballot process. A simple majority of the employees' vote determines the outcome.

10) Unions tend to call for employee slowdowns or strikes; they may also encourage employee boycotts of particular firms. Company managements tend to employ strikebreakers and impose lockouts (as an extreme measure); they also align themselves with other companies in the industry to create alliances and associations that can present a united front in support of the group's positions (e.g., with legislators).

CHAPTER 12
Producing Goods and Services

The production of goods and the providing of services are the bases of our economic system. This chapter addresses the fundamentals of these two important components of the economy.

■ AN OVERVIEW OF THE PRODUCTION OF GOODS AND SERVICES

When one party gives something of value to another individual for a good or a service, an exchange takes place. Millions of such exchanges occur everyday, whenever customers pay money ("something of value") for goods such as clothing, milk, and tires, and whenever they pay money for services (accounting, medical, or legal services, for example).

In all cases, the exchange should satisfy both the buyer and the seller, and this satisfaction is measured in terms of utility, the power of that good or that service to satisfy a human need. In this sense, the customer does not purchase a product or a service but a utility.

There are four types of utility: utility of form, utility of place, utility of time, and utility of possession. Production creates utility of form by processing inputs into finished products, whether those finished products are tangible goods, intangible goods, or services. Thus, utility of form is addressed in this chapter on the production of goods and services. The other kinds of utility are created by marketing and are examined in Chapter 13.

■ PRODUCING GOODS

Producing goods depends on production and operations management (POM), which is the systematic direction and control of the process that brings together the resources of raw materials, equipment, and labor and transforms those resources into finished goods. Production is the transformation process, and operations are the systems used to create goods in the production process.

Production Processes

Production processes can be classified in three ways: types of transformation, the methods in which resources are used to effect the transformation, and the arrangement of the transformation process (i.e., the product flow).

Types of Transformation

There are three processes that manufacturers use to transform raw materials into finished goods.

Chemical Transformation

Chemical transformation alters raw materials chemically. For example, petroleum is a raw material that can be transformed into plastics, gasoline, and other products.

Fabrication

Fabrication mechanically alters the form and/or the shape of the raw materials. Steel wire, for example, is transformed into nails or staples. Lumber can be turned on a lathe and transformed into chair arms or stool legs.

Assembly

Assembly involves putting together components into either a final product or a component product—that is, a product that will become part of a more-complex product. For example, fabricated lumber is formed into the arms of chairs that, along with other parts, are assembled into chairs. Electronic components are assembled along with other parts into computers.

Methods Used to Effect the Transformation

A second way to classify production processes is by the method in which resources are used to transform materials into finished goods.

Analytic Processes

Analytic processes break down basic resources into components. For instance, a flour mill breaks down a raw material, wheat, into a new product, flour.

Synthetic Processes

Synthetic processes combine a number of raw materials to produce a finished product. A bakery, for instance, transforms flour, eggs, shortening, and sugar into cake.

Product Flow

The third classification is based on how the plant, or production facility, is arranged and how the product moves through that plant.

Continuous Process

The continuous process describes any method where the flow of transformation from resources to finished product is smooth, straight, uninterrupted, and features long production runs. A manufacturer of chocolate candy bars uses the same process continuously to produce a steady product of consistent form, flavor, and quality.

Intermittent Process

The flow in an intermittent process is best described as stop-and-go, with short production runs. A printing plant, for instance, shuts down presses between product runs as it sets up the paper and inks needed for the next job. Although the manufacturing process—in this example, the printing process is the same—the finished product differs from print run to print run.

Types of Production

By following a series of steps or processes, production transforms resources into a form people need or want. Just as there are several types of production processes, there are several types of production.

Production Line and Assembly Line

In a production line, material is moved past teams or individual workers. Each worker or group of workers performs one specific step in the progression. If only assembly operations are performed (that is, nothing is manufactured from a raw material), the line is known as an assembly line. For example, brake pads may be produced from raw materials on a *production line*. But in an automobile manufacturing plant, the finished brake pads are just one of the components on an *assembly line* that turns out finished automobiles.

Automation

Mechanization, the substitution of machines for human labor, led to automation. In automated production, mechanical operations are performed with little or no human involvement. Automation was born during the Industrial Revolution, when machine-spinning replaced hand-spinning of textiles.

Although it has a high initial cost, automation reduces the cost of producing each unit (that is, unit cost) and ensures uniform high quality. A bakery or candy manufacturer may automate the measuring and mixing of ingredients along with baking.

Robotic and Computerized Production

Robots are machines that perform some of the mechanical functions of humans. Robotics, the use of robots in production processes, substitutes mechanical energy for human energy and is now common in many manufacturing processes.

Robots perform a single task, such as welding, with great accuracy and without the boredom or fatigue that human workers feel. Robots that can be adapted or directed by computers to perform several tasks are called flexible robots.

Computer-Aided Design (CAD)

Computer-aided design (CAD) allows a designer to rely on the powers of computer technology to produce blueprints, sketches, and various other kinds of product specifications. Aided by CAD, the designer can even check for design or engineering weaknesses.

Computer-Aided Manufacturing (CAM)

Computer-aided manufacturing (CAM) uses the computer to analyze product design. The computer helps determine the steps necessary for producing the product, as well as preparing and controlling the equipment used in making it.

Productivity

Productivity is the measure of the relationship between (1) the total amount of goods and services being produced, and (2) the resources needed to produce them. The inputs, the equipment, the materials, the planning, and the cost of labor all contribute to productivity as reflected in the value of the end product.

The major benefit of automation and mechanization has been increased productivity. However, the high cost of American labor has put domestic products at a disadvantage in world markets. In order to better compete in world markets, American companies attempt to increase efficiency of the production system and to develop technical innovations that establish new ways of producing goods.

■ OPERATIONS

Operations refers to the systems used to create goods: site selection, plant layout, purchasing, routing, scheduling, quality, inventory, and others, all discussed in the following sections.

Production Facility Planning

Once a decision to produce is made, management must decide where and how the production is to be carried out. Management must also decide where to locate the production facility and what the specific layout of the facility should be.

Site Selection

Site selection is the process of determining where the production facility is to be located. Some of the factors to be considered are location of the market; availability of suppliers and distribution channels, utilities, and labor costs; cost of land and development; and zoning, taxes, and regulations; and transportation. The site-selection process weighs the advantages and disadvantages of various sites.

Layout

Layout is the overall arrangement at the facility, the order in which machines, equipment, work stations, aisles, storage areas, and supply areas are arranged. The major patterns are process, product, and fixed-position layouts.

Process Layout

Process layout groups similar types of equipment or materials used in the process. A metal fabricating plant will generally group its drill presses, lathes, and welding equipment in separate locations.

Product Layout

Product layout follows an arrangement based on the successive production steps, from beginning to end, for a particular product. The automobile assembly line is a typical example of product layout.

Fixed-Position Layout

Fixed-position layout places the product in a fixed or stationary position in the plant; workers and equipment are brought to the product as work progresses. The fixed-position layout is common in the aircraft and construction industry, because of the large size of the product.

Operations Planning and Scheduling

The better a system is designed, the easier it will be to operate. However, no system runs by itself. A production system (or operation) that always turns out the same product, at the same rate, needs less ongoing planning and scheduling. A system that turns out a variety of products at different rates requires more ongoing planning and scheduling operations.

The function of operations planning is to determine the types and amounts of resources needed to produce specified goods and to plan for the purchasing, routing, scheduling, and dispatching of these resources. Resources include people, money, materials, and equipment.

Purchasing

Purchasing involves decisions concerning not only how much raw material or components to buy, but also where, when, and at what price. Suppliers must be considered on the basis of price, quality, reliability, and delivery. The quantity ordered depends on the rate the material is used, when it will be needed, and the time needed to deliver it to the production facility once the order is placed.

Routing

Routing determines the sequence in which all phases of production must be completed to produce the goods and, therefore, the path the materials must take through the plant. A plant producing frozen peas must take peas in, remove them from the pods, cook them, divide them into portions, and then freeze them.

Scheduling

Scheduling refers to the process of determining when an activity will take place and how long it will take to complete. Two commonly used scheduling techniques employ Gantt charts and program evaluation and review technique (PERT) charts.

Gantt Chart

Named for Henry Gantt, who developed the technique in the early 1900s, the Gantt chart is a graphic scheduling device in bar-graph format. A Gantt chart shows the progress graphically, indicating what has been done, what remains to be accomplished, and whether the time schedule is being met. Gantt charts (see Figure 12.1, below) can be used both as a planning and as a control tool.

Because drawer construction is the longest process, it must start earliest. Cutting and shaping the legs can begin half a week later, followed by cutting tops, so that assembly can begin the middle of the second week as a supply of all needed parts becomes available. Painting will not begin until assembly is completed.

Gantt charts are useful for repetitive projects or products that are made up of relatively few activities.

Program Evaluation and Review Technique (PERT)

Program evaluation and review technique (PERT) works like this: Suppose two activities, B and C, can be undertaken simultaneously. Activity B requires three days to complete, and activity C requires four days to complete. Both must be completed before production can move to activity D. If activity B is

Activity	Department	Week 1	Week 2	Week 3	Week 4
Cut Tops	1		▬▬		
Cut & Shape Legs	2	▬▬▬▬			
Build Drawers	3	▬▬▬▬▬▬▬▬			
Assemble	4			▬▬▬▬▬	
Paint	5				▬▬▬

Figure 12.1: A Gantt Chart for a Company Manufacturing Desks.

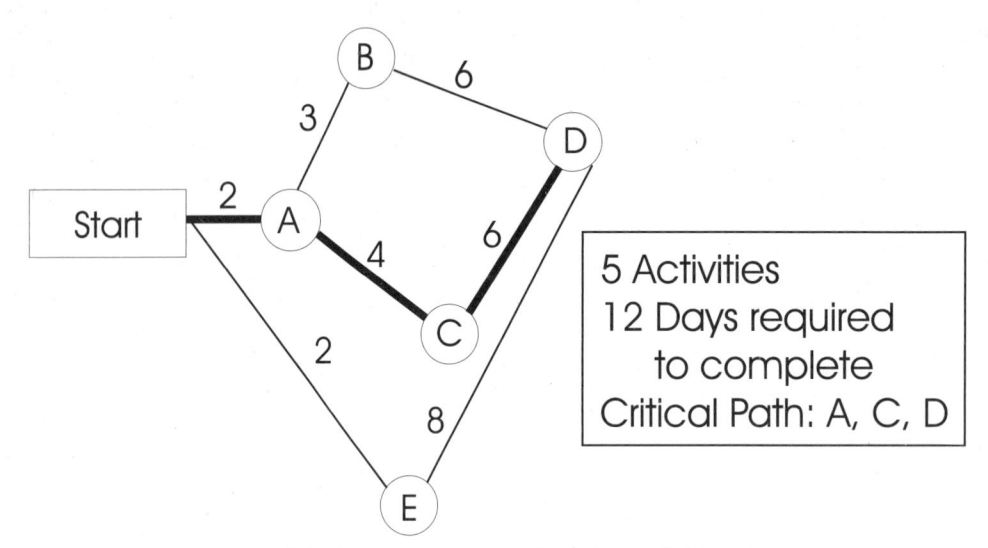

Figure 12.2: A PERT Diagram Showing a Critical Path

delayed, there is one day slack time available before activity C is completed. If, however, activity C is delayed, then the completion schedule is jeopardized. Keeping activity C on schedule is critical to maintaining the overall production schedule. The path of activities whose schedules must be maintained to avoid such delays is called the critical path. The planning method designed around these activities is the critical path method (CPM), and is a commonly used technique for scheduling complicated production processes (see Figure 12.2).

Dispatching

Dispatching, which means issuing detailed work orders, is based on the planning, scheduling, and routing decisions made to complete the production of goods. Dispatching takes the plans that have been made and makes those plans operational.

Materials Requirements Planning (MRP)

Materials requirements planning (MRP) is a computer-based coordination system that ensures the availability of needed parts and materials at the right time at the right place. By comparing customer orders, product specifications, and inventory of raw materials and parts, MRP can help determine what should be ordered, when it should be ordered, and which deliveries should be accelerated or delayed. MRP's major benefit is that it avoids downtime—that is, time when production is suspended because parts or materials are not available.

Controlling Production

Controlling, as indicated in Chapter 9, is closely related to planning. The control function enables production and operations managers to ensure that production proceeds as planned. Two key control areas in production and operations management (POM) are quality and inventory.

Quality Control

Quality control is the process of ensuring that final quality meets planned quality.

The Control Function

The control function must allow for adjustments and corrections, and at the right time. If, for instance, quality-control inspectors are placed at the end of the assembly line, all they can do is weed out products that fail to meet quality standards; they cannot adjust or correct problems. On the other hand, when purchasing departments ensure that parts purchased from suppliers are indeed high-quality parts, they have contributed strongly to quality control early in the process. The failure of many U.S. firms to compete in world markets has been blamed in part on inferior quality of American products, and inferior quality, in turn, can be blamed in part on ineffective quality control.

Statistical Quality Control

Statistical quality control is used to address only the percentage of final products deemed necessary to ensure quality of the entire batch. It involves taking samples from the process periodically. In the competitive world of the 21st century, the goal is to monitor the inputs to the process as far upstream as possible. Firms can no longer afford to detect bad quality after the final product is made.

Quality Circles

Developed in Japan, quality circles are small groups of workers who meet regularly to discuss and help solve problems related to quality. The group, usually fewer than twenty employees from the same work site or task area, focus on operational problems. The problems addressed can be either assigned by management or generated by the group. Solutions are presented to management, which, in turn, analyzes and accepts, rejects, or modifies the recommendations.

Inventory Control

Inventories tie up cash, and high inventories tie up a great deal of cash. Keeping inventories of inputs at the lowest levels necessary to meet customer demand reduces the amount of money invested in inventory and frees that cash for other uses. At the same time, it reduces inventory-related costs, such as inventory handling and storage. Materials requirements planning is one way managers control inventory (see the "Materials Requirements Planning (MRP)" section earlier on page 136).

Just-in-Time (JIT) Inventory Control

Just-in-time (JIT) inventory control reduces inventories to a minimum by arranging for materials to be delivered to the production facility "just in time" to be used in the manufacturing of a product. This method requires precise and complex coordination using MRP. JIT inventory control is widely used throughout the automotive industry and is being adopted in other industries.

In order to compete successfully in world markets in the future, the United States must increase productivity, the measure of efficiency that compares how much is produced with the resources used to produce it. In the battle to achieve lower production costs and higher productivity and quality, management is turning to more sophisticated methods of planning and control as well as to greater use of mechanization, automation, and computerization.

■ PRODUCING SERVICES

The service segment of the American economy has been growing rapidly in recent years and currently accounts for 60 percent of our gross domestic product GDP (see Chapter 1). In many ways, the production of services and the production of goods are similar, but they differ in a number of major ways.

First of all, goods are produced, services are performed. Further, all services are intangible. The raw materials for services are people with needs or with possessions that need care. The finished products are not goods, but people whose needs have been met or whose possessions have been cared for. These differences, and others, will become clear in the following discussion.

For goods, the focus of the production process is on the goods produced. For services, the goal of the production process is to create services rather than goods, and the focus of the production process is on the transformation process and on the outcome.

Service Production Processes

Production and operations management (POM) for services is concerned with the same categories as for goods—namely, types of transformation, the methods in which resources are used to effect the transformation, and the arrangement of the transformation process (i.e., service flow)—but the elements in each category vary.

Types of Transformation

Transformations are much more varied in producing services. Input for a service might be sick or injured people, the transformation process might be medical care, and the output, healthy people. Among the great variety of other services available are those provided by lawyers, consultants, entertainers, and educators.

Three transformation processes in producing services are assembly, transportation, and clerical.

Assembly

The assembly process involves putting together various components in an effort to service people's needs. A supermarket assembles meat, vegetables, groceries, to satisfy customers' need for food.

Transportation

The transportation process includes moving goods (for example, from the factory) and warehousing goods until sold. The transportation process includes other forms of shipping as well as moving people by airline, bus, or other means of transportation.

Clerical

The clerical process transforms information. The clerical transformation of data makes up a large segment of the service economy, and includes all the many services performed in data-processing and word-processing functions.

Methods of Transformation

Although few services can be characterized as analytic, many employ the synthetic process. The synthetic process entails combining a number of raw materials to produce a service. For example, MacDonald's combines rolls, meat, lettuce, and sauce into a hamburger, and thereby produces a service—feeding a hungry customer.

Service Flow

The flow of services tends to be intermittent rather than continuous. For example, a barber does not cut hair on a continuous basis. The service, a haircut, is delivered one at a time as customers arrive.

Types of Service Production

Service production tends to be labor-intensive, requiring more labor than does goods production. But service production is less capital-intensive, requiring less capital expenditure for plant and equipment, for example. Exceptions are hotels and airlines, which do require considerable capital. Service production does not lend itself to assembly-line or production-line organization.

Mechanization

Mechanization, the substitution of machines for human labor, is also found in the production of services. A car wash, for example, replaces handwork in washing and waxing an automobile with a mechanized process.

Automation

As we have already seen, mechanization led to automation. For example, one-hour film-developing services have automated most of the processes as a way of speeding up and standardizing their service. Bank ATMs (automated teller machines) are also examples of the automation of services.

Computerization

Computers contribute greatly to many of the transformation processes. Financial planners, brokers, catalog stores, and travel agents rely heavily on the use of computers. Interior decorators and contractors use computer-aided design, and many beauty shops utilize computer imaging to show how a new hairstyle will look.

Characteristics of Services

Unlike goods, services such as legal services or car repairs are intangible. There are other differences found in the special aspect of services.

Perishability

A service cannot be stored or inventoried. It cannot be produced in advance. If it is not used when available, it is wasted. An empty theater seat or an empty airline seat is a sale lost forever.

Customized Services

Many services are highly customized. There are differences not only between one service and another, but also within a single kind of service. For example, a haircut is unique—it is different from all other haircuts.

Customization

Services cannot be separated from the provider. Services are produced and consumed at the same time. The customer of a service has the ability to affect the transformation process to a degree that customers of goods essentially cannot. A potential customer for a good can only choose not to purchase the good if it is not suitable, but a customer of a service can complain, make suggestions, make requests, or otherwise affect the process. The degree of customer involvement depends upon whether the service is part of a high- or low-contact service.

High-Contact Services

High-contact services include the customer as part of the service. The customer who purchases a manicure must go to the beauty shop to receive the service; a passenger who purchases rail transportation must board the train. Both these examples illustrate high contact with the customer. High-contact services tend to reduce the extent to which a service can be standardized. Fast-food restaurants move toward greater efficiency through standardization by offering only a limited menu.

Low-Contact Services

For low-contact services, such as lawn care or television repair, the customer is not as closely involved with—does not become part of—the service.

Planning Services Operations

The planning and scheduling of service operations present some of the same problems as planning for products, but offer several additional challenges unique to services.

Site Location

Site location is a critical decision in any high-contact service. Because of the extra-close involvement with customers, the location must be convenient for the customers. In a low-contact service, proximity to suppliers or cost and availability of space may be more important than accessibility to or convenience of the customer.

Layout

For low-contact services, the arrangement of the facility should be designed to best accommodate the production of the service. The layout for high-contact services is designed around the customer's physical and psychological needs and expectations. Depending on the service involved, decor, waiting rooms, dressing rooms, and rest rooms are an important aspect of layout planning.

Scheduling Service Operations

Scheduling operations involve scheduling the workers, the work, and, in certain operations, the customer.

Scheduling High-Contact and Low-Contact Services

For high-contact services, the customer must be accommodated. A high-contact customer expects service on the spot. In a low-contact service, such as watch repair or dry-cleaning, the customer expects the service to be completed by a certain time, but is not concerned with specifically when the service is actually performed. In both low- and high-contact services, it is sometimes possible to employ part-time workers in periods of peak demand. As in producing goods, Gantt and PERT charts can help schedule services.

Queuing Theory

A queue is a waiting line. Queuing theory applies to organizing and controlling waiting time in lines to lessen customer waiting time and, at the same time, balance personnel cost. For example, a bank could open ten teller locations and have a very short waiting line, perhaps none, but the cost would be very high. Queuing theory helps determine how many tellers are needed to keep the line at an acceptable, reasonable length for customer satisfaction.

Appointment Scheduling

Where possible, appointment scheduling is effective. In a dental office, for example, patients are scheduled so as to allow minimum waiting time for patients and maximum flexibility for the dentist and staff. Without scheduling appointments, the waiting room might be full at one period and empty at other times, leaving the staff idly waiting for patients at times and overly busy at others.

Fixed Scheduling

Airlines or busses prepare detailed advance fixed schedules of their services, and customers then accommodate their needs according to the provider's schedule.

Routing

Routing is closely connected with layout. In producing goods, material is moved through the process. In producing services, the customer is often moved through the process.

For example, customers are routed through a cafeteria line and through the check-in, baggage, seat-assignment, and boarding procedures on an airline. Routing in a cafeteria should ensure that clean trays are available at the beginning of the line before the customer gets there, that food is available, and that tables are cleared as soon as possible, ideally, so that customers find tables when they finish paying.

Controlling Services Production

Both the quality and the quantity must be closely controlled in the production of services. In addition, prompt service and delivery dates are important if customers are to be satisfied.

Quality Control

Quality control in service operations, especially in high-contact services, is strongly dependent on the quality of the people who come into contact with the customer. Good human relations skills and the ability to work with people are of prime importance. Managers must hire the right types of workers, and then motivate them highly.

Quantity Control

Because services are intangible and cannot be inventoried, quantity control is a function-controlling demand. For greatest efficiency and cost effectiveness, demand must be balanced with the people and the facilities available. Quantity-control techniques include maintaining fixed schedules, as airlines do, using an appointment system, and delaying delivery in the case of low-contact services. Another technique is to provide incentives for moving demand to off-peak periods by offering off-peak fares in transportation, special prices for servicing air conditioners during the winter, and movie-theater discounts during weekdays.

Despite the difficulties involved, services are a growing factor in American business. Because services are intangible, it is necessary to provide as many tangible signs of each service's quality as possible.

Selected Readings

Albrecht, Karl. *At America's Service.* 1988.

American Management Association. *Best Practices in Customer Service.* 1999.

Anderson, Kristin, and Ron Zemke. *Delivering Knock Your Socks Off Service.* 2002.

Antis, David, C. M. Creveling, and J. L. Slutsky. *Design for Six Sigma in Technology and Product Development.* 2002.

Armstrong, Stephen C. *Engineering and Product Development Management: The Holistic Approach.* 2001.

Barlow, Janelle, and Paul Stewart. *Branded Customer Service: The New Competitive Edge.* 2004.

Bowen, David E. *Service Management Effectiveness: Balancing Strategy, Organization and Human Resources, Operations and Marketing.* 1990.

Davidow, William H., and Bro Uttal. *Total Customer Service.* 1990.

Deming, W. Edwards. *Quality Productivity and Competitive Position.* 1982.

Dilworth, James B. *Production and Operations Management: Manufacturing and Non-manufacturing.* 1986.

Fitzsimmons, James A., and Robert A. Sullivan. *Service Operations Management.* 1982.

Grant, Eugene L., and Richard Leavenworth. *Statistical Quality Control.* 1979.

Handscombe, Richard. *Product Management Handbook.* 1989.

Hayes, Robert H. *Dynamic Manufacturing: Creating the Learning Organization.* 1988.

Heskett, James. *Service Breakthroughs: Changing the Rules of the Game.* 1990.

Juran, J. H. *Juran on Planning for Quality.* 1987.

Lester, Richard K., Robert M. Solow, and Michael L. Dertouzos. *Made in America: Regaining the Productivity Edge.* 1989.

McCarthy, E. Jerome, and William Perreault. *Basic Marketing,* Fifteenth Edition. 2005.

McClain, John O., and L. Joseph Thomas. *Operations Management: Production of Goods and Services.* 1985.

McGrath, Michael E. *Setting the Pace in Product Development: A Guide to Product and Cycle-Time Excellence.* 1996.

Pisano, Gary P. *The Development Factory: Unlocking the Potential of Process Innovation.* 1996.

Robson, Mike. *Quality Circles: A Practical Guide.* 1988.

Shaw, John C. *Service Focus: Developing Winning Game Plans for Service Companies.* 1989.

Skinner, Wickham. *Manufacturing in the Corporate Strategy.* 1978.

Sloan, Alfred P., Jr. *My Years with General Motors.* 1963.

Suri, Rajan. *Quick Response Manufacturing.* 1999.

Thurow, Lester, and Louise Waldstein. *Toward a High Wage, High Productivity Service Sector.* 1989.

White, John A., editor. *Production Handbook.* 1986.

Woodward, Joan. *Industrial Organization.* 1965.

Wright, J. Patrick. *On a Clear Day You Can See General Motors.* 1980.

Wright, Kenneth. *21st Century Manufacturing.* 2001.

Zemke, Ron, and Dick Schaaf. *The Service Edge: Inside One Hundred One Companies That Profit from Customer Care.* 1989.

Test Yourself

1) What is production and operations management (POM)?

2) What are the three ways in which production processes can be classified?

3) What are the several types of production?

4) Production facility planning is an important first step in effective production. What are the major factors considered in selecting the correct site for the facility?

5) What is the purpose of operations planning?

6) Scheduling is the process of determining when an activity will occur and its duration. Describe how a Gantt chart supports scheduling.

7) What is just-in-time (JIT) inventory control?

8) What is materials-requirement planning (MRP)?

9) Production and operations management (POM) is often considered only in the context of the production of goods. How does POM relate to the providing of services?

10) What is queuing theory and how does it relate to scheduling services?

Test Yourself Answers

1) POM is the systematic direction and control of the process that transforms raw materials, equipment, and labor into finished goods.

2) One way to classify production processes is with transformation processes, including chemical transformation, fabrication, and assembly. Another way to classify processes is in terms of the method in which resources are used to transform materials into finished goods: analytic (breaking down resources into a finished-product component) and synthetic (combining of raw materials to produce the finished product). The final way to classify production processes is by the way in which product flow through the production facility: continuous process (flow from resource to finished product is smooth, straight, and uninterrupted and features long production runs), and intermittent process (stop-and-go processing, with short production runs).

3) Production line, assembly line, robotic and computerized production, computer-aided design (CAD), and computer-aided manufacturing (CAM) are all different types of production.

4) In selecting a site at which to locate the facility, the management must consider the location of the market for the product; the availability of suppliers and distribution channels, utilities and labor costs; the cost of land and development; and zoning, taxes, and regulation; and transportation.

5) The function of operations planning is to determine the types and amounts of resources required to produce specified goods and to plan for the purchasing, routing, scheduling, and dispatching of human resources, money, materials, and equipment.

6) A Gantt chart is a graphic scheduling device in bar-graph format. It shows the progress graphically, indicating what has been done, what remains to be accomplished, and whether the time schedule is being met.

7) JIT reduces inventory to a minimum by arranging for the delivery of materials to the production facility "just in time" for production. This method requires precise timing and control in producing the product, but results in minimum costs of holding inventories.

8) MRP is a computer-based coordination system that ensures the availability of required parts and materials at the right time and at the right place. It can assist in determining what should be ordered, when it should be ordered, and which deliveries should be either accelerated or delayed.

9) POM for services is concerned with the same categories as for goods: transformation, the methods in which resources are used to effect the transformation, and the arrangement of the transformation process (i.e., the flow of the process). The elements in each category, however, vary in one way or another.

10) A queue is a waiting line. Queuing theory applies to organizing and controlling waiting lines to minimize customer waiting time while balancing service costs. It helps determine how much service resource is required to keep the queue at a reasonable length to maintain customer satisfaction.

Part 4: Marketing Management

CHAPTER 13

The Marketing Concept

Companies that produce goods and provide services must engage in the marketing function to make their goods and services known to those whom they wish to purchase them. This chapter discusses the overall marketing concept and prepares readers for chapters 14 through 16.

■ AN OVERVIEW OF MARKETING

The American Marketing Association defines marketing as "the process of planning and executing the conception, pricing, distribution, and promotion of ideas, goods, and services to create exchanges that satisfy individual and organizational objectives."

Product decisions include package design, branding, and development of new products, while the pricing process includes setting profitable and justified prices; both are discussed in Chapter 14. Distribution, the physical distribution and selection of marketing channels, is discussed in Chapter 15. Promotion—the personal selling, advertising, and sales promotion—is discussed in Chapter 16.

The Concept of Utility

An exchange must have utility, the power of a good or service to satisfy a human need. In this sense, the customer does not purchase a product, but a utility.

Production gives form to utility by converting inputs into finished products, forms the buyer wants to have. There are three kinds of utility created by marketing: place, time, and possession.

Place Utility

Place utility satisfies a need by making a product available at a location or place where a customer wishes to purchase it. When customers visit a shoe store at a suburban shopping mall, they want the shoes they traveled for available at that store, not at the downtown store.

Time Utility

Time utility satisfies a need by making the product available when the customer wants it. If a customer wants a special-order product within a certain time frame—for example, three weeks—the order needs to be available within three weeks, not four weeks.

Possession Utility

Possession utility satisfies a need by transferring the title or ownership of the product to the customer.

Marketing Functions

Marketing functions involve exchange, physical distribution, and facilitation. These are further broken down into eight major functions, all of which are essential if the marketing process is to be successful.

The Exchange Functions

The exchange functions are any transactions in which two or more parties trade or swap something of value.

- **Buying:** Buying involves understanding what and why customers buy.
- **Selling:** Selling, the transfer of title from seller to customer, is the heart of marketing and creates possession utility.

Physical Distribution Functions

Physical distribution functions make it possible for the customer to buy a product and involve the flow of goods from producers to customers.

Transportation

Transportation, the movement of goods from the place of production to the place of purchase, provides place utility.

Storage

Storage supplies time utility by supplying a place to store goods until the final sale can be made, ensuring that the product is available when customers want it.

Facilitation Functions

Facilitation functions help (that is, facilitate) all the other functions.

Financing

Financing helps at all stages of marketing by advancing credit to wholesalers and retailers and supporting purchases by credit customers.

Standardizing and Grading

Standardizing and grading set uniform specifications for products or services, so that size and quality can be compared, and also facilitate production, transportation, storage, and sales.

Risk-Taking

Risk-taking enters marketing in various ways. Risk situations include new-product introductions, potential losses from bad debts (accounts receivable), obsolescence of product, and theft.

Gathering Market Information

Gathering market information through market research is necessary for implementing all marketing decisions.

■ THE DEVELOPMENT OF MARKETING ORIENTATION

From the Industrial Revolution to the early 1900s, business had a production orientation. Consumer demand grew at a rate that outpaced supply, enabling manufacturers to sell virtually all they could produce. Therefore, manufacturers' primary orientation was to improve the efficiency and capacity of production.

In the 1920s, supply began to overtake demand. Producers now found they had to sell goods to consumers whose basic demands were already satisfied. With production soundly in place, companies developed a sales orientation to ensure that their products were purchased over their competitors'. Business spent large amounts of money on advertising and sales.

By the 1950s, businesses began to realize that their sales depended on satisfying customer wants. Advertising and sales efforts were not enough. Businesses developed a customer orientation or marketing orientation, focusing on customer needs and wants and developing goods and services to meet those needs and wants.

■ MARKETS AND MARKET SEGMENTATION

Few companies try to sell their products to everyone in the United States. Instead, companies pick one or more groups within the overall population. Each group represents a market.

Markets

A market is a group of individuals, organizations, or both that has needs for a given product and has the ability, willingness, and authority to purchase the product. Markets can be described as consumer and industrial.

Consumer Market

The consumer market consists of people who buy products for their personal use or consumption, not to make a profit. Firms whose products are sold to the final user are engaged in consumer marketing.

Industrial Market

The industrial market includes organizations that buy products for use in day-to-day operations or in the production of other products to sell for profit. Within the industrial market are the producer, governmental, institutional, and reseller markets.

Producer Market

The producer market buys products to use specifically for manufacturing other products. For example, a pencil manufacturer buys wood to use in the production of pencils.

Governmental Market

The governmental market—that is, federal, state, and local governments—buys goods and services for internal operations or to provide citizens with highways, water, and other services. For example, a state highway department might buy reflective markers for use on roads, or the federal government might purchase parts for airplanes.

Institutional Market

The institutional market includes churches, schools, hospitals, clubs, and other institutions. Customers in the institutional market have different needs, and selling to the institutional market requires a different approach. For example, selling books to a school is different from selling books to an individual consumer in a one-on-one transaction.

Reseller Market

The reseller market consists of intermediaries, such as wholesalers and retailers, who buy finished products and sell them for profit (see Chapter 15).

Market Segmentation

Marketers further break down the overall market into target markets. A target market is any group of people that has similar wants and needs and may be expected to show interest in the same products. Categorizing markets according to common customer traits is called market segmentation.

By definition, the people in a market segment share common traits or behaviors that influence their buying decisions.

Industrial Segment

The segmentation of the industrial market is centered around the product; there is little likelihood that steel will be sold to a shoe manufacturer. Industrial markets are often concentrated geographically. For many industrial products or raw materials, the number of customers is limited.

It is also possible to target by industry. A bottle manufacturer can segment its market into drug manufacturing, food, or cosmetics industries.

Consumer Segment

The consumer market can be segmented several ways: for example, by geographic area, by product use, and by consumer motives (psychographics).

Geographic Areas

Where people live often affects buying decisions. Urban residents have less need for four-wheel drive vehicles than people in rural areas do. Warm, down parkas are sold more in Maine than in Alabama. By using ZIP codes, business marketers can segment a specific neighborhood with group characteristics as specific as income level.

Product Use

One way to segment a market is to examine product use—that is, how consumers will use the product. A shoe manufacturer will view the markets for athletic, casual, and dress shoes as separate markets. Truck dealers can segment the markets for pickup trucks, semi-trailers, panel trucks, or vans by end use of the vehicles.

Consumer Motives (Psychographics)

Information on motives, attitudes, activities, interests, and opinions of consumers helps segment the market. Psychographics, which describes the researching and gathering of such information, informs marketers that, for example, members of environmental organizations may be more likely to purchase hiking equipment than members of museum associations.

■ PRODUCTS

Marketing views the wide range of products by dividing them into two broad groups: consumer products and industrial products.

Consumer Products

Consumer products are goods or services produced for sale to individuals and families for personal consumption. Consumer products are either convenience goods, shopping goods, or specialty goods.

Convenience Goods

Convenience goods, products such as milk, candy, soap, and newspapers, are purchased frequently and with little shopping effort. Convenience goods are available at many outlets. Buyers pick up these products at the nearest store, without wasting energy and time shopping or comparing available brands. The seller's main marketing tool is location. Although the price may be higher at a convenience store than, say, at a grocery store, the unit price of convenience goods is generally low, as is the profit margin (the difference between the product's cost and its selling price). Stores use mass advertising rather than sales techniques to promote the fact that they carry convenience goods.

Shopping Goods

Shopping goods are products that consumers actively shop for, comparing prices, values, features, quality, and styles before finally making a purchase decision. Shopping goods include refrigerators, television sets, men's suits, and bicycles as well as nonconvenience-store groceries and meats.

Shopping goods are sold in different kinds of stores. They are often marketed both by national advertising on the part of the manufacturer and by local advertising on the part of the retailer. In many cases, especially with appliances and clothing, the efforts of salespeople come into play. Profit margins tend to be moderate (except with groceries) in order to cover the costs of promotion and personal selling. Margins on groceries tend to be low, with high volume making up for low margins.

Specialty Goods

Shoppers make extra efforts to find and purchase specialty goods, expensive items that are not purchased frequently, such as fine crystal, jewelry, automobiles, and clothing with high brand recognition and loyalty.

Specialty goods are stocked by few stores—or dealers, in the case of automobiles—and are promoted on the basis of quality, image, or unique characteristics. Selling is on a personal level, and profit margins are high.

Industrial Products

Industrial products are sold to private business firms or public agencies for use in the production of their goods or services. Industrial products include iron ore and other raw materials, chemicals, tools, textiles, and hardware. Advertising is generally limited to trade journals.

Industrial products are sold by sales representatives calling on the buyers personally. In industrial firms, purchases are frequently made by teams or committees.

■THE MARKETING CONCEPT

The marketing concept stresses the need for the entire organization to achieve customer satisfaction while achieving the organization's goals. All functional areas—product development, production, finance, and marketing—have a role in achieving customer satisfaction. The marketing concept starts with market research.

Market Research

Market research is the systematic gathering, developing strategies from, and analyzing of data concerning a particular marketing problem.

Gathering Information

Research helps to determine the needs of the ultimate user, how well these needs are being met by products on the market, and how products might be improved. After the problem is identified and the research planned, the factual information can be gathered in a variety of ways, including telephone and mail surveys, personal interviews, and observation.

Developing a Total Marketing Strategy

Marketers must interpret and analyze the factual information to determine the choices available and to establish a marketing strategy. The total marketing strategy must design and produce a product that will satisfy all customer needs. To achieve this goal, the marketing strategy must address four elements of the marketing concept, commonly called the four Ps: product, price, place (distribution), and promotion.

Product

The product must satisfy the final user's needs. Satisfying consumers may require changing the product frequently (as in the fashion industry), improving existing products to meet competition, introducing completely new products, or maintaining existing products that have strong consumer loyalty. (See Chapter 14.)

Price

The product must be priced at a level that will be acceptable to buyers and still yield an acceptable profit. A higher price may increase the unit profit but limit the number of sales. A lower price may raise sales volume. In some cases, a higher price may give shoppers the impression of higher quality and may, therefore, raise sales. (See Chapter 14.)

Place

The product must be place—that is, distributed—so that it is available where and when it is needed. Distribution also concerns choosing sales outlets and transporting the product from the producer to either the outlet or the customer.

Convenience items require wide distribution. Specialty items have fewer, more carefully selected outlets. Catalog and Internet items are sent directly from inventory to the consumer and require efficient means of distribution. (See Chapter 15.)

Promotion

The product must be promoted so that consumers will be aware that it is available to satisfy a particular need. Promotion includes advertising, personal selling, sales promotion, public relations, and publicity.

Automobile manufacturers rely on national television advertising to get customers into the showroom, and then personal selling makes the actual sale. Less-expensive products often rely on packaging to accomplish the sale, or on sales promotions such as coupons, samples, trading stamps, or rebates.

Public relations spreads goodwill about the company and its products or services by sponsoring public television programming or sports events. Public relations also includes information provided to the public in a planned fashion. Publicity, which is free communication to the public, can help a firm's public relations program if the publicity delivers a positive message. Bad publicity, on the other hand, can hurt a firm's image. (See Chapter 16.)

Evaluating the Marketing Mix

Having set objectives and established a strategy to meet these objectives, the firm must again return to market research for feedback to evaluate the effectiveness of their efforts. Feedback is intended to provide answers to questions such as: Is the product addressing customer wants and needs? Is it priced competitively and yet profitably? How effective is the distribution? Is the promotion effective?

Based on the evaluation of feedback, management will modify any of the elements in the marketing mix to improve performance.

■ CONSUMER AND INDUSTRIAL BUYING

Each consumer's buying decision is influenced by economic, demographic, psychological, and social factors, and marketing strategy must consider all those factors if the strategy is to be effective.

Economic Factors

Purchasing power is created by income, but not all income is available for spending.

Personal Income

Personal income represents total income from all sources, less Social Security or self-employment taxes.

Disposable Income

Disposable income is personal income less all personal taxes (such as income, estate, and property taxes). About 4 percent of all disposable income is saved, and about 50 percent is spent on necessities such as food, clothing, and shelter.

Discretionary Income

Discretionary income represents disposable income less savings and expenditures on necessities such as food, clothing, shelter, health, and necessary transportation. Knowing discretionary income is particularly important to marketers, because this is the income that consumers spend on vacations, luxuries, and nonnecessities and the income used to upgrade their food, clothing or automobile purchases.

Future Income

Americans spend not only present income, but also future income, income they have not yet earned, by using credit cards and by borrowing.

Demographic Factors

Demographic information offers data such as age, income, gender, ethnic background, race, religion, marital status, social class, education, and type of family. Using this information, marketers can target products or advertising to appeal to very specific groups of consumers, for instance, consumers in the 18- to 25-year-old age range, married couples with a combined income over $60,000, or retired widows with college degrees who live in the Southwest. Demographic studies show which groups are growing, where there are large numbers of people whose primary language is other than English, and much other helpful marketing information.

Psychological Factors

Psychological factors such as attitude or personality enter into the customer's buying decision. A decision may be rational or emotional, or it may be a combination of both.

Rational Motives

Rational motives are reasons for buying a product based on a logical evaluation of product attributes such as cost, quality, and usefulness.

Emotional Motives

Emotional motives, the subjective reasons for purchasing a product or a particular kind of product, include imitation of others and aesthetics. Buying coffee-flavored ice cream because of its taste or an automobile because it looks "sporty" are emotional reasons for making purchases.

Social Factors

Social factors enter into a consumer's decision to buy, for example, a deodorant to avoid unpleasant odors or the same brand of athletic shoe that others in the same peer group buy. Actions by a consumer's social class, subculture, or a fashion leader can serve as a motive for making a purchase decision.

Industrial Buying

Industrial buying is based on a more limited group of factors, such as cost, reliability, uniformity of product, delivery time, and service. In that sense, industrial buying is more rational than consumer buying.

Selected Readings

Aaker, David A. *Strategic Market Management*. 1988.
Bonoma, Thomas V., and Benson P. Shapiro. *Segmenting the Industrial Market*. 1983.
Dichter, Ernest. *Handbook of Consumer Motivations*. 1964.
Kinnear, Thomas C., and James R. Taylor. *Marketing Research: An Applied Approach*. 1983.
Kotler, Phillip, and Gary Armstrong. *Principles of Marketing*. 1989.
Levinson, Jay Conrad, and Charles Rubin. *The Guerrilla Marketing Handbook*. 1994.
Levitt, Theodore. *The Marketing Imagination*. 1983.
Lieberman, Al, and Pat Esgate. *The Entertainment Marketing Revolution: Bringing the Moguls, the Media, and the Magic to the World*. 2002.
Lilien, Gary L., and Philip Kotler. *Marketing Decision Making: A Model Building Approach*. 1983.
McCarthy, E. Jerome, and William Perreault. *Basic Marketing*. 2005.
Mitchell, Arnold. *The Nine American Lifestyles*. 1983.
Naisbitt, John. *Megatrends: Ten New Directions Transforming Our Lives*. 1984.
Porter, Michael E. *Competitive Advantage: Creating and Sustaining Superior Performance*. 1985.
Roseberry, Monica. *Marketing Massage*. 2002.

Test Yourself

1) An exchange must have utility, the power of a good or service to satisfy a human need. What are the three kinds of utility created by marketing?

2) What are the eight essential functions if marketing is to be successful?

3) What is a market and what are the two basic types of markets?

4) The consumer market consists of persons who buy products or services for their personal use or consumption, not to earn a profit. What are the types and thrusts of industrial markets?

5) Describe the concept of market segmentation.

6) What are some of the ways in which consumer markets might be segmented?

7) What are the four Ps of marketing?

8) Consumer products and services are provided for sale to individuals and families for personal consumption. What are the three broad categories of consumer products?

9) One of the major economic factors marketers must consider is the personal income of the target market. What are the three categories of personal income that the marketer must consider?

10) What psychological factors affect consumer spending?

Test Yourself Answers

1) Marketing creates the utilities of place (i.e., delivering where the customer needs the good or service), time (i.e., delivering the good or service when the customer needs it), and possession (i.e., transferring the title or ownership to the customer).

2) The eight essential functions are buying, selling, transportation, storage, financing, standardizing, risk-taking, and gathering market information.

3) A market is a group of individuals, organizations, or both that has needs for a given product or service and has the ability, willingness, and authority to purchase the product. Markets are generally classified as either consumer or industrial.

4) The producer market buys products to use specifically for manufacturing other products. The governmental market buys goods and services for internal operations or to provide citizens with public goods and services. The institutional market includes churches, hospitals, clubs, and other institutions. The reseller market consists of intermediaries, such as wholesalers and retailers, who buy finished products and then sell them for profit.

5) Market segmentation is the process of categorizing the major markets into smaller, more homogeneous markets of customers.

6) Consumer markets may be segmented by geography, by products used, and by consumer motives for purchasing (i.e., psychographics).

7) The four Ps are product, price, place, and promotion.

8) The three basic categories of consumer goods are convenience goods, shopping goods, and specialty goods.

9) The three types of personal income are disposable income, discretionary income, and future income (persons spend not only current income, but also future income, through credit cards, loans, etc.).

10) Psychological factors, such as attitude and personality, influence buying decisions, as do social factors.

CHAPTER 14

Product and Pricing Strategies

A very important part of marketing a product or service is the determination of appropriate product and pricing strategies. This chapter addresses the fundamentals of both concepts.

■ THE PRODUCT

Chapter 13 introduced the marketing concept and addressed various aspects of marketing goods and services—that is, of marketing products. This chapter focuses more closely on products and on the pricing strategies used to market products effectively.

To begin, what is a product? Products are goods or services that satisfy buyers' needs and demands. Products are, therefore, the focal point of business. Goods are tangible objects and devices (such as food, vacuum cleaners, and toothpaste), and services are deeds, acts, and performances (such as transporting materials, entertaining people, and banking). A product can be inventoried; a service cannot.

Product Line

A group of products is known as a product line. Companies may start with a single product or just a few products and then, over a period of time, develop additional products to expand their product lines and increase their revenues and profitability. The new products may be very similar to the company's "original" products. For example, General Motors offers a wide range of vehicles for different uses at differing prices, but all its products are vehicles and vehicle parts. On the other hand, the new products may be outside the company's original product line. For example, Proctor and Gamble expanded its original product line (soaps) to include a number of new product lines (including food, coffee, paper goods, and baby products).

To succeed in any industry, companies must be innovative and develop new products that meet consumers' needs, or at the very least, keep up with product advances in their industry.

Product Differentiation

Product differentiation is the process of developing and promoting differences between one company's product and all the other similar products that are available. The object is to create a specific demand for the firm's product by developing a special image of the product. For example, Perdue Farms, very effectively differentiated between its chickens and all other chickens available in the marketplace and therefore, created significant consumer demand for its products. Another example: Companies try to develop designer labels in an effort to promote product differentiation.

Product Mix

A company's product mix identifies all the products that the firm offers. The breadth of the mix is measured by the number of product lines it contains, and the depth of the mix is measured by the number of individual items in each product line.

Because customers' preferences and attitudes change, and because competitors develop and offer new products or change existing ones, a company's product mix does not usually remain unchanged for long. Instead, a company will alter its product mix by adapting an existing product, developing new products, or dropping existing products from its product line.

Product Life Cycle

A product's life cycle measures its longevity in the marketplace and describes its existence in terms of the four key stages of a product's "life"— namely, the product's introduction, growth, maturity, and decline.

Some products seem to retain their popularity and remain profitable forever; for example, Milky Way candy bars have been successfully marketed for many years. At the other end of the spectrum are fad items, products that complete their life cycles quickly, "living" perhaps only a few months from introduction to decline. For example, hula hoops—tubular hoops that were popular for a very short period in the 1960s—enjoyed a very short life cycle.

The Introductory Stage

During a product's introductory stage, consumer awareness and acceptance of the product is understandably low. As the company actively promotes and distributes the product, sales rise gradually, but the initial profit is low because development and marketing costs are high when a new product is introduced. During the introductory stage, all marketing decisions are critical to the product's success. The company must be very careful to set the price appropriately, choose distribution channels wisely, promote the product vigorously, and so on. Throughout the introductory stage, the company must be alert to any adjustments that may be needed to help establish the new product; for example, price adjustments and the addition of new distribution channels.

The Growth Stage

In the growth stage, sales increase more rapidly as consumers become more and more aware of, and familiar with, the product. And with increased sales come increased profits, thanks in part to greater production volume and lower manufacturing costs. However, in the early part of the growth stage, other firms are likely to enter the market with competitive products, and when they do, the new competition will cause prices and profits to drop for the original producer. To meet the needs of the growing market and to beat the competition, the original producer may alter the product, introduce new colors, models, sizes, or flavors, or promote it in a way that builds brand loyalty.

The Maturity Stage

The product's maturity stage begins while sales are still increasing, but at this stage, the rate of increase is slower. Because the product is established and mature, it will sell on its own and needs minimal promotion. As a result, profitability increases.

Later in its maturity stage, the product's sales will peak, and then begin to decline. Profits, too, decline throughout the maturity stage, and price competition increases. In order to bolster sales, manufacturers increase promotion of the product and offer dealers incentives and other assistance to help support mature products.

The Decline Stage

In its decline stage, a product's sales volume and profits decrease more rapidly. The number of firms offering competitive products also declines, leaving only "specialists" remaining in the marketplace. Now, production and marketing costs are the key elements that determine the product's profitability. New products, new technology, or the switching of consumers to competing brands may well lead the firm to drop the product from its line entirely.

Extending the Life Cycle

In a product's decline stage, marketers attempt to extend the product's life cycle and maximize short-term profits, for example, by developing new uses for the product, by attracting new users, and by making inexpensive alterations in packaging, labeling, or pricing. Sometimes, a product's life cycle may be extended by a temporary renewed interest in the product (as for a certain style of clothing).

New-Product Development

Marketing experts follow closely the life cycle of the products for which they are responsible. Perhaps the best defense against the loss of revenues and profits that results from aging and declining products is new-product development, replacing mature products with new products that have solid growth potential.

The "new" product may be an adaptation of an existing product, an imitation of an existing competitor's product, or a truly innovative new product. In any case, developing and introducing new products can be risky, time-consuming, and expensive. The evolution of new-product development follows the six steps discussed in the following sections.

Generate Ideas

Where do ideas for new products come from? Many companies have research and development (R&D) departments for the specific purpose of searching for new products. But ideas for new products may come from anywhere—from marketing managers, engineers, customers, competitors, consultants, or any other source.

Screen the Ideas

Screening is the process of evaluating ideas to determine whether the company should indeed implement ideas that are generated. Not all ideas are good ones. Even ideas that are profitable may not be appropriate to a particular organization for some reason—for example, developing the new idea may be too costly for one company but not for another, or the new product may require an additional sales force for one company but not for another company.

Prepare a Business Analysis

When the preliminary screening determines that a new product is worth pursuing, the company then prepares a business analysis. A business analysis evaluates and quantifies the product's potential by estimating sales, positioning the product among competitors (if any) in the marketplace, calculating costs, determining profitability, identifying the resources needed, comparing the cost with market alternatives, and evaluating the fit of the new product in the product line and in the firm's overall long-term objectives.

Develop the Product

When the business analysis is positive and promising, the company then proceeds to develop the product. The first questions to be answered concern technical and economical issues and are intended to test whether it is feasible to make the product. What will production costs be? Will unit costs be low enough to justify a reasonable selling price? When questions such as these are answered, the company uses the data to evaluate product development yet again. If it decides to continue, the next step is usually to develop a working model, or prototype, of the product.

Test the Market

Before the company begins full-scale production, it proceeds with limited production (based on the prototype) and test-markets the product. Typically, in test marketing the product, the firm introduces the product in a specially selected area, an area chosen specifically because it is representative of the entire market in terms of consumers' habits, lifestyles, and economic levels. From the data produced by test marketing, the company can determine how the larger total market might react to the product, packaging, and pricing.

Test marketing has many advantages; for example, it permits the company to experiment with pricing, advertising, and packaging. However, the costs of test marketing products can be high. As an alternative, therefore, companies will sometimes use focus groups and consumer panels to elicit information from potential consumers about the product, packaging, and pricing.

Commercialize the Product

The results of test marketing allow the company to further refine and fine-tune the product, packaging, and pricing and, finally, to commercialize the product. Commercialization is the introduction of the product into the market mainstream. Usually, companies introduce products not nationally but gradually, selecting geographical areas carefully, and then expanding from one area to an adjacent area, step by step, until the product reaches full commercialization.

This deliberate step-by-step approach allows the company to plan more precisely for full-scale manufacturing and national marketing and to prepare budgets accurately. In other words, this deliberate step-by-step process helps avoid product failure and ensure success. However, it cannot guarantee success. The business world has many examples of products that were very carefully researched and developed—and failed nonetheless. Two of the more famous stories concern the Ford Edsel, a classic failure from the mid-1950s, and Coca-Cola's "classic" story (the attempt to change the taste of Coke failed, forcing the company to return to the original flavor with a new name: Classic Coke).

Brands and Branding

Deciding on a name for a product is an important part of product development. Before discussing brands and branding, note the distinctions in the following terms.

- A **brand** is a name, term, or symbol that identifies one seller's products and distinguishes them from competitors' products.
- A **brand name** is the part of a brand that can be spoken; the brand name may include letters, numbers, words, or pronounceable syllables, such as "Proctor & Gamble," or "M&Ms."
- A **brand mark**, on the other hand, is a symbol or design that is part of a brand, for example, the CBS eye or the Playboy bunny.
- A **trademark** is a brand registered with the U.S. Patent and Trademark Office and protected from use by anyone except the trademark owner. The distinctive shape of the Coca-Cola bottle is protected by a trademark.

A brand name should be distinctive, easy to say, and easy to remember so that customers continue to buy that brand. Further, because brands and marks are assets, companies must carefully protect brands from misuse and unauthorized use, which can destroy the success of a brand and completely lose brand status for a product.

Once a brand becomes commonly used as a generic name, not a brand name, it loses its brand status, as cellophane, nylon, zipper, and band-aids have lost their brand status (they are now used generically to represent a class of products, not a particular company's brand of product). One way companies protect brands is to make sure that a brand name is always followed by the generic name of the product, as in "a Xerox copy," "a Xerox photocopier," "a Xerox machine," and so on.

Types of Brands

Many products have brand names, and these brand names are often classified according to who owns them.

Manufacturer (or Producer) Brands

Manufacturer (or producer) brands, also called national brands, are brands owned by the manufacturer. Most appliances, packaged foods, all automobiles, and clothing lines such as Levi's are examples of manufacturer brands. Establishing a brand name on a national level is expensive, but the rewards are great. For consumers, nationally known manufacturer brands represent consistently reliable quality and widespread availability. Consumers are confident that a box of Cheerios cereal will have a consistent quality wherever it is sold.

Licensed Brands

Licensed brands are brands that the owners have licensed to some other manufacturer, permitting that manufacturer to use its brand on another product. For example, Walt Disney Company licenses other manufacturers to market products such as watches or pajamas with the Mickey Mouse brand, which Walt Disney Company owns.

Store (or Private) Bonds

Store (or private) brands are brands owned by an individual retailer or wholesaler. Sears, Roebuck and Company has two well-known brands: Kenmore, its brand for appliances, and Craftsman, its brand for tools. Most major grocery chains have private brands for their food products.

Generic Brands

Generic brands are products with no brand name at all. Their plain packages merely identify the type of product "coffee," "peanut butter," "laundry soap." Some consumers are attracted by the lower price of generic brands, while others question the quality and consistency of generic brands (although most are produced by the same manufacturers of name brands).

Brand Loyalty

Companies spend large amounts of money to achieve brand loyalty, to create a following of regular buyers of their products. Consumer confidence and satisfaction are the major elements in the success of a brand, and companies work hard to earn consumers' confidence.

Developing Brand Loyalty

The first step in establishing brand loyalty is to develop brand recognition; that is, to educate consumers to identify one particular brand and to convince them that that brand consistently represents high quality. The tools for achieving brand recognition are advertising and promotion.

Once consumers recognize a particular brand, marketers next try to persuade them to exercise a brand preference when they make a purchase, a preference for their particular company's brand, of course.

The ultimate goal of brand loyalty is the final stage, brand insistence, which is very difficult to achieve. At this stage consumers will not accept substitutes; if the product is not available in one store, they will seek the product in another store. Convenience or shopping products seldom achieve brand insistence; specialty items may achieve brand insistence.

Maintaining Brand Loyalty

To maintain brand loyalty, the company must continue to offer a product that has a consistently high quality, is priced fairly, and represents a competitive value. The company must also support the same marketing efforts that established brand loyalty.

Branding Strategies

Any producer or retail store can brand its products. A producer may market products under its own brands, private brands, or both. Likewise, a store may choose to carry only its own brand, producer brands, or both. Producers and stores that choose to brand products may do so in one of two ways.

Individual Branding

Individual branding is a strategy in which a firm uses a different brand for each of its products. Proctor & Gamble, for example, uses a different brand name for Ivory, Zest, Safeguard, and each of its many other soap products. The advantage of individual branding is that a problem with one brand will not affect the others.

Family Branding

Family branding is a strategy in which a firm uses the same brand name for most or all of its products. For example, General Electric, Xerox, and Sony use family branding for all the items in their product mix. One advantage of family branding is that new products have a head start since the brand name is already known. Another advantage: Promoting one product helps promote all products in the product line. On the other hand, customer dissatisfaction (if any) is also shared by all products made by the company.

Packaging and Labeling

Packaging describes all aspects of the physical appearance of the product, including its container and wrappings. The package serves several useful purposes. First, the package provides a holder or container for the product. Second, it protects the product from damage or tampering. Third, the visual effect of the package (its shape, color, and printing) helps distinguish the product and influence purchasing decisions.

Frozen food is now commonly packaged in cardboard (instead of aluminum) to make the foods easy to cook in microwave ovens. Further, frozen foods are packaged in various sizes in an effort to target sales to specific markets (such as single portions for single-person households and giant economy sizes for large families).

Labeling describes the information on a product and/or its package—that is, both the actual copy and how it is presented. The Fair Packaging and Labeling Act of 1966 requires listing the product name, package size, contents, and the name and address of the manufacturer on all product labels. Additional information on product claims, directions for use, safety precautions, ingredients, and fiber content may also be required by various government regulations. In November 1990, President George Bush signed Public Law 101–535, which requires specific uniform nutrition labels for most processed foods. The law limits the manufacturer's ability to make health or nutrition claims and directs the Secretary of Health and Human Services to define terms such as *light* or *low fat* on food labels.

Labeling of many products now commonly includes the Universal Product Code (the bar code that identifies the price of each product) to facilitate automated checkout and inventory control.

Warranties

A warranty is a statement by a seller that a product meets certain standards of performance.

- An **express warranty** is a written explanation of the responsibilities of the producer in the event that the product is found to be defective or otherwise unsatisfactory.
- A **full warranty** is the producer's or seller's guarantee to repair or replace a defective product within a reasonable time at no cost to the customer.
- A **limited warranty** restricts the producer's or seller's offer in specific ways—for example, to certain problems or parts.

Warranties can be very effective in selling products. A number of auto makers (e.g., Hyundai, Volkswagon, and Isuzu), for example, have successfully used a 100,000-mile/10-year warranty on certain components to motivate consumers to buy their automobiles. L.L. Bean's lifetime guarantee on every item it sells assures its customers of satisfaction and allows them to buy with less hesitation.

To avoid the problems caused by unclear or confusing language in warranties, the Magnuson-Moss Warranty Act of 1975 requires warranties to meet certain minimum standards, stated in plain language. The act requires limited warranties to be clearly identified as such.

■ PRICING

Clearly, pricing is a very important aspect of business success. A product's price is the amount of money a seller will accept in exchange for that product at a given time under given circumstances. No matter how well a product is designed, if it is priced too high, consumers will not buy it, and if it is priced too low, it will earn little or no profit.

Price functions as an allocator. Producers make goods and services for consumers whom they believe are able and willing to buy those goods and services. Price allocates these goods and services among those consumers. Price allocates financial resources (sales revenue) among producers according to how well their products satisfy customers' needs. Price also helps customers to allocate their own financial resources among various products available to satisfy their needs and wants.

To put pricing in perspective, remember the basics of supply and demand. In Chapter 1, we define supply as the amount of output of a product that producers are willing and able to make available to the market at a given price at a given time. We define demand as the willingness of purchasers to buy specific quantities of a product at a given price at a given time. The point where supply and demand meet represents equilibrium; here, the supply at a given price equals the demand at that price.

In theory, equilibrium does not take into consideration whether the producer will make a profit at that price. In theory, in a system of pure competition, no producer controls the price of its product. All producers must accept the equilibrium price. If they charge a higher price, they will lose sales; if they charge a lower price, they will lose sales revenue.

In the real world, however, a producer tries to control pricing by creating perceived value among consumers. Through product differentiation and advertising, for example, a producer attempts to persuade consumers that its products are better, that its products have an additional value for some reason. If the producer is successful, consumers will perceive that a product has a value greater than its actual value, and the producer can then charge a higher price for that product.

Pricing Objectives

A company may have a variety of pricing objectives in setting the price of each product. Although making a profit is the primary concern, it is not the only consideration or objective.

Profit-Making Objectives

In an effort to maximize profit, a firm will charge the highest price it believes it can charge without causing sales volume to fall. If it sets prices too low, the firm will sell more units, but may lose money or miss the opportunity to make additional profit on the units sold. If it sets prices too high, the firm may make a greater profit on each unit, but it will sell fewer units and lose money. Because it is impossible to calculate in advance what the maximum profit might be, some firms target a return on investment (ROI) as their profit goal.

Market-Share Objectives

A firm's market share describes its percentage of total industry sales. When introducing a new product, a company will often deliberately set a low price, accepting lower profits in the short term in order to encourage consumers to try the new product. For an established product, a company may set a lower price to protect or to increase its market share. The assumption is that higher market share will help establish brand loyalty, hurt competitors, and pay off in the long run. An increased market share allows economies of scale that lead, among other things, to lower unit costs.

Loss-Containment and Survival Objectives

In an effort to survive an especially difficult problem or a particularly traumatic situation, a company may feel forced to accept a severe short-term pricing policy and lower its prices drastically in an effort to attract customers, contain losses, or remain in the market. For example, after the 9/11 terrorist attacks, airlines decreased airfares to entice travelers back to air travel.

Social and Ethical Concerns

The first company to develop a cure for AIDS would be in a position to charge any price, and demand for the product would still be extremely high regardless of price. However, only the very rich would be able to afford the high price tag.

For certain products, a company's pricing policy should address social and ethical concerns. In the case of a cure for AIDS, most companies would probably adopt a pricing strategy that provides a "reasonable" return. To do otherwise would be unacceptable and would probably raise a public clamor.

Company Image

A firm's pricing policy reflects the company image, how that firm is viewed by the public. Manufacturers try to establish pricing policies that will enhance their public image. For instance, Nieman Marcus has a well-established image for upscale, very expensive, high-quality merchandise, and it works hard to project and protect that image. Therefore, Nieman Marcus will not offer shirts for $6.95, suits for $99, or dresses for $20. Such low prices might connote low quality to its customers—clearly, an unacceptable image for Nieman Marcus. Similarly, Lacoste does not discount its clothing. Perfume manufacturers often adopt a pricing policy that sets a high price on their products in an effort to enhance the perception of glamour and exclusivity, a perception that a lower price tends to erase.

On the other hand, J.C. Penney, Sears, Target, and Wal-Mart have an entirely different company image. They offer merchandise at much more reasonable prices, prices that people earning average incomes expect to find—not $850 suits and $500 dresses.

Pricing Methods

Once a firm has established its pricing objectives, it must select a strategy and pricing method to reach its goals. The market (not the firm's unit cost) will ultimately determine the selling price of the product. Pricing methodology is often more art than science.

Cost-Based Pricing

Pricing may be cost-based: that is, established by the cost of producing one unit of the product.

Determining Total Cost

Cost-based pricing is based on covering variable costs and some fixed costs. Variable costs, mostly material and labor, are those costs that change or vary as more goods or services are produced. For example, in printing magazines, the cost of paper is a variable expense. If the paper cost per magazine is, say, $0.75, the cost of paper for printing 4,000 magazines will be twice as high as the cost of paper for printing 2,000 magazines. Yet the cost of paper per magazine remains the same—$0.75 a unit.

Fixed costs include rent, insurance, and management salaries. These costs remain constant (that is, fixed); they are unaffected by the number of units produced. The magazine's rent does not change whether it prints and sells 2,000 copies a week or 4,000 copies a week. Its rent is a fixed cost.

In cost-based pricing, the seller uses variable and fixed costs to determine the total cost of each unit.

Determining Markup and Gross Profit Margin

The seller determines the amount of profit or markup desired and adds this markup to the total cost. Together, the total cost plus the markup equals the selling price.

Markup is generally expressed as a percentage of the total cost or a percentage of the retail price. The difference between the total cost and the selling price is known as the profit margin. For a manufacturer, *cost* means production cost, and "selling price" is the wholesale price (that is, the manufacturer's selling price). For a retailer, *cost* means the wholesale price it pays for a product, and *selling price* means the retail or list price at which it sells the product.

For example, let's look at an item with a unit cost of $100, a markup of $20, and a selling price of $120. What is its markup percentage? The markup percentage is based on the unit cost; the mark-up amount divided by the selling price equals gross profit percentage.

In this instance, the markup percentage is 20 percent ($20/$100), while the gross profit percentage is 16.6 percent ($20/$120).

Calculating the Breakeven Point

The breakeven point is the number of units that must be sold at a given price to cover both fixed and variable costs—that is, the number of units that must be sold to recover expenses without making a profit. The calculations involved are part of what is known as a breakeven analysis.

To complete this analysis, the firm must know its fixed costs and its variable costs. Then, using demand estimates and other market data in conjunction with this analysis, the firm can establish the price for a product.

Let's look at the breakeven analysis for a firm that has fixed costs of $40,000 and variable costs of $60 per unit for a product selling at $120.

Breakeven # of units = Total fixed costs/(Unit selling price − Unit variable costs)
Breakeven # of units = $40,000/($120 − $60) = 667 units.

With this breakeven analysis, the firm can evaluate other prices:

Selling Price	Breakeven Quantity
$100	1,000
$110	800
$120	667
$140	500

In this way, the firm can establish its official price based on realistic costs.

Competition-Based Pricing

Companies often use their competitors' pricing as a guide in establishing their own prices. Competition-based pricing is most effective when competing products are very similar, or when price is the main differentiation between products. Competition-based pricing is popular among retailers, because it requires little analysis and is not likely to start a costly price war.

Pricing Strategies

Sellers must consider many factors in choosing a pricing method and setting a basic price—markets, goals, product differentiation, the life cycle stage of each product, and so on. All these factors contribute to the seller's pricing strategy. The specific strategy applied to a product varies, of course, depending on whether the product is new or is an existing product.

New-Product Strategies

When introducing new products to the market, companies consider two contrasting options: price skimming and penetration pricing.

Price Skimming

Price skimming is the strategy of charging a high price for a product during the introductory stage of its life cycle. The seller assumes the buyer is willing to pay the high price for some reason; for example, because of the novelty, prestige, or status associated with owning this new product. When the novelty wears off and competition increases, the company drops the price. Skimming is a strategy that helps the seller recover high development costs, but if it is successful, it creates a lucrative market that may attract competitors.

Penetrating Pricing

Penetration pricing takes an approach opposite to skimming. In applying the strategy of penetration pricing, the company sets a low price, anticipating that it will quickly garner a large market share for the product, achieve economies of scale, and reduce unit costs. Penetration pricing is often used by new companies because this strategy allows the firm to sell as many units as possible early in the product's life cycle, discourage competition, and quickly establish a name for the company. However, penetration pricing is less flexible than skimming; it is easier to lower prices than it is to raise them.

Pricing Existing Products

In pricing existing products, a firm can adopt one of three obvious strategies: It can set a price above, below, or at the existing market price.

Above the Market Price

Companies pricing products above the market imply that their higher price means higher quality. Godiva chocolates and Rolex watches are priced above the market.

Below the Market Price

Pricing below competitors' prices can effectively build market share if the quality of the product is acceptable. Budget, National, and Alamo all offer rental cars below the price of Hertz, for example.

At the Market Price

Pricing at the market is often most successful for products that differ little from one firm to another. Steel, processed foods, and gasoline often use market pricing; in such instances, companies compete through advertising or personal selling rather than price.

Pricing Tactics

For both new and existing products, marketers must choose pricing tactics that will implement their strategy for reaching their pricing objectives. A number of tactics can be utilized.

Psychological Pricing

Retailers who use psychological pricing believe that consumers react somewhat emotionally; for example, consumers will respond to odd pricing such as $9.95 or $49.99 more favorably than to $10 or $50. Adherents believe that customers focus on the whole dollar number and round down. This tactic is not limited to low-price items. Automobile manufacturers will price a car at $14,999 rather than $15,000.

Threshold Pricing

A related tactic is threshold pricing, which assumes that customers have a maximum price, a threshold, in mind and that they will not exceed that threshold level. At one time, when Hershey felt the threshold price for a chocolate bar was 10 cents, it chose to reduce the size of the bar rather than exceed the threshold price.

Price Lining

Following the strategy of price lining, retailers offer goods at a limited number of key prices that reflect definite price breaks. For example, a store may sell three lines of men's undershirts, one at $2.50, one at $3.50, and a third at $5.00, eliminating minor price differences and at the same time simplifying selection and checkout. A fast-food store or a movie-theater refreshment counter will offer small-, medium-, and large-sized soft drinks at three set prices, regardless of the flavor or the brand selected.

Multiple-Unit Pricing

Multiple-unit pricing, commonly used by supermarkets, sets a single price for two or more units, such as "2/99" (two cans for 99 cents), rather than 50 cents per can. To encourage multiple purchases, retailers will package merchandise in multiple units. Packaging items in multiple units and selling them as a single unit is likely to increase sales.

Prestige Pricing

Prestige pricing assumes that consumers will consider a higher price as evidence of higher quality. In an effort to keep prices at specific levels and avoid discounting, some manufacturers label their products with a suggested retail price. To prohibit retailers from remarking and discounting merchandise, some manufacturers sell only to retailers who agree to uphold the suggested retail price for their products.

Discount Pricing

Discount pricing offers a price reduction as an incentive to purchase a product. Retail stores often remark the suggested retail price to emphasize that the product is offered at a discount.

Some common discounts are cash, seasonal, trade, and quantity discounts.

Cash Discounts

To receive a cash discount, the customer must make payment in cash. Many gas stations will have one price for credit-card sales and a lower price (say, 4 cents per gallon less) for cash sales.

Seasonal Discounts

Seasonal discounts are offered in the off season; that is, during a season other than the expected season for purchasing the product or service. Buying lawn equipment in winter, ski equipment in summer, trips to Florida in the summer, or fur coats in July all represent opportunities for seasonal discounts.

Trade Discounts

Trade discounts are price reductions offered only to intermediaries and agents—wholesalers, distributors, and other people in the trade. A manufacturer, for example, may offer an appliance retailer a 40 percent trade discount on a microwave oven with a list price of $100. The net price (price after discount) to the appliance dealer: $60. (The role of intermediaries is covered more fully in Chapter 15.)

Quantity Discounts

Quantity discounts, similar to trade discounts, represent price reductions to buyers who purchase in large quantities. Retail examples include case prices for soft drinks, beer, motor oil, and wine, all lower per unit than if bought separately. Similarly, other products may be less expensive when purchased by the dozen, for example, donuts. Selling products in quantity often reduces packaging and other costs of the product, allowing those savings to be passed on to the buyer.

Selected Readings

American Marketing Association. *Marketing Definitions.* 1960.

Baker, Michael. *The Marketing Book.* 2002.

Bergdahl, Michael. *What I Learned From Sam Walton: How to Compete and Thrive in a Wal-Mart World.* 2004.

Buell, Victor P. *Handbook of Modern Marketing.* 1986.

Dolan, Robert J. *Strategic Marketing Management.* 1992.

Evans, Joel R. and Barry Berman. *Marketing.* 1987.

Ford, David. *Understanding Business Markets: Interaction, Relationships, Networks.* 1990.

Goldstucker, Jack L., and Otto R. Echemendia. *Marketing Information: A Professional Reference Guide.* 1987.

Lee, Ook. *Internet Marketing Research: Theory and Practice.* 2001.

Levitt, Theodore. *The Marketing Mode.* 1969.

Morris, Michael M., and Gene Morris. *Market Oriented Pricing: Strategies for Management.* 1990.

Nagle, Thomas T. *The Strategy and Tactics of Pricing.* 1987.

Phillips, Jerry J. *Products Liability in a Nutshell.* 1988.

Wilson, Robert B. *Nonlinear Pricing.* 1997.

Test Yourself

1) What is a product line?

2) A product's life cycle measures its longevity in the marketplace and describes its existence in terms of the four key stages of a product's life. What are the four key stages?

3) During a product's decline stage, a company may try to extend the product's life. What methods might a company use to accomplish this objective?

4) Identify the six steps in the new-product-development process.

5) What is a brand name and why is it important?

6) List the four types of brands discussed in this chapter.

7) Distinguish between individual and family branding.

8) What are the advantages of proper packaging of the product?

9) What are the minimum labeling requirements set by the Fair Packaging and Labeling Act of 1966?

10) List the many legitimate pricing objectives a company might try to achieve.

Test Yourself Answers

1) A product line is a group of products.

2) The four key stages are the introductory stage, the growth stage, the maturity stage, and the decline stage.

3) The company might develop new uses for the product, try to attract new users, make inexpensive alterations in packaging, labeling, or pricing.

4) The process includes generating ideas, screening ideas, preparing a business analysis, developing the product, testing the market, and commercializing the product.

5) A brand is a name, term, or symbol that identifies a seller's products and distinguishes it from competing products. It is the first step in developing brand loyalty and protecting the brand from misuse.

6) Manufacturer (or producer) brands, licensed brands, store (or private) brands, and generic brands.

7) Individual branding is a strategy in which a firm uses a different brand for each of its products. Family branding, on the other hand, entails a company's using the same brand for all its products.

8) Packaging provides a holder or container for the product, it protects the product from damage or tampering, and the visual effect of the package helps distinguish the product and can influence purchasing decisions.

9) The label must include the product name, package size, contents, and the name and address of the manufacturer.

10) Through its pricing, a company may try to achieve profit-making, market-share, loss containment and survival, social and ethical, and company image objectives.

CHAPTER 15
Supply Chains, Channels of Distribution, and Logistics

Every product begins with the producer and ends with the consumer, either an individual or an industrial consumer. A supply chain is the network created among different companies producing, handling, and/or distributing a specific product, beginning with the introduction of raw materials into the production process. The route the product travels from production to the end user is called the channel of distribution or the marketing channel. The channel of distribution is made up of a sequence of marketing organizations (intermediaries or agents) that link producers with consumers. Finally, the overall planning, implementing, and coordinating of the supply chain and channels of distribution is called logistics. Businesses employ these concepts in important ways to effect the production and ultimate distribution of products.

■ CHANNELS OF DISTRIBUTION

Distribution channels are sometimes referred to as the last link in the supply chain. The supply chain begins with the introduction of raw materials to the production process, continues through the production of the product, and concludes with the delivery to the ultimate customer, through the distribution channels.

Major Marketing Channels

The channels of distribution for consumer products and industrial products are different, and within each category the patterns of distribution are also different. The four most common channels for consumer products and the two most common channels for industrial products are listed in Figure 15.1

Consumer Channels

Channels of distribution of goods and services to ultimate consumers can be either direct or indirect. The route from producer to consumer is a direct channel. The route from producer to intermediary to consumer is an indirect route.

Consumer Product Channels				
Producer —	—	—	—	Consumer
Producer —	—	—	Retailer —	Consumer
Producer —	—	Wholesaler —	Retailer —	Consumer
Producer —	Agent —	Wholesaler —	Retailer —	Consumer
Industrial Product Channels				
Producer —	—	—	Industrial User	
Producer —	Agent/Intermediary —		Industrial User	

Figure 15.1: Major Marketing Channels

Producer to Consumer

The route from producer to consumer is a direct channel; it has no intermediaries. Most services travel the direct channel, from service provider to consumer. But most consumer goods arrive at their destinations through intermediaries; few goods travel the direct channel. Exceptions among consumer goods are producers such as Avon and Fuller Brush, which sell directly to the consumer to maintain close ties and to save intermediary costs.

Producer to Retailer to Consumer

Producer to retailer to consumer has one intermediary along the route, a retailer, who buys from the producer and sells to individual consumers. This channel of distribution is commonly used by retailers who buy large quantities and by retailers who deal in bulky products, such as furniture and other products that are costly to handle. This channel is equally popular for products that must reach the consumer quickly, either because they are perishable (produce, for example) or quickly outdated (for example, fashions).

Producer to Wholesaler to Retailer to Consumer

This is known as the traditional channel. Producers generally prefer dealing with wholesalers when the number of retailers is too cumbersome. In such cases, the wholesaler is a welcome intermediary, selling products to retailers or perhaps to other, smaller wholesalers.

Producer to Agent to Wholesaler to Consumer

This pathway is common for inexpensive products that reach millions of consumers, for example, candy bars. The agent, or distributor, may handle many different products from many different producers.

Industrial Channels

Industrial channels are those from producers directly to industrial users. They can be either direct or indirect.

Producer to Industrial User

This is a direct channel. The manufacturer uses its own sales force to sell directly to the industrial user. Manufacturers of heavy equipment such as mainframe computers often use the direct channel.

Producer to Agent/Intermediary to Industrial User

This channel uses the services of an agent/intermediary, who may be a wholesaler or an independent distributor representing the producer on a commission basis. Industrial companies distributing consumable supplies, small tools, accessories, or standardized parts often favor this channel of distribution.

Vertical Marketing Systems (VMSs)

Vertical channel integration results when two or more members of a channel are joined under a single management. The resulting channel is known as a vertical marketing system (VMS). Examples of VMSs are a large discount chain that buys directly from a manufacturer and warehouses its own stock, thereby doing away with the need for a wholesaler, and an oil company that owns its wells, refineries, terminals, and service stations.

There are three types of VMSs.

Administered VMS

In an administered VMS, one of the channel members dominates the other members, usually because of its great size. For example, Proctor & Gamble, one of the country's largest consumer products manufacturers, dominates the intermediaries that carry P&G products.

Contractual VMS

Under a contractual VMS, the rights and obligations of channel members are defined by contracts or other legal measures.

Corporate VMS

In a corporate VMS, production and distribution are joined by common ownership. A grocery chain that manufactures its own line of canned food is an example of a corporate VMS.

Market Coverage

To decide which distribution channel is best, producers must consider many factors, such as the nature of the product, production capability, consumer buying patterns, and marketing resources. For example, the nature of snowshoes limits market coverage to certain areas. If the producer's marketing resources are limited, the company may decide to use regional rather than national promotion. If production capacity is so limited that it curtails sales potential, the producer may opt for exclusive rather than widespread distribution. In any case, producers must evaluate such factors in order to develop the appropriate market coverage.

Intensive Distribution

Intensive distribution describes the efforts of a manufacturer to achieve the widest possible availability for a product. Manufacturers of candy, gum, cigarettes, and other convenience items will sell to any and all intermediaries or retailers willing to stock and sell the product.

Exclusive Distribution

Exclusive distribution uses only a single retail outlet in any one geographic area. Depending upon the merchandise, the area may be a neighborhood, a city, a suburb, or a larger area. Exclusive distribution is generally limited to prestigious and/or expensive products such as fine china, Rolex watches, or BMW automobiles. However, while the distributor may have exclusive rights for an area, there may be no limit on the number of retailers who can carry the product.

Selective Distribution

Selective distribution lies midway between intensive and exclusive distribution. Here, the manufacturer limits distribution to a selected portion or percentage of the available outlets in each geographic area. Clothing, major appliances, and furniture manufacturers selectively distribute their products. Franchisors such as McDonald's and Dairy Queen are selective in choosing franchise locations to avoid competing within their franchise families.

Marketing Intermediaries

Marketing intermediaries (often called distributors) are often the target of criticism from the press, consumers, and other marketers, who claim, generally, that intermediaries are inefficient and costly and simply add unnecessarily to the price that consumers ultimately pay for products. Undeniably, however, intermediaries perform an important service, and if they were eliminated, the functions they perform would then be performed by others, possibly raising, instead of lowering, costs.

Consider, for example, the added expense Hershey's would incur if it dealt individually with every outlet that carries its candy. Hershey's would then ship to hundreds of thousands of accounts instead of to a relatively few distributors. Its shipping costs and billing costs, for example, would increase as it hired additional people to handle the greater volume of smaller shipments and the increased number of customer accounts.

■WHOLESALERS

Wholesalers provide a number of services to retailers and to manufacturers.

Wholesalers' Service to Retailers

Wholesalers buy large quantities from manufacturers, stock the items in one location, and then sell and deliver smaller quantities to retailers. Wholesalers stock a variety of goods that the retailer would otherwise have to order from many producers rather than from one wholesaler. By maintaining inventories, wholesalers make products available to retailers on demand, with less waiting time and with greater economy than if the retailer had to order directly from the producer. In addition to stocking inventories of goods, wholesalers also supply several other services that are of value to retailers.

Promotion Assistance

In an effort to help retailers sell merchandise to consumers, wholesalers may supply—often free or, perhaps, at cost—promotion assistance. Wholesalers provide materials for window and counter displays, for example.

Market Information

Wholesalers also provide retailers with valuable market information concerning consumer demand, supply conditions, and new products. In the process of dealing with producers and retailers, wholesalers naturally gather useful information, which they gladly relay to retailers in the normal course of business.

Financial Aid

Wholesalers' prompt and frequent deliveries enable retailers to maintain lower inventories than would otherwise be possible and yet service their customers effectively. Thanks to this indirect form of financial aid, retailers need not tie up useful capital in large inventories. Many wholesalers provide generous credit terms; in some industries, they even extend loans.

Wholesalers' Service to Manufacturers

Manufacturers (even large, innovative, successful manufacturers) benefit from the services provided by wholesalers.

Instant Sales Force

Wholesalers provide the manufacturer with an instant sales force—and at a great savings. Imagine, for example, how the Campbell Soup Company or Proctor & Gamble might function without wholesalers. The size of, and, therefore, the expense of maintaining, a sales force capable of calling on the thousands of retail establishments that carry Campbell Soup Company or Proctor & Gamble products would be enormous without wholesalers.

Reduced Inventory Cost

By stocking goods for resale, wholesalers reduce inventory costs for manufacturers. Manufacturers' expenses are reduced for materials, storage, and other costs of maintaining a large inventory of finished goods.

Reduced Credit Risks

When wholesalers extend credit to retailers, wholesalers assume the credit risk, thereby reducing credit risks for manufacturers.

Information Network

Just as wholesalers provide retailers with an information network, they also provide manufacturers with the same kinds of valuable market information on consumer demand, buying trends, and so on.

Types of Wholesalers

There are three key types of wholesalers: (1) merchant wholesalers; (2) commission merchants, agents, and brokers; and (3) manufacturers' branch offices and sales offices.

The largest group is merchant wholesalers, which makes up more than half of all wholesalers.

Merchant Wholesalers

Merchant wholesalers are intermediaries who purchase goods in large quantities and resell them to retail and industrial users in smaller quantities. They take title to the goods and store them in their warehouses until the goods are sold. Merchant wholesalers maintain their own sales forces and function as independent businesses. Their range includes general merchandise wholesalers, who carry a wide range of different products; limited-line wholesalers, who carry only a few related lines; and specialty-line wholesalers, who carry a select group of products within a single line, such as gourmet foods.

Merchant wholesalers may provide full services or limited services to retailers.

Full-Service Wholesalers

Full-service wholesalers perform the entire range of wholesaler functions listed previously: selling, warehousing, delivery, financing, and promotion.

Limited-Service Wholesalers

Limited-service wholesalers, as the name implies, offer customers selected wholesaler functions. Limited-service wholesalers take title to the goods and warehouse them, but they have smaller sales forces. They are less likely to supply market information, credit, or promotion services.

Commission Merchants, Agents, and Brokers

Commission merchants, agents, and brokers also offer wholesaler services.

Commission Merchants

Commission merchants represent the manufacturers and are paid preset fees by manufacturers based on sales. Unlike merchant wholesalers, commission merchants do not take title to the goods they sell; instead, they arrange for delivery of merchandise from manufacturer to retailer.

Agents

Agents, sometimes called sales agents, represent one or more manufacturers within a specific territory. Agents work on a commission basis. They solicit orders but do not arrange for delivery. The manufacturer ships the merchandise and bills the customer directly.

Brokers

Brokers specialize in a particular commodity and represent either a buyer or a seller. They do not take title to the merchandise; instead, they receive a fee or commission, generally from the seller, for bringing the buyer and seller together, as real estate brokers do.

Manufacturers' Branch Offices and Sales Offices

Manufacturers may own and operate wholesaling operations of two kinds, branch offices and sales offices.

Branch Offices

Branch offices are merchant wholesale firms owned by the manufacturer. Branch offices perform all the merchant wholesale functions. Because they are owned by the producer, branch offices stock only goods manufactured by their own firms.

Sales Offices

Sales offices are also owned by the manufacturer, but unlike branch offices, sales offices act as agents, selling not only their company's products, but also other products that complement their company's product line. For example, a sales office for an automobile tire manufacturer may also carry car batteries and other car accessories manufactured by other companies.

■ RETAILERS

In the chain of distribution, retailers service the end customer, the consumer. Retailers range in size from small mom-and-pop operations to giants like Sears, Kmart, and Wal-Mart stores. Although individually owned stores account for 85 percent of all retail stores, they account for only slightly more than half of total retail sales. Retailers also vary in the services they offer and the merchandise they carry, as well as in their marketing approaches.

Retailers can be classified as in-store or non-store retailers, and shopping malls.

In-Store Retailers

In-store retailers maintain permanent locations where merchandise is regularly on display and available for purchase.

Department Stores

Department stores such as Macy's and Jordan Marsh carry a wide range of merchandise, from fashion items to kitchen appliances and furniture. Department stores are service-oriented, offering delivery service, sales help, credit, and liberal return policies to customers. Together, department stores (including all their branches in shopping malls or in the suburbs) account for the bulk of total store sales.

Specialty Stores

Specialty stores usually sell only one type of merchandise, for example, sporting goods and equipment. Specialty stores are designed to meet the needs of a particular market segment. Many are small, individually owned operations, but most of the larger specialty stores are part of a chain.

Chain Stores

Chain stores are groups of stores owned by one individual or one company. Ann Taylor, Toys "R" Us, and Barnes & Noble are examples of well-known chain stores. Their competitiveness lies in their ability to respond to trends more quickly than the larger department stores.

Discount Stores

Discount stores, such as Kmart, are self-service general-merchandise outlets offering products, including brand names, at lower prices. Discount stores have inexpensive decors, are open long hours, and offer limited services to reduce their expenses.

Warehouse Stores

Warehouse stores are minimal-service outlets that carry large inventories of foods, home furnishings, building supplies, and so on. In a warehouse store, such as Sam's Club and Costco, merchandise may sit in packing cases on pallets, and customers may even be expected to supply their own paper bags or cartons to carry their purchases home.

Convenience Stores

Convenience stores, as the name implies, offer customers a number of specific conveniences in return for which they charge higher prices than supermarkets charge for the same items. But customers are willing to pay the higher price for the "conveniences," which include store location (convenience stores are nearby, serving the needs of a neighborhood), product variety (they are small but carry a limited variety of products), and store hours (they are open very long hours—some, like 7-Eleven stores, are open 24 hours a day).

Supermarkets

Supermarkets such as Safeway and Kroger are the major sellers of food products in the United States. In addition to these national giants, independent smaller supermarket chains service regional areas.

Supermarkets operate on the basis of high volume and low margins. Competition is on the basis of price. In addition to canned, fresh, processed, and frozen foods, they stock items such as paper goods, cleaning products, and toiletries.

Scrambled Merchandising

Scrambled merchandising, a recent development, describes the odd mix of unrelated merchandise that a modern grocery store may offer in addition to traditional foods—for example, products such as motor oil, cosmetics, books and magazines, and housewares. Such stores may offer brand-name, generic, and unadvertised products.

Hypermarkets

Hypermarkets are an outgrowth of the trend toward scrambled merchandising. Developed in Europe and now common in the United States, hypermarkets are large-scale outlets that combine features of both supermarkets and discount stores and offer, for example, everything from cabbage to sporting goods under one roof (e.g., Wal-Mart and Costco).

Non-Store Retailers

Non-store retailers do not maintain conventional store facilities to which customers travel. Instead of customers traveling to stores, these retailers "travel" to their customers by television, telephone, door-to-door selling, mail order, home parties, vending machines, and the Internet.

Door-to-Door Retailers

Door-to-door retailers are sellers' representatives who sell directly to consumers in consumers' homes or offices. As part of the selling process, the representative may demonstrate the product; the representative may also deliver the product at the point of sale or after the sale. Encyclopedias, magazine subscriptions, even Girl Scout cookies are frequently sold door-to-door. Avon uses use this channel very effectively, while Mary Kay representatives sell primarily to persons they know (usually neighbors, family, and friends).

Mail-Order Retailing

Mail-order retailing is a reasonably strong segment of the retail market. Most American households receive catalogs of various kinds offering merchandise by mail order. The range of merchandise is virtually unlimited. Clothes, foods, furnishings, stationery, jewelry, appliances, books and magazines, tools, computers and computer supplies—all are available through mail order.

Each mail-order catalog contains an order form, which the customer completes and returns to the firm, although much of the current mail-order catalog business transpires via the Internet. Customers complete order forms on-line. Merchandisers such as L.L. Bean and Lands' End also provide toll-free numbers for ordering as well. Customers, generally, use credit and debit cards to transact mail-order catalog business.

Party Retailers

Some manufacturers—notably, Tupperware, Pampered Chef, and Mary Kay—maintain a network of part-time consultants who market the manufacturers' merchandise in customers' homes at parties. The consultant schedules a party with a customer at the customer's home. The customer invites friends, relatives, neighbors, or co-workers to the party, where the sales consultant demonstrates the merchandise and takes orders. As a reward for hosting the party, the customer earns a commission based on sales and receives free merchandise.

Vending Machines

Vending machines dispense many convenience goods such as candy, cigarettes, and beverages. Around-the-clock automatic teller machines (ATMs) are considered vending machines. Placed in convenient locations, ATMs require no sales personnel. On the other hand, they do require servicing, repairs, and maintenance due to vandalism and normal wear and tear, adding to the expense of operating vending machines.

E-Commerce (Business to Consumer)

E-commerce (electronic commerce) refers to business transacted over the Internet. It is the fastest growing non-store retailing options for consumers. The two major forms of e-commerce are business-to-consumer (B2C) and business-to-business (B2B). Web sites such as Amazon.com cater mostly to consumers. (The terms *e-business* and *e-tailing* are often used synonymously with *e-commerce*.) Virtually every retailer has a Web site through which customers can order goods.

Television Marketing

Everyone who watches television with any regularity is very familiar with commercials, advertisements of varying lengths that attempt to persuade viewers to buy a product or service. Some commercials try to elicit an immediate response, offering toll-free numbers and Web sites to order books, magazines, recordings, and many other products. These commercials are part of television marketing, a long- and well-established means of reaching consumers.

With the success of cable television and all the additional channels available through cable, television selling is no longer limited to commercials. Television broadcasts home-shopping channels devoted exclusively to selling merchandise, which is displayed on screen while a salesperson describes the merchandise in great detail, all the while urging viewers to call the toll-free telephone number or visit the Web site and place an order.

Shopping Malls

Built by private developers, shopping malls are self-contained retail centers that offer a variety of stores serving diverse consumer needs. The shopping-center management tries to assemble a coordinated mix of stores that will generate consumer traffic. In an effort to attract shoppers, malls provide adequate parking and pleasant surroundings. Shopping malls are neighborhood, community, or regional.

Neighborhood Shopping Malls

Along many major roads are neighborhood shopping malls, sometimes called strip malls, which consist of convenience and specialty stores such as drugstores, fast-food outlets, and grocery stores. The key to success for the neighborhood mall is the convenience it provides to consumers in the immediately surrounding area, the neighborhoods that lie within a few minutes' driving time of the mall.

Community Shopping Malls

In addition to specialty and convenience stores, community shopping malls may offer one or two medium-sized department stores. Because they offer more stores with a larger assortment of products and specialty items, community malls draw shoppers from a wider area than neighborhood malls do. Here, too, the mall management tries to achieve a balance in the mix of stores and products and will often stage special events such as art shows and handicraft fairs to increase customer traffic.

Regional Shopping Malls

With the growth of the suburbs, most large stores have followed the leads of Sears and Montgomery Ward, which pioneered the movement to branch stores in regional malls. In addition to branches of large department stores, regional malls may feature numerous specialty stores, restaurants, multi-screen movie complexes, national chain stores, and a range of franchise operations. Located on major traffic arteries, regional malls compete effectively with, and frequently outdo, the downtown shopping areas. Marketing and advertising for regional malls is well coordinated, and many special events are held to attract consumers.

■ PHYSICAL DISTRIBUTION

Physical distribution includes all the orderly and economic activities required to move goods from the producer to the ultimate consumer. It combines the functions of inventory control (that is, warehousing, order processing, and materials handling) and transportation. Marketers have integrated all these functions in an effort to achieve greater efficiency and get the right merchandise to the right place at the right time and at the right (lowest) cost.

Inventory Control

Holding costs describe all the expenses incurred in buying and storing inventory. Keeping inventory at the "right" level keeps holding costs at a minimum and avoids stockout costs, the sales losses that result when merchandise is unavailable and out of stock. Inventory control is the art and science of balancing holding costs against stockout costs. Understandably, the computer is now an invaluable tool in all aspects of managing inventory, including order processing, warehousing, and materials handling.

Order Processing

Order processing includes all activities involved in receiving and filling customers' orders as well as procedures for shipping, billing, and granting credit. Delivery time is a function of order processing. Whether the order is for a sofa to be delivered to an individual or for precision parts to be delivered to a manufacturer, prompt and certain delivery is important because (1) it gives the seller a competitive advantage in the marketplace, and (2) it reduces the costs of maintaining large inventories. The shorter the delivery time from the supplier, the smaller the inventory that must be maintained.

Warehousing

Warehousing combines several operations—not only the receiving, sorting, storing, and holding of goods, but also the assembling and shipping of goods when needed. All these operations are linked by order processing.

Private Warehouses

A company may have its own private warehouse, or it may rent space in a public warehouse. One obvious benefit of owning a private warehouse is that a firm can design it and operate it to meet the company's specific needs. But the costs of operating a warehouse are high, and only certain firms can justify the expense.

Public Warehouses

Public warehouses supply various warehousing services and charge clients accordingly. Most public warehouses are large facilities located on the outskirts of metropolitan areas, accessible to rail and truck transportation.

Distribution Centers

Unlike warehouses, distribution centers are in-and-out operations. Their purpose is not to store goods for indefinite periods, but to receive bulk shipments and reship or distribute the goods, usually quickly and in smaller quantities. For example, when a large retail chain like Sears receives a shipment of 5,000 power saws from a manufacturer, the shipment is delivered to a Sears distribution center, where smaller quantities of the saws are reshipped to Sears outlets nationwide.

Materials Handling

Materials handling, the physical handling of goods in warehousing as well as transporting, is an important element in distribution costs. Proper materials-handling procedures can increase usable warehouse capacity, reduce breakage and spoilage, and save time.

One goal of materials handling is to reduce the number of times a product is handled by using techniques such as unit loading. Unit loading combines smaller items and packages into single standardized loads that can be efficiently handled by trucks or forklifts. Containerization, a variation of unit loading on a grand scale, combines sizable numbers of individual items or unit loads, packs them in large containers or trailers, and handles and ships the container as a single unit.

Transportation

Transportation involves all aspects of shipping products through the channels of distribution to the ultimate consumers.

Carriers

Firms supplying transportation services are called carriers. The following sections describes various types of carriers.

Common Carriers

A common carrier is a firm whose service is available to all shippers. Railroad lines, airlines, and most long-distance trucking firms are common carriers.

Contract Carriers

Contract carriers do not serve the general public; they are available for hire only by commercial shippers. The number of firms they can service is limited by law.

Private Carriers

A private carrier is one owned and operated by a shipper for its own business use.

Package Carriers

Package carriers provide delivery services for many retail stores, e-tailers, businesses of all kinds, and individuals. The oldest package carrier is the U.S. Postal Service, which offers a variety of services. Many private carriers compete with the U.S. Postal Service in delivering packages, for example, United Parcel Service, Federal Express, and DHL. All offer overnight delivery throughout the country and, in many cases, overseas. In addition to these national services, many small, specialized package delivery services operate in metropolitan areas.

Freight Forwarders

Shippers can hire agents called freight forwarders to pick up the merchandise from the shipper and assume responsibility for delivery. The forwarder selects the carrier, frequently combining small shipments into one large load for which the carrier charges a lower rate.

Means of Transportation

There are several means of transportation, each with its own advantages and disadvantages.

Railroads

Almost all railroads are common carriers, except for a few operated by coal mining companies. Railroad freight volume has decreased in recent years, but railroads still transport a greater volume than any other type of carrier, principally because railroads are the least expensive form of transportation for many products. Railroads are routinely used for transporting heavy equipment, raw materials, commodities, foodstuffs, and lumber.

Rail transportation now offers a piggyback service: Loaded truck trailers are put on a special railroad car and transported by rail to a depot near their destination, where they are off-loaded to complete the rest of the journey by truck.

Trucks

Trucks are more expensive than railroads, their primary competition, but trucks offer several advantages, including door-to-door service, flexible scheduling, greater convenience, and added accessibility to rural or suburban areas not serviced by rail.

Airfreight

Because airfreight is the most expensive carrier, air transportation is often restricted to high-value, lightweight, perishable, and rush-delivery goods (for example, flowers and pharmaceuticals). Jumbo jets now enable airlines to carry bulk or containerized cargo. All certified airlines are common carriers. Charter lines and some freight lines are contract carriers.

Ships

Cargo ships and barges are the least expensive but the slowest form of transportation. As a result, water transport is used for nonperishable bulk goods such as ore, grain, and oil and petroleum products, as well as for many kinds of international cargo. Shipping destinations are, of course, limited to locations on inland waterways or seaports, and weather conditions present additional problems.

Pipelines

Pipelines, a highly specialized form of transportation, are used primarily for moving petroleum and natural gas. Pipelines are completely automated, are unaffected by weather, and allow the product to move slowly, constantly, and dependably.

Telecommunications

For many service companies, the product is information, which can be transported by means of telecommunications—computer networks, cable, and wireless networks.

Couriers

Couriers provide messenger services for delivering small parts and important documents quickly and safely.

Choosing a Carrier

Factors to consider when choosing a carrier include the size, weight, and type of the merchandise; the distance involved; the firm's overall distribution system; the speed required; the flexibility of the carrier; and of course, costs. When goods are in transit or are in storage, they incur carrying costs for inventory and insurance, for example.

Japanese manufacturers have developed a just-in-time inventory system, which ensures a continuous flow of materials from suppliers and thereby minimizes the amount of goods held in inventory. Just-in-time inventory systems require fast, reliable transportation. See Chapter 12.

Selected Readings

Arthur Andersen & Co. *Future Trends in Wholesale Distribution: A Time of Opportunity.* 1982.

Barger, Harold. *Distribution's Place in the American Economy Since 1869.* 1955.

Bolen, William H. *Contemporary Retailing.* 1988.

Bucklin, Louis P., editor. *Vertical Marketing Systems.* 1970.

Christopher, Martin, and Helen Peck. *Marketing Logistics.* 2002.

Handfield, Robert B., and Ernest Z. Nichols. *Introduction to Supply Chain Management.* 1998.

Lambert, Douglas, James R. Stock, and Lisa M. Ellram. *Fundamentals of Logistics Management.* 1997.

Lewis, Robert L. *Information Technology in Physical Distribution Management.* 1986.

McKinnon, Alan. *Physical Distribution Systems.* 1988.

Rein, Irving, Philip Kotler, Michal Hamlin, and Martin Stoller. *High Visibility: Transforming Your Personal and Professional Brand.* 2005.

Robeson, James F., and Robert C. House. *The Distribution Handbook.* 1985.

Rolnicki, Kenneth. *Managing Channels of Distribution.* 1998.

Sigafoos, Robert A. *Absolutely Positively Overnight.* 1984.

Shapiro, Jeremy F. *Modeling the Supply Chain.* 2000.

Stem, Louis W., and Adel I. El-Ansary. *Marketing Channels.* 1988.

Stroh, Michael B. *Practical Guide to Transportation and Logistics.* 2001.

Test Yourself

1) What are the two major marketing channels?
2) What is a vertical marketing system (VMS)?
3) Distinguish among intensive distribution, exclusive distribution, and selective distribution.
4) Wholesalers provide a number of services to retailers. What are they?
5) Wholesalers provide a number of services to manufacturers. What are they?
6) List and describe the different types of merchant wholesalers.
7) In the chain of distribution, retailers service the end customer. They can be classified as in-store and non-store retailers, and shopping malls. List the types of in-store retailers.
8) What is scrambled merchandising in the context of in-store retailing?
9) What is e-commerce and what in what category of retail outlets does it fit?
10) What is inventory control?

Test Yourself Answers

1) The major marketing channels are consumer and industrial.

2) Vertical channel integration results when two or more members of a channel are joined under a single management. The resulting channel is known as a vertical marketing system. There are three types of VMS: administered, contractual, and corporate.

3) Intensive distribution describes the efforts of a manufacturer to achieve the widest possible availability of its product. Exclusive distribution, on the other hand, uses a single retail outlet in any one geographic region. Finally, selective distribution lies between intensive and exclusive distribution; the manufacturer limits distribution to a selected portion or percentage of the available outlets in the region.

4) They provide retailers promotion assistance, market information, and financial aid.

5) They provide manufacturers an instant sales force, reduced inventory costs, reduced credit risks, and an information network.

6) Merchant wholesalers are intermediaries who purchase goods in large quantities and resell them to retail and industrial users in smaller quantities. They come in two types. Full-service wholesalers perform the entire range of wholesaler functions: selling, warehousing, delivery, financing, and promotion. Limited-service wholesalers offer only selected wholesaler services.

7) Department stores, specially stores chain stores, discount stores, warehouse stores, convenience stores, supermarkets, scrambled merchandising, and hypermarkets.

8) Scrambled merchandising describes the odd mix of unrelated merchandise that a modern grocery store may offer in addition to traditional foods, for example, motor oil, cosmetics, books and magazines, and housewares.

9) E-commerce (electronic-commerce) refers to business transacted over the Internet. It is the fastest-growing non-store retailing option for consumers.

10) Holding costs include all the expenses of buying and storing inventory. Stockout costs are the sales losses associated with not having the inventory available when required. Inventory control is the art and science of balancing holding costs and stockout costs.

CHAPTER 16
Promotional Strategy

Promotional strategy includes all techniques and devices designed to induce customers to buy products or services. Promotion may communicate, inform, influence, or remind people in the markets about the organization and/or its products.

■THE PROMOTIONAL MIX

The promotional mix describes the particular combination of methods that each firm uses in its promotional campaign to reach its target market(s).

Promotion Methods

There are four basic methods of promotion: advertising, personal selling, sales promotion, and publicity and public relations.

Advertising

Advertising is a paid message communicated through a mass medium to a wide general audience by an identified sponsor.

Personal Selling

Personal selling includes personal communication aimed at informing one or more prospective purchasers and persuading them to buy a firm's products.

Sales Promotion

Sales promotion describes all activities or materials that directly influence customers or salespeople. Although advertising uses media such as newspapers and television, sales promotion uses displays, demonstrations, samples, coupons, and other selling efforts.

Publicity and Public Relations

Publicity is a nonpersonal message delivered through mass media, free-of-charge, usually in a news story. The marketer cannot control the content of the publicity. Company-influenced publicity is known as public relations.

These four areas of promotion are discussed in detail later in this chapter in their own individual sections.

Promotional Objectives

The broad, basic objective of promotion is to create sales; which, in turn, generates profits. But promotion performs several additional functions: It communicates information, positions products, and controls sales volume.

Communicating Information

Consumers cannot buy a product unless they have been informed that the product exists. The information communicated to consumers may take many different forms. The information may be direct, as in an announcement concerning a product's availability, or it may be indirect, as in a flier, brochure, or article on technological advances. The information may be targeted to a specific group or to several groups. It may be communicated in print media (through letters, fliers, brochures, newspapers, magazines, or billboards), in broadcast media (radio or television), by telephone, or by computer.

Positioning Products

Companies position products by establishing a clearly identifiable image and identifying that image of the product in consumers' minds. Before a company can position a product, the company must identify which segments of the market are potential purchasers and which other products it will compete against.

Controlling Sales Volume

Companies that experience seasonal sales patterns can often effectively promote their products during slow periods in an effort to increase sales during those slow periods and to stabilize sales volume throughout the year. For some seasonal products, such as sleds, promotional efforts are designed to maximize sales volumes at certain times of the year.

Promotional Strategies

Once a firm has established its promotional objectives, it must develop a promotional strategy to achieve those objectives. The company may use a push strategy, a pull strategy, or a combination of both.

Push Strategy

The idea behind a push strategy is to drive or push the company's product through wholesalers and retailers, who will then persuade customers to buy the product. The product is presented to the potential customer, as opposed to the customer's demanding the product. The push strategy stresses personal selling (on the part of wholesalers and retailers) over advertising (on the part of the manufacturer) and is widely used by marketers of higher-priced goods and industrial equipment.

Pull Strategy

A pull strategy emphasizes mass advertising to move goods into consumers' hands. This strategy is designed to create a demand on the part of the consumers and pull them into retail outlets to purchase the product. Marketers of lower-priced convenience goods rely on the pull strategy to market their products.

ADVERTISING

Advertising is a paid, nonpersonal message delivered through a mass medium. Advertising has great flexibility; it can be aimed very effectively to reach a very broad general audience or targeted to reach a narrower, carefully chosen niche group. Advertising also provides flexibility in delivering various kinds of messages.

Types of Advertising by Purpose

Advertising can be categorized according to its purpose and its message as selective, institutional, primary-demand, and advocacy advertising.

Selective Advertising

Selective advertising, also called brand advertising, promotes specific brands of products and services. This is the most widely used form of advertising, accounting for the major portion of advertising budgets.

Immediate-Response Advertising

Selective advertising for the purpose of persuading consumers to make purchases within a short time is called immediate-response advertising. Most local advertising is for this purpose.

Reminder Advertising

Selective advertising aimed at keeping a firm's name before the public is called reminder advertising.

Comparative Advertising

Selective advertising that compares specific characteristics of two or more identified brands is called comparative advertising.

Institutional Advertising

Institutional advertising is designed to enhance a firm's image or reputation, to build goodwill rather than sell merchandise. For example, for twenty-four years, General Electric used the phrase "We bring good things to life" in all its institutional advertising in an effort to enhance GE's public image. Now it uses the tagline "imagination at work." Nike has become famous for its tagline of "Just do it!"

Primary-Demand Advertising

Primary-demand advertising is designed to increase consumer demand for all brands of a good or service. Trade and industry groups such as the American Dairy Association or the Beef Growers Association use primary-demand advertising to build consumer demand for milk and meat, respectively, without mentioning any brand names or company names.

Advocacy Advertising

Advocacy advertising attempts to influence individuals' or organizations' attitudes and opinions. Companies and trade associations such as the Building Owners and Managers Association (BOMA) often use advocacy advertising to encourage public support for, or public opposition to, specific legislation.

Types of Advertising by Message

The message underlying product advertising often depends on that particular product's life cycle stage. The message can be described as informative, persuasive, or reminder.

Informative Advertising

The goal of informative advertising, used primarily in the introductory stage of a product's life cycle, is to make potential customers aware of both the new product and the company. Informative advertising can help establish a primary demand for a product.

Persuasive Advertising

During the growth stage of a product's life cycle, when the product is already established, persuasive advertising is used to influence consumers to buy the company's product as opposed to competitors' products. During the maturity stage of a product's life cycle, persuasive advertising can help maintain the level of sales.

Reminder Advertising

Reminder advertising reinforces brand loyalty and keeps the product's name before the consumer during the later part of the maturity stage and all of the decline stage of the life cycle.

Advertising Media

An advertising medium is the specific communication vehicle used to carry the firm's message to potential consumers. The main media are television, newspapers, direct mail, radio, magazines, outdoor advertising and, increasingly, the Internet. As Table 16.1 shows, television receives the largest share of advertising expense dollars, closely followed by newspapers and direct mail.

Note that telephone, sponsorship of sports entertainment, telephone directories, neon signs, displays on bus stops, score boards, and shopping bags are included in the "Other Media" percentage.

Each medium has its own advantages and disadvantages, which are discussed in the following sections.

Television

Television allows advertisers to combine color, sound, and motion and to create effective, dramatic presentations. Television has many pluses. Stations and networks can provide advertisers with very

Table 16.1: Media's Share of Advertising Dollars

Medium	Allocation
Television	25%
Newspapers	19%
Direct Mail	19%
Radio	8%
Magazines	5%
Outdoor	2%
Online and Interactive	2%
Other Media	20%
Total	100%

detailed information on viewer demographics, allowing advertisers to choose carefully the most appropriate program for the advertiser's particular message. National advertisers are able to reach huge numbers of people using national or regional networks, and local advertisers can buy time on a local station.

Television also has some negatives. The cost of television advertising is very high. Broadcasting a thirty-second commercial during a Super Bowl game costs more than $2.5 million. Because there are many commercials—running ten, fifteen, thirty, or sixty seconds each—viewers may not pay close attention to the commercials, or they may ignore them altogether (by leaving the room, using the mute button on the remote control, using the time to talk with someone, and so on). And once the commercial has been broadcast, it is gone.

Newspapers

Newspapers are the most widely used advertising medium. Almost every market is covered by at least one daily newspaper. Newspapers offer flexible, rapid coverage, and they are read by many people. However, papers are discarded after they are read and reproduction quality is poor although many papers are now printing in color. Also, newspaper messages are difficult to target to specific audiences.

Direct Mail

Direct mail includes letters, fliers, cards, and so on, sent directly to consumers' homes or their places of business. Generally, fliers attempt to pull the customer to the store, while letters push for an immediate direct order. Direct mail allows advertisers to select target audiences rather precisely, and direct mail can be easily personalized.

True, much direct mail is considered junk mail and thrown away, but what is read is taken seriously. When used skillfully, direct mail is cost effective and successful. Recognizing its effectiveness, many businesses are allocating a growing proportion of their advertising budgets to direct mail.

Radio

Radio offers advertisers a number of advantages, including a very large audience and relatively inexpensive commercials. Further, most programming is local and is segmented into categories such as rock, country and western, talk, news, and classical, offering advertisers the opportunity to select target audiences. Drawbacks include the fact that many listeners use radio as background noise, paying little attention to the ads, or listen in their cars, where they can easily change stations during commercials.

Magazines

Magazines offer the ability to select and reach specific consumer targets because there are magazines for every interest imaginable. Artwork reproduction is excellent in all major magazines, and there is plenty of space for product information. Many magazines publish different regional editions, giving advertisers more flexibility in selecting target markets. Magazines have a long life; because they tend to be passed on, they are read by more than one person.

Two disadvantages of magazine advertising are that ads must be submitted well in advance of the publication date, and an ad's location is not guaranteed. Advertising in the major magazines is also relatively expensive.

Outdoor Advertising

Billboards and other outdoor advertising are relatively inexpensive and offer high repeat exposure. However, targeting is nearly impossible, giving advertisers no control over who sees the ad.

Online and Interactive Advertising

This category of advertising includes Web sites, compact discs (CDs), information kiosks, and many others. It is the fastest growing segment of the advertising market. In fact, Nike uses this form of advertising as one of its primary strategies.

One of the major negative aspects of online advertising is that consumers clearly deplore the pop-up ads that suddenly appear on their screens. As a consequence, a number of services and software packages have been developed to combat pop-ups. However, pop-ups are not the only way to advertise online.

Other Media

Advertisers, always innovative, have used various other media to communicate their messages, including telephoning, skywriting, electronic scoreboards at sports stadiums, blimps, balloons, ski lift stanchions, bus shelters, phone book directories, shopping bags, and displays on supermarket shopping carts. Indeed, even product packaging is a form of advertising.

Planning the Advertising Campaign

An advertising campaign is a detailed strategy organized in stages. The stages may vary somewhat, but they should include the following basic steps.

Identify and Analyze the Target

Identifying the target precisely is crucial to the success of the campaign. To pinpoint the target, advertisers must first analyze the geographic distribution of consumers, demographic information such as age, sex, income, and level of education completed, and consumers' attitudes both toward the product and toward competing products.

Define the Advertising Objectives

Advertising goals must be stated precisely and in measurable terms, including the time span, the sales-increase goals (expressed in either dollar revenue or market share), and the specific information to be conveyed.

Create the Advertising Platform

The advertising platform includes the key selling points or features that are to be incorporated into the ad campaign.

Determine the Advertising Appropriation

The advertising appropriation is the total amount of money budgeted for advertising in a given period. Appropriations may be based on a percentage of existing sales, projected sales, or competitors' spending on advertising.

Develop the Media Plan

A media plan specifies exactly which media will be used, which ads will be featured, and when the advertisements will appear. A typical goal might be to reach the most people in the target audience for each dollar spent or to make the strongest impact in the selected target market.

Create the Advertising Message

The product's features, the characteristics of the target audience, the object of the campaign, the choice of media—all help determine the content and the form of the advertisement message, including the copy (that is, the words used in the message) and the artwork used to illustrate the message. For radio and television, the message will also include sound, of course.

Evaluate the Effectiveness of the Advertising

The success of a campaign should be measured both during and after the campaign. Feedback permits adjustments during the campaign and provides valuable information to guide future campaigns.

Advertising Agencies

An advertising agency is a professional business organization equipped to undertake all phases of the preparation, development, and execution of advertising campaigns for its clients. Among the services that agencies provide are identifying and analyzing target audiences, writing copy, preparing artwork, creating and preparing commercials, casting talent, media buying, budgeting campaigns, and identifying spokespersons.

The agency bills the client for all production services and media expenses, and then adds the agency's commission (up to 15 percent) on total billings. Although large companies and companies that advertise a great deal have their own in-house advertising departments, they still use independent agencies to handle their ad campaigns.

Regulation of Advertising

Advertising claims for products and services are often exaggerated, deceptive, or blatantly stretched beyond what can be proven. As a result, advertisements and advertisers have been criticized, along with their companies. Some industries, the government, and consumers have taken steps to prevent such excesses and monitor advertisements.

Industry Self-Regulation

In an effort to preclude further government interventions, certain industries (the cosmetics and toiletries industries, for example) have established Trade Practice Rules, which prohibit false or deceptive advertising. Most media have ethical standards such as the Radio Code and the Television Code of the National Association of Broadcasters. The Better Business Bureau (BBB) also attempts to police misleading advertising or deceptive practices.

Government Regulations

The two principal agencies involved in fighting fraudulent advertising of foods, drugs, or cosmetics are the Federal Trade Commission (FTC) and the Food and Drug Administration (FDA). The FTC has authority over false advertising, and the FDA has the power to prohibit false labeling and deceptive packaging. The Federal Communications Commission (FCC) has established policies concerning the types of products that can be advertised on radio and television as well as the content of ads.

Consumer Action

A number of consumer groups have been successful in influencing advertising. A group of parents called Action for Children's Television (ACT) monitors commercials directed at children. Other groups have, in some cases, successfully convinced sponsors to discontinue support for television shows that they feel have excessive violence or sex, or that advocate political and moral messages with which they disagree.

■ PERSONAL SELLING

Personal selling describes all individual communications intended to inform consumers about—and persuade them to buy—the company's products or services. Of all promotional methods, personal selling is the most adaptable, but it is also the most expensive. Thus, personal selling is used more often to sell higher-priced items.

Personal selling can take one of two forms:

- **Industrial sales**, which is selling products to other businesses, includes many multimillion-dollar sales (of heavy equipment, for instance).
- **Retail sales** involves selling consumer products to individual buyers.

Basic Tasks in Personal Selling

Personal selling is made up of three basic tasks: order processing, creative selling, and missionary selling. A specialized form of personal selling is telemarketing.

Order Processing

Order processing describes sales that require little persuasion but in-depth service, including handling all steps from order placement to delivery as well as any follow-through that may be necessary. The salesperson's main responsibility is servicing the account and ensuring customer satisfaction. In some cases, the salesperson is a route salesperson, someone who calls on customers regularly (daily, weekly, monthly); for example, route salespeople for bread and milk companies call on retail stores daily, checking each store's supply of merchandise and restocking shelves immediately from inventory carried on their delivery trucks.

Creative Selling

Creative selling requires that salespeople apply a variety of techniques to persuade customers to buy a product, often because the benefits are not readily apparent to customers or because the price is high. Automobile sales and sales of new brands or new products require creative selling. Creative selling is more complicated than other forms of selling. The steps in creative selling are described in the following sections.

Prospecting and Qualifying

Prospecting is the process of finding and identifying potential customers (called prospects, short for prospective, or likely, customers). Salespeople find the names of prospects in a number of ways, for example, from company records, customers, friends, business associates, and mailing list companies.

Then salespeople must qualify each prospect; that is, the salesperson must evaluate potential customers to determine whether each has the authority to buy and the ability to pay. Each potential customer who passes this initial screening is a qualified prospect.

Making the Approach

The approach describes the first few minutes a salesperson spends with the qualified prospect. In personal selling, these first few minutes are crucial, because during this short time, the salesperson makes that important first impression, which affects the salesperson's credibility and rapport with the customer.

Presenting and Demonstrating

The presentation is the salesperson's delivery of the promotional message; his or her full explanation of the product, its features, its uses, and its benefits to the prospect. If possible, during the initial conversation with the customer, the salesperson tries to discover the customer's needs so that he or she can then tailor the presentation to that particular customer's needs. When appropriate, the salesperson should demonstrate the product.

Answering Objections

No matter what the product or its price, prospects will usually have some objections; that is, prospects will question the need for the product or show uncertainty about buying it. The reasons for objections may not always be clear, but objections often show that the buyer is interested. An experienced salesperson "reads" objections to learn the customer's feelings and attitudes and to determine which selling points to reinforce with each customer. Strong objections, of course, show that the customer is not interested.

Closing the Sale

The closing is the most critical part of the personal-selling process. This is the point when the salesperson asks the prospect to buy the product. Professionals use a wide range of techniques to close sales. For example, some salespeople "assume the sale" and begin their close by completing an order form or asking indirect questions such as "Which delivery date is best for you?" or "Would you like to start with a small order?"

Following Up the Sale

Follow-up activities after the sale include processing the order quickly, delivering the order on time, providing instructions on the care and use of the product, and if necessary, providing maintenance and repairs. Good follow-up helps establish customer loyalty and is an important source of market research information.

Telemarketing

Telemarketing is a specialized form of personal selling; namely, using the telephone for any or all steps in the selling process, from the approach to the close. The use of telemarketing has been growing steadily because it provides a less-expensive alternative to face-to-face personal selling. Telemarketing may be used instead of outside salespersons, or it may be used in conjunction with outside salespersons, for example, for prospecting or for scheduling sales calls.

The National Do Not Call Registry was created in response to complaints about the high volume of "nuisance" telemarketing calls received by consumers. The registry gives consumers an opportunity to prohibit telemarketing calls at their homes. Once the phone number has been listed on the registry for 31 days, telemarketers cannot call that telephone number; the prohibition against calling lasts for five years. Consumers may file complaints with the Federal Trade Commission against telemarketers who violate the prohibition.

Missionary Selling

The objective of missionary selling is to promote the company's long-term image, rather than make a quick sale. Sales representatives for drug companies, for example, promote their products by calling on doctors, who, in turn, prescribe the company's pharmaceuticals to their patients. But the actual buying and selling of pharmaceuticals is done in pharmacies, not doctor's offices.

■ SALES PROMOTION

Sales promotion, an important part of the promotional mix, includes all the related activities that companies sponsor in an effort to persuade customers to make purchases. Sales promotion can take a variety of forms, including coupons, point-of-purchase displays, trade shows, and purchasing incentives (free samples, trading stamps, and premiums).

Coupons

Coupons are certificates that entitle the bearer to a savings off a product's regular price. Coupons appear in newspapers and magazines, are sent through direct mail, and are enclosed with packages of products to encourage repeat purchases. Coupons are often effective both in attracting new customers and in inducing present users to buy more of the product.

Point-of-Purchase (POP) Displays

Point-of-purchase (POP) displays are designed to catch customers' attention at specific, prominent locations—for instance, at the ends of aisles or near the checkout counter at supermarkets.

Trade Shows

Trade shows—exhibits sponsored by industries and associations—allow companies to display and demonstrate their products to customers who have a special interest in a specific type of product. For example, computer software shows, furniture shows, and gift merchandise trade shows attract buyers who are already interested in a given type of product.

Purchasing Incentives

Free samples, trading stamps (and now trading points), and premiums are all used as purchasing incentives. Free samples also allow the customer to try the product without cost or risk; they may be given out by local retailers or sent directly to the consumer. Trading stamps and points, such as S&H greenpoints, are offered as a bonus for patronizing certain stores. Premiums are gifts given to consumers in return for buying a specific product.

■ PUBLICITY AND PUBLIC RELATIONS

Publicity and public relations are two very important methods by which businesses can enhance the public's awareness of their goods, services, and community contributions. They are critical to the overall marketing of an enterprise.

Publicity

Publicity refers to all unpaid messages about a company, its products, or its personnel that appear in magazines and newspapers or are broadcast on radio and television. Note the distinction between advertising, which is purchased, and publicity, which is free.

All media are eager to print or broadcast news that will be of interest to readers, listeners, or viewers, and business organizations are equally eager to provide the media with publicity releases, bulletins specially written and designed to satisfy media needs for news. Because publicity releases follow the format of newspaper stories or columns, they are easier for the media to use "as is," with few or no changes. At the same time, their news format makes publicity releases appear objective, and therefore, more believable than company-paid advertising. For marketers, therefore, publicity is a form of free advertising. In the hands of expert publicists, publicity can be used to show the company at its best advantage or to downplay a negative image.

Because it is free for the company, the firm has less control over the media's use, or nonuse, of news releases. For many different reasons, the media do not use all the releases they receive from various organizations.

Public Relations

Public relations defines company-influenced publicity, publicity that the firm pays for, and therefore, controls. The goal of public relations is to establish a positive image and a sense of goodwill between the company, its customers, and the general public. To achieve this goal, companies contribute to public television, sponsor Little League teams, provide financial support for charitable and community organizations, and so on.

As this chapter shows, promotional strategy is part of the greater marketing picture. Marketing is involved in all decisions related to determining a product's characteristics, price, production quantities, sales, and service.

Selected Readings

Baker, Michael. *The Marketing Book*. 2002.

Carnegie, Dale. *How to Win Friends and Influence People*. 1998.

Cutlip, Scott M., Allen H. Center, and Glen M. Broom. *Effective Public Relations,* Ninth Edition. 2005.

Goodrum, Charles, and Helen Dalrymple. *Advertising in America: The First 200 Years*. 1990.

Hanssens, Dominique, Leonard J. Parsons, and Randall L. Schultz. *Market Response Models*. 2003.

Herold, Jean. *Marketing and Sales Management: An Information Source Book*. 1988.

Hopkins, Tom. *How to Master the Art of Selling*. 1988.

Lazarsfeld, P. F., Bernard Berelson, and Hazel Gaudet. *The People's Choice: How the Voter Makes Up His Mind in a Presidential Campaign*. 1944.

McLuhan, Marshall. *Understanding Media*. 1964.

Manning, Gerald L., and Barry L. Reece. *Selling Today*. 1987.

Nash, Edward L., editor. *Direct Marketing Handbook*. 1984.

Ogilvy, David. *Ogilvy on Advertising*. 1983.

Reynolds, Jonathan, and Christine Cuthbertson. *Retail Strategy: The View from the Bridge*. 2004.

Ridgway, Peggi. *Successful Website Marketing: Worksheets, Forms & Easy Steps for Web Success*. 2005.

Seiden, Hank. *Advertising Pure and Simple*. 1990.

Smith, Paul Russell, and Jonathan Taylor. *Marketing Communications: An Integrated Approach*. 2004.

Stern, Louis W., and Thomas L. Eovaldi. *Legal Aspects of Marketing Strategy*. 1984.

Yeshin, Tony. *Integrated Marketing Communications*. 1999.

Test Yourself

1) Promotion includes all techniques designed to induce customers to buy products. List and describe the four basic methods of promotion.

2) In addition to generating profits, promotion performs several additional functions. What are these functions?

3) Distinguish between a push promotional strategy and a pull promotional strategy.

4) Advertising has many purposes. List the different advertising purposes discussed in this chapter.

5) What are the main media outlets for advertising?

6) What are the major steps in planning an advertising campaign?

7) What is an advertising agency and what services does it provide?

8) What mechanisms are in place to discourage exaggerated and outright false or misleading advertising and promotional claims for products and services?

9) Creative selling is considered more complex than other forms of personal selling. What are the steps involved in creative selling?

10) Sales promotion can take a variety of forms. What are they?

Test Yourself Answers

1) The four basic methods of promotion are advertising, personal selling, sales promotion, and publicity and public relations. Advertising is a paid message communicated by a mass medium. Personal selling is aimed at informing one or more prospective purchasers and persuading them to buy a firm's products. Sales promotion includes a number of activities and materials that directly influence customers or salespersons, including displays, demonstrations, samples, coupons, and other selling efforts. Public relations is the art of establishing and promoting a favorable relationship between an entity and the public.

2) Promotion also communicates information to potential customers, positions the company's product, and provides a mechanism for controlling sales volume (especially during off seasons for seasonal products).

3) The push strategy entails a company's driving the product through wholesalers and retailers, who, then, persuade customers to buy the product. The pull strategy, on the other hand, emphasizes mass advertising to move the goods to consumers.

4) Advertising may be used to achieve the following purposes: to promote specific brands of products and services (selective advertising); convince persons to make purchases within a short period of time (immediate-response advertising); keep the firm's name in front of potential customers (reminder advertising); compare specific characteristics of its product with one or more competing products (comparative advertising); enhance a firm's image or reputation (institutional advertising); increase consumer demand for all brands (primary-demand advertising); and influence individuals' and organizations' attitudes and opinions (advocacy advertising).

5) The main advertising outlets are television, newspapers, direct mail, radio, magazines, outdoor advertising, the Internet and others (e.g., telemarketing, phone directories, etc.).

6) Planning the advertising campaign includes the following: identifying and analyzing the target market; defining the advertising objectives; creating the advertising platform; determining the advertising appropriation (budget); developing the media plan; creating the advertising message; and evaluating the effectiveness of the advertising.

7) An advertising agency is a professional business organization equipped to undertake all phases of the preparation, development, and execution of advertising campaigns for its clients.

8) Certain industries self-regulate, developing rules that prohibit false advertising and establish ethical minimum standards for advertising. The government is also involved: the Federal Trade Commission (FTC), the Food and Drug Administration (FDA), and the Federal Communications Commission (FCC) provide rules and guidelines that prohibit and address false and misleading advertising. Finally, consumer groups have also been successful in influencing advertising regulations.

9) Creative selling includes the basic following tasks: finding and identifying potential customers (prospecting and qualifying); making the approach; presenting and demonstrating the product; answering any objections expressed by the potential customer; and closing the sale.

10) Sales promotion can take the following forms: coupons that entitle the bearer to a reduced price for the product; point-of-purchase (POP) displays, designed to capture the attention of potential customers; trade shows; and purchasing incentives (e.g., free samples, trading stamps, and premiums and gifts to consumers).

Part 5: Management Tools

CHAPTER 17
Management Information and Statistical Analysis

In business, managers must make decisions, and decisions are based on information. Whether the decision is complicated and critically important (e.g., whether to merge with another company) or simple and routine (e.g., which supplier to use for general office products), managers need to evaluate information. This chapter addresses how managers use information systems and statistical analyses to make informed decisions.

■ DATA, INFORMATION, AND INFORMATION MANAGEMENT

Information sources, which are many and diverse, offer "hard" information and "soft" information. "Hard" information describes factual information such as actual sales figures from the past, newspaper articles, government reports and surveys, actual production costs, actual expenses paid, and so on. "Soft" information describes nonfactual information such as opinions, feelings, and beliefs. In any case, whatever the source, today's business managers have a wealth of information at their fingertips—such a massive amount of information, in fact, that today's company needs a management information system (MIS), preferably computerized, to help collect, organize, analyze, and distribute the overwhelming quantity of information available to its managers. Without its MIS, the data and the information available to a company is often useless.

The first step in understanding the role of information in general, and of the MIS in particular, in business management is to distinguish between information and data.

■ DATA VERSUS INFORMATION

When managers complain that they receive too much "information," they are often referring not to information but to data. Data are raw facts and figures, the raw material of information, which usually have little or no meaning on their own. For example, knowing the current unit cost of a product, say, $2.50, may be meaningless by itself. However, if a manager also knows that the estimated unit cost for product and unit costs in the past, the manager has useful information that he or she might use in pricing the product or making other product decisions.

To be useful, then, data must be collected, sorted, organized, and presented in a meaningful form, a form that managers can use to make decisions. In this transformed state, data become information.

Kinds of Data
Data can be classified according to their source.

Internal Data
Internal data are the data available from the company's records. For example, a company's financial statements and accounting records provide data on creditors and suppliers, its personnel files offer information on salaries and employee turnover, its invoices and sales reports contain data that can be valuable in establishing and understanding sales patterns, and so on.

External Data
External data originate from sources outside the company. Newspapers, radio, and television keep managers informed of events and trends—data that could affect the company's business. Government agencies, such as the Department of Labor or the Census Bureau, can provide valuable data concerning current and projected unemployment, income and educational levels within market areas, and so on. Customers, suppliers, bankers, even friends are sources of business data.

Data can also be classified as primary or secondary.

Primary Data
Primary data describe data gathered through original research on a specific problem or situation. A company may, for example, conduct a formal, thorough survey of its customers to find out customers' attitudes, preferences, and opinions in an effort to collect primary data.

Secondary Data
Secondary data originate not from the company, but instead from other sources (for example, from economic and industrial surveys or from electronic information services such as Reuters and UPI). Thus, secondary data describe data that are already available. If the secondary data are inadequate, the company may decide to update the original source of the data.

Methods of Data Collection
The three basic methods used to collect primary data are observation, experimentation, and survey.

Observation
Observation is the process of watching and observing behavior and performance. For example, to decide whether trucks should be redirected to other highways, the Department of Transportation may monitor a particular stretch of road to observe how many large trucks use the road each day. A detergent manufacturer may set up video cameras in a supermarket to observe customers' selection process—how long customers look at different brands, how many different boxes they pick up before making their final selection, and so on.

Experimentation
Experimentation is a process of controlled observation and testing, often conducted in a laboratory. A detergent manufacturer uses lab experiments to compare the ability of its detergent, against competitive products, to remove oil and grease stains, for example. Companies may also use experimentation to evaluate the effectiveness of training methods. The experiment may expose one group of employees, the control group, only to on-the-job training, but the other group, the experimental group, to classroom

training in addition to on-the-job training. After training is completed, the company then compares the job performance of both groups on identical tasks. In this way, the experiment can establish which training method was more effective.

Survey

The survey method elicits opinions and attitudes and/or gathers facts from a specific group by means of questionnaires or telephone interviews. A manufacturer may easily be able to survey all of the thirty or fifty wholesalers it deals with, but in many cases it is impossible or impractical to survey all users (consider, for instance, surveying all users of a particular brand of toothpaste or soft drink). In most cases, therefore, researchers sample the total population. A sample is a small group that, ideally, is representative of the larger group. From this sample of the larger group, researchers can forecasts or draw conclusions with some degree of accuracy.

Television and newspaper election polls, for instance, sample voters and use the results of their sample to forecast the outcome of the election.

■ MANAGEMENT INFORMATION AND THE MIS

Data collection produces vast amounts of figures, statistics, and other facts. But not all data—and, as a result, not all information—available to managers are useful, accurate, or relevant.

The Need for Management Information

If managers are to make the best decisions, they must have information that is timely, complete, concise, relevant, and accurate.

- **Timely:** Information must be based on current or recent data.
- **Complete:** *Complete* here does not mean "exhaustive," but instead, that the information is sufficient for making this particular decision without guesswork.
- **Concise:** Although information should be complete, it should be presented concisely in order to be more easily and more quickly understood.
- **Relevant:** Extra information, data above and beyond the presents needs for making the decision, detracts from the decision-making process and should be excluded.
- **Accurate:** The information should have no errors. Inaccurate information provides no foundation for making decisions.

Information that is timely, complete, concise, relevant, and accurate gives managers a significant advantage in making decisions. Information that is vital to decision making is called management information.

The MIS

To transform data into vital information and to use that information to the company's best advantage are responsibilities of the firm's MIS.

The Role of the MIS

The MIS comprises all the tools and procedures that transform data into information that can be used for decision-making at all levels within an organization. For example, the MIS helps track (that is, record) daily sales and provides reports comparing actual daily sales both to (1) actual daily sales in the same time period last year, and (2) estimated (or budgeted) daily sales for this current period. Managers can then compare this information with other reports that track, for example, the cost of goods sold. Together, these sales and cost reports help managers decide whether they should adjust their operations in any way. Without such MIS-generated information, managers would, indeed, be working at a disadvantage.

Today, of course, computers are mandatory parts of any company's MIS. Computers facilitate the handling of financial, accounting, production, sales, and cost data, all of which are vital to the effective operation of a modem business. The significant role that computers play in the MIS is discussed in detail below.

Functions of the MIS

The MIS has four main functions, discussed in the following sections.

Collecting Data

One key MIS function is to collect data. Data, as already discussed, originate from a variety of sources, and computers make it possible to gather data in unique new ways. For example, while bar code scanners allow checkers to total a customer's purchases, at the same time, the scanners track sales and inventory data for the MIS.

Organizing and Storing Data

The MIS organizes data efficiently to make data easily accessible, and stores data in databases. A database is an organized collection of data. A company usually has many databases, for example, a payroll database, an accounts payable database, an inventory database, and a database of customers' names and addresses.

In fact, an ordinary handwritten address book is an example of a simple, manually maintained database. In this case, the data are organized alphabetically by name. If the same address book were stored in a computerized database, the data could be accessed not only by name but also by city, state, and ZIP code.

Of course, today even small companies can afford to computerize their databases. Computerized databases enable users to save (that is, store), view, update, manipulate, and print the data stored.

Processing Data into Information

Once data have been collected, organized, and stored, the data can be processed to make the information useful to management. The data can be printed as the information appears on the computer screen, or the data can be manipulated in a variety of ways. For example, let's assume that a database lists (1) the names and addresses of fifteen hundred retail stores, and for each store, its (2) last purchase (amount, date, and code numbers of products purchased), (3) total dollar purchases for the last twelve-month period, (4) amount currently owed and how long this amount is outstanding, and (5) the sales representative's name or code number. Once this information has been stored in the database, the data can be sorted and manipulated to yield printed reports:

- by store name in alphabetical order
- by date of purchase, either in chronological or in reverse-chronological order
- by quantity of last purchase
- by total annual purchases, either from greatest to least or vice versa
- by ZIP code to show sales by geographic region
- by product-code numbers, showing sales for each product, and/or which stores purchased which products

- by amount owed, either from the largest amount to the smallest or vice versa; and
- by sales representative, showing the dollar amount of sales for each sales representative and/or the products sold by each representative

Further, the data can be summarized in any of several ways as well as calculated for, say, tax or commission purposes. All of this information can be derived from a single database.

Presenting Data

The data, however organized, must be presented in a meaningful and useful form. Information is most often presented in the form of reports and graphs, which often can be tailored to the specific needs of the people who receive the report.

Decision-Support Systems

MIS systems that are specifically designed to support complex decision-making are called decision-support systems. Decision-support systems are often intended for high-level decision-making and long-term planning, as opposed to daily or monthly operational processing or information needs. For example, managers use decision-support systems in investment analysis, cash management, and sales force deployment.

■ STATISTICAL ANALYSIS

Much of the information that management uses is statistical in nature—financial audits and cash flows, percentages and ratios, productivity levels, inventory levels, averages and means, probabilities and risks, increases and decreases, and on and on. To understand the meaning of the numerical data requires statistical analysis.

Statistics

Statistics are figures that summarize and represent factual data and are, therefore, especially meaningful. Statistics include the total quantity of goods sold in a particular period, the number of chocolate bars eaten in one year, a company's return on investment, a baseball player's batting average, and the infant mortality rate in the United States. Many statistics are expressed as percentages, for instance, an inflation rate of 9.5 percent and an unemployment rate of 6.2 percent.

Probability

Probability attempts to measure the likelihood that an event will occur. For instance, in coin tossing the probability of landing on heads as opposed to tails is one in two, or 50 percent. Given this probability, if a coin is tossed one hundred times, the most likely number of heads is fifty.

Probability has a significant impact on everyday business operations. In a given sales group, for example, suppose that out of every ten demonstrations given to qualified customers, sales representatives make four sales. Knowing this probability, the sales manager will be alerted to a problem when a sales representative suddenly makes, say, only one or two sales in ten demonstrations.

Sampling

Collecting and storing data can be expensive. Therefore, researchers often rely upon a representative sample. As already discussed, a sample is a small group that, ideally, is representative of the larger group (called the population). A random sample is a sample in which any person or item in the population has an equal chance of being selected.

Table 17.1: Frequency Distribution Table

Average Weekly Wage of 100 Workers	Frequency
250–275	7
276–300	12
301–325	20
326–350	46
351–375	10
376–400	4

Table 17.2: An Array

Sales (Year)	Product X	Product Q
20X0	100	94
20X1	120	75
20X2	135	105
20X3	128	110

Displaying Statistical Information

However statistical data are collected, statistical information is often easier to communicate graphically rather than by lists of numbers. The types of diagrams most often used to display statistical data are frequency distribution tables, line graphs, bar charts, pie charts, and pictographs.

Frequency Distribution Tables

A frequency distribution is a table in which possible values for a variable are grouped into classes, and the number of times a value falls into each class is recorded. For example, Table 17.1 shows a frequency distribution of the weekly wages of one hundred workers.

A table (sometimes called an array) is a diagram that displays information in columns and rows. It is most often used to show the relationship between two or more related variables. (See Table 17.2.)

Line Graphs

A line graph shows a line connected by dots at various points plotted on a graph. Line graphs are very effective for showing changes in the value of a variable or trend over a period of time. (See Figure 17.1.)

Bar Charts

A bar chart uses either horizontal or vertical bars to measure and compare several values, with the longest bar representing the greatest value. (See Figure 17.2.)

Pie Charts

A pie chart is a circle (a "pie") that has been divided into sections, each section representing (and measuring the value of) a different item. The whole pie represents 100 percent of the value being measured, and each slice represents the percentage of the whole for one particular item.

For example, a pie chart showing the distribution of a college's students by regional area might have one slice for each region of the country, the size of each slice depending on the distribution of students in that particular region. If the college has 20,000 students and one-fourth or 5,000 are from the Northeast,

Daily Sales Information

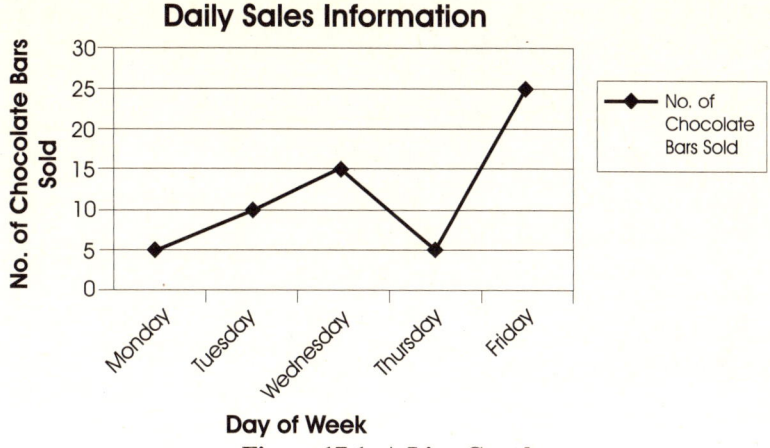

Figure 17.1: A Line Graph

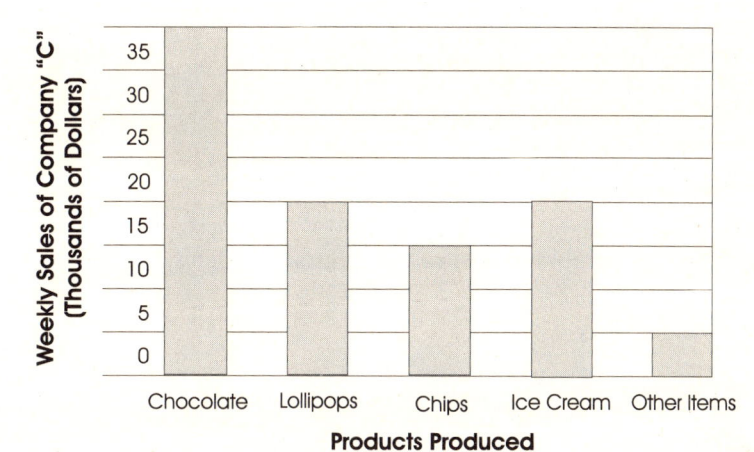

Figure 17.2: A Bar Chart

then the "Northeast slice" would take up one-quarter or 25 percent of the pie. If 2,500 students are from the South, then a smaller slice, representing 12.5 percent of the total, would represent this group. Together, all slices would account for the total of 20,000 students.

Pie charts are particularly effective at underscoring the relative importance of items. (See Figure 17.3.)

Analyzing Statistical Data

An important starting point for analyzing data is to determine some kind of center point or some measure of central tendency. Measures of central tendency describe numbers that are "most representative" of the data. The three most common measures of central tendency are the mean, the median, and the mode.

Mean

The mean, commonly called the average, is the sum of all the items in a group divided by the number of items. Consider the data in Table 17.3. The total sales in a seven-day period was $1,463. To compute mean sales per day, divide $1,463 by 7, to get $209.

Number of Students

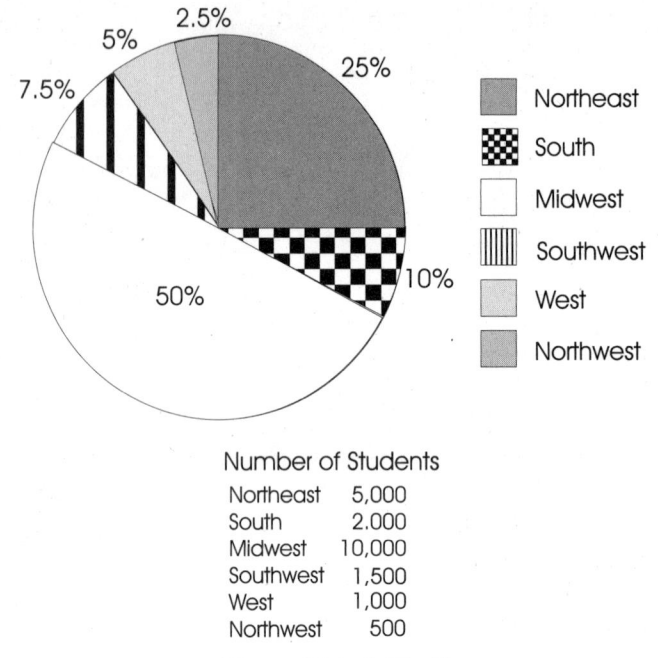

Northeast	5,000
South	2.000
Midwest	10,000
Southwest	1,500
West	1,000
Northwest	500

Figure 17.3: A Pie Chart

The mean is the most reliable measure of central tendency when data are fairly evenly distributed.

Median

When all items in a group are arranged in order from the lowest to the highest, the median is the item in the middle. Thus, half the data will be lower than the median; the other half will be higher. When there are an odd number of items, the median works out perfectly: There will be only one midpoint. When there is an even number of data, the median is the mean of the two middle numbers.

The median is useful when data are not very evenly distributed. In Table 17.3, the median, or midpoint, is $215. (Remember to arrange the numbers from lowest to highest!)

Mode

The mode describes the item or number that occurs most frequently in a group. In Table 17.3, the mode is $270, since it occurs twice. If no item occurs more than once, then there is no mode.

Index Numbers

An index number is a percentage representing the degree of change between a base number in one period (such as cost or price) and the current number in the current period. The Consumer Price Index (CPI), the best known index number, is used in economic forecasts. Published monthly by the U.S. Department of Labor, the CPI compares the current value with the base value of a "market basket" of goods and services purchased by the typical American household. The base value is the value of the same basket of goods and services in a specific base year (currently 1987). Other indexes include the Dow Jones Industrial Average, the Standard and Poor's 500 Index, and the New York Stock Exchange Index.

Table 17.3: Daily Sales

Day	Daily Sales
Monday	$111
Tuesday	$225
Wednesday	$215
Thursday	$170
Friday	$270
Saturday	$270
Sunday	$202

Total = $1,463
Mean = $209
Median = $215
Mode = $270

Time-Series Analysis

Measurements fluctuate from one period of time to another, and managers must often explain such fluctuations. A time-series analysis, also known as a trend analysis, is a useful statistical technique for observing changes in data over time and basing forecasts on those observations.

Time-series analyses are used to forecast sales trends or utility costs. Changes are often explained in terms of three factors: seasonal, cyclical, and secular variations.

Seasonal Variations

Seasonal variations are predictable, repetitive changes closely tied to particular seasons of the year. In summer, for instance, ice cream sales increase; in winter, sales of ice skates and skis increase; in the Christmas season, most retail stores enjoy higher-than-average sales.

Cyclical Variations

Fluctuations that occur over a period of several years or more and that are linked to the business cycle are referred to as cyclical variations. Cyclical variations result from changes in economic activity—for example, a change from economic prosperity and growth to recession and high unemployment.

Secular Variations

A consistent pattern of growth or decline in a particular industry or economy over a long period of time is known as a secular variation. An example of a secular trend is the steady growth in the number of DVD players over the past seven years.

Correlation Analysis

Correlation analysis is a statistical technique that measures the relationship between two or more variables. Variables are the factors that change in a situation. Correlation analysis helps managers predict fluctuations in one variable when the levels of change in another variable are known. Variables in which the changes are already known or have been controlled are independent variables. Variables that change in response are dependent variables (that is, their change is dependent on the fluctuations of another, different variable).

Correlations are identified as being either positive or negative.

Positive Correlations

A positive correlation exists when an increase in one variable is linked with an increase in another variable. For example, an increase in movie attendance accompanied by an increase in popcorn sales shows a positive correlation between the two variables. Similarly, a decrease in movie attendance and a decrease in popcorn sales shows a positive correlation because both variables are changing in the same direction.

Negative Correlations

A negative correlation exists when an increase in one variable is accompanied by a decrease in a second variable—that is, when variables change in opposite directions. For example, the value of a car decreases as it gets older, showing a negative correlation between its value and its age.

Selected Readings

Cassidy, Anita. *A Practical Guide to Information Systems Strategic Planning.* 1998.

Freund, John, and Frank J. Williams. *Modern Elementary Statistics.* 1988.

Gallagher, Charles A., and Hugh J. Watson. *Quantitative Methods for Business Decisions.* 1980.

Garrity, Edward, and G. Lawrence Sanders. *Information Systems Success Measurement.* 1998.

Kazmier, Leonard J. *Schaum's Outline of Theory and Problems of Business Statistics.* 1988.

Kendall, M. G., and W. R. Buckland. *A Dictionary of Statistical Terms.* 1986.

Kovacich, Gerald. *The Information Systems Security Officer's Guide: Establishing and Managing an Information Systems.* 2003.

Landon, Kenneth C., and Jane P. Landon. *Management Information Systems: A Contemporary Perspective.* 1991.

Larsen, Tor, and Eugene McGuire. *Information Systems Innovation and Diffusion: Issues and Directions.* 1998.

Liebowitz, Jay. *Introduction to Expert Systems.* 1988.

Lucas, Amy and Kathleen Young Marcaccio, editors. *Encyclopedia of Information Systems and Services,* three volumes. 1987.

Lucas, Henry C., Jr. *Information Systems Concepts for Management.* 1990.

Morgan, Tony. *Business Rules and Information Systems: Aligning It with Business Goals.* 2002.

Murray, John P. *Managing Information Systems as a Corporate Resource.* 1984.

Strassman, Paul A. *Information Payoff.* 1985.

Triola, Mario F. *Elementary Statistics,* Ninth Edition. 2003.

Umbaugh, Robert. *Handbook of MIS Management.* 1988.

U.S. Department of Commerce, Bureau of the Census. *Statistical Abstract of the United States.* Annual publication.

U.S. Department of Commerce, Bureau of Economic Statistics. *The Handbook of Basic Economic Statistics.* Annual, with monthly supplements.

Von Neuman, John, and Oskar Morgenstern. *Theory of Games and Economic Behavior.* 1980.

Zuboff, Shosmana. *In the Age of the Smart Machine: The Future of Work and Power.* 1988.

Test Yourself

1) Distinguish between data and information.
2) What are the basic kinds of data?
3) What are the basic methods of data collection?
4) What are the prerequisites of information if it is to be useful for management decision-making?
5) What is a management information systems (MIS) and what is its major purpose?
6) What are the four major functions of the MIS?
7) What is sampling and why is it important?
8) What are some of the ways in which statistical information can be effectively displayed?
9) List and describe the three measures of central tendency described in the chapter.
10) What is time-series analysis and when is it most useful?

Test Yourself Answers

1) Data are raw facts and figures; that is, the raw materials of information. Information, on the other hand, is data properly collected, sorted, organized, and presented in a meaningful form—a form that management can use to make decisions.

2) Internal data are available from the company's records. External data originate from sources outside the company. Primary data describes data gathered through original research by the company itself. Secondary data originate not from the company, but instead, comes from other sources.

3) The basic methods of data collection are observation, experimentation, and survey.

4) To be useful for decision-making, information must be timely, complete, concise, relevant, and accurate.

5) The MIS comprises all the tools and procedures that transform data into information that can be used for decision-making at all levels within an organization.

6) The MIS must collect data, organize and store the data efficiently, process the data into information, and then present it in ways that are useful to management.

7) A sample is a small group that, ideally, represents the larger group of which it is a part. Examining all the data would be very expensive; sampling makes it much more cost-effective to analyze the data.

8) Statistics may be presented in the following ways: frequency distributions tables, line graphs, bar charts, pie charts, and pictographs.

9) The mean (or average) is the sum of all the items in a group divided by the number of items; it is the most reliable measure of central tendency when data are normally distributed. The median is the middle item in a group when all the items are arranged from the lowest to the highest value; the median is most useful when items are not normally distributed. The mode describes the item or number that occurs most frequently in a group.

10) Time-series analysis, or trend analysis, is useful for observing changes in data over time, and then basing forecasts (predictions) on those observations.

CHAPTER 18
Accounting and Financial Statements

Accounting is a management tool used in the control function of management. More specifically, accounting is the systematic collecting, analyzing, classifying, recording, summarizing, reporting, and interpreting of business transactions. Bookkeeping is routine recordkeeping, a necessary part of accounting and producing financial information.

■ THE ROLE OF ACCOUNTING IN BUSINESS

In the accounting process, the input is raw data and the output is financial statements. Financial statements are essential for management because they provide information needed to make day-to-day business decisions. Managerial accounting is concerned with providing information to be used within the firm. Financial accounting is concerned with reporting to outside users such as stockholders, potential investors, the government, or lenders.

Accounting procedures and reports are highly standardized and are regulated by the Securities and Exchange Commission (SEC), the American Institute of Certified Public Accountants (AICPA), and the Financial Accounting Standards Board (FASB).

■ THE ROLE OF ACCOUNTANTS

Accountants are classified as either private or public accountants.

Private Accountants

Private accountants are employed by a specific organization and provide services only to that organization's management. Specifically, they provide management with advice and assistance, and they prepare reports required by management or by law.

Public Accountants

Public accountants may be hired by the general public, individuals, or firms that require their services. Public accountants may be self-employed, or they may work for an accounting firm. Accounting firms range in size from one person to thousands of employees. They may service the local community or they may operate internationally. Most accounting firms include at least one certified public accountant.

Certified Public Accountants (CPAs)

Certified public accountants are those who have met state education and experience requirements and have passed a rigorous accounting examination. Certification brings both status and responsibility. Only a CPA, for example, can officially verify the contents of a corporation's annual report and express an opinion (as required by law) concerning the acceptability of the corporation's accounting practices.

■ USERS OF FINANCIAL INFORMATION

The primary purpose of financial information is, of course, to inform people both inside and outside the organization. The primary users are managers. In addition to the company's managers, other users include government taxing agencies and regulatory agencies, stockholders and potential stockholders, and suppliers and lenders.

Managers

Finances affect every company decision. Managers need financial information concerning sales revenues, costs, and accounts receivable to make decisions about pricing, resource allocation, investment in plant or equipment, and a wide range of other decisions. Much of this information is proprietary; that is, restricted to use within the firm, and therefore, not disclosed to outsiders.

Government Taxing Agencies

Government taxing agencies, including the Internal Revenue Service (IRS) and city and state taxing agencies, require businesses and individuals to substantiate their income for the purpose of confirming tax liabilities.

Government Regulatory Agencies

Government regulatory agencies such as the Securities and Exchange Commission (SEC) require public corporations to file detailed quarterly reports of income. In addition, each state has its own securities regulation agency that requires public companies to file similar data.

Stockholders

By law, a company must supply stockholders with a summary of the firm's position, and firms comply by providing an annual report. Stockholders analyze the information provided in the annual report to make a number of decisions about the firm, for example, investment decisions and voting decisions concerning company management.

Potential Stockholders

Potential stockholders use financial information to evaluate the present financial position of the company, make decisions about the company's future potential, determine the likely return for their investments, evaluate the risks involved, and so on.

Suppliers and Lenders

Before they extend credit or approve loans, suppliers and lenders require financial statements from the company. They use financial statements to determine whether a company is credit worthy.

■ THE ACCOUNTING PROCESS

The accounting process transforms raw financial data into useful reports. The process requires three distinct steps: capturing the data, processing the data, and communicating the results in the form of financial statements. The financial statements, in turn, provide information on sales revenues, costs, money payable and money receivable, and other financial data.

Central to understanding the accounting process are the accounting equation, double-entry bookkeeping, and the accounting cycle.

The Accounting Equation

The accounting equation forms the basis for the accounting process:

$$\text{Assets} = \text{Liabilities} + \text{Owners' equity}$$

This equation shows the relationship of assets, liabilities, and owners' equity.

- **Assets** are things of value owned by the firm. Assets include cash, land, inventories, equipment, and other items of value, including goodwill—that is, the firm's reputation.
- **Liabilities** are the firm's debts and obligations, what the firm owes to others.
- **Owners' equity** is the difference between assets and liabilities; that is, the amount that would remain for the firm's owners if the assets were used to pay off the liabilities.

Double-Entry Bookkeeping

Double-entry bookkeeping describes a system in which each financial transaction is recorded as two separate accounting entries in order to maintain the balance of the accounting equation. A loan, for example, is entered as follows: The cash received is recorded as an asset, and the loan itself (that is, the outstanding debt) is recorded as a liability. Only by making both entries can the equation be kept in balance.

The Accounting Cycle

The typical accounting system uses five steps, collectively known as the accounting cycle, to transform raw data into financial statements.

Analyzing Source Documents

Basic accounting data originates from receipts, invoices, sales slips, order forms, and other records or source documents of business transactions. Transactions must be analyzed to identify how they are to be entered into accounting journals and ledgers.

Entering Transactions in the General Journal

Each transaction is first recorded in a general journal by date; that is, in the order that transactions occur. The journal, therefore, offers a chronological list of all original transactions.

Posting Transactions to the General Ledger

Entries in the general journal are made chronologically. These entries are then copied or posted to the general ledger not by date, but according to categories or accounts.

The general ledger is a book of accounts; it has separate pages or sections for each income account (such as sales) and for each expense account (such as telephone, rent, or supplies).

Determining a Trial Balance

A trial balance is the summary of the balances of all the general ledger accounts at the end of the accounting period. If the totals are correct, the accountant can prepare financial statements, the final step.

Preparing Financial Statements

The firm's financial statements are prepared from the information contained in the trial balance. Financial statements are organized and presented in a standardized format designed to make the information accessible to all interested parties. Financial statements comply with regulations and standards set by the FASB: generally accepted accounting principles.

■ FINANCIAL STATEMENTS

Financial statements are periodic summarizations of a business's transactions. The most important financial statements are the balance sheet, income statement, and statement of cash flows (also called the cash flow statement).

Balance Sheet

In the accounting equation, assets are listed on the left side of the equal sign; liabilities and owner's equity are listed on the right side (see Figure 18.1). Both sides must be equal—that is, they must balance. The balance sheet, as its name suggests, shows a summary of all accounts and reflects that the total of assets equals the total of all liabilities and owners' equity. The balance sheet shows the financial position of the firm on a specific date.

Assets

Assets are listed on the balance sheet according to their liquidity, the most liquid first. Liquidity measures the ease with which an asset can be converted to cash. Land and inventories are both assets, but inventories are more liquid because inventories can be sold much more quickly than land can be sold and converted to cash.

Assets are described as current, fixed, or intangible.

Current Assets

Current assets are cash and other assets that can be quickly converted to cash, or assets that will be used in one year. Cash is the most liquid asset, followed by marketable securities (investments in stocks or bonds) that can be readily sold. Next in order of liquidity is accounts receivable, money due to the firm within thirty to ninety days from customers, followed by any reserve allowance for doubtful accounts. Current inventory of merchandise that is expected to be sold within the year is the next asset listed, and finally prepaid expenses, assets that have been paid for in advance, but not yet used, such as the balance of the year's insurance premiums.

Fixed Assets

Fixed assets are assets that will be held or used longer than one year. Typically, fixed assets include land, buildings, and equipment. Because the value of many fixed assets decreases each year, this devaluation is accounted for through depreciation, a method of distributing the cost of fixed assets over a period of years. For each fixed asset, the amount depreciated is treated as an expense for that year and is subtracted from the value of that fixed asset.

Intangible Assets

Not all assets are tangible. Intangible assets such as patents, copyrights, franchises, trademarks, and goodwill have a financial value because they offer legal rights, advantages, or privileges.

GOOLD CORPORATION
Balance Sheet
December 31, 20__

ASSETS

Current assets
Cash		$118,000	
Marketable securities		20,000	
Accounts receivable	$80,000		
Less allowance for bad debts	4,000	76,000	
Notes receivable		64,000	
Merchandise inventory		82,000	
Prepaid expenses		4,000	
Total current assets			$364,000
Fixed assets			
Delivery equipment	$220,000		
Less depreciation	40,000	$180,000	
Furniture and equipment	124,000		
Less depreciation	30,000	94,000	
Total fix assets			$274,000
Intangible assets			
Patents		$12,000	
Goodwill		30,000	42,000
Total assets			$680.000

LIABILITIES AND OWNERS' EQUITY

Current liabilities
Cash		$118,000	
Accounts payable	$70,000		
Notes payable	50,000		
Salaries payable	8,000		
Taxes payable	12,000		
Total current liabilities		$140,000	
Long-term liabilities			
Mortgage payable	$80,000		
Total long-term liabilities		80,000	
Total liabilities			$220,000
Owners' equity			
Common stock: 20,000 shares at $15 Par Value		$300,000	
Retained earnings		160,000	
Total owners' equity			460,000
Total liabilities and owners' equity			$680,000

Figure 18.1: Balance Sheet

Liabilities
Liabilities are grouped into current and long-term liabilities.

Current Liabilities
Current liabilities are debts that will be paid within one year. On the balance sheet, current liabilities are listed in order from shorter-term to longer-term liabilities. Accounts payable are short-term obligations incurred in making credit purchases. Notes payable, taxes payable, debts secured by promissory notes, and other obligations due within the year are also considered current liabilities.

Long-Term Liabilities
Long-term liabilities are debts that will come due in one year or more. Mortgage payable (for property or equipment, for instance) is the most common long-term liability. Bonds and other long-term loans are listed under long-term liabilities.

Owners' Equity
Owners' equity can appear on the balance sheet in different ways, depending on the legal form of the business. If the business is a sole proprietorship owned, for example, by William Smith, owners' equity is listed as "William Smith, capital." In a corporation, owners' equity is identified as "stockholders' equity." Stockholders' equity contains two listings:

- **Capital stock** includes the amount the stockholders invested in the company, and
- **Retained earnings** represents the increase in stock-holders' equity that results from profitable operations.

Income Statement
An income statement, also called a profit-and-loss (P&L) statement, is a summary of revenues and expenses for a certain period of time—say, one month, one quarter, or one year (see Figure 18.2). An income statement covering the previous year must be included in a corporation's annual report.

Just as there is an equation for the balance sheet, there is one for the income statement:

$$\text{Revenues} - \text{Expenses} = \text{Net income (or Net loss)}$$

Net income is also referred to as profit.

Revenues
Revenues, also called gross sales, are all receipts from customers' purchases, the money received for goods and services sold. Goods returned, sales allowances, and sales discounts are deducted from gross sales to yield net sales, the actual dollar amount received.

Companies may record their revenues (as well as their costs) on either an accrual or a cash basis. However, those companies reporting in accordance with Securities and Exchange Commission rules must use accrual accounting.

Accrual Basis Accounting
An accrual basis records revenues and costs in the year in which the sale is made, whether or not payment is received in that year.

Cash Basis Accounting
A cash basis records revenues and costs in the year in which the payment is received.

Revenues received from the company's main business are listed separately from other revenues (for example, rent paid to the company, interest received from banks, or dividends received from securities).

GOOLD CORPORATION
Income Statement
For the Year Ended December 31, 20__

Revenues			
Gross sales		$930,000	
Less sales returns and allowances	$19,000		
Less sales discounts	9,000	28,000	
Net sales			$902,000
Cost of goods sold			
Beginning inventory, Jan. 1, 20__		$80,000	
Purchases	$692,000		
Less purchase discounts	22,000		
Net purchases		$670,000	
Cost of goods available for sale		$750,000	
Less ending inventory, Dec. 31, 20_		82,000	
Cost of goods sold			$668,000
Gross profit on sales			$234,000
Operation expenses			
Selling expenses			
Sales salaries	$60,000		
Advertising	12,000		
Sales promotion	5,000		
Depreciation—store equipment	6,000		
Miscellaneous selling expenses	3,000		
Total selling expenses		$86,000	
General expenses	$37,000		
Office salaries			
Rent	17,000		
Depreciation—Delivery equipment	8,000		
Depreciation—Office equipment	3,000		
Utilities expense	5,000		
Insurance expense	2,000		
Miscellaneous expense	1,000		
Total general expense		$73,000	
Total operating expense			$159,000
Net income from operations			$75,000
Less interest expense			4,000
Net income before taxes			$71,000
Less federal income taxes			10,650
Net income after taxes			
			$60,350

Figure 18.2: Income Statement

Expenses

Expenses fall into two general categories: cost of goods sold and operating expenses.

Cost of Goods Sold

Cost of goods sold is computed according to this formula:

Cost of goods sold = Beginning inventory + Net purchases − Ending inventory

For a manufacturing firm, the calculation of cost of goods sold includes a determination of raw materials inventory, work in progress inventory, direct manufacturing costs, and manufacturing overhead.

Raw Materials Inventory

Raw materials inventory includes the cost of lumber, steel, and other raw materials used to manufacture products.

Work in Progress Inventory

Work in progress inventory highlights the cost of materials for all unfinished products now in some stage of the manufacturing process but not yet completed.

Direct Manufacturing Costs

Direct manufacturing costs include materials costs and labor costs that can be traced directly to the product. If this product were not produced the direct manufacturing costs would not be incurred.

Manufacturing Overhead (Indirect Manufacturing Costs)

Manufacturing overhead includes all those costs of producing the product that cannot be traced directly to the product, either because they are incurred, at least in some measure, irrespective of whether the product is produced or because the difficulty of tracing them directly to the product is too difficult.

Determining Inventory Costs

Inventories can be valued by any one of four methods.

- The **specific-identification method** assigns an actual dollar cost to each item.
- The **average-cost method** assumes that the cost for each inventory item is the same, and therefore, assigns an average cost to each item.
- The **first-in, first-out (FIFO) method** assigns the costs of the first item inventoried to be the first item sold.
- The **last-in, first-out (LIFO) method** assigns the cost of the most recent or last inventoried item to the first item sold.

Each system of valuation makes different assumptions. Although all four systems are acceptable, each valuation system affects the balance sheet, income, and taxes differently. Companies must choose from among these systems carefully.

Operating Expenses

Operating expenses includes all other costs beyond costs of goods sold. Two broad categories of operating expenses are selling expenses and general expenses.

Selling Expenses

Selling expenses include all costs related to the firm's marketing activities, for example, salaries of sales representatives and advertising and promotion expenses.

General Expenses

General expenses, sometimes called administrative expenses or overhead, are general costs incurred in running a business, as opposed to costs specifically and directly associated with a particular item or service sold. General expenses include salaries of office workers and all the expenses of operating an office (rent, the cost of office supplies, electricity, insurance, equipment) and other miscellaneous expenses (charitable donations and contributions, for example).

Net Income before Taxes (NIBT)

Net income before taxes (NIBT) or net operating income (NOI) is the profit earned (or the loss suffered) by a firm during the accounting period. All expenses except tax expense have been deducted from net income before taxes.

Net income after taxes is derived by deducting tax expense. Since this figure appears at the end (or bottom) of the statement, net income after taxes is sometimes referred to as the bottom line.

Statement of Cash Flows

The Securities and Exchange Commission requires all public corporations to issue a statement of cash flows (funds flow) (see Figure 18.3). This statement describes the company's cash receipts (money coming into the firm) and cash payments (money going out of the firm) for a specific period. It provides a detailed picture of the company's ability to generate and use cash.

The cash flows statement is concerned only with actual cash, while the income statement also includes noncash items such as depreciation expenses and income earned but not yet received.

The cash flows statement summarizes three areas in which cash is received and disbursed: operations, investing, and financing.

Cash Flows from Operations

Cash flow from operations shows cash generated by and expended for the buying and selling of goods and services as part of the firm's main operating activities. It also includes the effect of inventory changes, accounts receivable, and accounts payable on cash flows.

Cash Flows from Investing Activities

Investing activities reflects cash income from—and payments for—buying and selling securities, property, or equipment.

Cash Flows from Financing Activities

Financing activities includes cash flows from borrowing and from issuing stock as well as from repaying loans and paying dividends.

■ ANALYZING FINANCIAL STATEMENTS

On the surface, the information offered in balance sheets and income statements help answer a variety of questions about a firm's ability to do business, its profitability, or its value as an investment. Just

GOOLD CORPORATION
Statement of Cash Flow
Year Ended December 31, 200_

Cash flows from operations		
Net Income		$75,000
Adjustments		
Depreciation	$6,000	
Inventory increase	(2,000)	
Accounts receivable decrease	1,000	
Accounts payable increase	1,000	
Total adjustments		$6,000
Net cash provided by operations		$81,000
Cash flows from investing		
Payments for purchase of equipment	(15,000)	
Net cash used in investing		(15,000)
Cash flows from financing		
Proceeds from long-term note	10,000	
Net cash provided by financing		10,000
Net increase in cash		$76,000
Cash at beginning of year		42,000
Cash at end of year		$118,000

Figure 18.3: Cash Flow Statement.

beneath the surface of these statements lies a wealth of information that can be easily uncovered by computing certain financial ratios.

Financial Ratios

A financial ratio shows the relationship between two elements of a balance sheet or income statement. Financial ratios offer keen insights into a firm's present health and its future potential. Like baseball statistics, ratios are most useful in comparisons. For example, comparing the same ratio for the same company for several consecutive years may uncover a trend, a weakness, or a strength in that company. Comparing a specific ratio for two companies in the same industry may show why Company A is stronger or weaker than Company B.

The most common and most useful financial ratios are explained in the following sections.

Liquidity Ratios

Liquidity ratios indicate a firm's solvency and its ability to meet its short-term liabilities. Liquidity ratios are especially meaningful to short-term lenders.

Working Capital

Working capital is the difference between current assets and current liabilities:

$$\text{Working capital} = \text{Current assets} - \text{Current liabilities}$$

Working capital indicates how much liquidity would remain if a firm immediately paid off all its current liabilities.

Current Ratio

The current ratio, one of the most commonly used measures of liquidity, is found by dividing current assets by current liabilities:

$$\text{Current ratio} = \text{Current assets/Current liabilities}$$

Acid-Test Ratio

The acid-test ratio, also called the quick ratio, is very similar to the current ratio. The acid-test ratio is calculated by dividing quick assets by current liabilities:

$$\text{Acid-test ratio} = \text{Quick assets/Current liabilities}$$

Unlike current assets, quick assets do not include either inventories or prepaid expenses, because these are not immediately liquid. Quick assets includes cash and only those current assets that can be readily converted to cash—namely, marketable securities, accounts receivable, and notes receivable.

Debt Ratios

Debt ratios indicate the extent to which the firm's operations are financed through borrowing. Debt ratios are, therefore, of special interest to long-term lenders and investors.

Debt-to-Assets Ratio

The debt-to-assets ratio indicates the extent to which the firm's borrowing is backed by its assets. It is calculated by dividing total liabilities by total assets:

$$\text{Debt-to-assets ratio} = \text{Total liabilities/Total assets}$$

Debt-to-Equity Ratio

The debt-to-equity ratio compares the amount of equity supplied by creditors with the amount of equity furnished by the owners. It is found by dividing total liabilities by owners' equity:

$$\text{Debt-to-equity ratio} = \text{Total liabilities/Owners' equity}$$

Profitability Ratios

Profitability ratios indicate how effectively the firm's resources are being used.

Net Profit Margin

Net profit margin indicates how effectively the firm is transforming sales into profits:

$$\text{Net profit margin} = \text{Net income after taxes/Net sales}$$

Return on Equity

Return on equity, also called return on investment, indicates how much income is generated by each dollar of equity:

$$\text{Return on equity} = \text{Net income after taxes/Owners' equity}$$

Earnings Per Share

Earnings-per-share, a widely used indicator of a corporation's success, is calculated by dividing net profit after taxes by the number of shares outstanding:

$$\text{Earnings per share} = \text{Net profit after taxes}/\text{Number of shares outstanding}$$

■ BUDGETING AND PLANNING

Budgeting and planning are important aspects of managing and leading an organization. Budgeting is the process of translating decisions into specific projected financial plans for both short-term and long-term periods. It focuses on projected accomplishments and estimates the resources necessary to attain those accomplishments.

Budgets

While financial statements capture a view of the past, budgets look forward to the future. Budgets are financial plans for a specific future period, usually one year. Managers use budgets to guide them in their day-to-day operations, and investors use budgets to evaluate future plans and future potential. The master budget includes several individual budgets that, together, summarize planned financial activities.

Operating Budgets

An operating budget addresses a specific area of day-to-day business activities—that is, addresses a specific area of operations. Together, operating budgets of all operating divisions or groups make up an overall financial plan. An operating budget is typically developed for areas such as sales, production, and operating expenses.

Sales Budgets

The sales budget projects sales income and sales expenses for all items listed in the income statement (that is, for all sales items that will generate income). The production budget and the operating expense budget will pick up the sales estimates used in the sales budget. As a result, these budgets are interdependent. When combined, these budgets comprise the budgeted income statement that gives the firm the total budget picture for a given period. Like all budgets, if it is not satisfactory to management, it may need to be revised.

Cash Budgets

The cash budget is a plan that shows cash receipts and cash payments for a given period. The cash budget shows not only how much, but also when cash is anticipated to be coming in and going out of the firm. Thus, the cash budget is an important tool for projecting borrowing needs. The cash budget is the last budget prepared.

Capital-Expenditure Budgets

While operating budgets are concerned with the purchase of current assets, capital-expenditure budgets detail a company's long-term plans for investments in long-term assets, such as property and equipment. Capital-expenditure budgets often involve large sums and reflect key management decisions.

The Budgeting Process

Approaches to budgeting are traditional and zero-based budgeting.

Traditional Budgeting

Traditional budgeting uses as its base the dollar amounts in the preceding year's budget. Managers modify the individual items to reflect increased costs, revised goals, and so on, and they provide justifications for any new expenditures. As a result, traditional budgeting often overlooks outdated or wasteful programs.

Zero-Based Budgeting

Instead of using the preceding year's budget as a base, zero-based budgeting starts without a base, requiring managers to justify all expenses, in every budget, in every year. Zero-based budgeting often reduces unnecessary spending, but it requires additional time-consuming paperwork.

Planning

A company's plan is an outline of a firm's intended future actions needed to accomplish its goals.

Long-Range Plans

A long-range plan covers actions over a two- to five-year period, and sometimes longer. Alternatively, a long-range plan may be made up of a series of one-year plans.

Short-Range Plans

A short-range plan covers one year or less and tends to be more specific than a long-range plan. As conditions change, the short-range plan will update, modify, and adapt the long-range plan.

Selected Readings

Anthony, Robert N. *Essentials of Accounting.* 2006.
Dixon, Robert. *The McGraw-Hill 36-Hour Accounting Course.* 1990.
Eisen, Peter. *Accounting.* 2000.
Estes, Ralph. *Dictionary of Accounting.* 1984.
Fields, Edward. *The Essentials of Finance and Accounting for Nonfinancial Managers.* 2002.
Flesor, C. N., editor. *How to Read a Financial Report.* 1985.
Graham, Benjamin, and Charles McGolrick. *The Interpretation of Financial Statements.* 1987.
Kieso, Donald D., Jerry J. Weygandt, and Terry D. Warfield. *Intermediate Accounting.* 2005.
Morse, Wayne J., James R. Davis, and Al L. Hartgraves. *Management Accounting.* 1990.
Pinson, Linda. *Keeping the Books: Basic Record Keeping and Accounting for the Successful Small Business.* 2004.
Porter, Gary A., and Curtis L. Norton. *Financial Accounting: The Impact on Decision Makers.* 2003.
Simini, Joseph P. *Balance Sheets for Non-Finance Managers.* 1990.
Solomon, Lanny M., Larry M. Walther, and Richard J. Vargo. *Financial Accounting.* 1991.
Spurga, Ronald C. *Balance Sheet Basics.* 1987.
Stickney, Clyde P. *Financial Statement Analysis: A Strategic Perspective.* 1990.
Tracy, John A. *How to Read a Financial Report.* 1989.
Wildaysky, A. *The Politics of the Budgetary Process.* 1984.
Note: See also publications by the American Institute of Certified Public Accountants (AICPA).

Test Yourself

1) What are the two basic types of accountants and their roles?

2) What is a certified public accountant?

3) Who are the major users of financial statements?

4) What is the basic accounting equation?

5) Describe the components of the accounting cycle.

6) Financial statements are periodic summarizations of business transactions. What are the three most important financial statements?

7) What is the major difference between the income statement and the statement of cash flows?

8) What is a financial ratio and what are the most commonly used?

9) How do budgets differ from the balance sheet, income statement, and statement of cash flows?

10) What are the two basic types of budgeting approaches?

Test Yourself Answers

1) The private accountant is employed by one organization and provides accounting services only for that organization. The public accountant, on the other hand, provides services for the general public, individuals or firms that require the service. A public accountant may be self-employed or work for an accounting firm that performs accounting services for the public.

2) A certified public accountant (CPA) is one who has met state education and experience requirements, and has passed a rigorous qualifying examination. Only a CPA can officially audit the contents of certain corporate financial statements and express an opinion (as required by law) concerning the fairness of those financial statements.

3) Managers of companies use the financial statements to make day-to-day operating decisions. Government taxing agencies use financial statements to determine taxable income, for example (e.g., Internal Revenue Service). The Securities and Exchange Commission, a governmental regulatory agency, requires the production of financial statements for the public. Suppliers and lenders utilize financial statements to assess the credit worthiness of companies. Stockholders and potential stockholders require financial statements so that they can know and assess the financial condition of the company, for purposes of determining whether to invest or to hold the company's stock.

4) Assets = Liabilities + Owners' equity.

5) The accounting cycle includes the following steps: analyzing source documents, entering transactions in the general journal, posting transactions in the general ledger, determining a trial balance, and preparing the financial statements.

6) The most important statements are the balance sheet, the income statement, and the statement of cash flows.

7) The income statement includes noncash items, such as depreciation expense, income earned but not yet received, and expenses incurred but not yet paid. The statement of cash flows, on the other hand, includes only the cash effects of the year's business transactions.

8) A financial ratio shows the relationship between two elements of a balance sheet or income statement. Financial ratios can offer keen insights about a company, especially in comparison with the company's ratios over time or with the ratios of competitors or with the industry norms. The most commonly used financial ratios are liquidity ratios (e.g., working capital, current ratio, and acid test ratio), debt ratios (e.g., debt-to-assets and debt-to-equity ratios), and profitability ratios (e.g., net profit margin, return on equity, and earnings per share).

9) The traditional financial statements (balance sheet, income statement, and statement of cash flows) focus on past transactions, while budgets represent looks forward (i.e., plans for revenues and expenditures).

10) Traditional budgeting uses as its base the dollar amounts used in the preceding year's budget, which means that management must only justify the changes. Zero-based budgeting, on the other hand, begins each budget year with zeros as beginning balances, which means that every dollar of the new budget must be justified by management.

Part 6: Financial Management

CHAPTER 19

Money, Banking, and Credit

Money, banking, and credit are human contrivances that have evolved over the years. These contrivances are critical to contemporary commerce because they trump "barter" by bridging the gap between human wants/needs and resources by providing virtually universally acceptable mediums of exchange.

■ MONEY

Money is defined as anything used by a society to purchase goods, services, or resources. Today, most countries use metal coins and paper bills, but items as varied as gold and silver, beads, and clam shells have been used as money.

Functions of Money

Money is used to purchase—that is, used in exchange for—goods, services, or resources. The power to purchase, or exchange, is the basis of money's three principal functions, described in the following sections.

Medium of Exchange

A medium of exchange is anything accepted as payment. The key word is *accepted*. At one time, barter, the trading of goods for other goods, was acceptable. Money permits selling (rather than trading) goods and using the money received in exchange for desired goods. As long as sellers are willing to accept money from buyers, this medium-of-exchange function is being fulfilled.

Measure of Value

Because the value of all products and resources are stated in terms of money, money provides the means to compare value. Money serves as the standard for the measure of value.

Store of Value

Money does not need to be spent immediately; instead, money can be saved and spent later. Thus, the value of money can be stored, and storing value allows wealth to be accumulated.

This stored value is not constant, however. The value of money fluctuates with the economy, losing value in periods of inflation and gaining value in periods of deflation.

Characteristics of Money

Money must meet certain criteria in order to be acceptable. First, money must be trusted. Also, money must be convenient to use. For example, when the U.S. Treasury issued the Susan B. Anthony silver dollar coin, the public trusted the coin but found it inconvenient. As a result, this particular coin was never widely circulated.

The five important characteristics of money are portability, divisibility, stability, durability, and authenticity.

Portability

Money must be portable—small enough and light enough to be carried easily. Paper money is easier to carry in large amounts if it is available in denominations of one, five, ten, twenty, fifty, and one-hundred dollars.

Divisibility

Money must be divisible into smaller units to permit purchases of less than one dollar and purchases in odd amounts over one dollar. To make such purchases possible, coins in fractions of one dollar—pennies, nickels, dimes, quarters, halves—are circulated.

Stability

Money should be stable—that is, it should retain its value over time. In periods of very high inflation, people may tend to lose faith in their money; as a result, they may try to store value in assets such as gold, jewels, or real estate.

Durability

Whether it is in coin or paper form, money should be durable enough to withstand reasonable usage without disintegrating.

Authenticity

Part of the trust people feel in their money lies in the difficulty of counterfeiting money. If currency were easy to counterfeit, even authentic or genuine currency would lose value.

Types of Money

Money exists in several different forms, which are discussed below.

Currency

Currency comprises not only all paper money and coins issued by the government, but also money orders, travelers' checks, personal checks, and bank checks or cashier checks, issued by banks against secure bank funds. All these forms of currency are acceptable for payments.

A check is a written order to a bank or other financial institution to pay a stated amount to the person indicated on the face of the check.

Demand Deposits

Demand deposits are funds that are deposited in banks and that can be withdrawn at any time by writing personal checks against the funds.

Other Checkable Deposits

There are a number of other checkable deposits, deposits against which checks can be drawn. NOW (negotiable order of withdrawal) accounts function like demand deposits but pay interest, provided users maintain a minimum balance.

Time Deposits

Time deposits, such as certificates of deposit (CDs) and money-market certificates, are savings accounts that require notice prior to withdrawal. Checks cannot be written against time deposits. Although the funds are not readily available, as demand deposits are, time deposits earn a higher rate of interest.

Money-Market Funds

Money-market funds pool the funds of many individual investors. The funds are used to buy short-term, low-risk financial securities in large denominations—for example, 90- or 120-day notes from large secure banks or from the U.S. Treasury.

Savings Accounts

Savings accounts are traditional time-deposit passbook accounts. Savings accounts have declined in recent years because of the greater flexibility offered by NOW accounts and the higher interest paid by money-market accounts.

Plastic Money

Plastic money, credit-card or debit (check) card purchasing, has become a major factor in purchasing goods and services. Although credit cards serve as a substitute for money, they are, as their name implies, really an extension of credit, not money. More recently, debit cards have become popular. They are not extensions of credit. Instead, modern technology allows access directly to amounts on deposit at financial institutions.

Money Supply

The overall supply of money helps determine its value. If there is too much money in circulation, its value or purchasing power drops, leading to inflation. However, it is difficult to measure the amount of money in circulation.

Three specific measurements of the money supply—M-1, M-2, and M-3—are discussed on the following page.

M-1

M-1 is a measure of money supply that includes only the most liquid forms of money. M-1 measures currency, demand deposits, and other deposits against which checks can be drawn.

M-2

M-2 includes M-1 plus other types of money that can be easily converted to spendable forms, namely, time deposits, money-market funds, and savings deposits.

M-3

M-3 includes M-2 plus time deposits over $100,000 plus short-term repurchase agreements. On November 10, 2005, the Board of Governors of the Federal Reserve System decided to cease publishing the M3 monetary aggregate. It decided that it does not provide sufficiently appreciable information than M-2.

■ THE AMERICAN BANKING SYSTEM

Merchants, rather than banks, were the sources of money and credit in early American history. After independence, however, the Bank of North America was established (1781). By 1789 three commercial banks existed, the Bank of North America, and two state banks, those of Massachusetts and New York. The primary function of a commercial bank is to make short-term loans, by either issuing its own bank notes or by creating deposits in the names of borrowers (i.e., opening an account to the person's credit) and allowing the writing of checks to draw against it.

Financial Institutions

Many forms of money, especially demand deposits and time deposits, depend on the existence of financial institutions such as commercial banks, savings and loan associations (S&Ls), mutual savings banks, credit unions, and non-deposit institutions such as pension funds, insurance companies, and finance companies.

Commercial Banks

Commercial banks are profit-making organizations that accept deposits, make loans, and supply related services to their customers. Their input is the deposits they receive, for which they pay depositors interest. Their output is the loans they grant, on which they charge interest. If successful, their income exceeds expenses, and they earn a profit.

National Banks

National banks are commercial banks chartered by the U.S. Comptroller of the Currency. These banks must conform to all federal banking regulations and are subject to unannounced visits by federal auditors.

State Banks

State banks are commercial banks chartered by the states in which they operate. State banks tend to be smaller than national banks. State banks are subject to unannounced inspections by both state and federal auditors.

Savings and Loan Associations (S&Ls)

Savings and loan associations (S&Ls) are chartered either by the federal government or by state governments. As their name suggests, their input is savings deposits, and their output is home-mortgage loans.

During the early 1980s, S&Ls went through a very difficult period. Both interest and inflation were high. As a result, fewer people were borrowing at the higher rates. At the same time, the S&Ls were not producing sufficient interest income because they had made their loans during periods of lower interest rates. In addition, depositors demanded higher interest on their deposits.

Under deregulation, in an effort to increase their income, S&Ls began to offer loans on higher-risk mortgages. By itself, this practice was risky enough, but unfortunately, added to this practice were serious abuses in the system. At a number of S&Ls, loans with unacceptably high risks were authorized for friends and associates for ventures that failed, predictably; thus, forcing many S&Ls to close.

As a result of the failed S&Ls, the federal government, which had insured individuals' deposits under the Federal Savings and Loan Insurance Corporation (FSLIC), was forced to expend huge amounts of money to repay depositors.

Mutual Savings Banks

Mutual savings banks are owned by their depositors. They accept deposits, and they make home-mortgage loans. There are no stockholders; the profits are distributed to the depositors. Almost all mutual savings banks are state-chartered; they are mainly found in the East.

Credit Unions

Like mutual savings banks, credit unions are owned by the depositors (called members). Credit unions accept deposits only from members and offer loans only to members. Credit unions are generally formed by the employees of a company, a union, or an institution such as a college or university. Two of the country's largest credit unions are those for the employees of the U.S. Navy and of the Pentagon.

Non-Deposit Institutions

Non-deposit institutions, which comprise pension funds, insurance companies, and finance companies, are also part of the banking system.

Pension Funds and Insurance Companies

Pension funds and insurance companies accept funds and invest them in stocks, bonds, or other securities, or they lend the funds in the form of mortgages for large commercial real estate projects.

Finance Companies

Finance companies lend smaller amounts of money, generally to individual consumers.

Services Provided by Banks

As they compete to attract customers, banks offer a wide range of services to both individuals and firms, including cash-handling services, financial advice, transfer of funds, certified checks, and safe-deposit boxes. Bank services can be divided into deposit-side services and lending-side services.

Deposit-Side Services

Deposit-side services are based on deposits received from customers. Services include checking accounts (demand deposits) and NOW accounts. Time-deposit services include certificates of deposit (CDs) and passbook accounts.

CDs are deposits that the customer agrees to freeze (that is, allow to remain on deposit) for a specific period of time, such as three, six, or twelve months. In return, the depositor receives a fixed, stated rate of interest. If the depositor makes a withdrawal before the end of the agreed-upon period, the depositor pays a penalty (usually a large part of the interest).

Passbook accounts are deposits from which depositors may withdraw money whenever they wish.

Lending-Side Services

Lending-side services are based on loans made to customers. Banks offer short- and long-term loans both to businesses and to individuals. Short-term loans are usually repaid within one year; long-term loans, one year or longer.

Many firms establish a line of credit before they need funds. A line of credit is a loan approval for a specific total amount before the money is needed. In this way, businesses or individuals needing money quickly do not need to wait until a loan is approved. In exchange for granting the loan or the line of credit, most lenders require the borrower to pledge collateral (real or personal property such as stocks, bonds, or real estate) as security for the loan.

Credit Cards

Many banks issue credit cards, which are a form of loan extended to the card-holder. When a customer charges a purchase to a credit card, the bank advances payment to the merchant on behalf of the customer and then bills the customer at a later date. Debit cards are similar to credit cards. With debit cards, however, the money is electronically deducted from the customer's account at the time of the sale; no credit is issued to the customer. Debit cards essentially serve the same function as checks.

Trust Services

When banks offer trust services, they play the role of trustee. In return for a fee, the bank manages funds left in trust, for example, for minors, or as part of the estate of a deceased person.

Automated Teller Machines (ATMs)

Automated teller machines (ATMs) allow users to make cash withdrawals, deposit cash or checks, and transfer funds electronically, all by machine, twenty-four hours a day (depending on the location).

The Federal Reserve System

The Federal Reserve System—or the Fed, as it is generally known—is the government agency responsible for regulating the U.S. banking industry. The Fed was created by Congress on December 23, 1913, to maintain an economically healthy and financially sound business environment.

The Structure of the Fed

The Federal Reserve System is controlled by a seven-member Board of Governors appointed by the President and confirmed by Congress for over-lapping fourteen-year terms. From among the members the President selects the chairman and vice chairman, who serve renewable four-year terms.

The Federal Reserve System consists of twelve regional Federal Reserve District Banks, one in each Federal Reserve District. In addition, there are twenty-five branch territory banks. Each District Bank is owned, but not controlled, by the commercial banks that are members of the Federal Reserve System.

All federally chartered national banks must be members of the Federal Reserve System. State banks may join if they wish—and if they meet membership requirements.

The Role of the Fed

The Fed's role is primarily to regulate the supply of money, and in so doing, fulfill its mandate, which is to maintain a healthy economy. The Fed also serves as the federal government's bank and the banker's bank. It fulfills these roles in a number of ways.

The Government's Bank

The Fed performs two important functions for the government. First, it produces the nation's paper currency (U.S. dollar bills bear the legend "Federal Reserve Note"). Thus, the Fed controls the money supply by printing and issuing new money.

Second, the Fed lends money to the federal government by buying bonds issued by the Treasury Department. By making these loans to the Treasury Department, the Fed finances the federal deficit.

The Banker's Bank

When a bank needs money, it can borrow from the Federal Reserve bank and pay interest on the loan. Banks that belong to the Fed are required to maintain a reserve; this reserve money is kept on deposit at Federal Reserve Banks.

The Reserve Requirement

The Fed's Board of Governors establishes and controls the reserve requirement, which is a percentage of a bank's total deposits that the bank is required to maintain either in its own vaults or on deposit with the Fed. By increasing reserve requirements, the Fed can reduce the amount of money available for lending. This reduction, in turn, tends to slow the economy and is a powerful anti-inflation tool. On the other hand, by reducing reserve requirements, the Fed makes more money available for lending, and thereby, stimulates the economy.

The Discount Rate

The discount rate is the interest rate that the Federal Reserve System charges member banks for loans. The lower the discount rate, the easier it is for member banks to obtain money, and therefore, to make money available for loans at low rates. Because a low discount rate increases the money supply, it stimulates the economy. The Fed's discount rate to member banks directly affects the banks' rate, of course—specifically, it affects the prime rate, the rate that member banks set for loans to their best, most secure borrowers (such as blue chip corporations).

Open-Market Operations

The Fed engages in open-market operations; that is, it sells and buys U.S. government securities for the purpose of controlling the money supply. Because financial institutions are major purchasers of government securities, the Fed's open-market operations have a direct and immediate effect on lending. By selling government securities to financial institutions, the Fed takes that institution's money out of circulation, reducing the money supply. By buying government securities back from financial institutions, the Fed returns money to circulation, increasing the money supply.

Selective Credit Controls

The Federal Reserve System has, although it seldom uses, the power to set the necessary down payment and credit terms for real estate loans and for loans involving consumer durables, such as automobiles.

The Fed is also responsible for setting margin requirements for stock purchases. When an investor buys stock on margin, the investor is required to put down only a percentage of the total selling price, not the full price, in cash. The remainder of the selling price is covered by loans. Margin requirements specify what that percentage must be.

Check-Clearing

Checks presented for payment to other banks must be cleared through a clearinghouse, which serves as an intermediary in the transaction. Local checks presented for payment at other local banks are processed through a local clearinghouse. The Federal Reserve Systems acts as the clearinghouse for checks drawn on a bank in a different city or state. It will debit one bank and credit the other for the amount of the check, usually by electronic equipment, which enables checks to be cleared in most cases within two or three days.

Deposit Insurance

Faced by bank failures during the Depression, the government responded with deposit insurance. The Federal Deposit Insurance Corporation (FDIC) was created by Congress in 1933. All commercial banks that are members of the Federal Reserve System are required to belong to the FDIC and pay insurance premiums. The FDIC insures an account against bank failure for up to $100,000 per depositor.

Similarly, S&L depositors formerly protected by the Federal Savings and Loan Insurance Corporation (FSLIC) are now protected by the Savings Association Insurance Fund (SAIF).

■ CREDIT

Credit provides immediate purchasing power in exchange for a promise to repay the total amount, with or without interest, at a later date.

Credit Transactions

Borrowers take loans to get immediate purchasing power; that is, the ability to buy something at a time when they do not have the available funds to make the purchase. The lender—a bank or a business—supplies the credit.

A bank is in the business of lending money; its profit is the interest it receives on its loans. Businesses also extend credit, either to compete with other firms that extend credit or to increase their customer base by attracting customers who cannot pay the entire purchase amount in one payment, but can make smaller payments over a period of time.

Credit Management

The primary purpose of a business is to earn a profit by selling goods or services. As part of its sales effort, a business extends credit to customers, and in so doing, takes on the responsibility of credit management.

The Five Cs of Credit

In extending credit, a business is aware of and accepts, but tries to limit, the risk that some of its customers will be either unwilling or unable to pay for their credit purchases. One way lenders try to limit credit losses is by setting standards for lending based on the five Cs of credit: character, capacity, capital, collateral, and conditions. The first tool lenders use to determine how likely the borrower is to repay the loan is the borrower's credit application. From this completed form and from other key sources, the lender can learn critical information about the five Cs.

Character

Character refers to the borrower's attitude toward his or her debts. Have past debts been repaid in a timely fashion? Have other lenders been forced to request payment repeatedly, to threaten to sue or to actually sue, all in order to obtain payment?

Capacity

Capacity is the borrower's financial ability to meet the scheduled payment obligations in the credit agreement. An individual's capacity is reflected, in part, by his or her salary statements and other sources of income. A business's capacity can be measured—again, in part by its income statement. In both cases, of course, other factors (for example, outstanding obligations and expenses) must be considered.

Capital

Capital refers to the borrower's assets or net worth. Capital can be determined from a business's financial statements (those prepared by a certified public accountant) or from an individual's credit application.

Collateral

Collateral is real property (such as stocks, bonds, or real estate) pledged as security that the loan will be repaid. If the borrower fails to live up to the terms of the credit agreement, the collateral can be sold to satisfy the debt. A loan that is backed by collateral is more secure than other loans; oftentimes, the borrower will be charged a lower interest rate if the loan is backed by collateral.

Conditions

Lenders know that general economic conditions can affect a borrower's ability to repay the loan or other credit. In a falling economy or in a recession, for example, loans for expensive consumer items carry an added risk.

Checking Credit Information

Credit applications must be checked for accuracy. For a business, credit information can be obtained from several sources. National credit-reporting agencies (such as Dun & Bradstreet Reports) or local credit-reporting agencies supply information for a fee. Other sources of information are industry associations and other firms that have dealt with the applicant. For individuals, many credit bureaus (such as TRW Information Services) supply credit information on a fee basis. Credit bureaus are subject to provisions of the Fair Credit Reporting Act of 1970, which safeguards consumers' rights by making the information in an individual's file available to the individual and by offering the individual the opportunity to correct inaccurate statements in his or her file.

■ CHANGES IN THE MONEY AND BANKING SYSTEM

The Depository Institutions Deregulation and Monetary Control Act of 1980 brought about many changes in the money and banking system. Previously, only commercial banks could offer checking accounts, S&Ls and mutual banks could not make consumer loans, and interest rates were regulated. Deregulation ended these restrictions and opened an era of fierce competition among banks and financial institutions based on their various products and services and their interest rates.

Deregulation also increased the number of players in the financial markets. Not only brokerage firms such as Merrill Lynch, but also retail chains such as Sears have now become financial supermarkets, offering a range of products and services in the areas of consumer finance, real estate, insurance, and stockbrokerage services.

Banking is entering a new era. There were many bank failures as a result of deregulation, but to economists some of these failures were part of the weeding-out process of inefficient units; others were due to unscrupulous management or criminal activities. There will undoubtedly be new winners and losers in this newly competitive market.

Selected Readings

American Bankers Association. *Banking Terminology.* 1981.
Bessis, Joel. *Risk Management in Banking.* 2002.
Board of Governors of the Federal Reserve System. *Federal Reserve Bulletin,* Monthly. 1915–.
Chancellor, Edward. *Crunch Time for Credit?* 2005.
Chernow, Ron. *The House of Morgan.* 1990.
Edmister, Robert O. *Financial Institutions: Markets and Management.* 1986.
The Federal Reserve System: Purposes and Functions. United States. Congress. Joint Economic Committee. 1984.

Financial World Publishing. *Dictionary of International Banking and Finance Terms.* 2001.

Laidler, David. *Taking Money Seriously.* 1990.

Miller, Roger Leroy, and Robert W. Pulsinelli. *Modern Money and Banking.* 1989.

Mrkvicla, Edward F., Jr. *The Bank Book.* 1989.

Munn, Glenn G. *Encyclopedia of Banking and Finance.* 1983.

Rachlin, Harvey, editor. *The Money Encyclopedia.* 1984.

Rose, Peter S. *Commercial Bank Management.* 1999.

Rouse, Nicholas. *Bankers' Lending Techniques.* 2002.

Sampson, Anthony. *The Money Lenders.* 1981.

West, Robert Craig. *Banking Reform and the Federal Reserve, 1863–1923.* 1974.

Wynn, Anthea, and Helen McNab. *Principles and Practices of Consumer Credit Risk Management.* 2003.

Test Yourself

1) Money is used in exchange for goods and services. This power is the basis of the three principal functions of money. What are they?

2) List the five important characteristics of money.

3) What are the different forms of money?

4) What are three specific measures of the money supply?

5) How are credit unions different from commercial banks?

6) What are the two major types of services provided by banks?

7) Describe the role of the Federal Reserve System.

8) What are the five Cs of credit? Describe each one.

Test Yourself Answers

1) Money's three principal functions are as a medium of exchange, a measure of value, and a store of value.

2) The five important characteristics are portability, divisibility, stability, durability, and authenticity.

3) Money comes in the following forms: currency, demand deposits, other checkable deposits, time deposits, money-market funds, savings accounts, and plastic money (e.g., credit and debit cards).

4) M-1 is a measure of money supply that includes only the most liquid forms of money. M-2 includes M-1 plus other types of money that can be easily converted to spendable forms, namely, time deposits, money-market funds, and savings deposits. M-3 includes M-2 plus time deposits over $100,000 plus short-term repurchase agreements.

5) Commercial banks are profit-making organizations that accept deposits, make loans, and supply related services to the public-at-large; they are owned by their stockholders. Credit unions, on the other hand, are owned by the depositors (called members). They accept deposits from, and make loans, only to these members.

6) Banks provide deposit-side services (e.g., checking accounts, NOW accounts, savings accounts) and lender-side services (e.g., short-term loans, long-term loans, and open lines of credit).

7) The Federal Reserve System's role is primarily to maintain a healthy U.S. economy by controlling the supply of money. It serves as the government's bank (producing the paper currency and buying bonds issued by the Treasury Department) and as the banker's bank (by lending money to the banks). It also establishes the reserve requirement for banks that borrow money and the discount rate it charges for borrowing its money. The Fed engages in open-market operations; that is, buying and selling U.S. government securities. It can set the necessary down payment and credit terms for real estate and consumer durables loans. Finally, it provides check clearing services for the banking system and provides deposit insurance for bank depositors.

8) Character, refers to the borrower's attitude toward his or her debts. Capacity is the borrower's ability to meet the scheduled payment obligations. Capital refers to the borrower's assets or net worth. Collateral is property pledged as security that the loan will be repaid. Conditions refers to the lenders knowledge of the general economic conditions that can affect a borrower's ability to repay the loan.

CHAPTER 20

Financial Strategies: Short- and Long-Term Financing

Money is required both to start a business and to keep it going. Ideally, the original investment is sufficient to get the company started, and then income from operations pays for continued operations and provides a profit.

■ THE NEED FOR FINANCING

In actual practice, income and expenses might vary from season to season and from year to year, forcing companies to seek temporary funding during such periods to finance opportunities for expansion or to take advantage of an opportunity to purchase a new facility. Corporate expansion is most often financed through borrowing.

The decision to borrow money does not mean the firm is in trouble. Astute financial management uses regular responsible borrowing to meet needs. Some firms limit their growth, or miss profitable opportunities by not borrowing or by borrowing too little. In any case, financial planning and control is critical to the success of any firm.

■ FINANCIAL PLANNING AND CONTROL

Every business, regardless of size, has concerns about money—how to get it and how to use it—and these concerns fall to the financial manager, the person responsible for planning and controlling the acquisition and dispersal of the firm's financial assets and resources. The financial manager's overall goal is to increase the value of the firm by increasing its profits, and in so doing, to increase stockholders' wealth. To achieve this goal requires a financial strategy, which is reflected in the manager's financial plan.

A financial plan is a plan for obtaining and using the money needed to implement the organization's goals. The financial plan controls spending in line with the firm's priorities, ensures the availability of financing, and controls the efficient use of financial resources. The plan establishes priorities that are compatible with the organization's objectives.

A financial plan has four basic steps, described in the following sections.

Establishing Valid Objectives

Financial objectives are specific, realistic statements detailing financial goals for a specific period.

Budgeting Income and Expenses

A budget is a statement that projects income and expenses over a specified future period. The budget process begins by constructing individual budgets for each area of activity—production, sales, promotion, and so on—and then combining these budgets into a master budget. With the master budget, the financial planner can determine whether outside funding will be required, and if so, when it will be required.

Identifying Sources of Funds

Financial managers identify funding sources in advance so that they are sure the funds will be available when needed. The four basic sources of funds are sales revenue, sales of assets, and equity and debt capital.

- **Sales revenue** is the income from future sales and is the primary sources of funds for a firm.
- **Sales of assets** that are no longer needed by the firm can be a source of capital. If the company has no other source of funds, it may need to sell assets that are still utilized—a drastic but sometimes necessary step.
- **Equity and debt capital** are discussed in the "Equity Financing" and "Debt Financing" sections, respectively.

Monitoring and Evaluating Financial Performance

Financial plans must be monitored on an ongoing basis to ensure they are being properly implemented. By comparing reports of actual sales and actual expenses with budgeted sales and budgeted expenses, managers can often uncover minor problems before they become major ones.

■ SHORT-TERM FINANCING

Financial managers use a variety of short- and long-term strategies to finance the company's operations. Short-term financing describes money that will be used within a year or less, and then repaid. A company's need for short-term financing is closely related to its cash flow, the movement of money into and out of a firm. Ideally, the company wants to have enough money coming in during any period to cover expenses for that period, but this is not always possible.

For example, if the company has not yet received payments for its credit sales, it may need short-term financing to pay its bills while it waits for its customers to pay their bills. Slow sales or unexpected expenses may also cause a cash flow problem. Short-term financing may also be needed to support inventory. Holding inventory incurs a considerable expense for many businesses. Because inventory is often manufactured well in advance of the actual sale, manufacturers need short-term financing to buy materials and pay for production. Wholesalers and retailers need short-term financing to pay for the inventory they must have on hand to make sales. In both cases, manufacturers and wholesalers will repay the money when sales are made.

Sources of Unsecured Short-Term Financing

Most firms have a close working relationship with their short-term lenders. Generally, the shorter the term of the loan, the less risk to the lender.

Short-term loans are usually for smaller amounts than long-term loans and are generally unsecured; the borrower is not required to pledge collateral. The major sources of unsecured short-term financing are trade credit, promissory notes, bank loans, commercial paper, and commercial drafts.

Trade Credit

Trade credit is a payment delay that a firm grants to its customers. When a business buys a product from a supplier, the business receives a bill stating the supplier's credit terms. If the bill is paid on time, the supplier charges no interest.

To encourage prompt payment, suppliers often offer a cash discount. The invoice may read "2/10, net 30," a standard abbreviation meaning that the customer (1) may take a discount of 2 percent off the total if the bill is paid within 10 days or (2) must pay the total, or net, amount (without a discount) in thirty days.

Promissory Notes

A promissory note is a borrower's written pledge to pay a certain sum of money to a creditor at a specified future date. Unlike trade credit, promissory notes carry interest. In addition, a promissory note is legally enforceable.

Promissory notes are negotiable—that is, the lender can sell the note, at a slight discount, to the lender's bank; the bank, in turn, then advances the money to the lender and collects the full amount of the loan from the borrower when the note becomes due. The discount becomes the bank's profit.

Bank Loans

Unsecured bank loans are offered by commercial banks to their customers at interest rates that vary according to the firm's credit rating. Many firms maintain a line of credit, which is a prearranged short-term loan that the firm can access quickly (because the credit has already been approved). A revolving credit agreement is a guaranteed line of credit.

Commercial Paper

Commercial paper is a short-term promissory note issued by large corporations and secured only by the reputation of each individual firm. Commercial paper is usually issued in large denominations, generally $50,000 to $100,000.

Commercial Drafts

Commercial drafts are written orders requiring the customer (the payee) to pay a specified sum to a supplier (the drawer) for goods or services. Commercial drafts are used when the supplier is unsure of the customer's credit standing.

Sources of Secured Short-Term Financing

Borrowers that cannot obtain enough capital through unsecured loans may be required to pledge collateral, most often inventory and accounts receivables, to secure their loans.

Inventory Loans

A company's inventory can be used to secure an inventory loan. As part of the loan agreement, the lender may require that the inventory be stored in a public warehouse, and the lender holds the warehouse receipt. The lender releases the merchandise only when the loan is paid.

Accounts Receivables

A firm may pledge its accounts receivables as collateral. The lender establishes the quality of the receivables and then advances 70 to 80 percent of the value of the accounts receivables to the borrower. When the borrowing company receives accounts receivable payments, it must give that money to the lender in payment of the loan.

Factoring

A factor is a firm that specializes in buying receivables at a discount. Factoring, the selling of accounts receivables, is basically a variation of pledging receivables. By selling its receivables, the company receives money immediately, although it receives less than the face amount of the receivables. Then, when the account is due, the company pays the full amount of that receivable to the factor. Although the selling firm receives less than the face value of the account receivable, it does not have to wait for payment, but instead, gets the cash at once.

■ LONG-TERM FINANCING

Long-term financing describes money that will be needed longer than one year. Long-term financing might be needed for starting a business, for new-product development, for long-term marketing activities, for purchasing or replacing capital assets, or for mergers or acquisitions. All of these activities require large amounts of money, too large to be repaid within the year.

Sources of Long-Term Financing

Sources of long-term financing vary according to the size and type of business. For a corporation, equity financing includes selling stock and retaining earnings. Debt financing includes long-term loans and the sale of corporate bonds. Stocks and bonds are discussed in Chapter 22.

Equity Financing

Equity financing marks the beginning of every business, whether sole proprietorship, partnership, or corporation. Sole proprietorships and partnerships acquire equity when the owners invest their own money to start the business. Corporations acquire equity when stockholders buy shares in their corporations.

Equity financing has two main advantages for corporations. First, equity financing does not have to be repaid; thus, issuing new shares of stock is one way a corporation can finance its long-term operations.

Second, the corporation is under no legal requirement to pay dividends, distributions of earnings, to stockholders.

Issuing New Shares of Stock

The corporation may issue new shares of stock to provide equity financing. Many states grant present stockholders preemptive rights: When new stock is to be issued, the present stockholders have the first right to buy the new stock before it is publicly offered.

Retained Earnings

Retained earnings are the portion of a business's profits that is not distributed to stockholders. These funds are reinvested in the business and are considered a form of equity funding. Stockholders gain because this reinvestment tends to increase the value of their stock. By retaining earnings for future operations, the corporation does not have to pay for the use of equity capital.

Debt Financing

Debt financing is accomplished through long-term loans and issuing bonds. Small business is usually limited to long-term loans, whereas large corporations may also issue bonds.

Long-Term Loans

Long-term loans are available from commercial banks, insurance companies, pension funds, and other financial institutions. Long-term loans run from three to seven years and call for regular quarterly, semi-annual, or annual payments. Interest rates and other terms depend on the credit rating of the borrower. The loans are generally secured by real estate, machinery, or equipment.

Bonds

A bond is a corporation's written pledge to repay a specified amount of money at a specified date at a specified interest rate.

■ INTEREST FACTORS

The interest rates corporations pay to borrow money are determined by many factors, the most important of which are the financial health and credit record of the firm, the general level of interest rates (as reflected in the prime rate), and the overall economic outlook.

The prime rate is the lowest rate charged by a bank for a short-term loan to its best customers, usually large corporations with the highest credit ratings. Less-sound or smaller firms will pay higher rates, depending on the amount of risk to the lender and the collateral pledged.

Selected Readings

Altman, Edward I., editor. *Handbook of Corporate Finance.* 1986.
Aragon, George. *Financial Management.* 1989.
Bruck, Connie. *The Predators' Ball.* 1988.
Burrough, Bryan, and John Helyar. *Barbarians at the Gate: The Fall of RJR Nabisco.* 1990.
Crane, Dwight, and Robert Eccles. *Doing Deals: Investment Banks at Work.* 1988.
Financial World Publishing. *Dictionary of International Banking and Finance Terms.* 2001.
Gitman, Lawrence J., and Carol McDaniel. *Future of Business: The Essentials.* 2005.
Institutional Investor Editors. *The Way It Was: An Oral History of Finance, 1967–1987.* 1988.
Johnson, Hazel J. *Handbook of Financial Institutions and Markets.* 2000.
Krism, James E., and Susan Z. Diamond. *Finance Without Fear.* 1984.
Kross, Herman E., and Martin R. Blyn. *A History of Financial Intermediaries.* 1971.
Levin, Dick. *Buy Low, Sell High, Collect Early and Pay Late: The Manager's Guide to Financial Survival.* 1983.
Luecke, Richard. *Finance for Managers.* 2003.
Rouse, Nicholas. *Bankers' Lending Techniques.* 2002.
Silver, A. David. *The Bankruptcy, Workout, and Turnaround Market Directory and Source Book.* 1991.
Train, John. *The Money Masters.* 1980.
Weaver, Samuel C., and J. Fred Weston. *Finance & Accounting for Non-Financial Managers.* 2004.
Weston, Fred J., and Eugene Brigham. *Essentials of Managerial Finance.* 1989.

Test Yourself

1) Theoretically, company operations should generate income sufficient to allow the company to operate and to continue to grow as well as to earn a profit. Why, then, might a company need to secure either short- or long-term financing?

2) What are the basic steps in developing a financial plan?

3) What is the difference between unsecured and secured financing?

4) What are the five sources of unsecured short-term financing discussed in this chapter?

5) Secured short-term financing requires the pledging of collateral, usually either inventory or accounts receivable. What are the two basic types of secured financing sources?

6) What are the basic types of long-term financing?

Test Yourself Answers

1) Income and expenses vary from season to season and from year to year, sometimes forcing the company to seek temporary funding.

2) A successful financial plan includes the establishing of valid objectives, the budgeting of income and expenses, the identifying of sources of funds, and the monitoring and evaluating of financial performance.

3) Unsecured financing does not require collateral (usually property) as security for the loan, while secured financing does require collateral.

4) Trade credit, promissory notes, bank loans, commercial paper, and commercial drafts constitute sources of short-term financing.

5) The typical short-term secured financing options are inventory loans and accounts receivable, using either a traditional lender or a factor.

6) Equity financing (i.e., the sale of common stock, preferred stock, and the use of retained earnings) and debt financing (i.e., the borrowing of money on a long-term basis and the sale of bonds) are the two basic approaches available for a company to secure long-term financing.

CHAPTER 21

Risk Management and Insurance

Risk management is the systematic application of management policies, procedures, and practices to the tasks of identifying, analyzing, evaluating, and monitoring risk. Insurance is one of the mechanisms available to a company as a form of risk management, primarily used to transfer the risk of a potential loss, from one entity to another, in exchange for a fee.

■ RISK IN BUSINESS

For businesses, risk is part of every decision. The essence of business decisions is balancing the risks and potential gains involved in any course of action. Insurance cannot guarantee safety, but it can limit the financial damage of an accident or misfortune. This chapter deals with insurance and other techniques available for managing risk.

The Nature of Risk

Risk is the possibility that a loss or injury will occur. The greatest risk exists not when the odds are very high, but when they are unknown, because there is no way to insure against or manage an unknown risk.

For an individual, risk is involved in driving an automobile, investing in stocks or bonds, and skiing. For a business, risk is part of every decision. Risks can be classified as either speculative or pure risks.

Speculative Risk

A speculative risk is accompanied by the possibility of earning a profit. Investing in stocks or bonds involves risk, but investments also have the possibility of making a profit. Business decisions such as whether to market a new product involve speculative risks. If the new product is successful, the business reaps profits; if not, the business suffers losses.

Pure Risk

A pure risk involves the possibility only of loss; it offers no possibility of profit or gain. Hurricanes and fires present pure risks: There is no gain if they do not occur, but there is certain loss if they do.

Risk Management

Risk management is the process of identifying exposure to risk, identifying possible ways to handle each exposure, and acting to establish protection against the risk. The responsibility for managing speculative risks belongs to the entire management team. The responsibility for managing pure risks in most firms lies with specific individuals, generally called risk managers. Their concerns are property risks and liability risks.

Property risks include fire, flood, and other damage to property. Liability risks are related to the firm's liability for losses suffered by an individual or another company as a result of, for example, an accident or product liability.

Techniques of Risk Management

The four basic methods for handling risk are risk avoidance, risk assumption, risk transfer, and risk reduction. The risk manager chooses the appropriate technique or combination of techniques.

Risk Avoidance

Risk avoidance recognizes that not all risks are avoidable and that the costs of attempting to avoid all risks might be high. A company can avoid the risk of product failure by not introducing new products, but such a course would ensure eventual failure. A firm can, however, attempt to avoid engaging in activities that lead to an exposure to risk. For example, many companies avoid operating in politically volatile countries to avoid risks associated with political instability. Jewelry stores place their merchandise in vaults at night to avoid losses through robbery.

Risk Assumption

Risk assumption describes a company's acceptance of responsibility for loss resulting from a particular risk. Knowing and accepting that risks are part of doing business, a firm may reasonably assume risks in certain situations, for example: (1) if the potential loss is too small to be of concern; (2) if effective risk management has reduced the risk; (3) if insurance coverage is either very expensive (too costly in relation to the potential cost of the loss) or unavailable; and (4) if there is no other way of protecting against loss.

One kind of risk assumption is self-insurance, a company's attempt to protect itself against the risk of loss by establishing a fund to cover a loss. Self-insurance is practical only in situations where the company is large enough to spread the cost over a large operation. For example, rather than pay insurance premiums for truck repairs or damages, a large trucking company may opt instead to pay any damages itself, using the money it sets aside each year as part of its self-insurance.

Risk Transfer

Risk transfer, the most common method of dealing with risk, consists of transferring the risk to an insurance company. The insurance company estimates the potential loss of a given risk and assumes the financial responsibility for that specific risk, in return for which the insurance company charges a fee called a premium.

Risk Reduction

Risk reduction assumes that since risk cannot be avoided, perhaps it can be reduced. For example, a company may sponsor employee safety programs and provide safety equipment in an effort to reduce risk of injury to its workers, and it may install fire alarms, smoke alarms, and sprinkler systems to reduce the risk of fire loss.

■ INSURANCE AND INSURERS

An insurance company is a business whose product is protection from loss. An insurance policy is a contract between the company and the insured that reduces the risk of loss to the insured.

Principles of Insurance

An insurance policy requires the insured to pay a fee, called a premium, in return for which the insurer will pay a specified amount to the insured should an event occur that has been identified in the policy. Insurance generally works on five basic principles, discussed in the following sections.

The Law of Large Numbers

The law of large numbers is a statistical principle that states that as the number of units in a group increases, predictions about the group become more accurate and certain. Although insurance companies cannot predict whether a particular house will burn down within the year, they can project within close range how many houses will be destroyed by fire in a twelve-month period.

By using the law of large numbers, probability, and statistical analysis (see Chapter 17), insurance companies can reduce the risk for an entire class of insured entities—for example, single-family wood homes—and profitably offer protection at a reasonable cost.

Indemnification

The principle of indemnification requires the insurer to pay only for the actual cash value of the loss. The standard property insurance policy, for instance, will pay only the purchase price of an item less its depreciation. A building may be insured for $200,000, but if its value is only $150,000, the insurer will pay only that amount. It is possible to purchase replacement-value insurance, but since the replacement cost of a depreciated building is higher than its cash value, the cost of the insurance is higher. In life insurance, dollar value for a death is difficult to determine, so life policies pay a specific predetermined amount at the death of the insured.

Uninsurable Risk

An uninsurable risk is a risk that few, if any, insurance companies will assume because of the difficulty of calculating the probable loss. Market risks, such as price or style change; political risks, such as revolution or war; and acts of God, such as tornadoes, blizzards, and droughts are generally considered uninsurable risks.

Insurable Risk

Insurance policies can be purchased only for insurable risks, risks that are financial, measurable, and predictable. Emotional or sentimental values are not insurable. Insurable risks must generally meet the following requirements.

- **Losses must not be under the control of the insured**. An insurance company will not pay for the damage that was intentionally caused by the insured party. A building owner cannot collect damages for a fire deliberately set by the owner.
- **Losses must be measurable**. Property insured must have a value measurable in dollars, not in sentimental or emotional value, because insurance firms reimburse losses with money.
- **The insured hazard must be widespread**. The insurance company must be able to write many policies covering the same hazard throughout a wide geographic area. Unless the insurance company spreads its coverage in this way, a single disaster in a particular area—a hurricane, for example—could cause it to pay out on all its policies at one time.

- **A sufficiently large number of similar situations must have previously occurred.** The probability of loss, using the law of large numbers, can then be calculated to arrive at an accurate estimate of risk due to a specific cause.

When the insurable risk is too large, an insurer will utilize a process called reinsurance; that is, sell off portions of the coverage to other insurance companies. In this way, insurance companies, too, transfer risk. Reinsurance, then, is actually an insurance policy limiting the potential loss to the insurance company.

Insurable Interest

In order to purchase insurance, an individual or company must have an insurable interest; that is, must be the one to suffer a measurable dollar loss. Thus, an individual cannot, for example, purchase insurance on a house owned by a neighbor hoping to profit if that house suffers a fire.

Public Insurance

Although we do not think of the government as being in the insurance business, the federal and state governments are an important source—and in some cases, the only source—of many types of insurance.

Unemployment Insurance

Unemployment insurance provides partial, temporary replacement of income to eligible former workers who become unemployed. Unemployment insurance is funded by a state payroll tax on employers; the actual amount of the tax varies according to the rate of claims among each company's employees. The program is administered by the state, but during periods of high unemployment, the federal government offers supplemental benefits.

Worker's Compensation

Worker's compensation, which is also state-administered, offers employees protection against losses caused by injury or illness resulting from their employment. It is a form of no-fault insurance: It compensates for losses regardless of who, if anyone, is responsible for the occurrence. In some states, the employer may buy the insurance from a private insurer.

The Social Security Act of 1935

The Social Security Act of 1935 provides for retirement, survivors', disability, and health benefits from the federal government. It is funded by a payroll tax, which is paid for by both the employee and the employer.

- **Retirement benefits:** are based on the covered worker's income during his or her years of employment.
- **Survivors' benefits:** are paid to the spouse, dependent children, or dependent parents if the worker dies before retirement.
- **Disability benefits:** are paid in the event that a person covered under Social Security becomes disabled. In certain situations, Social Security will also cover hospital and medical costs for a person over age 65.

Other Public Insurance

Federal and state governments also offer a number of other insurance programs, including the following.

- **Federal Deposit Insurance Corporation (FDIC) and Savings Association Insurance Fund:** provide insurance protection for deposits up to $100,000 in banks, savings and loan associations, and credit unions.
- **The Federal Crop Insurance Corporation:** protects farmers from loss through natural disasters such as flood, drought, etc.
- **Federal Flood Insurance:** protects homes and small businesses against damage caused by floods.
- **Federal Home Mortgage Loan Insurance:** protects private savings and loans and banks from losses resulting from default on the part of the borrower.
- **Federal Crime Insurance:** protects businesses and homes against burglary, robbery, and theft (other than auto theft) in certain high-crime areas.
- **Employee Retirement Income Security Act of 1974 (ERISA):** created the Pension Benefit Guaranty Corporation for the specific purpose of guaranteeing pension plans.

Private Insurance

The insurance industry has more than 6,000 private insurance companies employing over two million people. Private insurers control enormous assets, making the insurance industry one of the major investors in real estate, government securities, and corporate securities.

There are two major types of insurance companies: stock insurance companies and mutual insurance companies.

Stock Insurance Companies

Most of the insurance companies in the United States are stock insurance companies, owned by stockholders and operated for profit. Like other profit-making companies, they pay dividends to stockholders. Aetna Life and Casualty Co. and All-State are stock insurance companies.

Mutual Insurance Companies

Mutual insurance companies, such as Mutual of New York (MONY) and Metropolitan Life, are owned by their policyholders, who receive any profits earned in the form of reduced premiums or insurance dividends. The policyholders elect the board of directors, which, in turn, chooses the executives who run the firm.

■TYPES OF INSURANCE COVERAGE

Effective risk management ensures that insurance coverage is adequate. Considerations include the hazards to be insured against, the cost of the coverage, and the risk-management techniques that can be utilized. Insurance coverage can be classified as business insurance or employee insurance.

Business Insurance

The major loss exposures for businesses are loss of property, liability, loss of income, and loss of services of key employees.

Loss of Property

Property owners run the risk that their property may be lost or destroyed by accident, natural disaster, or theft.

Fire Insurance

A fire insurance policy protects the insured building and its contents against financial loss caused by fire, smoke, or water damage. The larger the risk, the larger the premium. Thus, a wooden building without a sprinkler system will cost more to insure than a brick building with a sprinkler system. Fire insurance does not cover (1) new plant additions if the insurance company has not been previously informed of them, (2) buildings that have been left vacant sixty days or more, (3) fire caused by explosion or riot, or (4) fires deliberately started by the owner of the property.

Most fire policies on commercial buildings carry a co-insurance clause, which requires the policyholder to purchase enough insurance to cover a specified percentage (usually 80 percent) of the value of the building in order to obtain full reimbursement for loss in the event of a fire. For example, assume that as a result of fire a commercial building valued at $1 million sustains $400,000 in damages. If the building were insured for $800,000 (80 percent of its value), the insurance company would pay the full $400,000 in damages. If the building were insured for only $600,000 (which is 75 percent of the co-insurance requirement of $800,000), the insurance company would pay only $300,000, which is 75 percent of the loss.

Natural Disaster Insurance

Extended coverage of a fire policy will protect against risks other than fire. For example, extended coverage can protect a building and its contents against damage caused by windstorm, hail, explosions, smoke, aircraft or vehicles, and riot resulting from a strike. The extended coverage can be purchased separately, but it is much less expensive if it is added as extended coverage to an existing policy.

Marine Insurance

There are two kinds of marine insurance, ocean and inland. Ocean marine, the oldest kind of insurance, protects ship owners and shipments against damage to vessels and property being transported by ships at sea.

Inland marine covers most moveable property being transported from ports on inland waterways, rather than on the ocean. It may also cover rail or truck transportation.

Burglary, Robbery, and Theft Insurance

Burglary is the illegal taking of property through forcible entry. Robbery is the unlawful taking of money or property by force or threat of violence on a person. Theft (or larceny) is a general term for the wrongful taking of property that belongs to another. Insurance policies are available to cover each individually, or all three. A fidelity bond is an insurance policy that protects a business from theft, forgery, or embezzlement by its employees.

Self-Insurance through a Captive Insurance Company

Companies evaluate on a regular basis other risk-transferring options available, including self-insurance. More and more companies are choosing to self-insure through captive insurance companies.

A captive insurance company is owned by the company it insures and organized for that specific purpose. It may not offer insurance coverage to non-owners. Most jurisdictions allow two types of captives: pure and group. A pure captive is owned by one parent company, while a group captive is owned by a small number of unaffiliated companies that are generally in the same type of business (e.g., law firms).

Captive insurance companies are generally less regulated and taxed differently than traditional insurance companies.

Motor Vehicle Insurance

There are over 20 million automobile accidents in the United States each year, resulting in 50,000 deaths and billions of dollars in losses. Businesses purchase automobile insurance because it is required by state law and by the companies that finance the automobile purchase or lease. Businesses also buy auto insurance to protect their investment.

The two broad areas covered are physical damage and liability insurance.

- **Physical damage insurance** covers damage to the insured vehicle. Collision insurance pays for damage caused during an accident. Most policies include a deductible (of $50 or more) that the policyholder must pay. The insurance company then pays either the remaining cost of repairs or the actual cash value of the car if it is destroyed beyond repair (also called "totaled"), whichever is less. Comprehensive insurance covers damage to the insured vehicle due to fire, theft, vandalism, and almost anything else except collision and wear and tear. Comprehensive insurance also covers the contents of the car, such as radio, luggage, CBs, and so on. As with collision insurance, comprehensive generally includes a deductible.
- **Liability insurance** covers financial losses resulting from injuries or damages caused by the insured vehicle. Bodily-injury liability coverage pays medical bills and other costs in the event that injury or death results from an accident in which the policyholder is at fault. Liability limits are typically stated as "20/50/20," which means policy limits are (1) up to $20,000 for each individual, (2) up to a total of $50,000 for all those injured in a single accident, and (3) up to $20,000 in property damage. Because of the costs of medical treatment and the size of legal settlements, insurance companies recommend 100/300/100. The property liability coverage pays for any damage caused by the insured vehicle to the property of another person.

Business Liability Insurance

As a result of consumerism, new laws, and court decisions, businesses are increasingly responsible for losses sustained by others as a result of using a company's products or of a company's actions. Such losses are covered by business liability insurance. Business liability insurance of several types is available.

Public Liability Insurance

Public liability insurance protects the policyholder from financial losses due to injuries suffered by others as a result of negligence on the part of a business owner or employee. A notable example is the chemical accident at Union Carbide's plant in Bhopal, India.

Malpractice—or professional liability insurance purchased by physicians, lawyers, accountants, engineers, and other professionals—is another form of public liability insurance.

Product Liability Insurance

Product liability insurance protects the policyholder from financial losses due to injuries suffered by others as a result of using the policyholder's products. Because recent court settlements have been very large, business management now gives a great deal of attention to risk management of product liability.

Precautions include the following: (1) including thorough and explicit directions with products; (2) including hazard warnings to avoid using products incorrectly; (3) removing potentially hazardous products from the market; and (4) testing products in-house to reduce both the risk of product liability losses and the cost of insurance.

Worker's Compensation Insurance

Worker's compensation insurance, a form of liability insurance, covers medical expenses and salary continuation for employees who are injured while they are at work. It also pays benefits to dependents of workers killed on the job. Coverage is mandated by every state, and the benefits are set by the state. Premiums are paid by the employer and are generally computed as a small percentage of the worker's salary. Premiums vary according to the type of job and the risk involved.

Loss-of-Income Insurance

Insurance that pays benefits to policy holders because they lose income is called "Loss of-Income Insurance. It comes in a number of forms to meet a myriad of loss-of-income needs.

Business-Interruption Insurance

Business interruption insurance provides protection for a business whose operations are interrupted by fire, storm—or some other natural disaster, in some cases, even interruptions from employee strikes. Specifically, if the business cannot operate, the policyholder is reimbursed for loss of profits and for expenses such as salaries, interest payment, and rent. Generally, business-interruption insurance is an endorsement to the fire policy.

Loss-of-Services Insurance

In some businesses, one person, or perhaps a few executives or employees, are crucial to the company's operation. Key-executive insurance protects the company against the financial impact of the death or disability of a key employee. (This type of insurance is also discussed in the "Life Insurance" section on the following pages.)

Employee Insurance

In addition to insuring their property and assets, most businesses buy insurance for coverage of risks to employees. Federal law mandates payment of half of Social Security taxes, and all fifty states mandate worker's compensation. Most businesses provide additional coverage.

Medical Insurance

As a benefit to employees, most employers pays part or all of employees' medical insurance, which covers hospital care, physicians' and surgeons' fees, prescription drugs, and related services. Major medical insurance can be purchased to extend medical coverage beyond the dollar limits of the standard policies. Coverage for dental or mental health expenses are sometimes included.

To control premiums at a time when medical care costs are escalating rapidly, insurers have developed less-expensive plans (for example, plans that provide less than full coverage) or have required the employee to pay a larger share of the cost (for example, by paying a higher deductible).

Another method is to encourage the use of health maintenance organizations (HMOs). An HMO is a group of private doctors who provide HMO members with medical and hospital care under one roof on a prepaid basis. By setting fixed fees, HMOs provide doctors with an added incentive to be good managers; in this way, HMOs help control costs (in other plans, costs are set by the doctors and hospitals).

Disability Income Insurance

Disability income insurance protects an individual employee against loss of income while he or she is disabled as a result of illness or accident. The amount of the monthly payments to the disabled employee depends on whether the disability is permanent or temporary and on whether the disability is partial or full.

Life Insurance

Life insurance pays a stated amount of money on the death of the individual. The money is paid to one or more beneficiaries, individuals, or organizations named in the policy. Premiums vary according to age, sex, health, occupation, and type of insurance. Many companies offer group life insurance to employees.

There are a number of different types of life insurance available. Choosing the right policy depends upon the policyholder's specific needs and the particular situation.

Term Life Insurance

Term life insurance provides protection to beneficiaries for a stated period of time—usually one year—and no other benefits; the cost remains constant over the period covered. Level-term insurance, on the other hand, can be renewed each year at a slightly higher cost, reflecting the increasing age of the insured. Term is the least expensive form of life insurance. Most term policies are convertible into other forms of life insurance at the option of the policyholders so that they can adjust their insurance coverage as their circumstances change.

Whole Life Insurance

Whole life insurance provides both protection and savings. Premiums are higher than term insurance, but the premiums remain constant. Over the years, the policy accumulates savings, called the cash surrender value, which is payable to the policyholder if the policy is canceled. In addition, the policyholder may borrow money (up to the surrender value) from the insurance company at attractive rates. Whole life policies are available in three forms.

- **Straight life,** for which the policyholder pays premiums as long as the insured is alive or the policy is not canceled.
- **Limited-payment life,** for which the premiums are paid only for a specified number of years. Premiums are higher than straight life, as is the cash value.
- **Single-payment life,** for which one lump-sum payment is made at the time of the purchase.

Endowment Life Insurance

Endowment life insurance provides protection and guarantees payment of a stated amount to the policyholder after a specified number of years. The term of the policy is generally twenty years or until the insured reaches the age of 65. If the insured dies while the policy is in force, the beneficiaries are paid the face amount of the policy. Both the premiums and the values are higher than whole life policies.

Universal Life Insurance

Universal life insurance provides protection and offers a tax-deferred savings account that pays flexible interest. Policyholders can choose to make larger or smaller premium payments, to increase or decrease coverage or take out the cash value without canceling the policy. The premium, often called the contribution, is used only partly to buy insurance; the rest (after deducting certain expenses and fees) is invested by the insurance company on behalf of the policyholder.

Key-Executive Life Insurance

Companies purchase key-executive life insurance to protect their organizations from the financial disruption that would result from the death of a senior executive. In the same manner, many partnerships insure the partners so that upon the death of one, money will be available for the surviving partner(s) to purchase the deceased partner's share of the business from his or her estate.

Credit Life Insurance

As part of their loan agreements, many lenders, especially commercial banks, require a special life insurance policy, called credit life insurance, to be paid by the borrower as part of the monthly payment. In the event that the borrower dies before the loan is repaid, the insurance company then makes the monthly loan payment, removing the burden from the borrower's estate.

Selected Readings

Abraham, Kenneth S. *Distributing Risk.* 1986.

Allan, Steve L. *Financial Risk Management: A Practitioner's Guide to Managing Market and Credit Risk.* 2003.

Bloch, Annette, editor. *Insurance Almanac: Who, What, When and Where in Insurance: An Annual of Insurance Facts.* Annual, 1912.

Borodovsky, Lev, and Marc Lore. *The Professional's Handbook of Financial Risk Management.* 2000.

Crane, Frederick G. *Insurance Principles and Practices.* 1984.

Crawford, Samuel H., and Paul M. Sacks. *New Product, New Risks.* 1991.

Crouhy, Michael, Robert Mark, and Dan Galai. *Risk Management.* 2000.

Davids, Lewis E. *Dictionary of Insurance.* 1983.

Jess, D. J. *Insurance of Commercial Risk: Law & Practice.* 1986.

Lam, James. *Enterprise Risk Management: From Incentives to Controls.* 2003.

Rejda, George E. *Principles of Risk Management and Insurance.* 2004.

Schroeck, Gerhard. *Risk Management and Value Creation in Financial Institutions.* 2002.

Tobias, Andrew. *The Invisible Bankers.* 1982.

Whiting, Richard M. *A Guide to the Federal Law of Banking and Insurance.* 1989.

Williams, C. Arthur, and Richard M. Heins. *Risk Management and Insurance.* 1988.

Test Yourself

1) Distinguish between speculative and pure risks.

2) What is risk management?

3) What are the four basic methods of handling risk?

4) Discuss the concept of risk assumption.

5) What are the sources of public insurance?

6) What is the difference between a stock insurance company and a mutual insurance company?

7) Describe worker's compensation insurance.

8) If a company is concerned with the loss of services of its key executives and the effects on the business, what kind of insurance should the company purchase?

9) Distinguish between a term life insurance policy and a whole life insurance policy. Which would you recommend to a person attempting to purchase a large insurance policy for as low a premium as possible?

Test Yourself Answers

1) Speculative risk is accompanied by the possibility of earning a profit or gain. Pure risk involves only the possibility of loss; it offers no possibility of profit or gain.

2) Risk management is the process of identifying exposure to risk, identifying possible ways to handle each exposure, and acting to establish protection against the risk.

3) The four basic methods of handling risk are risk avoidance, risk assumption, risk transfer, and risk reduction.

4) Risk assumption occurs when a company decides that it will simply assume the risk of loss. A firm may decide to assume the risk in certain situations, including the following instances: the potential loss is too small to be of concern; effective risk management has already reduced the risk to an assumable level; insurance coverage is either very expensive or not available; or if there is no way of protecting against the loss. One kind of assumption of risk is self-insurance; this approach is only reasonable when the company is large enough to spread the risk over a large operation.

5) The following are sources of public insurance: unemployment insurance, worker's compensation, the Social Security Act of 1935, and other public insurance (e.g., FDIC and SAIF insurance).

6) Stock insurance companies are owned by stockholders and operate for profit. Mutual insurance companies are owned by the policyholders, who receive any profits earned in the form of reduced premiums or insurance dividends.

7) Worker's compensation insurance is a type of liability insurance. It covers medical expenses and salary continuation for employees who are injured while on the job. It also pays benefits to dependents of workers killed on the job. Coverage is mandated by every state and the benefits are set by the state. Premiums are paid by the employer, at a small percentage of employee salaries and wages.

8) The company should purchase loss-of-services insurance. It will protect the company against the financial impact of the death or disability of a key employee.

9) Whole life insurance policies provide insurance benefits and savings (investments). Premiums are higher than for term policies. Over the years, the policy accumulates savings, which are payable to the policyholder if the policy is cancelled. In addition, the policyholder may borrow against the policy. Term life insurance policies provide protection for a stated period of time (ten years, twenty years, etc.). The term policies are the least expensive types of life insurance.

CHAPTER 22
The Securities Markets

Securities such as stocks and bonds play vital roles both for companies and for investors. As key elements of the American economy, securities are bought and sold in the securities markets.

The securities markets are important to both companies and individual investors. For companies, the markets make possible the establishment and growth of business by supplying the capital needed to fund their operations. For individuals, the markets provide opportunities to earn interest, dividends, and capital gains and to share in American business.

■ THE ROLE OF SECURITIES AND THE SECURITIES MARKETS

This chapter examines what securities are, distinguishes among the most common types of securities, explains the process for buying and selling securities, and discusses the need for securities from both the individual and the company's investor's point of view.

The Investor's View

More than 56.9 million households in the United States own shares of stock in U.S. corporations (that is up from 54.1 million, in 2002, and 40 million, in 1995). They range from the proverbial "widows and orphans" who want maximum security to speculators whose aim is to make a short-term "killing." When approaching the stock market, one must decide if he or she is an investor or a speculator. The investor buys stock in a company, hoping to make a reasonable profit. The greater the uncertainty and risk, the greater profit or risk of loss. The speculator accepts this greater risk in the hopes of making a greater and quicker profit. In this chapter, the securities markets are viewed through the eyes of individual investors whose aim is to make a reasonable return on their investment.

Income describes the money that investors receive through dividends paid to them as shareholders. Many corporations have long, uninterrupted histories of paying regular quarterly dividends year after year, making their stocks more desirable to the investing public.

Capital gains describes the profits, if any, that an investor realizes by selling a security at a price higher than the investor's purchase price.

The Company's View

The securities markets supply two essential services for American corporations. First, the securities markets sell original new issues of corporate securities, thereby supplying the capital for companies to launch a new business or expand an existing one. Second, the securities markets also provide the marketplace for investors to buy and sell previously issued securities. Original issues are sold in what is called the primary market; previously issued securities, in the secondary market.

■ THE PRIMARY AND SECONDARY MARKETS

Corporations raise funds for operations and expansion in the primary market. Generally, they utilize an investment banking firm to facilitate the sales. Indeed, the investment banking firm buys the stock from the company, and then, sells it in the open market to individual and other institutional investors.

In the secondary market, previously issued stocks and bonds are bought and sold. The secondary market exists to make it possible for both individual and institutional investors to sell or buy securities they already own.

The Primary Market

Corporations raise funds in the primary market with the help of an investment banking firm, a company that underwrites the offering of stocks or bonds on behalf of the corporation. An investment bank is a firm that acts as an agent or intermediary between the issuer of securities (that is, the corporation) and the investing public (that is, each individual investor). Underwriting the new issue means that the investment bank buys the new stocks or bonds (that is, pays the company for the securities) and then sells them to the public through dealers and brokers. In practice, more than one investment banking firm underwrites a new offering because of the large sums of money involved.

As underwriters of the new issue, the investment banks assume a risk and make a profit. Their profit is the difference between the price paid to the issuing corporation and the price received from the public offering price. The underwriters attempt to sell the new issue of stocks or bonds to institutional investors (large organizations such as insurance companies, pension funds, or mutual funds) and to brokerage companies, which, in turn, resell the securities to individual investors. To promote sales, the underwriters will advertise the new issue in the financial sections of major newspapers and list all the firms underwriting the issue.

The Secondary Market

Investors finance first the birth, then the growth and success, of American corporations with the money they invest when buying securities. Investors are willing to buy and are willing to risk, but only if they will be able to sell their securities if and when they decide to do so. If investors were not able to sell their stocks and bonds, they would not have bought them. The ability to sell a security is provided by the secondary market.

In the secondary market, previously issued stocks and bonds are bought and sold. The secondary market exists to make it possible for both individual and institutional investors to sell or buy securities they already own.

■ TYPES OF CORPORATE SECURITIES

The most common types of corporate securities are bonds, common stock, and preferred stock. Each category has a number of variations. Many corporations issue all three types of securities.

Bonds

Corporations issue bonds to provide them with needed capital. A bond is a loan contract between the bond issuer (the corporation) and the bond buyer (the investor). The amount of the loan is the purchase price of the bond. In return for the loan, the corporation promises to make regular interest payments in specified amounts for a specified period of time, the end of which is the bond's maturity date. At the maturity date, the corporation repurchases or redeems the bond at the specified price. All terms are set forth in a document called the bond indenture.

Bonds are usually sold in units of $1,000, $5,000, $10,000, or $100,000, which is the face value of the bond; that is, the amount of money the issuing company must repay at maturity. Depending on the company, economic conditions, and other factors, the actual price a purchaser pays for a bond may be lower or higher than its face value. Whatever the price the bondholder pays, the issuing company must pay the face value at maturity.

There are a number of types of bonds, each with unique characteristics, discussed in the following sections.

Debentures

When a company issues debentures, it does not pledge any specified assets. Instead, the buyer depends on the good name and the earning power of the issuer as a guarantee that interest payments will be made on time and that the bonds will be redeemed at the maturity date.

Subordinated Debentures

Subordinated debentures, which are also unsecured bonds, specify that in case the issuer defaults, bondholders' claims on company assets will be subordinate or second to claims by regular debenture holders. Thus, because subordinated debentures are riskier, they typically pay higher interest.

For debentures and subordinated debentures, the company must make its interest payments whether or not it makes a profit. If the company does not meet its obligations to make interest payments, it is in default. The same is true of mortgage bonds, discussed in the following section.

Mortgage Bonds

Mortgage bonds, unlike debentures, are secured with fixed assets, which are specifically named in the bond agreement. The asset is generally a building, equipment, or land. In case the issuer is unable to repay the loan, the bondholder is entitled to the secured property.

Income Bonds

Income bonds, generally issued during the reorganization of a bankrupt company, require the issuing firm to meet its obligations to make interest payments only if it has sufficient money to do so. If the firm fails to pay the required interest to bondholders, the company is not in default; the balance due is carried over to the next year and added to the interest due then. Because of the uncertainty underlying income bonds, the investment risk is high.

It is important to note that issuers of bonds other than income bonds must pay the interest whether they have a profit or not. If a company fails to meet the payments on a debenture or mortgage bond, the company would then be in default.

Industrial Development Bonds

Industrial development bonds are issued by an industrial development agency of a state or local government to finance plants and facilities, which are then leased to private business. Raising money through industrial development bonds attracts industry, and helps state and local governments to energize the local economy.

Convertible Bonds

Convertible bonds can be exchanged for or converted to a company's stock at the option of the bondholder. The number of shares of stock and the price per share are clearly stated in the original agreement.

If the firm's stock increases in value, the investor can exercise his or her option to convert the bonds to stocks, and then, as an owner/stockholder, share in the firm's profits. Convertible bonds usually carry a lower interest rate than nonconvertible bonds.

Zero-Coupon Bonds

Zero-coupon bonds make no periodic interest payments. Instead, zero-coupon bonds are sold at a deep discount from their face value, and then, at maturity, the issuer buys back, or redeems, the bond at the full face value.

For example, U.S. government savings bonds having a face value of $50 are purchased at a deep discount, at $25. At maturity, these bonds are redeemed at their full face value of $50.

Junk Bonds

The term junk bond gained popularity as a result of takeovers and leveraged buyouts. These high-yield bonds, as investment bankers prefer calling them, carry yields several points higher because the bonds are issued by less-secure companies, which are forced to pay higher interest in order to attract investors and compensate them for accepting the higher risk.

Callable Bonds

Callable bonds may be redeemed before the maturity date at the option of the issuing company. If, for example, a corporation must issue bonds at a time when it must pay high interest rates, the firm may choose to issue callable bonds, and then, if interest rates do drop, call back the higher-interest bonds and issue bonds at a lower interest rate. The call price, the price at which the issuer redeems the bond, is higher than the amount of the bond, and the difference is the call premium.

Sinking-Fund Bonds

Sinking-fund bonds carry a sinking-fund provision—that is, the issuer makes regular payments into a fund or a savings account, and these funds accumulate over time and earn interest. The payments are planned so that there will be exactly enough money available to redeem the bond in full at the maturity date.

Serial Bonds

Serial bonds belong to a single bond issue but mature on different dates. For example, a corporation may issue a series of twenty-five-year bonds that it plans to redeem over a period of years, rather than all at once. The issuer may stipulate that at the end of fifteen years it will begin redeeming 10 percent of the total issue each year so that after twenty-five years, the entire issue will have been redeemed.

Bond Ratings

Investors evaluate bonds on the basis of two criteria: risk and return.
- **Risk** is the possibility that the issuing firm will not be able to meet its obligation.
- **Return** refers to the rate of interest payments.

The higher the risk, the higher the return. The lower the risk, the lower the return.

Bond-Rating Services

To help investors evaluate risk, two organizations publish bond ratings: Standard & Poor's Corporation (S&P) and Moody's Investment Service Inc. Table 22.1 shows the range of ratings each service uses to rate bond issues.

Table 22.1: Bond Ratings

Standard & Poor's	Moody's	
AAA	Aaa	Best Quality
AA	Aa	High Grade
A	A	Upper Medium Grade
BBB	Baa	Medium Grade
BB	Ba	Speculative
B	B	Not Desirable
CCC	Caa	In Default or Danger of Defualt
CC	Ca	Highly Speculative
C	C	Extremely Poor

Both S&P and Moody's give their highest ratings (AAA and Aaa, respectively) to the most secure bonds, bonds that rank second only to U.S. government securities (considered in the investment community to be the highest-rated, safest securities). Bonds with S&P ratings from AAA to BBB are referred to as investment grade. Many institutional investors, such as pension and retirement funds, are restricted from buying bonds rated BB or lower (junk bonds are rated BB and lower).

Common Stock

A share of common stock represents the most basic form of corporate ownership. Holders of common stock are the owners of the corporation. The total number of shares held by all the investors represents the total ownership of the company. Stocks have no maturity date and can be held permanently or sold, as the owner chooses.

As owners of the company, common stockholders are entitled to a share of the after-tax earnings, if any. When distributed to these shareholders, the earnings are called dividends. A corporation is not legally required to pay dividends.

Corporations may also reward stockholders with non-cash dividends. A stock dividend gives stockholders additional shares of stock in proportion to the number of shares they own. For example, the company's board of directors may elect to issue a 10 percent stock dividend, which gives stockholders one additional share for every ten already owned. Under a stock split, the company may issue one or more shares of additional stock to stockholders for each share they currently own.

Preferred Stock

Preferred stock is a cross between a corporate bond and common stock and shares some features of both. Like a bond, preferred stock pays a fixed income payment or dividend, but in the case of preferred stock the dividend represents a distribution of profit, not a payment of interest on a debt (as bond dividends represent). Preferred-stock dividends must be paid before common-stock dividends, if any, are paid. However, nonpayment of preferred-stock dividends does not put a company in default. Preferred stocks have no maturity dates.

If a firm is liquidated, the order of priority for payments is bondholders first, followed by preferred stockholders, and then common stockholders.

Cumulative preferred stock pays cumulative dividends—that is, if the dividend is not paid one year, the dividend is carried over to the next year. Again, common-stock dividends cannot be paid until all money due the preferred stockholders has been paid.

Convertible preferred stock, like convertible bonds, may be exchanged for common stock at a specified conversion price, allowing preferred stockholders to take advantage of a price rise in the common stock.

Mutual Funds

Mutual funds provide a vehicle for many small investors to combine their funds and act like one large investor. Investors buy shares in funds, and professional fund managers then invest the money accumulated (the types of investments will vary from one fund to another). The major advantages to individuals are the ability to buy a widely diversified range of stocks through the mutual fund and to have professional management oversee the investment. Mutual fund managers buy and sell stocks in extremely large quantities, making up a substantial portion of the institutional market.

There are many different kinds of mutual funds, offering investors a wide variety of investment opportunities. Mutual funds are described as closed-end or open-end funds, and as load or no-load funds.

Closed-End Funds

A closed-end fund sells shares in the fund only when the fund is first organized, at which time only a specified number of shares are made available. Once all the shares are sold, the fund is closed: An investor can buy or sell shares only from other investors—that is, on the secondary market, where the share price is based on the net asset value (NAV). The NAV is computed by dividing the total value of all stocks owned by the fund by the number of shares outstanding. The selling price will vary above or below the NAV, depending on the future outlook for the fund's holdings.

Open-End Funds

Open-end funds issue and sell shares to any willing investor. As investors purchase shares in the fund, the fund manager utilizes the additional cash to buy more securities. The value of each share in the fund varies according to the value of the fund's total investment portfolio. An open-end fund is always willing to repurchase all or any of the shares a fund owner wishes to sell, a feature that contributes to the wide popularity of open-end funds.

Load and No-Load Funds

Mutual funds are also described according to whether they charge sales fees (loads). Load funds charge investors a sales fee of from 7 to 8.5 percent for each purchase. No-load funds have no sales charge, but may charge a redemption fee of 1 to 2 percent. Both load and no-load funds charge a management fee of 0.5 to 1 percent of the total dollar amount invested. Because they have no sales fees, no-load funds generally charge higher management fees.

Investment Goals of Mutual Funds

Mutual fund managers tailor their portfolios to their investment goals, which are either to achieve growth or to provide income—or a combination of both. Mutual funds have grown to the point that funds now cover all types of investments, from the most speculative to the most conservative. Specialized funds exist that invest only in government bonds, only in utilities, only in specific industries, in specific countries, in gold, in growth companies or in high-income securities. There is a fund to meet almost every investment preference.

■ THE EXCHANGES

Stocks and bonds are bought and sold through stock exchanges. The New York Stock Exchange (NYSE) and the American Stock Exchange (AMEX) are two national exchanges. So, too, is the National

Association of Securities Dealers Automated Quotation (NASDQ). In addition, there are regional and several specialized exchanges.

The New York Stock Exchange (NYSE)

The New York Stock Exchange (NYSE) is an association of 1,469 members: 1,366 members own seats on the exchange, while 103 members pay an annual fee that allows them to use the trading floor of the NYSE.

The purpose of the NYSE is to help its members buy and sell stock for their customers. Toward this end, the NYSE building contains a trading floor for conducting transactions. On the trading floor, electronic equipment reports, controls, and facilitates trading. Millions of shares are traded each day on the NYSE; indeed, a 100-million-share day is considered slow.

The governors of the exchange set regulations governing all transactions. The stocks and bonds of over 1,500 corporations with a market value over $1.5 trillion are listed and traded on the NYSE. To be listed, a firm must meet these minimum requirements: (1) annual earnings of $2.5 million before taxes; (2) 1 million shares outstanding with a market value of $16 million; and (3) at least 2,000 shareholders who own at least one-hundred shares each.

The American Stock Exchange (AMEX)

The American Stock Exchange (AMEX), also a national exchange, is a smaller version of the NYSE. The 780 companies listed on the AMEX tend to be small- or middle-sized corporations with growth potential. As these companies grow, they may meet the requirements of the NYSE, and if accepted, move to that exchange. To meet the minimum requirements for listing on the AMEX, a firm must have pretax annual earnings of $750,000 and 500,000 shares outstanding.

The NASDAQ

The term over-the-counter (OTC) is misleading because the OTC market has no central location. OTC is a *way* of trading stocks rather than a *place* for trading stocks. There are no requirements for listing OTC stocks; most of the firms listed are small.

Originally, OTC stocks were traded by a network of brokers who communicated with one another by telephone. Today, the OTC market has an automated computer service called the National Association of Security Dealers Automated Quotations (NASDAQ, pronounced "NAZ-deck").

The NASDQ stock market is an electronic marketplace and the second largest equity market in the United States. It operates over multiple competing market-makers and has a greater volume than the American Stock Exchange. It is divided into two markets: (1) the National Market System (NMS), in which shares are quoted in financial newspapers and major general-circulation newspapers; and (2) the Small Capital (Small Caps) Market.

NASDAQ uses a network of computer terminals in dealers' offices to collect and display the prices of about 4,000 of the most actively traded stocks. Non-listed OTC stocks are still traded by telephone. While the NYSE trades fewer than 2,000 stocks and the AMEX fewer than 1,000, the OTC trades about 30,000 different stocks.

Regional Exchanges

Regional exchanges serve as trading places for companies in specific local areas. The main regional exchanges, in order of size, are the Midwest, Pacific, Philadelphia, and Boston Exchanges. Recently, a few large national corporations that are traded on the national exchanges have begun to be traded on regional exchanges.

■ THE OVER-THE-COUNTER MARKET (OTC)

Buying and Selling Securities

Buying and selling any good or service, including securities, requires a buyer, a seller, and an agreed-upon price. For stocks, however, the price is not set by the seller alone, as the following discussion shows.

The Stockbroker's Role

The stockbroker can perform a number of functions and services for investors. Full-service brokers supply research material, analysis, and advice. Discount brokers only execute buy and sell orders, but they offer no other services, allowing discount brokers to charge lower commission and transaction fees.

To place a client's order to buy or sell securities on an exchange, the stockbroker places the order with a commission broker.

The Commission Broker's Role

Most exchanges use a post trading system, whereby each stock traded on the exchange is assigned a "post" or a trading area. A commission broker who has either a buy order or a sell order for a stock goes to the post for that stock and attempts to make a trade. Price is set by the supply and demand. The selling price depends on the balance between how much a seller is willing to accept and how much a buyer is willing to pay.

The Specialist's Role

The specialist is an important person in "making a market" for securities. The specialist stays at the post in the trading area of the exchange where that specialist's stock is traded, and monitors the trades of that particular stock. The specialist is responsible for maintaining an "orderly and fair" market in that company's stock. In an effort to minimize large price fluctuations, the specialist will regularly buy and sell that particular stock in his or her own account. Thus, for example, if a commission broker has a buy order for Company A stock at $37 dollars and sellers are currently not accepting less than $38, the specialist will offer to buy or sell stock at some price between $37 and $38 to complete the trade.

Orders and Lots

Commission brokers receive various instructions or orders for buying and selling stocks.

Orders

Most orders are market orders, which authorize the sale or purchase at the best possible price at that moment, generally very close to the price of the last trade for a particular stock. A limit order, however, limits the commission broker to buy only at a specified price or lower, or to sell only at a specified price or higher.

Lots

Stocks are typically traded in round lots; that is, in multiples of one hundred shares. A transaction of fewer than one hundred shares—for example, a buy order for fifty-two shares—is called an odd lot. Finding a seller who wants to sell precisely fifty-two shares is not always possible. An odd-lot broker gathers and combines several odd lots to make up a round lot, which can then be sold at once.

A Typical Transaction

A typical transaction is illustrated in Figure 22.1. Assume, for example, that a female stockholder in Cleveland, Ohio, wants to sell one hundred shares of General Motors stock and that another investor, a man in Miami, Florida, wishes to buy one hundred shares of General Motors stock. Each person calls a local broker, one to place a sell order; the other, a buy order. Each local broker wires instructions to a commission broker on the floor of the NYSE, where General Motors is traded. (Commission brokers often work for the same company as the broker.) The two commission brokers individually go to the specialist at the trading post and execute the trade.

Once the trade is made, the price per share and the number of shares traded appear on the ticker tape, and the brokers are notified that the trade has been made. The broker in Cleveland then informs his or her customer that her one hundred shares of General Motors have been sold. The broker in Miami informs his or her customer that he now owns one hundred shares of General Motors.

Buyer → Stock Broker → Commission Broker → Trading Area → Commission Broker → Selling Broker → Seller

Figure 22.1: Typical Stock Trading Process

Trading Tactics

A number of sophisticated trading tactics have been developed, many of which fall into the area of speculation rather than investing.

Selling Short

When investors speculate that a stock price will fall, they may choose to sell short, which is a strategy that relies on borrowing stock from the broker and then selling the borrowed stock. The broker holds the proceeds of the sale as collateral. For example, assume that an investor believes stock in Company A, now selling at $50 a share, will soon drop to $35 a share or lower. The investor borrows one hundred shares from the broker, orders the broker to sell those one hundred shares at the current price of $50 a share, and promises to replace those shares in the future. If the investor's speculation pays off and two months later, the stock drops to, say, $36, the investor buys one hundred shares of Company A at $36 a share and returns those shares to the broker, repaying the debt to the broker of the borrowed stock (namely, one hundred shares of Company A). The investor's profit is the difference between the price sold ($50) and the price paid ($36), multiplied by one hundred shares, less commission fees, of course.

On the other hand, if the price rises instead of falls, the investor must then buy shares to repay the broker at a higher price than he or she sold and suffers a loss.

Buying on Margin

Buying on margin permits an investor to finance part of a stock purchase with borrowed money. At the present time, investors may borrow up to 50 percent of the purchase price from the broker. When buying on margin, the investor is speculating that the stock price will rise. If a $50 stock purchased on margin for $25 rises, say, from $50 to $60, the investor realizes a $10 per share profit on a $25 investment (a 40 percent profit), less the interest on the borrowed money. If the investor had purchased the stock outright at $50 a share, profit on the $50 investment would be $10, or 20 percent.

But buying on margin presents great risks. If the stock falls to $40 a share, a $10 drop, and the investor sold, he or she would still have to repay the broker the borrowed sum, $25 a share, out of the proceeds. The net of $15 a share represents a 40 percent loss on the $25 originally invested.

Options

Options give the holder the right, but not the obligation, to buy or sell a specified stock at a specified price for a specified period of time. The option, which may cost only a small amount, represents only the right to buy; it does not represent ownership.

Calls

A call is the right to buy a specified stock at a specified price for a specified period, for example, three months. The person selling the option is called the writer. Assume that a speculator has purchased a call—that is, a right to buy one hundred shares of Company A stock at $50 a share. If the price of Company A stock rises to $60, the investor can exercise his or her right to purchase the stock at $50, or if the investor prefers, sell the option, which now has a greater value and can be sold for a profit to someone who wishes to buy the stock at this special price. Either way, the call will realize a substantial profit for the investor.

But remember, the option expires at the end of a specified period. If the stock has not risen, or has fallen in price, at the end of the option period the speculator allows the option to expire. The speculator's loss is then the fee paid for the option. The writer's profit is the option fee received.

Puts

A put is the right to sell a specified stock at a specified price for a specified period. Because a put is the right to sell, its value increases as the price of the stock falls. If the price of the stock rises above the stated price, the put expires without being exercised.

■ READING THE FINANCIAL NEWS

Nearly every newspaper has a financial section that offers financial news and long tables of very small print. A few papers are devoted entirely to business news. In addition, several periodicals supply general economic news as well as detailed financial information about companies. Besides newspapers and periodicals, there are many other sources of financial news and advice. Full-service brokers prepare detailed analyses, including buy and sell recommendations, and they make these analyses available to their customers. Many brokers and other financial institutions now offer "real time" stock quotations on the Internet. Corporations issue quarterly and annual stockholders' reports that are available to the general public.

Investors may also subscribe to services that provide financial information and advice to their readers for an annual subscription fee. Among the best known are Bloomberg, Value Line, Moody's Investment Service, and Standard & Poor's Reports. The transactions for listed stocks, bonds, and the OTC markets are listed separately, and the tables listing the transactions are different.

Listed Stocks

The NYSE and AMEX stock listings also include preferred stocks in their alphabetical listings. Table 22.2 shows a listing for Merck, Inc., a global pharmaceutical company.

NASDAQ

The information in NASDAQ quotes include the same information as the NYSE and AMEX:

Bond Prices

The face value of bonds is generally $1,000, but in bond quotations, prices are listed on a basis of 100. Thus, for example, the actual price for a $1,000 bond may be listed at 97 1/2, which means $975: $97.5 \times 10 = \$975$

Stock Averages

Financial journals also publish stock averages or stock indexes, which give investors general stock market information. In addition to those listed in the following sections, there are various other indexes such as the Russell 2000 and the Wilshire 500, but these are not as closely watched or as well known.

Table 22.2: Merck Listing as of October 1, 2005

52-Week Hi	52-Week Lo	Stock	Sym	Div	Yld %	PE	Vol in 100s	Hi	Lo	Close	Net Chg
35.36	25.50	MERCK	MRK	1.52	5.7	13	100387	27.20	26.20	26.75	−0.15

The 52-week Hi and Lo columns show the highest and lowest price of the issue during the past 52 weeks, plus the current week.

Stock column shows the company name.

Sym column shows the company stock symbol.

Div column shows dividend rates are annual disbursements.

Yld is the dividends paid by a company on its securities, expressed as a percentage of the stock price.

PE is the price-earnings ratio, which is determined by dividing the price of a share of stock by the company's earnings per share of that stock.

Vol in 100s is the unofficial daily total of shares traded quoted in hundreds (two zeros omitted).

Hi is the highest price at which the stock traded on the day listed.

Lo is the lowest price at which the stock traded on the day listed.

Close is the price at which the last trade of the day was made.

Net Chg is the difference between the close of the day listed and the close of the previous day.

Table 22.3: Dow Jones Industrial Average Companies

3M Company	Home Depot, Incorporated
Alcoa Incorporated	Honeywell International, Inc.
Altria Group, Incorporated	Intel Corporation
American Express Company	International Business Machines
American International Group, Inc.	Johnson & Johnson
AT&T, Inc.	J.P. Morgan Chase & Company
Boeing Company	McDonald's Corporation
Caterpillar, Incorporated	Merck & Company, Incorporated
Citigroup, Incorporated	Microsoft Corporation
Coca-Cola Company	Pfizer, Incorporated
E.I. du Pont de Nemours & Co.	Procter & Gamble Company
ExxonMobile Corporation	United Technologies Corporation
General Electric Company	Verizon Communications, Inc.
General Motors Corporation	Wal-Mart Stores, Incorporated
Hewlett-Packard, Company	Walt Disney Company

The Dow Jones Industrial Average

Perhaps the best-known of the stock averages, the Dow Jones Industrial Average, simply called the Dow, is an adjusted average of the prices of thirty leading industrial companies. The companies comprising the Dow have changed over time; as of October 1, 2005, the companies listed in Table 22.3 comprised the Dow.

The Dow Jones Company also publishes a Transportation Average, made up of twenty transportation-industry stocks, a Utility Average made up of fifteen utility stocks, and a Composite Average made up of the sixty-five stocks included in the Industrial, Transportation, and Utility Averages.

The Standard & Poor's Index (S&P 500)

Although the Dow is the best known, it is not the broadest average available. The Standard & Poor's Index (S&P 500) covers 500 NYSE companies in 88 industries. It is made up of 400 industrial companies, 40 public utilities, 20 transportation companies, and 40 financial institutions. Because of its wide coverage, many people consider the S&P 500 a more representative reflection of market activity.

The New York Stock Exchange Composite Index (NYSE Composite)

The New York Stock Exchange Composite Index (NYSE Composite) is computed from a weighted average reflecting the number and value of all outstanding shares of common stocks listed on the exchange.

The NASDAQ Composite Index

The NASDAQ Composite Index measures all NASDAQ common stocks listed on the NASDAQ Stock Market. The index is market-value weighted. The NASDAQ-100 Index includes only the 100 largest domestic and international nonfinancial companies listed on The NASDAQ Stock Market. It reflects companies across major industry groups, including computer hardware and software, telecommunications, retail/wholesale trade, and biotechnology. It does not include any financial companies.

The American Stock Exchange Value Index

The American Stock Exchange Value Index is made up of the value of all the stocks listed on the AMEX.

■ REGULATION OF SECURITIES TRADING

Government regulation of securities began as a response to fraudulent practices and abuses in the sale of stocks and bonds to the public as well as to rigging of the markets. Huge sums of money are involved in securities trading. In an effort to protect investors from unfair treatment, both state and federal governments have acted to regulate the industry.

State Regulation

In 1911, Kansas enacted the first state law to regulate the sale of securities. Within a few years, several other states followed. Today, most states have regulations requiring that a new stock issue be registered with a state agency and that brokers and dealers be licensed. Laws also provide for prosecution and penalties for fraudulent sales of stocks or bonds.

Federal Regulation

Federal regulation, much more detailed and extensive than state regulation, originally came into being as a reaction to abuses and excesses leading to the market crash of 1929 and the Depression that followed.

The Securities Act of 1933

The Securities Act of 1933 required full disclosure of important facts about a corporation issuing new securities. The act required a corporation to file a registration statement containing specific information about earnings, assets, liabilities, its products or services, and the qualifications of its top management. It also required the corporation to publish a prospectus containing a summary of the information.

The Securities Exchange Act of 1934

The Securities Exchange Act of 1934 created the Securities and Exchange Commission (SEC) to enforce federal securities regulations. The 1934 act gives the SEC the power to regulate the trading on the NYSE and AMEX and to require brokers and dealers to pass an examination before they are allowed to sell securities. It also required registration statements to be updated periodically.

Other Federal Regulations

Since the Securities Exchange Act of 1934, a number of other laws have been enacted extending the jurisdiction of the SEC to protect investors.

The Maloney Act of 1938

The Maloney Act of 1938 established the National Association of Securities Dealers (NASD) for self-regulation of the OTC market.

The Investment Company Act of 1940

The Investment Company Act of 1940 placed companies that sell mutual funds under SEC jurisdiction.

The Federal Securities Act of 1964

The Federal Securities Act of 1964 extended the SEC's jurisdiction to cover stocks sold on the OTC market of companies with assets of at least $1 million or more than 500 stockholders.

The Securities Investors Protection Act of 1970 (SIPC)

The Securities Investors Protection Act of 1970 (SIPC) provides investors with insurance up to $500,000 for securities or $100,000 for cash left on deposit with a brokerage firm that fails.

Selected Readings

Beim, David O. *Emerging Financial Markets.* 2000.
Darst, David M. *The Handbook of the Bond and Money Markets.* 1981.
Fabozzi, Frank, and Franco Madigliani. *Capital Markets.* 2002.
Fabozzi, Frank J., and Frank G. Zarb, editors. *Handbook of Financial Markets: Securities, Options, Futures.* 1981.
Graham, Benjamin. *Security Analysis.* 1951.
Hayes, Samuel L. III, editor. *Wall Street and Regulation.* 1987.
Investment Company Institute and Security Industry Association. *Equity Ownership in America.* 2005.
MacKay, Charles. *Extraordinary Popular Delusions and the Madness of Crowds.* 1932.
Malkiel, Burton. *A Random Walk Down Wall Street.* 1981.
Mayer, Colin, editor. *Financial Innovation & the Regulation of Capital Markets.* 1990.
New York Stock Exchange. *The NYSE Fact Book 2001.* 2001.
Peters, Edgar E. *Patterns in the Dark.* 1999.
Pring, Martin. *Technical Analysis Explained.* 1985.
Shilling, A. Gary. *After the Crash: Recession or Depression? Business Investment Strategies for a Deflationary World.* 1988.
Smith, Adam. *The Money Game.* 1976.
Sobel, Robert. *The Big Board: A History of the New York Stock Exchange.* 1965.
Sobel, Robert. *The Curbstone Brokers: The Origins of the American Stock Exchange.* 2000.
Westerfield, Ross S., and B. Jordan. *Essentials of Corporate Finance.* 2004.

Test Yourself

1) Why are securities markets important?

2) Distinguish between the primary and secondary securities markets.

3) List the different types of bond investments available to the public.

4) What is the usual risk relationship with returns?

5) If an investor is primarily concerned with earning the highest return, would he or she prefer to own common stock, preferred stock, or bonds? Why?

6) It is often said that preferred stock is a hybrid of a common stock and a bond. Why?

7) Why would a small investor prefer to invest in a mutual fund rather than trying to invest in individual stocks and bonds?

8) Investor X believes the price of Vogt Company stock will rise. He borrows $30 per share to pay for 100 share of stock at a price of $60 per share. Investor X sells the stock at a price of $80 per share. In securities-market parlance, what is this type of transaction called? Ignoring the interest on the borrowed funds, what percentage return did Investor X earn?

9) The Dow Jones is much more often quoted than the S&P 500. Which of the two provides the better indication of general economic conditions of the securities market? Why?

10) Why is the Securities Exchange Act of 1934 important?

Test Yourself Answers

1) The markets make possible the establishing and growing of businesses by supplying the capital needed to fund operations. For individuals, they are important in that they provide opportunities to earn interest, dividends, and capital gains, and to share in American business.

2) The primary market includes newly issued securities by the company. The secondary market provides a mechanism for securities holders to buy and sell securities already owned by individuals.

3) Available bonds include debentures, subordinated debentures, mortgage bonds, income bonds, industrial development bonds, convertible bonds, zero-coupon bonds, junk bonds, callable bonds, sinking-fund bonds, and serial bonds.

4) Ordinarily, the higher the risks, the higher the returns, and vice versa.

5) The investor would prefer the common stock. The preferred stock and the bonds are relatively assured of receiving returns but they are limited.

6) Preferred shareholders are entitled to receive dividends based on a constant percentage (similar to a bond's interest), if any, prior to the common shareholders' receiving anything. On the other hand, if the board of directors does not declare a dividend, the preferred shareholders are not entitled to any dividend for the year (similar to a common stock).

7) Mutual funds provide an opportunity for small investors to combine their funds to act as one large investor. Investors buy shares in the fund and professional fund managers invest the money and manage the fund.

8) The transaction is termed "buying on margin." It is a risky approach to buying stock, but can result in significant earnings. In this transaction, Investor X earned a 67 percent return ($20 return/$30 investment = 67%).

9) The Standard & Poor's Index (S&P 500) provides a much better indication of the overall securities market because it is much bigger and broader in scope; it includes 500 companies across 88 industries. The Dow Jones Industrial Average, on the other hand, includes only 30 companies across fewer distinct industries.

10) The 1934 Securities Exchange Act created the Securities and Exchange Commission (SEC), with a charge to enforce securities regulations. In addition, it gives the SEC the power to regulate the trading on the NYSE and AMEX, and to require brokers and dealers to pass an examination before they are allowed to sell securities.

Part 7: The Challenge of the Future

CHAPTER 23

Business Careers

A business career can be quite rewarding. In addition to earning a good living, business professionals can make a huge difference in the economic well-being of a region, through the work they do on a day-to-day basis and the broader leadership abilities they can contribute to the communities in which they live.

■ WHAT IS A "CAREER"?

A career is a life-work chosen by a person to use his or her personal talent, education, and/or training, to provide some service or goods, earn money, and contribute to society.

There is an important difference between a job and a career. Your job belongs to your employer. It is a specified function, a set of tasks that an organization needs a person to perform. If you don't do it, someone else will. Your career belongs to you. You will have many jobs, even if you only have one employer, and these jobs will make up your career. Each job is a step toward establishing a satisfying and successful career. One job is "better" than another only if it moves you toward that goal. Your career is human resources management from your point of view.

This chapter will help you attain your personal definition of success by identifying information about yourself and by gathering information about organizations that are most likely to have career opportunities for you.

■ CHOOSING A CAREER

Some people choose their careers. In other cases, careers choose people—that is, their careers happen by chance. Some wait for an opportunity, recognize it, and take advantage of it as best they can. Some accept the recommendation or advice of parents, friends, or counselors.

The people who take charge of their future forge their own careers. In some cases, the path is a straight line; once the career decision is made, the individual may spend a lifetime in that chosen occupational field. Most times, however, interests and needs change, as do business environments. As a result, an individual will choose to, or be forced to, shift jobs, locations, and careers.

In any case, a career is a journey and not a destination. Career decisions are part of a broader set of decisions that include lifestyle, family, and other personal matters. As important as career decisions are, they are not made on a one-time permanent basis. Rather, they are part of a continuing, lifelong process.

There is no set route. The only constant is change. The better the understanding you have of yourself, work tasks and environments, and career paths, the greater control you will have of your own career.

Choosing a career is an information-gathering process involving a series of steps and searches. The process starts with self-assessment, moves to an assessment of the business world, and then finds the best fit between you and the organizations that need you and that offer the kinds of jobs you want.

Understanding Self-Assessment

The first step in choosing a career is self-assessment. Before you can choose a career, you need to know who you are, what skills you have, what motivates you, and what you find satisfying. The process of self-assessment is based on your examination of your own personal characteristics—your interests, personality characteristics, skills and abilities, values, and lifestyle.

Interests

Interests are anything you enjoy doing. It can relate to work or play, to career or hobby. The Strong Interest Inventory is frequently used to elicit a person's interests or attitudes. It does not measure intelligence, aptitudes, or skills. Rather, it produces a profile based on the work of John Holland, a career-development theorist who classified six broad categories marked with simple letters.

- **R:** Realistic occupations, which deal with things rather than with ideas or people. Examples include computer repair and construction.
- **I:** Investigative occupations, which center around science and scientific activities to better understand the physical world. Examples include medical research and oceanography.
- **A:** Artistic occupations, which provide many opportunities for self-expression. Examples include commercial art and acting.
- **S:** Social occupations, which are concerned with the welfare of others. Examples include social work and nursing.
- **E:** Enterprising occupations, which require persuading others. Examples include sales and advertising.
- **C:** Conventional occupations, which are highly ordered. Examples include secretarial work and accounting.

Personality Characteristics

Personality characteristics determine to a large extent who you are. The Myers-Briggs Type Indicator (MBTI), based on the theories of Carl Jung, examines the preferences that determine your personality predispositions. The categories are arranged in scales representing opposites in four dimensions.

- The **Extraversion-Introversion** scale describes where one likes to focus attention: the outer world of people or one's own inner world.
- The **Sensing-Intuitive** scale describes the opposite ways a person perceives or acquires information. A sensing person depends on physical senses (hearing, seeing, etc.), while an intuitive person relies on feelings.
- The **Thinking-Feeling** scale describes how a person reaches conclusions or makes decisions once he or she has appropriate information.
- The **Judging-Perceiving** scale describes one's adaptation to the outer world. A judging person likes things planned and in place, while a perceiving person is more spontaneous.

The MBTI divides people into sixteen combinations of these distinguishable personality types, and identifies preferences in jobs and work arrangements that will provide people with the opportunity to express and use those preferences.

Skills and Abilities

Skills and abilities are your talents. Academic skills, mechanical aptitude, dexterity, language fluency, and social skills all contribute to the total picture. These skills may already be present, but they can be developed or enhanced through education and training.

Values

Values are the principles or standards that represent what is important to you. Life values include, for example, financial independence, family, religious freedom, and marriage. These values are influenced by people such as your parents, teachers, and peers and by social, cultural, and economic factors. Work-related values include recognition, security, challenge, meaningful job tasks, commitment to quality, and working conditions.

Lifestyle

Lifestyle describes the way a person chooses to live. The interactions of your work, leisure, and interpersonal relationships make up your lifestyle. You can choose to be near family or not, to live in an apartment or a single-family house, and so on. Lifestyle decisions include choices such as the geographic location of where you live—urban, suburban, or rural. Lifestyle goals can change as personal needs and circumstances in life change.

The Job Seeker

There are several standardized tests that can help you with the process of self-assessment and with determining vocational interests. The Myers-Briggs Type Indicator and the Strong Interest Inventory have already been mentioned. Others are the Jackson Vocational Interest Survey and the System of Interacting Guidance and Information Plus (SIGI Plus), a computerized career-information system.

Conscientiously executed, the self-assessment process is very informative and develops a great deal of data. In addition to an inventory of skills, the process will give you a good idea of the work-styles you prefer. You will learn whether you:

- Like to work alone or in teams.
- Prefer to have autonomy or work at clearly defined tasks.
- Would rather organize or execute.
- Prefer to work with detailed analyses or with broader ideas.

You will also have an understanding of the sort of environment you prefer, what pace of work, how much variety you require, and the other aspects of work that are important to you.

Understanding the Business World

In order to make an intelligent choice, you must know what the options are. The U.S. Department of Labor's *Occupational Outlook Handbook* lists 225 occupations, 80 percent of all jobs in the economy. For each area, the handbook describes the nature of the work, working conditions, qualifications required, and an overview of broad trends. The information is very useful, but to make a meaningful choice you will need a narrower focus. The screening process starts with the broad choice of industry, narrows to the occupation, and finally to the job. All three areas are discussed in the following sections.

Industry

The examination of career opportunities begins with a broad view of industries, which can be classified as either goods-producing or service-producing industries.

Goods-Producing Industries

Goods-producing industries are divided into four main categories: manufacturing, agriculture, construction, or mining. In recent years, the number of jobs in goods-producing industries has not grown appreciably, due partly to automation and partly to improved productivity resulting from better-trained workers.

Service-Producing Industries

Service-producing industries comprise retail and wholesale trade, government (local, state, and federal, including education), repair and maintenance services, transportation and public utilities, finance, insurance, real estate, advertising, and health care. Service-producing industries have shown continuing growth in recent years.

Occupations

Occupations can be divided into four groups: white collar, blue collar, service, and farm. In evaluating any of these groups, you should consider whether it shows a trend for growing or contracting.

White Collar

White-collar jobs, or nonfactory jobs, include professional and technical workers—teachers, engineers, doctors, accountants, clergy, managers and administrators, sales workers, clerical workers, and more.

Managers and administrators are increasingly in demand as firms come to depend on trained management specialists more and more. Because of needs in electronic data processing, the demand for computer-literate clerical workers is rapidly expanding. Sales workers—people selling goods and services for retail, wholesale, insurance, and real estate firms—also represent a growth area.

Blue Collar

Blue-collar workers include craft workers, semiskilled workers, and laborers. Craft workers include carpenters, machinists, and electricians. Semiskilled workers assemble goods, operate machines in factories, and drive vehicles such as trucks or buses. Laborers perform unskilled work and include truck loaders and stock clerks.

Service Occupations

Service-occupations workers are employed in service fields such as health care, appliance maintenance and service, and a wide range of personal-services occupations (for example, beauty shops). Many white-collar workers such as secretaries are employed in service industries, but the phrase *service occupations* refers only to those who perform the actual services.

Farm Occupations

Farm occupations include farmers, farm managers, and farm supervisors. As mechanization of farms continues, the number of farm occupations is shrinking.

Jobs

Ultimately, an individual works at a job within an occupation in an industry. The chapters throughout this book help make you aware of the diverse jobs existing in business, helps you understand the nature of some of those jobs, and assists you in identifying career opportunities that are appropriate for you. Therefore, we now discuss representative job titles of occupations as they were presented in this book.

Part I: The Challenge of American Business

Job opportunities include analysts, advocates and lobbyists, economic geographers, government inspectors (including health inspectors), food and drug inspectors, meat and poultry inspectors, wage and compliance officers, and bank economists.

Part II: Business Formation

Job opportunities include lawyers specializing in government regulatory work; litigation; labor law; equal employment opportunity; banking; criminal law; environmental, bankruptcy, corporate law; and product liability law.

Part III: Managing the Enterprise

Job opportunities include work supervisors, analysts, management consultants, hotel managers, hotel assistants, health-services administrators, and medical-records administrators.

Part IV: Managing People and Production

Job opportunities in managing people include personnel specialists, recruiters, trainers, wage and salary compensation specialists, recreational safety and health workers, labor relations specialists, labor union business agents, and interviewers in employment agencies.

Job opportunities in production management include computer-assisted manufacturing-production supervisors, manufacturing inspectors, engineering technicians, industrial planners, purchasing agents, and technical writers. Drafters and industrial designers are employed in product development. Production and operations departments are headed by a vice president of operations at the top management level and a plant manager in middle-level management.

Part V: Marketing Management

Job opportunities include special-events coordinators, retail, wholesale, and manufacturer's sales workers, retail buyers, displayers, promotion assistants, public relations workers, advertising space salespeople, product or brand managers and assistants, account executives, market research analysts, interviewers, and statisticians.

Part VI: Management Tools

Job opportunities include bookkeepers and accounting clerks, credit managers, internal and external auditors, public and corporate accountants, tax accountants, controllers, data processing clerks, computer operators and programmers, application support workers, computer service technicians, customer services representatives, computer designers, computer engineers, documentation specialists, statisticians, and operations analysts.

Part VII: Financial Management

Job opportunities include bank tellers, bank branch officers and/or managers, trust and estate administrators, loan counselors, credit analysts, claims adjustors, insurance agents, brokers, actuaries, securities sales workers or stockbrokers, financial analysts, underwriters, and treasurers.

By researching the job description for a particular job title, you will gather much valuable information. For example, in most occupations, jobs will require different levels of skill and responsibility. The job description details the responsibilities for a particular job. The job specifications outline any requirements for training, education, and prior work experience needed to perform the responsibilities; at entry level, people with good general skills and the ability to learn are sought. The job outlook describes the anticipated future for a particular job.

Opportunities for getting a particular job depend on the relationship between the number of openings and the number of qualified people for that job. At any time, economic forces, government programs, and geographic imbalances can cause a shortage or a surplus for a particular job. In general, jobs in the future will require increasing levels of training and education.

■ MAKING THE MATCH

Once you have identified a job that matches your interests, abilities, and career goals, your next step is to identify companies where you would like to work and that have, or will have, job openings, and then persuade those companies to hire you. You begin this stage by learning more about specific companies.

The Company and Its Culture

Just as people have individual identities, so do organizations. The "personality" of an organization can be seen in its corporate culture. Corporate culture evolves from many aspects of each corporation's environment: the way people dress; the way they act; the management style; the expected number of work hours; and attitudes toward teamwork, risk-taking, and work-life balance. Moreover, some firms encourage independence, while some emphasize close adherence to established procedures and policies. All these factors, and more, contribute to a company's corporate culture.

Different areas of business have different cultures; for example, advertising agencies and accounting firms tend to have very different cultures. But even within the same industry—in advertising, for example—different firms have different styles.

Gathering information on an industry and on specific companies within an industry involves research. Libraries have a variety of useful directories that describe industries by company, location, sales volume, and other characteristics. Trade journals are a source of industry information. Dun and Bradstreet's *The Career Guide, America's Corporate Families,* and *Million Dollar Directories* (Volumes I, II, and III) contain a wide range of information on specific companies. The U.S. Department of Labor's *Occupational Outlook Handbook,* which offers information on occupations, has already been discussed.

As you narrow your choice to specific companies, you will that find magazines and newspapers are a source of current information. The company's annual report contains much information. Even more helpful, if available, is the more-detailed 10K report, which the Securities and Exchange Commission (SEC) requires every publicly-owned corporation to file. Financial information on companies can also be found in Moody's Manuals, Standard & Poor's Corporate Records, and the Value Line Investment Survey.

Privately-held companies and partnerships are more difficult to research. However, the local Chamber of Commerce, the Better Business Bureau, and trade publications can be very informative.

The Match

Armed with job and career goals and having a sense of what companies you might want to work for, your next step is to find a good match. Sometimes, you'll find a position that seems perfect for you, but the company may not be interested in you, or it may have other candidates it prefers. Other times, you'll find a company that is interested in you, but does not offer the work environment, salary, or opportunity that you want. Neither of these situations is a good match. Instead, a good match is a job opportunity that meets your requirements in a company you like that has a need for someone with your qualifications.

The Job Search

Newspaper classified ads are one good source of position openings. College placement offices, newsletters, trade publications, and specialized job-bank services also list openings. In today's technological world, the Internet probably offers the broadest selection of job opportunities through one of the hundreds of International, National, or local job-search websites. A job search can be a numbers game: The more people you contact for jobs or leads, the wider your contact list and the more likely it is that your search will be successful.

Networking

Networking, a proven, effective strategy, is the process of using contacts to make more contacts. The key to networking is to develop contact lists. Write lists of the names of businesspeople you know, people in companies you are interested in, people in professions of interest, and friends and relatives who might provide the names of additional contacts or information about industries, companies, or jobs. Then select from your list the names of those people who can most likely provide you with help in the form of additional contacts, company information, career objectives, and so on.

Before you call, develop a short sample presentation, in which you introduce yourself, explain how you acquired the person's name, and state the purpose of the call. Note that your purpose is not to ask for a job; you must make this clear immediately. The purpose is to get information—about their fields, companies, contacts, and the labor market. You are calling to schedule a brief meeting—an informational interview—at a convenient time to discuss career opportunities.

Before the meeting, prepare your key questions. At the meeting, ask for suggestions for your job search and for names of others who might be of assistance. Respect the person's time: Keep the meeting brief, as you promised. In using this approach, you present yourself as a knowledgeable person who has a professional manner.

The more people you meet for an informational interview, the greater your odds of obtaining job leads and expanding your contact list and there lies the strength of networking, getting referrals from each person you contact. Sometimes you learn about job opportunities during the informational interview. If you act on any suggestions given to you, be sure to inform the originator of the suggestion about the results.

Employment Offices

Employment offices are operated by city, state, and federal governments, and by private agencies. They list job openings and charge no fee to either the employee or the hiring company.

Employment Agencies

Employment agencies, which include both private employment agencies and executive recruiters, do charge fees. Many employment agencies specialize in a single industry banking or advertising, for example. Agency fees may be paid by either the company or the individual. Employment agencies are most useful for those who already have some work experience.

Direct Mailings

Direct mailings to companies can also result in interviews, although according to estimates, you may need to send one hundred letters to generate five interviews. Including a customized cover letter with the résumé is much more effective than sending the résumé alone. Direct your mailings to a specific person, preferably one in a position to hire you.

The Résumé

Your résumé represents you. Thus, the information it contains and its physical form are very important and deserve your careful attention.

In addition to saying what you want about yourself, your résumé should present the information your prospective employer will want to know about you. The best résumés are directed to a specific audience for a specific purpose. If your job search covers several industries or occupations, you may need to develop a résumé for each target audience.

There is no single "correct way" to design a résumé, but there are guidelines. Neatness counts, as do spelling and grammar. If you must submit a hard copy of your résumé use white or off-white paper and a matching envelope. (Of course, many résumé are now submitted online.) If possible, limit the résumé to one page—no more than two pages unless you have years of experience.

The résumé should contain the following information.

Personal Data

Include your personal data—your name, address, telephone number(s), and e-mail address.

Career Objectives

State your career objectives in a way that does not limit possible jobs. Customize your objective for the particular company and job for which you are applying.

Potential

Demonstrate your potential. Highlight the skills, talents, and capabilities that give you an advantage compared to other applicants. Stress your accomplishments and achievements.

Experience and Education

List information related to your experience and education that are pertinent to the position sought. Use action words such as accomplished, demonstrated, increased, managed, and initiated.

References

Make a note that references will be made available upon request; do not include the names of references in the résumé, but prepare a list of references for those employers who request references and have it readily available. In your list of references, include the names of teachers and employers. Before you list any names, however, be sure to get each person's permission.

Other Information

Try to differentiate yourself from other applicants. Add information about activities, language skills, travel, or personal interests related to the specific job. Remember that your purpose is to convince the prospective employer to grant you an interview.

Many books have been written about writing effective résumés. Writing a résumé is not a light undertaking; it is hard work. Write, rewrite, refine, and polish your résumé—both its content and its format until you are proud to have it represent you. Finally, ask persons whose opinions you value to critique your résumé.

The Cover Letter

Never mail a résumé without a cover letter, a letter whose purpose is to accompany the résumé and highlight key points of information that are pertinent to the job. No matter how you find out about a job opening, learn as much as you can about the employer and the job, and use this information in the cover letter. The appearance, form, style, and content all contribute to the message you convey. The letter should be on the same type of paper as your résumé.

Here is a brief outline for a cover letter.

1. In the first paragraph, clearly identify the specific job you are applying for and why you are interested in that job. If you have been recommended by an individual, mention his or her name. If you are replying to an ad, mention the source of the ad.
2. In the second paragraph, discuss your qualifications, expanding on the experience described in your résumé. Make clear your knowledge and interest in the company and the particular job.
3. In the closing paragraph, express your interest in meeting with the employer to discuss the requirements of the job and your qualifications.

The cover letter and résumé have one purpose: to get an interview. They should convince the prospective employer to grant you an interview.

If you do not hear from the prospective employer in a reasonable length of time (say, two weeks), telephone the person you wrote to and inquire how the search is progressing. This will indicate your continuing interest and could lead to an interview.

The Interview

Dress according to industry practice. If you do not know, visit the company in advance to see how people dress. Your dress should underscore the impressions you want to make and the image you want to project: neat, clean, enthusiastic, capable, motivated, and responsible.

Think of the interview as a conversation with a purpose, and be prepared for that conversation. Actually, there are two purposes: to sell yourself to the interviewer, and to get information about the company and the job.

To prepare, find out everything you can about the company—and if possible, the job—in advance, and anticipate the kinds of questions you expect the interviewer to ask. The interviewer will, of course, want to know about your work experience. Moreover, he or she may want to see a portfolio of your work, when appropriate. Be prepared to answer questions about whether you can do the job, why you are interested in that specific job, what skills or experience you have that specially suit you for the position, why you have chosen this field, and what your career objectives are. Don't be afraid to ask questions. You might ask questions related to the self-assessment information you gathered through the Myers-Briggs Type Indicator or the Strong Interest Inventory. For example, you might ask whether you will have the opportunity to apply your specific skills and talents and whether you will work alone or in a group.

The information exchanged in an interview is not all verbal. In addition to your appearance, your manner, your voice, and your presence communicate, too. Make eye contact. Be friendly, honest, and sincere. Try not to answer all questions with just "yes" or "no," but don't do all the talking either.

After the interview, write the person who interviewed you, expressing your thanks for his or her time and your continued interest in the job. If you omitted any pertinent information in the interview, mention it in your letter.

The job-search process is not easy. Gathering the information needed will take much time and effort, and the job search may not have instant success. But because your work constitutes a major part of your life, finding a satisfactory job and career is well worth the effort.

Selected Readings

Adams, G. Marilee. *Change Your Questions, Change Your Life: 7 Powerful Tools for Life and Work.* 2004.

Arthur, Michael B., Douglas T. Hall, and Barbara S. Lawrence, editors. *Handbook of Career Theory.* 1989.

Bolles, Richard. *What Color Is Your Parachute?* 1987.

Dyer, Wayne W. *The Power of Intention.* 2004.

Handy, Charles. *The Age of Unreason.* 1990.

Harrell, Keith. *The Attitude Is Everything Workbook: Strategies and Tools for Developing Personal and Professional Success.* 2003.

Hyatt, Carole, and Linda Gottlieb. *When Smart People Fail.* 1987.

Korn, Lester. *The Success Profile.* 1988.

Schein, Edgar H. *Career Dynamics: Matching Individual and Organizational Needs.* 1978.

Sheehy, Gail. *Passages.* 1976.

Stumpf, Stephen A. *Choosing a Career in Business.* 1984.

Throop, Robert K., and Marion B. Castellucci. *Reaching Your Potential: Personal and Professional Development.* 2003.

Test Yourself

1) What is the first step in choosing a career?

2) How might you use the U.S. Department of Labor's *Occupational Outlook Handbook* in conducting a job search?

3) In identifying a compatible company, culture is so important. What are the aspects of a company's environment that determine its culture?

4) What are some resources and agencies that are useful in job searches?

5) Describe the concept of networking and how it can affect a job search.

6) What are the main categories of information an effective resumé should include?

7) What should be included in a cover letter?

8) What are the key ingredients of a successful interview?

Test Yourself Answers

1) The first step is conducting a self-assessment, during which you take stock of who you are, what skills you possess, what motivates you, and what you find satisfying.

2) The *Occupational Outlook Handbook* contains lists of more than 225 occupations, including the nature of the work, working conditions, qualifications required, and an overview of broad trends.

3) The way employees dress, the way they act, the management style, the expected number of work hours, and their attitudes toward teamwork, risk-taking, and work-life balance are key components of a company's culture.

4) Newspapers, college placement offices, newsletters, trade publications, and job-bank services are useful resources for identifying jobs. In addition, networking is a critical resource. Finally, employment offices, employment agencies, and direct mailings are also great resources for identifying job opportunities.

5) Networking is the process of using contacts to make more contacts. In a job search, the idea is to share job search plans with members of the network, asking them for other contacts who might prove helpful.

6) An effective resumé should include the following information: personal data (i.e., name, address, telephone numbers, and e-mail address), career objectives (adapted for a particular company and job), experience and education (those relevant to the job sought), other information that distinguishes the candidate from others, and a note that references will be made available upon request (a separate listing should be readily available).

7) The first paragraph should identify the specific job of interest and why the candidate is interested. Mention the source of knowledge about the position. The second paragraph should include a discussion of the candidate's particular qualifications, while making clear the interest in and the knowledge of the company. The final paragraph should request a meeting to discuss the requirements of the job.

8) First, the candidate must conduct appropriate research to equip him- or herself with sufficient knowledge of the company and the specific job. The candidate should also anticipate questions and prepare a list of questions to ask the interviewer. The candidate should dress in accordance with industry practice, emphasizing the impression the candidate wishes to make and the image he or she wishes to project. During the interview, the candidate should project a pleasant personality, making effective eye contact and being friendly, honest, and sincere. Finally, the candidate should follow up the interview with a thank-you note, including an expression of continued interest in the position.

GLOSSARY

Absolute advantage
A country's or a region's inherent superiority in producing a product more efficiently than any other country or region.

Accounting
Systematic collecting, analyzing, classifying, recording, summarizing, reporting, and interpreting of business transactions.

Accounting cycle
System of five steps used to transform raw data into financial statements.

Accounting equation
Assets = Liabilities + Owners' Equity.

Accounts payable
Amounts owed by a company and payable in one year or less.

Accounts receivable
Amounts owed to a company, usually receivable within one year or less.

Accrual basis
Method of recording revenues and costs in the year they are incurred.

Acid-test ratio
Financial measure found by dividing quick assets by current liabilities.

Advertising
Paid messages communicated through a mass medium to a wide general audience by an identified sponsor.

Advertising campaign
Detailed advertising strategy organized in stages.

Advertising platform
Summary of key selling points or features that are to be incorporated into the advertising campaign.

Affirmative action
Programs instituted by businesses to increase the number of minority employees.

Agency shop
Workplace that requires workers to pay union dues whether or not they are members.

Agent
Person who acts for, and in the name of, a second person, who is known as the principal.

Arbitration
Procedure in which a neutral third party hears both sides of a dispute and renders a decision.

Assembly-line production
Transformation of resources by moving materials through a series of work areas, where different groups of workers perform specific assembly operations.

Assets
Anything of value, either tangible or intangible, owned by a firm.

Autocratic leadership
Style describing managers who make decisions without consulting employees, and then announce their decisions and expect or demand compliance.

Automated teller machine (ATM)
Machine that allows users to make common banking transactions electronically without human assistance.

Automation
Production that maximizes the use of mechanical operations and minimizes human involvement.

Balance of payments
A country's payments to other countries minus payments received from those countries.

Balance of trade
A country's total exports minus its total imports.

Balance sheet
Financial statement summarizing all accounts and showing the financial position of the firm on a specific date.

Bankruptcy
Court-granted relief from paying certain outstanding debts.

Bartering
Exchanging goods and services for others' goods and services, not for money.

Beneficiary
Individual or organization named in a life insurance policy to receive payments in the event of the insured's death.

Bond
Long-term loan contract between a corporation or municipality and investors.

Bonus
Compensation in addition to wages, salary, or commissions.

Bookkeeping
Recordkeeping of accounting and financial information.

Boycott
Commitment to not to do business with a particular firm.

Branch office
Merchant wholesale firms that are owned by the manufacturer and stock only that manufacturer's goods.

Brand
Name, term, or symbol that identifies one seller's products and distinguishes them it from competitors' products.

Breach of contract
Failure of one party to fulfill the terms of a contract.

Breakeven point
Number of units that must be sold at a given price to cover both fixed and variable costs.

Broker
Intermediary who executes clients' trades for a securities firm.

Budget
Financial plan that projects income and expenses over a specified future period.

Business-interruption insurance
Insurance that protects a business against loss of income from interruptions caused by fire, storm, or other natural disaster.

Buying on margin
Buying stock by borrowing part of the money from a broker, using the borrowed stock as collateral, and then repaying the broker with interest.

Call
Right to buy a specified stock at a specified price for a specified period.

Callable bond
Bond that may be redeemed before the maturity date.

Capital
Money or funds needed to operate a business; buildings, machinery, and other productive assets owned by a business.

Capital gains
Profits realized by selling a security at a price higher than the purchase price.

Capitalism
Economic system that relies on free markets.

Cash basis
Method of recording revenues or costs in the year they are received or paid.

Cash discount
Price reduction offered to customers who make cash payments.

Catalog showroom
Outlet that features a wide assortment of merchandise, samples of which are displayed in the showroom.

Centralized organization
One in which most of the decision-making authority is retained by upper-level management.

Certified public accountant (CPA)
Accountant who has met state education and experience requirements and has passed a rigorous accounting examination.

Chain of command
Flow of authority within an organization, from the top-most level through all lines of authority.

Chain store
Group of retail establishments owned by one individual or one company.

Channel of distribution
Route that a product travels from producer to consumer.

Check
Written order for a bank or other financial institution to pay a stated amount to the person indicated on the face of the check.

Closed shop
Workplace that requires an employee to be a union member as a condition of employment.

Collective bargaining
Process of negotiating a contract between labor and management.

Commercial bank
Profit-making organization that accepts deposits, makes loans, and supplies related services to its customers.

Commercial paper
Short-term promissory note issued by large corporations and secured only by company reputation.

Commission
Payment based on a percentage of sales revenues.

Common law
Law based on precedents established by prior decisions.

Common stock
Certificates that represent ownership in a corporation.

Comparative advantage
A country's or a region's greater efficiency in producing certain products as compared to another country or region.

Compensation
Monetary payment employees receive in exchange for their labor.

Computer-aided design (CAD)
Use of computer technology to design and produce blueprints, sketches, and various other kinds of product specifications.

Computer-aided manufacturing (CAM)
Use of computer technology to analyze product design as part of the manufacturing process.

Conglomerate
Corporation that operates in widely diverse fields.

Consideration
Something of value (not necessarily money) that each party must receive in order for a contract to be legally binding.

Consumerism
All activities intended to protect consumers in their dealings with business.

Consumer market
People who buy products for their personal use or for consumption, not for profit.

Contract
Legally enforceable agreement between two or more parties.

Convenience goods
Low-priced products that consumers purchase frequently and with little shopping effort.

Convenience store
Retail outlet that offers customers goods at higher prices than supermarkets charge.

Convertible security
Convertible preferred stock or convertible bond, which may be exchanged for common stock at a specified conversion price.

Cooperative
Nonprofit corporation owned collectively by its members to supply services for the distribution, marketing, and purchasing of goods.

Copyright
Exclusive rights to publish, perform, or sell an original book, article, design, illustration, computer program, film, or other creation.

Corporate culture
Personality and environment of an organization.

Corporation
Organization that is formally and legally chartered as a business and has the rights of an individual; that is, to own and sell property, borrow money, and be sued.

Correlation analysis
Statistical technique that measures the relationship between two or more variables.

Cost-of-living adjustment (COLA)
Automatic employee wage increases intended to keep pace with inflation.

Cottage business
Business operated by an individual who works in his or her home.

Craft union
Early union made up of workers with specialized skills, such as electricians and carpenters.

Credit union
Depositor-owned institution that offers services only to members.

Critical path method (CPM)
Technique for scheduling complicated production processes that focuses on the one step, activity, or "path" that requires the longest time to complete.

Currency
All paper money and coins issued by the government plus money orders, travelers' checks, personal checks, and bank checks or cashier checks.

Current assets
Cash and other assets that can be quickly converted to cash.

Current liabilities
Debts that will be paid within one year. Current ratio measure of liquidity found by dividing current assets by current liabilities.

Data
Raw facts and figures.

Debenture
Bond not backed by the issuer's assets.

Debit card
Plastic card used to deduct money electronically from the customer's account at the time of sale.

Debt financing
Borrowing through long-term loans or the selling of corporate bonds.

Debt-to-assets ratio
Measure found by dividing total liabilities by total assets.

Debt-to-equity ratio
Comparison of equity supplied by creditors with equity furnished by the owners, found by dividing total liabilities by owners' equity.

Decentralized organization
One in which authority is delegated to lower management.

Decision-support system
MIS system that is specifically designed to support complex decision-making.

Deed
Written document transferring ownership of real property.

Deflation
General decline in the prices of goods and services.

Demand
Willingness of purchasers to buy specific quantities of a good or service at a given price at a given time.

Demand deposit
Bank account funds that can be withdrawn at any time.

Demography
Statistical study of the characteristics of human populations.

Departmentalization
Grouping jobs into manageable work units, or departments, usually based on function, geography, product or service, customer, process, matrix, or a mixture or combination of these.

Department store
Large, service-oriented retail establishment that offers a wide range of merchandise.

Depreciation
Method of distributing the cost of devaluation of fixed assets over a period of years.

Deregulation
Reduction of the complexity and quantity of regulations that affect business.

Devaluation
Arbitrary downward adjustment of one country's currency in terms of another country's currency.

Direct mail
Advertising through letters, fliers, cards, and so on, sent directly to consumers' homes or their places of business.

Disability income insurance
Insurance that protects an employee against loss of income while he or she is disabled as a result of illness or accident.

Discount rate
Interest rate the Federal Reserve System charges member banks for loans.

Discount store
General-merchandise outlet that offers products at reduced prices.

Discretionary income
Disposable income less minus savings and expenditures on necessities.

Disposable income
Personal income less all personal taxes.

Dividends
Earnings distributed to shareholders.

Double-entry bookkeeping
System in which each financial transaction is recorded as two separate accounting entries.

Earnings per share
Net profit after taxes divided by the number of shares outstanding.

Embargo
Government law or regulation forbidding trading in a specified good or with a certain country.

Entrepreneur
Person who assumes the risks, accepts the responsibilities, and takes the steps necessary to create a business and make a profit.

Equilibrium
Point at which supply and demand are in balance.

Equity financing
Selling stock or retaining earnings.

Exchange
Giving something of value to another individual as part of a transaction for a good or a service.

Exchange rate
Value of a particular currency expressed in terms of another currency.

Exchanges
National, regional, and other associations established for the specific purpose of trading securities.

Exclusive distribution
Distribution by only one retail outlet in any one geographic area.

Expenses
Costs involved in creating and selling products or services and operating a business.

Exporting
Selling and shipping goods or raw materials from the home country to another country.

External data
Data that originate from sources outside the company.

Factoring
Selling the firm's accounts receivable at a discount in order to secure capital.

Factors of production
Resources from which all goods and services are produced; namely, land, labor, capital, information resources, and entrepreneurs.

Financial accounting
Reporting accounting information to outside users, such as stockholders, potential investors, the government, or lenders.

Fixed assets
Assets that will be held or used longer than one year.

Fixed costs
Costs that remain constant regardless of the number of units produced.

Flat organization
One with few levels of management, a high degree of decentralization, and frequent delegation of authority.

Form utility
Value of products to consumers resulting from transformation of inputs into finished products.

For-profit corporation
A corporation formed to make profits for its owners, who receive these profits in the form of dividends.

Four Ps
Four elements of the marketing concept: product, price, promotion, and place (distribution).

Franchise
License to sell another company's products or to use another company's name or both.

Franchisee
Person or company that buys the rights to another company's logo, methods of operation, national advertising, and products in exchange for fees and payments.

Franchisor
Company that sells a license to use its name or products.

Free-enterprise system or free-market system
Economic system in which individuals (not governments) control all or most of the factors of production and make all or most of the production decisions.

Frequency distribution
Table in which possible values for a variable are grouped into classes, and the number of times a value falls into each class is recorded.

Gantt chart
Scheduling device in bar-graph format that shows what has been done and what remains to be accomplished.

General expenses
Costs incurred in running a business other than production costs and selling expenses.

General partner
Co-owner who bears full liability for the debts of the business.

Globalization
Trend among businesses to operate worldwide, as multinational organizations.

Goals
Measurable steps in a plan.

Goods
Tangible products (such as automobiles and shoes).

Governmental market
The part of the industrial market (namely, federal, state, and local governments) that buys goods and services either for internal operations or to provide citizens with highways, water, or other services.

Grievance procedure
Formal process for resolving employees' complaints against management.

Gross domestic product (GDP)
Total market value of all goods and services produced in the United States, irrespective of the source. GDP includes profits earned by foreign companies inside the United States, but excludes profits earned by U.S. companies abroad.

Gross national product (GNP)
Total value of all goods and services produced by U.S. companies during a one-year period, whether inside or outside the country.

Health maintenance organization (HMO)
Group of private doctors who provide patient members with medical hospital care under one roof on a prepaid basis.

High-contact services
Services that include the customer as part of the service (for example, haircuts and manicures).

High-growth venture
Small business that has the potential to grow into a large company.

Holding company
Corporation organized to own stock in and manage another company.

Horizontal merger
Combination of two direct competitors in the same industry.

Human resources management
Management of personnel, including planning, recruiting, hiring, training and development, performance appraisal, and compensation.

Importing
Bringing in goods or raw materials from other countries.

Income statement
Summary of revenues and expenses for a certain period of time.

Index number
Percentage showing the degree of change between a base number (such as cost or price) in one period and the current number in the current period.

Industrial market
Organizations that buy products for use in day-to-day operations or for making into other products to sell for profit.

Industrial products
Products sold to private business firms or public agencies for use in the production of their goods or services.

Industrial union
Organization made up of workers in a particular industry, regardless of skills or jobs.

Information
Data transformed and presented in a meaningful form.

Information sector
The part of the service sector that includes people employed in the computer and information-processing technologies.

Institutional market
The part of the industrial market that includes institutions such as churches, schools, hospitals, and clubs.

Insurable risks
Risks that are financial, measurable, and predictable.

Intangible assets
Assets having financial value because they grant legal rights, advantages, or privileges.

Intensive distribution
Distribution to all intermediaries or retailers willing to stock and sell the product.

Internal data
Data available from the company's records.

International trade
Trading between countries.

Inventory control
Maintaining inventories of inputs at the lowest levels necessary to meet customer demand.

Job analysis
Detailed study of the jobs to be performed and the specific duties entailed in each job.

Job description
Key tasks and responsibilities of each position as well as the relationship of one job to another.

Job specification
Statement summarizing the knowledge, skills, education, and experience required to perform a job.

Joint venture
Separate corporation owned by two or more corporations and established for the purpose of working on a specific project or in specific markets.

Junk bonds
Bonds offering higher yields because they are issued by less-secure, higher-risk companies.

Just-in-time (JIT) inventory control
Technique for reducing inventories by delivering materials "just in time" to be used in the manufacturing process.

Key-executive insurance
Insurance that protects the company against the financial impact of the death or disability of a key employee.

Labor union
Workers' organization formed to achieve common goals in the areas of wages, hours, and working conditions.

Laissez-faire
Economic system that calls for private ownership of property, free entry into markets, and an absence of government intervention.

Laissez-faire leadership
Style describing managers who allow employees to make decisions.

Law of demand
Principle stating that people will buy more of a product at a lower price than at a higher price.

Law of large numbers
Statistical principle stating that as the sample of units in a group increases, predictions about the group become more accurate and certain.

Law of supply
Principle stating that producers are willing to produce and offer for sale more goods at a higher price than at a lower price.

Leadership
Ability to influence organization members to attain the organization's objectives.

Lease
Agreement for the temporary transfer or use of property from owner to tenant.

Leveraged buyout (LBO)
Purchasing a company by borrowing money, using the company itself as collateral.

Liabilities
Firm's debts and obligations to others.

Licensing
Contractual agreement in which one firm permits another to produce and market its product or to use its brand name in return for a royalty or other compensation.

Life-style business
Modest business operation that has little growth potential but provides the owner(s) with modest income.

Limited partner
Co-owner whose liability is limited to the amount of his or her investment in the firm.

Line management
The part of the chain of command that has direct responsibility for achieving the organization's goals.

Line of credit
Loan approval for a specific total amount before the money is needed.

Liquidation
In bankruptcy cases, selling the assets of the business.

Liquidity
Ease with which an asset can be converted to cash.

Load fund
Mutual fund that charges investors a sales fee.

Lobbyist
Representative for a special-interest group who attempts to influence legislators to approve legislation favorable to the group and oppose legislation that is not.

Local area network (LAN)
Communication system that links computers in a small geographical area; for example, in one building.

Lockout
Company's refusal to allow workers to enter the workplace.

Long-range plan
Covers actions over a two- to five-year period, sometimes longer.

Long-term liabilities
Debts that will come due in one year or more.

Low-contact service
Service that does not directly and closely involve the customer (for example, lawn care and television repair).

M-1
Money supply that includes currency, demand deposits, and other checkable deposits.

M-2
Money supply that includes M-1 plus time deposits, money-market funds, and savings deposits.

M-3
Money supply that includes M-2 plus time deposits over $100,000 plus short-term repurchase agreements.

Mail-order retailing
Selling merchandise by mail.

Major medical insurance
Insurance that provides medical coverage beyond the dollar limits of the standard policies.

Management
Process of working with and through people and other organizational resources to achieve organizational goals and objectives.

Management development
Specialized form of training, designed to improve the skills and talents of present managers or to prepare future managers.

Management information
Information that is vital to decision-making.

Management information system (MIS)
All the tools and procedures that transform data into information that can be used for decision-making at all levels within an organization.

Managerial accounting
Reporting accounting information to people within the firm.

Margin requirement
Percentage of total purchase price an investor is required to put down to buy stock on margin.

Market
Group of individuals, organizations, or both that have needs for a given product and have the ability, willingness, and authority to purchase the product.

Marketing
According to the American Marketing Association, "The process of planning and executing the conception, pricing, distribution, and promotion of ideas, goods, and services to create exchanges that satisfy individual and organizational objectives."

Marketing concept
Principle stressing the need for the entire organization to achieve customer satisfaction while achieving the organization's goals.

Marketing mix
Combination of the four Ps in a particular marketing strategy.

Marketing orientation or customer orientation
Business approach that focuses primarily on customer needs and wants and developing goods and services to meet those needs and wants.

Market order
Client's authorization to a broker to buy or sell at the best possible price at that moment.

Market research
Gathering, recording, and analyzing data concerning a particular marketing problem.

Market segmentation
Division of a market into various smaller groups or target markets.

Market share
Percentage of total industry sales.

Markup
Amount added to the total cost of a product to determine its selling price.

Materials handling
Transporting, handling, and inventorying goods.

Materials-requirements planning (MRP)
Computer-based coordination system that ensures the availability of needed parts and materials at the right time at the right place.

Mean
Sum of all the items in a group divided by the number of items.

Mechanization
Replacement of human labor with machine labor.

Median
Midpoint of a group of numbers.

Media plan
Detailed description of media, ads, schedules, and costs.

Mediation
Use of a neutral third party in management-labor negotiations.

Merchant wholesaler
Intermediary who takes title to goods in large quantities and resells them to retail and industrial users in smaller quantities.

Merger
Combination of two companies in related industries.

Mission
Company's broad, general business purpose.

Missionary selling
Long-term sales strategy that emphasizes the company's positive image.

Mixed economy
Economic system that shares some of the features of both the market economy and the planned economy.

Mode
Number that occurs most frequently in a group of numbers.

Modem
Communications device that allows computers to transmit and receive information over ordinary telephone lines, broadband, or cable.

Money
Anything used by a society to purchase goods, services, or resources.

Money-market fund
Mutual fund that invests in short-term, low-risk securities.

Monopoly
One company's control of market, industry, or area.

Multinational company
Corporation that operates on a worldwide scale.

Mutual fund
Company that sells shares to investors and uses the combined funds to make specific investments (as in stocks or bonds).

Mutual insurance company
Company owned by its policyholders.

National bank
Commercial bank chartered by the U.S. government.

Natural monopoly
Monopoly permitted and regulated by the government.

Negotiable instrument
Any form of business paper used instead of cash; for example, checks, bank drafts, certificates of deposit, and promissory notes.

Net income
Profit earned (or loss suffered) by a firm during an accounting period.

Net profit margin
Measure of how effectively sales are transformed into profits, found by dividing net income after taxes by net sales.

Network
Communication system that links computers and other devices.

Networking
Process of using personal contacts to make new, contacts for a specific purpose, such as obtaining a job.

No-load fund
Fund that charges no sales fees.

Nonprofit or not-for-profit corporation
Corporation set up for charitable, educational, or fraternal purposes.

Nonstore retailer
Retailer that does not maintain conventional store facilities.

Objective
Statement of how an organization plans to achieve its mission.

Oligopoly
Market dominated by only a small number of very large firms.

Open shop
Workplace where union membership has no effect on hiring or firing.

Operating expenses
Costs other than those of goods sold.

Operations planning
Determining the types and amounts of resources needed to produce specified goods and to plan for the purchasing, routing, scheduling, and dispatching of these resources.

Opportunity cost
Value of a resource as measured against the best alternative use for that resource.

Option
Right to buy or sell a specified stock at a specified price for a specified period of time.

Order processing
All activities involved in receiving and filling customers' orders and in shipping, billing, and granting credit.

Organization chart
Blueprint of a company's structure, showing all components, their relationship, and the chain of command.

Orientation
Process of acquainting new employees with the company, its policies and procedures, and its personnel.

Over-the-counter (OTC) market
Network of dealers who trade stocks.

Owners' equity
Difference between assets and liabilities; amount that would remain for the firm's owners if the assets were used to pay off the liabilities.

Partnership
Business owned and managed by two or more persons.

Patent
Exclusive rights to a machine, a process, or other useful invention.

Penetration pricing
Strategy of setting a low price in order to garner a large market share.

Performance appraisal
Formal program comparing employees' actual performance with expected performance.

Personal property
Property other than real property.

PERT (Program Evaluation and Review Technique) chart
Chart showing activities to be done, time required for each activity, and relationships among the different activities.

Physical distribution functions
Functions that involve the flow of goods from producers to customers.

Picket
March conducted by striking employees in front of their workplace, holding signs notifying the public that a strike is in progress.

Place utility
Value of a product to consumers resulting from the product's availability at a place where a customer wishes to purchase it.

Planned economy
Market system in which the government controls the factors of production.

Planning
Process of establishing objectives, and then setting policies, procedures, and a course of action to accomplish these objectives.

Point-of-purchase (POP) displays
Product displays designed to catch customers' attention at specific, prominent locations.

Policy
Broad, general guidelines for making decisions and taking actions.

Positioning
Establishing in consumers' minds a clearly identifiable image for a product.

Possession utility
Value of a product to consumers resulting from transferring the title or ownership of the product to the customer.

Preferred stock
Stock that shares some features of both corporate bonds and common stock.

Primary data
Data gathered through original research.

Prime rate
Loan rate that banks give to their most credit worthy borrowers.

Principal
Person whom an agent represents.

Private accountant
Accountant employed by a specific organization.

Private corporation
Corporation formed by private individuals or companies and chartered for a specific business purpose.

Private law
Law that deals with the relationships between two or more individuals or businesses.

Producer market
The part of the industrial market that buys products for the purpose of manufacturing other products.

Product differentiation
Process of developing and promoting differences between one company's product and all the other similar products that are available.

Product line
Group of related products.

Product mix
All the products that one firm offers.

Production
Transformation process for converting resources into goods or services.

Production and operations management
Systematic direction and control of the transformation process.

Production orientation
Business approach that focuses primarily on improving manufacturing efficiency.

Productivity
Measure of efficiency that compares the total amount of outputs and the resources needed to produce them.

Product life cycle
Four key stages of a product's life: introduction, growth, maturity, and decline.

Profit
Selling price minus production and marketing costs.

Profit margin
Difference between selling price and total cost.

Promissory note
Borrower's written pledge to pay a certain sum of money to a creditor at a specified future date.

Promotion
All persuasive techniques designed to induce customers to buy products or services.

Promotional mix
Combination of specific methods a firm uses to market its products or services.

Property
Anything tangible or intangible that can be owned.

Prospecting
Process of finding and identifying potential customers (or "prospects").

Protectionism
Creation of artificial barriers to free international trade.

Prototype
Working model of a product.

Psychographics
Profiles of consumers according to their motives, attitudes, activities, interests, and opinions.

Public accountant
Accountant who may be hired by the general public, by individuals, or by firms.

Public corporation
Corporation set up by Congress or a state legislature to provide a specific public service.

Publicity
Nonpersonal, unpaid mass media messages about an organization, its products or services, or its personnel.

Public law
Law that deals with relations between individuals or businesses and society.

Public relations
Company-influenced publicity.

Pull strategy
Promotional technique that relies on mass advertising to convince consumers to buy goods.

Purchasing
Operations-planning function that deals with all aspects of buying raw material or components.

Pure competition
Situation in which a large number of small firms are producing identical, or nearly identical, products.

Pure risk
Risk that involves only the probability of loss with no possibility of profit or gain.

Push strategy
Promotional technique that encourages wholesalers and retailers to push products to customers.

Put
Right to sell a specified stock at a specified price for a specified period.

Quality circle
Small group of workers that meets regularly to solve problems related to quality.

Quality control
Process of ensuring that final quality meets planned quality.

Quantity discount
Price reduction to buyers who purchase in large quantities.

Quasi-public corporation
Corporation with a government-granted monopoly to provide certain services to the public.

Random sample
Sample in which any person or item in the population has an equal chance of being selected.

Real property
Land and anything permanently attached to it, such as housing or other structures.

Recruiting
Process of finding and attracting sufficient qualified job applicants.

Regulatory law
Business law formed by the decrees and regulations of government agencies.

Reserve requirement
Percentage of a bank's total deposits that the bank is required to maintain on hand.

Résumé
Summary of a job applicant's work experience, education, and other relevant information.

Retailer
Business that sells directly to consumers.

Return on investment
Measure of how much income is generated by each dollar of equity, found by dividing net income after taxes by owners' equity.

Revaluation
Arbitrary upward adjustment of one country's currency in terms of another country's currency.

Revenues
Gross sales; all receipts from customers' purchases.

Right-to-work laws
Legislation prohibiting union shops and agency shops.

Risk
Possibility that a loss or injury will occur.

Risk management
Process of identifying potential risks and ways to protect against each.

Round lot
Stock transaction in one-hundred-share multiples.

Salary
Compensation at a specified rate regardless of time worked or output.

Sales agent
Commission sales representative for one or more manufacturers within a specific territory.

Sales office
Manufacturer-owned office that acts as agent, selling both the manufacturer's products and other products that complement the manufacturer's product line.

Sales promotion
Activities or materials designed to influence customers to buy products or services.

Sample
Small group that, ideally, is representative of a larger group.

Savings account
Traditional demand-deposit passbook account.

Savings and loan association (S&L)
Bank that offers savings accounts and home-mortgage loans.

Scrambled merchandising
Offering an odd mix of unrelated merchandise in addition to a store's traditional merchandise.

Seasonal discounts
Price reductions offered in the off-season.

Secondary data
Data that originate from sources outside the company.

Selection
Process of identifying appropriate job applicants and selecting from among them.

Selective distribution
Distribution to a selected portion or percentage of the available outlets in each geographic area.

Selling expenses
Costs related to marketing, advertising, and promotion.

Selling price
Total cost plus markup.

Selling short
Selling stock borrowed from a broker and replacing the borrowed stock later, when the price is anticipated to be lower than the current price.

Serial bonds
Bonds in a single issue that mature on different dates.

Sinking-fund bond
Bond for which the issuer regularly makes payments into a fund in preparation for payment at maturity.

Service
Intangible item, such as professional advice and assistance.

Service business
Business that does not produce goods, but instead, provides intangible professional assistance or advice.

Shopping goods
Products that consumers shop actively for, comparing prices, values, features, quality, and styles before finally making a purchase decision.

Shop steward
Person elected by union members to represent them at a particular work location.

Short-range plan
Plan that covers one year or less.

Situational leadership
Style of managers who adapt as appropriate to each specific situation and to the people involved in that situation.

Small business
Business that is independently owned and operated for profit and is not dominant in its field.

Socialism
Economic system in which the government controls key industries and major natural resources.

Social Security
Federal government insurance that provides for retirement, survivors', disability, and health benefits.

Software
Computer programs—sets of instructions, procedures, and rules—that tell a computer what to do.

Sole proprietorship
Business that is owned and managed by one person.

Specialist
Intermediary who works on the floor of an exchange for the purpose of making a market (trading) in a particular stock.

Specialization
Division of labor into smaller work tasks.

Specialty store
Retail establishment that sells a limited line of merchandise.

Speculative risk
Risk accompanied by the possibility of earning a profit.

Staffing
Supplying an organization with the human resources it needs through recruitment, selection, and employee orientation.

State bank
Commercial bank chartered by the state in which it operates.

Statement of cash flows
Statement describing the company's cash receipts and payments for a specific period.

Statistics
Figures that summarize and represent factual data.

Statutory law
All laws enacted by federal, state, or local legislatures under their constitutions.

Stock average or stock index
Adjusted average of stock prices of selected companies, used to measure performance.

Stockbroker
Person who executes clients' orders to buy and sell securities and receives a commission for services rendered.

Stock insurance company
Insurance company owned by stockholders and operated for profit.

Stock split
Issuing one or more shares of additional stock to stockholders for each share they currently own.

Strike
Work stoppage by employees.

Subsidiary
Corporation that is owned by another corporation and operated as a separate entity.

Supercomputers
World's fastest, most expensive computers.

Supermarket
Large retail food outlet.

Supply
Amount of output of a good or service that producers are willing and able to make available to the market at a given price at a given time.

Survey
Method of eliciting opinions and attitudes and/or gathering facts by means of questionnaires or telephone interviews.

Sustainable Business
The planning, implementing, and conducting of business operations in a manner that balances economic viability, environmental responsibility, and social equity. The aim is to conduct business in a manner that allows the business to meet today's needs without compromising its ability to serve future generations in an equally effective manner.

Syndicate
Group of firms operating together, usually on one large project.

Tall organization
One with many levels of management, a high degrees of centralization, and less delegation of authority.

Target market
Group of people with similar wants and needs.

Tariff
Tax imposed on imported goods.

Telemarketing
Personal selling that uses the telephone for any or all steps.

Theory X
Management theory that employees can be motivated only by fear (of job loss, for example).

Theory Y
Management theory that employees can be motivated by better challenges, personal growth, and improved work performance and productivity.

Theory Z
Management theory that employees should be involved, should participate, and should be treated like family.

Time deposit
Savings account that requires notice prior to withdrawal.

Time-series analysis or trend analysis
Statistical technique for observing changes in data over time and basing forecasts on those observations.

Time utility
Value of a product to consumers resulting from the product's availability when the customer wants it.

Tort
Noncriminal injury to person or property.

Trade credit
Credit granted by a supplier to a business.

Trade deficit
Negative balance of trade.

Trade discounts
Price reductions offered to wholesalers and distributors.

Trademark
Brand legally protected from use by anyone except the trademark owner.

Trade show
Exhibit sponsored by an industry or association to promote sales.

Trade surplus
Positive or favorable balance of trade.

Transportation
Moving products through the channels of distribution to the ultimate consumers.

Unemployment insurance
Insurance funded by a state payroll tax on employers to provide partial, temporary income replacement to eligible workers who become unemployed.

Uninsurable risk
Risk that presents an incalculable loss.

Union shop
Workplace that requires an employee to join the union.

Unsecured loan
Loan not backed by collateral.

Utility
Power of a good or service to satisfy a need.

Value-added tax (VAT)
Tax assessed at each level in the chain of distribution.

Variable
In statistics, a factor that changes in a situation.

Variable costs
Costs that change as more goods or services are produced.

Vertical marketing system
Integration that results when two or more members of a channel of distribution are joined under a single management.

Vertical merger
Combination of two companies in the same chain of supply.

Wages
Compensation based on the number of hours worked or units produced.

Warehouse store
Minimal-service outlets that carry large inventories of merchandise.

Warehousing
Activities that ensure the availability of products when needed.

Warranty
Seller's promise (either expressed or implied) that a product meets certain standards of performance.

Wholesaler
Business that buys and then resells products to other businesses.

Workers' compensation
Insurance covering medical expenses and salary continuation for employees injured at work.

Yellow dog contract
Contract that includes, as a condition of being hired, a statement that the worker is not a union member and will not join a union while employed at the firm.

Zero-based budgeting
Method of budgeting that starts with no base from the preceding budget period.

Zero-coupon bond
Bond sold at a deep discount from its face value and redeemed at full face value.

Index

A

Absolute advantage (of a country), 53
   see also Comparative advantage
Accountants, 3, 11, 36, 72, 76, 88, 89, 94, 213, 214, 215, 227, 238, 256, 282, 283
   certified public accountants (CPAs), 72, 213, 214, 227, 238
   corporate, 283
   private, 213, 227
   public, 213, 227
   tax, 283
Accounting and financial statements, 202, 213–216, 218, 219, 221–224, 227, 238
   accounting cycle, 215, 227
   accrual basis, 218
   acid-test ratio, 223
   analyzing financial statements, 221
   balance sheet, 216–218, 220–224, 227
      assets, 216, 217, 222–224, 227
         current, 216, 217, 222–224
         fixed, 216, 217
         intangible, 216, 217
         see also Assets
      liabilities, 216, 217, 218, 222, 223
         current, 217, 218
         long-term, 217, 218
         see also Liabilities
      owners' equity, 215–218, 223, 227
   budgeting and planning, 224
      budgets, 224
         budgeting process, 224
         capital-expenditure budgets, 224
         operating budgets, 224
      long-range plans, 225
      short-range plans, 225
      see also Budget
   cash flow, statement of, 216, 221, 222, 227
      difference with income statement, 221, 227
   financial ratio, 222, 223, 227
      debt ratios, 223, 227
         debt-to-assets ratio, 223, 227
         debt-to-equity ratio, 223, 227
      liquidity ratios, 222, 227
   format, standardized, 216
   general journal, 215, 227
   general ledger, 215, 227
   income statement, 216–225, 227, 234, 238
      expenses, 216–221, 223–225, 227, 234, 238
         cost of goods sold, 220
            direct manufacturing costs, 220
            raw material inventory, 220
            work in progress inventory, 220
         operating, 216, 217, 219–221, 223, 224, 227
            depreciation, 221, 227
            general (or administrative), 219, 221
            insurance, 219
            interest, 219
            miscellaneous, 219
            prepaid, 216, 217, 223
            selling, 219, 221, 224
            tax, 221
            utilities, 219
      net income before taxes (NIBT), 219,
      revenues, 214, 215, 218, 219, 227, 244
      accrual basis accounting, 218
      cash basis accounting, 218
   payable, 215, 217, 218, 221, 222
      accounts, 217, 218, 221, 222
      mortgage, 217, 218
      notes, 217, 218
      salaries, 217
      taxes, 217, 218
   preparing, 215, 216, 227
   process, 213, 215, 216, 227
      accounting cycle, 215, 227
      accounting equation, 215, 216
      double-entry bookkeeping, 215
   profit and loss statement, see Accounting and financial statements, income statement
   profitability ratios, 223, 227
      earnings per share, 227
      net profit margin, 223, 227
      return on equity, 223, 227
   receivable, 148, 214–217, 221–223, 245, 246, 249
      accounts receivable, 148, 214, 216, 217, 221–223, 245, 246, 249
      notes receivable, 217, 223
   role in business, 213
   trial balance, 215, 216, 227
   users of financial information, 214
   see also Marketing, tools, accounting and financial statements
Advertising, see Promotion, methods, advertising
Agency shop, 123, 125, 130
Agent, 34, 59, 124, 139, 168, 171–173, 175, 176, 181, 263, 283
American banking system, see Money, American banking system
American economic system, see Economic systems, American
American Law Institute, 32
American Stock Exchange (AMEX), see Securities, exchanges, American Stock Exchange (AMEX)
Annual Report, 48, 52, 214, 218, 284
   see also Accounting and financial statements
Assets, 8, 19, 20, 26, 34, 35, 39, 59, 60, 69, 71, 76, 97, 160, 215–217, 222–224, 227, 232, 238, 242–244, 246, 257, 264, 267, 273, 274
   accounting equation, in, 215
   capital, 246
   company and corporate, 59, 60, 97, 160, 215, 216, 222–224, 227, 243, 244, 246, 264, 273, 274
   current, 216, 217
   fixed, 216, 217, 264
   intangible, 216, 217
   long-term, 224
   marks and brands, as, 160
   net asset value (NAV), 267
   personal, 69, 71, 76
   purchase of, 19, 20, 26, 246
   sales of, 35, 39, 244, 246
Automation, 133, 137, 139, 282

B

Balance of Trade, see Trade, balance of
Banking, see Financial management, banking
Bankruptcy, 8, 28–30, 34–36, 39, 41, 125, 264, 283
   Bankruptcy Abuse Prevention and Consumer Protection Act (2005), 35, 36
      filing limit, 36
      financial counseling, 36
      luxury goods and cash advances, 35
      student loans, 35
   Bankruptcy Reform Act (1978), 35
   involuntary, 34
   resolving, methods of, 35, 39, 264
      liquidation, 35
      reorganization, 35, 264
      repayment, 35, 39
   voluntary, 34
Bartering, 9, 231
   see also Economic systems, American, bartering
Beneficiary, 258
Bond, 13, 22, 31, 39, 74, 161, 216, 218, 235, 236, 239, 242, 246, 247, 249, 250, 255, 262–268, 271, 273, 276
Bonus, 96, 115, 195
Bookkeeping, 69, 88, 213, 215
   double-entry, 215
Budget, 100, 116, 119, 160, 166, 188, 190–192, 198, 203, 224, 225, 227, 244
   advertising, 188, 190–192, 198
   budgeting and planning, 224
   budgeting process, 224, 225, 227, 244
      traditional, 224, 225, 227
      zero-based, 224, 225, 227
   capital-expenditure, 224
   cash, 224
   compensation, 116, 119
   income and expenses, 244
   master, 224
   operating, 224
   production, 224
   sales, 224, 244
Business careers, 69, 70, 74, 78, 115, 279–287, 290
   advancement, 69, 280
   choosing, 279–284, 286, 287, 290
      job seeker, 281
      understanding the business world, 280–284, 286, 290
         industry, 281, 282
            goods-producing industries, 281, 282
            service-producing industries, 281, 282
         jobs and job opportunities, 70, 74, 78, 279, 281, 282, 285
         occupations, 279, 280–284, 286, 290
            artistic, 280
            blue collar, 282
            conventional, 280
            enterprising, 280
            farm occupation, 282
            investigative, 280
            Occupational Outlook Handbook (published by U.S. Department of Labor), 281, 284, 290
            realistic, 280
            service occupation, 282
            social, 280
            white collar, 282
      understanding self-assessment, 279–281, 284, 286, 287, 290
         Jackson Vocational Interest Survey, 281
         interests, 279–281, 284, 286
         lifestyle, 280
         Myers-Briggs Type Indicator (MBTI), 280, 281, 287
         personality characteristics, 280
         System of Interacting Guidance and Information Plus (SIGI Plus), 281
         skills and abilities, 280
         values, 280
   computerized career-information system, 281

Business careers *(Continued)*
　making the match, 284, 285–287, 290
　　company and its culture, 284
　　interview, 287, 290
　　job search, 285, 286, 288, 290
　　　direct mailing, 285, 290
　　　employment agencies, 285
　　　employment offices, 285
　　　networking, 285
　　The Résumé, 284–287, 290
　　　career objectives, 285–287
　　　cover letter, 285–287
　　　experience and education, 284–287, 290
　　　other information, 286, 290
　　　potential, 286
　　　references, 286, 290
　objective, 286, 287, 290
　resignation, 115
Business ethics, 27, 36
　generally accepted auditing standards (GAAS), 36
　Sarbanes-Oxley Act (2002), 36
Business formation, *see* Formation and Structure, of business
Business law, 8, 27–30, 32–36, 39, 41, 125, 283
　agency, law of, 34
　　agents, 34
　　principals, 34
　bankruptcy, *see* Bankruptcy
　categories of, 27, 28, 39
　　common law, 28, 39
　　regulatory law, 28, 39
　　statutory law, 39
　private law, 28
　public law, 28
　sources of, 27
　tort law, 28, 29, 32–34, 39
　　intentional tort, 33
　　negligence, 33
　　product liability, 34
Business structure, *see* Formation and Structure, of business

C

Capital, 4–8, 10, 12, 16, 19, 26, 59, 71, 74, 80, 82, 84, 95, 97, 139, 174, 218, 222–224, 227, 238, 242, 244–246, 262, 263, 268, 276
　assets, 246
　debt, 244
　equity, 244, 246
　expenditure, 224
　market, 268
　small, 268
　working, 222, 223, 227
Capital gains, 262, 276
Capital goods, 6
Capital stock, 218
Capitalism, *see* Economic systems, capitalism
Careers, business, *see* Business Careers
Cash basis accounting, 218
Cash discount, 168, 245
Celler-Kefauver Act (1950), *see* Economic systems, American, government regulation, antitrust legislation, Celler-Kefauver Act (1950)
Centralized structure of organization, 90, 94
　see also Decentralized structure of organization
Clayton Act (1914), *see* Economic systems, American, government regulation, antitrust legislation, Clayton Act (1914)
COD (collect on delivery), *see* Property, tangible personal property, transfer of, COD (collect on delivery)
Commercial law, 32, 33, 39, 48
　negotiable instruments, 32, 33
　　endorsement, 33
　　　blank, 33
　　　restrictive, 33
　　　special, 33
　uniform commercial code (UCC), 32
　　National Conference of Commissioners on Uniform State Laws, 32
　warranties, 32, 39, 48
　　express warranties, 32, 39
　　implied warranties, 32, 39
　see also Warranty
Communism, *see* Economic systems, communism
Comparative advantage (of a country), 53
　see also Absolute advantage
Competition, 7, 8, 11, 16–20, 26, 44, 47, 55, 91, 152, 158, 163, 166, 177, 182, 239
　foreign, 55
　free, 44
　government, 17–19, 26
　　role of consumer, 17
　　role of regulator, 17–19, 26
　monopolistic, 7, 16
　monopoly, 7, 16
　oligopoly, 7, 8
　pricing, competition-based, 166
　pure, 7, 16, 163
　unfair, 26
Conglomerate, *see* Legal forms, corporations, acquisitions, conglomerate
Consumer, 3, 4, 6, 7, 10, 13, 17, 18, 21, 26, 35, 36, 40–45, 47, 48, 52, 56, 81, 83, 84, 149–154, 156–164, 167, 171–176, 178–181, 185, 187–195, 198, 208, 235, 237, 239, 242
　consumer action, 192
　consumer-advocacy groups, 44
　consumer awareness, 158, 195
　consumer channels, 171, 185
　consumer goods, *see* Goods, consumer goods
　consumer issues, 47
　consumer loyalty, 152, 161
　consumer market, 149, 150, 156
　Consumer Price Index (CPI), 13, 208
　consumer-protection, 35, 36, 44, 47, 48
　consumer right, 47, 52, 239
　　choose, right to, 47, 52
　　heard, right to be, 47, 52
　　informed, right to be, 47, 52
　　safety, to, 47, 52
　consumer segment, 150
　　consumer motives (psychographics), 150
　government as, 17, 26
Consumerism, 47, 256
Contract, 17, 19, 26, 29–33, 34, 39, 59, 82, 115, 122, 124–127, 173, 185, 252, 263
　breach of, 30
　cancellation of, 32
　contract laws and regulations, 17, 19, 26, 29
　government contracts, 82
　grievance procedures, 125
　licensing, 59
　requirements of, 29, 30
　　agreement, 29
　　capacity, 29
　　consideration, 30
　　lawful purpose, 30
　　proper form, 30
　　real consent, 29
　transfer of real property, 31
　tying, 19, 26
　union contracts, 115, 122, 124, 126
　yellow dog contracts, 122
Convenience store, 151, 177, 179, 185
Cooperative, 73
Copyright, 28, 31, 39, 216
Corporate culture, 284
Corporation, 18, 19, 21, 22, 36, 39, 45, 47, 59, 67, 70–76, 78, 79, 87, 214, 218, 221, 224, 245–247, 262–266, 268, 271, 273, 284
　'adoption' by, 45
　advantages of, 74
　alien, 71
　board of directors, 72
　bond-rating services, 265
　commercial paper, 245
　corporate ethics, 36
　corporate income tax, 22
　corporate securities, 247, 263–265
　　bond, 247, 263, 265
　　　serial bonds, 265
　　common stock, 263, 266
　　preferred stock, 263, 266
　　debentures, 264
　　　subordinated debentures, 264
　domestic, 71
　direct investments overseas, 59
　disadvantages of, 74
　equity financing, 246
　foreign, 71
　forming of, 71
　　certificate of incorporation, 71
　　corporate charter, 71
　framework, 72
　limited liability corporations (LLC), 67, 76
　management, 72
　shareholders, 72, 262
　stockholders' equity, 218
　types of, 72, 73, 78, 214, 221
　　private, 73, 78
　　　closely held, 73
　　　cooperative, 73
　　　for profit, 73
　　　holding company, 73
　　　joint venture, 73
　　　nonprofit, 73
　　　professional, 73
　　　subchapter S, 73
　　　subsidiary, 73
　　　syndicate, 73
　　public, 72, 78, 214, 221, 284
　　quasi-public, 73, 78
Correlation analysis, 209
Cost-of-living adjustment (COLA), 125
Cottage business, 80, 81, 86
Craft union, 120, 121
Credit, *see* Financial management, credit
Credit card, 48, 153, 156, 168, 233, 236
Critical path method (CPM), 136
Currency, 54–56, 58, 60, 63, 232–234, 236, 242
　adjusting currency values, 55
　　devaluation, 55
　　revaluation, 55
　exchange rates, 54
　international currency fluctuations, 60
　foreign-exchange control, 56
　U.S. Comptroller of the Currency, 234
Current assets, *see* Accounting and financial statements, balance sheet, assets, current
Current liabilities, *see* Accounting and financial statements, balance sheet, liabilities, current

D

Debenture, 264, 276
　subordinated, 264, 276
Debit card, 178, 233, 236, 242
　see also Credit card
Debt financing, 244, 246, 249
Debt-to-assets ratio, 223, 227
Debt-to-equity ratio, 223, 227
Decentralized structure of organization, 90, 94
　see also Centralized structure of organization
Decision-support system, 205
Deed, 31, 157
Deficit, 12, 13, 16, 23, 25, 26, 54, 55, 63, 236
　federal, 12, 13, 16, 23, 25, 26, 236
　　deficit spending, 23
　　Emergency Deficit Control Act (1985), 23
　　trade, 13, 54, 55, 63
Deflation, 12, 13, 231
　see also Inflation
Demand, *see* Economic forces, demand
Demand deposit, 232–235, 242
Demography, 18, 42, 43, 153, 190, 191
　demographic factors, 153
Departmentalization, 88, 89
Department store, 177, 179, 185
Depository Institutions Deregulation and Monetary Control Act (1980), 239
Depreciation, 216, 217, 219, 221, 222, 227, 252

Deregulation, 10, 20, 21, 28, 234, 239
Devaluation, 55, 216
  see also Revaluation
Direct mail, 189, 190, 195, 198, 285, 290
Discount store, see Distribution, marketing intermediaries, retailers, discount stores
Discretionary income, 153, 156
Disposable income, 153, 156
Distribution, 6, 10, 11, 13, 18, 20, 44, 48, 52, 59, 80, 81, 86, 134, 137, 138, 141, 144, 147, 148, 150, 151, 153, 156, 161, 162, 165–168, 171–183, 185, 187, 191, 195, 198, 202, 203, 239, 244, 255, 272, 273, 276, 282
  channels of, 171–173, 185
    major marketing channels, 171–173, 185
      consumer channels, 171
      industrial channels, 172
      vertical marketing systems (VMSs), 173, 185
  market coverage, 173, 174
    exclusive, 173
    intensive, 173
    selective, 174
  marketing intermediaries, 11, 13, 48, 52, 59, 80, 81, 86, 138, 147, 148, 150, 151, 156, 161, 165–168, 172–80, 182, 185, 187, 191, 195, 198, 202, 203, 239, 244
    wholesalers, 13, 59, 80, 81, 86, 148, 150, 156, 161, 168, 172–176, 185, 187, 198, 203, 244
      types of, 175, 176, 185
        branch offices and sales offices, 175, 176
        commission merchants, agents, and brokers, 175, 176
        merchant wholesalers, 175, 176, 185
    retailers, 11, 48, 52, 81, 138, 148, 150, 151, 156, 161, 165–168, 172–180, 182, 185, 187, 191, 195, 198, 202, 239, 244
      chain stores, 177, 180, 185
      convenience stores, 151, 177, 179, 185
      department stores, 177, 179, 185
      discount stores, 177, 178, 185
      hypermarkets, 178, 185
      in-store (non-store) retailers, 48, 52, 176, 178, 179, 182, 185
        door-to-door retailers, 48, 52, 178, 182
        e-commerce, 179, 185
        mail-order retailing, 178
        party retailers, 178
        vending machines, 178, 179
      scrambled merchandising, 177, 178, 185
      specialty stores, 177, 179
      supermarkets, 138, 167, 177, 178, 185, 191, 195, 202, 239
      warehouse stores, 177, 185
      shopping malls, 147, 176, 177, 179
  physical, 6, 10, 18, 20, 44, 134, 137, 138, 141, 144, 148, 153, 156, 162, 180–183, 185, 202, 255, 272, 273, 276, 282
    inventory control, 137, 162, 180, 185
    transportation, 6, 10, 18, 20, 44, 134, 138, 141, 144, 148, 153, 156, 180–183, 202, 255, 272, 273, 276, 282
Dividends, 8, 72–74, 78, 218, 221, 246, 254, 261, 262, 266, 272, 276
Double-entry bookkeeping, 215
Dow Jones Industrial Average, 208, 272, 276

E

Earnings per share, 224, 227, 272
Economic forces, 6, 7, 11, 12, 15–17, 32, 33, 39, 54, 73, 75, 78, 79, 111, 112, 119, 134, 135, 137, 140, 141, 148, 149, 157, 163–165, 171, 174, 175, 181, 187–189, 193, 198, 233, 234, 236, 237, 239, 242, 269, 284
  demand, 6, 7, 12, 15–17, 32, 33, 39, 54, 79, 111, 112, 119, 137, 140, 141, 149, 157, 163–165, 174, 175, 187–189, 198, 269
    see also Equilibrium of supply and demand
  supply, 6, 7, 11, 16, 17, 54, 73, 75, 78, 111, 112, 119, 134, 135, 148, 149, 163, 171, 174, 181, 193, 233, 234, 236, 237, 239, 242, 269
    see also Equilibrium of supply and demand
  see also Equilibrium of supply and demand
Economic goals, 11, 12
  full employment, 12
  stability, 12
Economic performance, 12
Economic systems, 5–12, 16, 18–20, 26, 43, 53, 60, 73, 78, 120, 121, 127, 133, 149
  American, 5–12, 16, 18–20, 26, 43, 53, 60, 73, 78, 120, 121, 127, 133, 149
    bartering, 9
    colonial era, 8
    economic expansion, 10
    industrial revolution, 8–10, 120, 133, 149
    monopolies, 7, 16, 18–20, 26, 73, 78
    New Economy, 11, 12, 19, 43, 53, 60, 127
      globalization, 11, 12, 19, 43, 53, 60, 127
      information sector, 11
      service sector, 11, 43
      politics and economics, 9
      trade, growth of, 9
    capitalism, 5, 6, 121
    communism, 6
    market economy or free-market economy, 5, 6, 10, 17, 60
    mixed economy, 5
    planned economy, 5
    socialism, 6
Embargo, 9, 56, 63
Emergency Deficit Control Act (1985), see Government, role of, deficit, federal, Emergency Deficit Control Act (1985)
Employee Retirement Income Security Act (ERISA, 1974), see Insurance, public insurance, other, Employee Retirement Income Security Act (ERISA, 1974)
Enterprise, 4–6, 8, 9, 17, 26, 60, 70, 72, 97, 195, 283
  free, see Free-enterprise system
Entrepreneurs and entrepreneurship, 3, 4, 6, 8, 9, 16, 79, 81
Equilibrium of supply and demand, 6, 7, 163
Equity, 215–217, 218, 223, 227, 244, 246, 249, 268
  financing, 244, 246, 249
  market, 268
  return on, 223, 227
European Free Trade Association (EFTA), see International economic communities, European Free Trade Association (EFTA)
European Union (EU), see International economic communities, European Union (EU)
Exchange, 8, 30, 31, 54, 55, 131, 147, 148, 163, 231, 235, 238, 242, 250, 264, 267
  exchange rate, 54, 55
  medium of, 231, 242
  see also Trade, international, currency, foreign exchange control
Exchanges, see Securities, exchanges
Exclusive distribution, 173, 174, 185
Expenses, 216–221, 223–225, 227, 234, 238, 243, 244, 257, 258, 261
  budgeting, 244
  cost of goods sold, 220
    direct manufacturing costs, 220
    raw material inventory, 220
    work in progress inventory, 220
  operating, 216, 217, 219–221, 223, 224, 227, 257, 261
    depreciation, 221, 227
    general (or administrative), 219, 221
    insurance, 219
    interest, 219
    medical, 257, 261
  miscellaneous, 219
  prepaid, 216, 217, 223
  selling, 219, 221, 224
  tax, 221
  unexpected, 244
  utilities, 219
Exporting, 9, 13, 54–56, 58, 59, 63
External data, 202, 212

F

Factoring, 246
Factors of production, 4, 5, 40, 97, 100
Federal Aviation Administration (FAA), see Government regulation, federal regulatory agencies, Federal Aviation Administration (FAA)
Federal Communications Commission, (FCC), see Government regulation, federal regulatory agencies, Federal Communications Commission, (FCC)
Federal Crime Insurance, see Insurance, public insurance, other, Federal Crime Insurance)
Federal Energy Regulatory Commission (FERC), see Government regulation, federal regulatory agencies, Federal Energy Regulatory Commission (FERC)
Federal Railroad Commission (FRC), see Government regulation, federal regulatory agencies, Federal Railroad Commission (FRC)
Federal Communications Commission (FCC), 20, 192, 198
Federal Crop Insurance Corporation, see Insurance, public insurance, other, Federal Crop Insurance Corporation
Federal Deposit Insurance Corporation (FDIC), see Insurance, public insurance, other, Federal Deposit Insurance Corporation (FDIC)
Federal Flood Insurance, see Insurance, public insurance, other, Federal Flood Insurance
Federal Home Mortgage Loan Insurance, see Insurance, public insurance, other, Federal Home Mortgage Loan Insurance
Federal Trade Commission (FTC), see Trade, Federal Trade Commission (FTC)
Federal Trade Commission Act (1914), see Government regulation, antitrust legislation, Federal Trade Commission Act (1914)
Federal Unemployment Tax Act (FUTA), see Taxation, other taxes, unemployment tax, Federal Unemployment Tax Act (FUTA)

Index

Finance and financing, 16, 47, 148, 156, 175, 185, 216, 222, 243–246, 249
   'debt financing', 244, 246, 249
   'equity financing', 244, 246, 249
   long-term, 246, 249
   need for, 243
   short-term, 244, 245, 249
Financial accounting, 204, 213
   Financial Accounting Standard Board (FASB), 213
Financial management, 3, 4, 6, 10, 11, 13, 20, 22, 31, 33, 39, 47, 48, 52, 69, 71, 73, 74, 76, 81, 90, 100, 115, 116, 124, 125, 134, 137, 144, 148, 149, 153, 156, 157, 161, 163, 168, 174, 175, 177, 178, 180, 185, 191, 214–218, 221–223, 227, 231, 233–239, 242–252, 255, 259, 262–68, 270, 271, 273, 276, 283, 285
   banking, 6, 10, 20, 73, 157, 231, 234–236, 239, 242, 263, 283, 285
   credit, 11, 13, 22, 47, 48, 52, 69, 90, 116, 148, 153, 156, 168, 174, 175, 177, 178, 180, 185, 214, 218, 227, 231, 233–239, 242, 244, 245, 247, 249, 254, 259, 283
   financial strategies, 13, 22, 31, 33, 39, 74, 148, 161, 214, 216–218, 221–223, 235, 236, 239, 244–250, 255, 262–268, 271, 273, 276
      long-term financing, 13, 22, 31, 39, 74, 161, 216–218, 235, 236, 239, 242–244, 246, 247, 249, 250, 255, 262–268, 271, 273, 276
      sources of, 13, 22, 31, 39, 74, 161, 216–218, 235, 236, 239, 242, 244, 246, 247, 249, 250, 255, 262–268, 271, 273, 276
      debt financing, 13, 22, 31, 39, 74, 161, 216, 218, 235, 236, 239, 242, 244, 246, 247, 249, 250, 255, 262–268, 271, 273, 276
      bonds, 13, 22, 31, 39, 74, 161, 216, 218, 235, 236, 239, 242, 246, 247, 249, 250, 255, 262–268, 271, 273, 276
      long-term loans, 218, 235, 242, 244, 246, 247
      equity financing, 217, 218, 246, 249
         issuing new shares of stock, 246
         retained earnings, 217, 218, 246, 249
      short-term financing, 31, 33, 39, 148, 214, 216–218, 221–223, 244–246, 248, 249
         unsecured, 33, 218, 244, 245, 249
         sources of, 33, 218, 244, 245, 249
            bank loans, 244, 245, 249
            commercial drafts, 244, 245, 249
            commercial paper, 244, 245, 249
            promissory notes, 33, 218, 244, 245, 249
            trade credit, 244, 245, 249
         secured, 31, 39, 148, 214, 216, 217, 221–223, 245, 246, 249
         sources of, 31, 39, 148, 214, 216, 217, 221–223, 245, 246, 249
            accounts receivables, 31, 39, 148, 214, 216, 217, 221–223, 245, 246, 249
            inventory loans, 245, 249
   interest factors, 247
   money, 3, 4, 69, 71, 74, 76, 81, 100, 124, 125, 134, 137, 144, 149, 161, 191, 215, 216, 218, 221, 243–247, 249, 251, 252, 255, 262–267, 270, 273, 276
   objectives, 3, 100, 115, 163, 214, 215, 244, 249
      budgeting income and expenses, 244
      financial performance, monitoring and evaluating, 244, 249
      source of funds, identifying, 3, 100, 115, 163, 214, 215, 244
      equity and debt capital, 244
      sales revenue, 3, 100, 115, 163, 214, 215, 244
   planning and control, 137, 243
   securities market, 10, 262, 263
Financial ratio, 222, 227
Fixed assets, 216, 217, 264
Fixed costs, 165
Flat organization, 91, 94
FOB (free on board), *see* Property, tangible personal property, transfer of, FOB (free on board)
Food and Drug Administration (FDA), 192, 198
Foreign direct investment, *see* Trade, international, levels of involvement, direct investment
Form utility, 131
Formation, *see* Formation and Structure, of business
Formation and Structure, of business, 65–108
For-profit corporation, 73
Four Ps, 152, 156
Franchising, 79, 83, 84, 86, 174, 180, 216
   advantages, 83, 86
   disadvantages, 84, 86
   franchisee, 83, 84
   franchisor, 83, 84, 86, 174
Free enterprise system or free-market system, 5, 6, 8, 9, 10, 17, 55, 60
Frequency distribution, 206, 212

G

Gantt Chart, *see* Production, goods, of, operations, Gantt Chart
Gantt, Henry, *see* Production, goods, of, operations, Gantt Chart
General Agreement on Tariffs and Trade (GATT), *see* Trade, international, agreements, General Agreement on Tariffs and Trade (GATT),
General expenses, 219–221
General partner, 69, 70
Global economy, 1, 11
Global marketplace, 53
Globalization, 11, 12, 19, 43, 53, 60, 127
Goals, 6, 8, 11, 12, 20, 21, 23, 44, 49, 80, 68, 87, 89, 94, 95, 97, 99–104, 114, 115, 120, 121, 130, 137, 138, 151, 152, 162, 164, 166, 181, 189, 191, 196, 225, 243, 244, 267, 279, 281, 284
   advertising, 191
   economic, 11, 12
Goods, 3–6, 9–13, 17–19, 22, 26, 27, 29, 30, 32, 35, 41–43, 53–57, 59, 60, 63, 73, 79, 86, 89, 94, 97, 104, 126, 131–141, 144, 147–149, 151, 156, 157, 163, 165, 167, 171, 172, 174–183, 185, 187, 195, 198, 204, 205, 208, 218–221, 231, 233, 238, 245, 279, 281, 282
   consumer goods, 6, 17, 151, 156, 172, 178, 187
      convenience goods, 151, 156, 178, 187
      shopping goods, 151, 156
      specialty goods, 151, 156
   intangible goods, 131
   luxury goods, 35
   sporting goods, 177, 178
   tangible goods, 131
   see also Production, goods, of
   see also Services
Government regulation, 10, 17–21, 26, 28, 30, 44, 46–48, 52, 56, 60, 63, 70, 82, 134, 144, 162, 192, 198, 214, 216, 234, 239, 268, 273, 274, 276
   advertising, regulation of, 192, 198
   antitrust legislation, 18, 19, 26, 44
      Celler-Kefauver Act (1950), 19
      Clayton Act (1914), 19, 26, 44
      Federal Trade Commission Act (1914), 19, 26
      Robinson-Patman Act (1936), 19, 26
      Sherman Antitrust Act (1890), 18, 26, 44
   business regulation, 21, 52
   consumer protection, 35, 36, 44, 47, 48
   Bankruptcy Abuse Prevention and Customer Protection Act, 35, 36
   deregulation, 10, 20, 28, 234, 239
   environmental and safety, 17, 20, 26, 46
   federal banking regulations, 234
   federal regulation, 273, 274
   federal regulatory agencies, 20, 192, 198
      Federal Aviation Administration (FAA), 20
      Federal Communications Commission (FCC), 20, 192, 198
      Federal Energy Regulatory Commission (FERC), 20
      Federal Railroad Commission (FRC), 20
      Interstate Trade Commission (ICC), 20
      Nuclear Regulatory Commission (NRC), 20
   licensing regulation, 30
   lobbyists, role of, 21, 26
   monopolies, regulation of, 19
   political action committees (PACs), 21
   securities trading, regulation of, 273
   state regulation, 273
   trade regulation, 48
Government, role of, 8, 12, 13, 16–18, 20, 21, 23, 26–28, 39, 42, 44, 46, 74, 116, 153, 214, 236, 253, 257, 261, 283
   debt, federal, 26
   deficit, federal, 12, 13, 16, 23, 26, 236
      Emergency Deficit Control Act (1985), 23
      see also Taxation,
   fiscal policy, 21, 42
   free-market system, in, 8, 17, 18, 20, 26–28, 39, 46, 74, 214, 283
      business supporter, 17, 18, 26
      consumer, role of government as, 17, 26
      regulator, 17, 20, 26–28, 39, 46, 74, 214, 283
         federal regulatory agencies, *see* Government regulation, federal regulatory agencies
         law, regulatory, 28, 39, 46
         Fuels Regulatory Relief Act (1999), 46
   regulatory reports, 74
   regulation, *see* Government regulation
   social security system, 23, 26, 44, 116, 153, 253, 257, 261
      Social Security Act (1935), 253, 261

Index

disability benefits, 253
retirement benefits, 253
survivors' benefits, 253
tax, 23, 26, 257
Governmental market, 149, 156
Gramm-Rudman-Hollings Act, *see* Deficit, federal, Emergency Deficit Control Act (1985),
Grievance procedure, 115, 125
Gross Domestic Product (GDP), 12, 79, 137
Gross National Product (GNP), 12
Growth, measuring of, 12

H

Health maintenance organizations (HMO), 257
High-contact services, 139–141
see also Low-contact services
High-growth venture, 80, 86
Holding company, 73
Horizontal merger, 75, 78
Human resources management, 111, 117, 279

I

Import, 13, 22, 54–56, 59, 60, 63
import quota, 56, 63
import taxes/duties, 56, 60
Income statement, 216, 218, 219, 221, 222, 224, 227, 238
Index number, 208
Industrial market, 149, 150
Industrial products, 150, 151, 171
Industrial revolution, 8–10, 120, 133, 149
Industrial union, 120, 121
Congress of Industrial Union (CIU), 121
Inflation, 11–13, 42, 57, 125, 205, 231–234, 237
anti-inflation tools, 237
consumer price index, 13
producer price index, 13
see also Deflation
Information, 4, 8, 11, 12, 16, 18, 34, 36, 40–43, 47, 60, 68, 71, 82, 90–92, 101, 104, 108, 111–113, 138, 148, 150, 152, 153, 156, 160, 162, 174, 175, 182, 185, 187, 190–192, 194, 198, 201–206, 212–216, 221, 222, 233, 238, 239, 271, 273, 279–281, 284–287, 290
Age, 4
communicating, 187, 198
credit information, 239
data versus, 201, 212
demographic, 153, 191
electronic information services, 202
financial information, 68, 213–215, 271, 273
financial statements, 216, 221
flow of, 91
"hard", 201
information-based economy, 8
management information, 201–206, 212
market information, 148, 153, 156, 160, 174, 175, 185, 194
network, 175, 185
resources, 4, 40

sector, 11
"soft", 201
statistical information, 205, 206
Institutional market, 149, 156, 267
Insurance, 72, 116, 237, 238, 251–259, 261
coverage, types of, 251, 253–259, 261
business insurance, 251, 253–257, 261
business liability insurance, 253, 256, 257, 261
product liability insurance, 256
public liability insurance, 256
worker's compensation insurance, 253, 257, 261
loss-of-income insurance, 257
business-interruption insurance, 257
loss of property, 251, 254–257, 261
burglary, robbery, and theft insurance, 254, 255
fire insurance, 255
marine insurance, 255
motor vehicle insurance, 256, 257, 261
liability insurance, 256, 257, 261
physical damage insurance, 256
natural disaster insurance, 255
self-insurance, 251, 255, 261
loss-of-services insurance, 257, 261
employee insurance, 257–259, 261
disability income insurance, 257
life insurance, 258, 259, 261
credit life insurance, 259
endowment life insurance, 258
key-executive life insurance, 259
term life insurance, 258, 261
universal life insurance, 258
whole life insurance, 258, 261
medical insurance, 257
insurers, 252–254, 257
principles of, 252, 253
indemnification, 252
insurable interest, 253
insurable risk, 252, 253
law of large numbers, 252, 253
uninsurable risk, 252
private insurance, 254, 261
mutual insurance companies, 254, 261
stock insurance companies, 254, 261
public insurance, 72, 116, 237, 238, 253–255, 257, 261
other, 72, 237, 238, 253–255

Employee Retirement Income Security Act (ERISA, 1974), 254
Federal Crime Insurance, 254
Federal Crop Insurance Corporation, 254
Federal Deposit Insurance Corporation (FDIC), 72, 237, 254
Federal Flood Insurance, 254
Federal Home Mortgage Loan Insurance, 254
Savings Association Insurance Fund, 238, 254
unemployment insurance, 116, 253, 261
worker's compensation, 253, 257, 261
Social Security Act (1935), *see* Government, role of, social security system, Social Security Act (1935)
see also Risk
Insurers, *see* Insurance, insurers
Intangible assets, *see* Assets, intangible
Intensive distribution, 173, 185
Internal data, 202, 212
Internal Revenue Service (IRS), 21, 214, 227
International economic communities, 57, 58, 59, 63
European Free Trade Association (EFTA), 58
European Union (EU), 57, 58, 63
Latin American Integration Association (LAIA), 58
North American Free Trade Agreement (NAFTA), 58
Organization of Petroleum Exporting Countries (OPEC), 58, 59, 63
U.S./Canada Free Trade Agreement, 58
International firms, *see* Trade, international, levels of involvement, international firms
International Monetary Fund (IMF), *see* Trade, international, agreements, United National Agencies, International Monetary Fund (IMF),
International trade, *see* Trade, international
Interstate Commerce Act (1887), *see* Social responsibilities, Interstate Commerce Act (1887)
Interstate Trade Commission (ICC), *see* Economic systems, American, government regulation, federal regulatory agencies, Interstate Trade Commission (ICC)
Inventory, 220
cost, determination of, 220
average-cost method, 220
first-in first-out method (FIFO), 220

last-in first-out method (LIFO), 220
specific-identification method, 220
Inventory control, 137, 162, 180, 185

J

Job analysis, 111
Job description, 111, 284
Job specification, 111, 284
Joint venture, *see* Trade, international, levels of involvement, joint venture
Judicial system, 19, 28–30, 33–35, 39, 122, 126, 256
appellate courts, 28, 29
federal courts, 28, 29
other courts, 28, 29
special courts, 29
state and local courts, 28, 29
supreme court, U.S., 28, 29, 39
trial court, 28
Junk bonds, 265, 266, 276
Just-in-time (JIT) inventory control, 137, 183

K

Key-executive insurance, 257

L

Labor, 44, 49, 52, 117, 119–127, 130, 202, 208, 255, 257, 281, 284
Department of Labor, U.S., 202, 208, 281, 284, 290
Occupational Outlook Handbook, 281, 284, 290
labor-management relations, 120, 123–125, 130
organized labor, evolution of, 120–122
AFL-CIO, 121, 122
American Federation of Labor (AFL), 121, 122
Congress of Industrial Unions (CIO), 121, 122
Industrial Workers of the World (IWW), 121
knights of labor, 120
organized labor today, 44, 49, 52, 117, 119, 121–127, 130, 255, 257
management weapons, 126, 127, 130
lockouts, 126, 130
strikebreakers, 126, 130
mediation and arbitration, 127
pro-labor legislation, 49, 117, 119, 122–125, 130
Fair Labor Standards Act (1938), 49, 117, 119, 123
Federal Service Labor-management Relations Statute (1978), 124, 130
Labor-Management Relations Act (1947), 123, 125
Landrum-Griffin Act (1959), 123

Labor *(Continued)*
  National Labor Relations Act (1935), 122, 130
  National Labor Relations Board (NLRB), 122, 124, 130
  Norris-LaGuardia Act (1932), 122, 123, 130
  Postal Reorganization Act (1970), 123
  unions, 44, 49, 52, 121–127, 130, 255, 257
    formation of, 124
    future of, 127
    negotiations with management, 44, 49, 52, 102, 121, 123–125
      collective bargaining, 121, 124
      contract issues, 124
      grievance procedures, 115, 125
      job security, 102, 124, 125
      management rights, 125
      working hours and overtime, 44, 49, 52, 123–125
    union membership, 122–124, 127, 130
    weapons, 121–124, 126, 127, 130, 255, 257
      boycotts, 126, 130
      slowdowns, 126, 130
      strikes, 121–124, 126, 127, 130, 255, 257
      picket, 122, 126
Laissez-faire, 9, 10, 44, 101, 102, 108
Laissez-faire leadership, 101, 102, 108
Land, 4, 8, 16, 22, 29–31, 46, 48, 95, 97, 120, 134, 144, 215, 216, 264
Latin American Integration Association (LAIA), *see* International economic communities, Latin American Integration Association (LAIA)
Law of demand, 6, 54
Law of large numbers, 252, 253
Law of supply, 6, 54
Leadership, 10, 95, 101, 102, 108, 279
Lease, 30, 31, 256, 264
Legal forms, 9, 19, 26, 42, 44, 52, 59, 67, 69, 70–74, 76, 78, 98, 214, 221, 243, 246, 262, 265, 266, 268, 276
  corporations, 19, 26, 42, 44, 52, 59, 67, 71–76, 78, 98, 214, 221, 243, 246, 262, 265, 266, 268, 276
    acquisitions, 19, 75, 78, 243, 246
    conglomerate, 19, 75, 78
    advantages, 72, 74
    disadvantages, 72, 74
    alien, 71
    domestic, 71
    foreign, 71
    framework, 42, 44, 52, 72–76, 78, 262, 266, 268, 276

Board of Directors, management, 72, 76
    shareholders, 42, 44, 52, 72–76, 78, 262, 266, 268, 276
    mergers, 19, 26, 75, 78, 246
      horizontal merger, 75, 78
      vertical merger, 75, 78
    takeovers, 75, 76, 265
      friendly, 76
      hostile, 75
    types of, 59, 67, 72–74, 76, 78, 98, 214, 221
      cooperative, 73
      holding company, 73
      joint venture, 59, 73
      limited liability corporation (LLC), 67, 74, 76, 78
      private corporations, 73, 78
        closely held corporation, 73
        for-profit corporation, 73, 78
        nonprofit corporation, 73, 78
        professional corporation (PC), 73
        subchapter S corporation, 73
      public corporations, 72, 73, 78, 214, 221
      quasi-public corporations, 73, 78
      subsidiary, 73, 98
      syndicate, 73
  partnerships, 67, 70, 71
    limited liability partnership (LLP), 67, 70, 71
  sole proprietorships, 9, 67, 69, 70, 72, 246
Leveraged buyout (LBO), 75, 76, 78, 265
Liabilities, 34, 67, 69–72, 74, 76, 78, 214–218, 222, 223, 227, 251, 254, 256, 257, 261, 273, 283
  accident liability, 251
  accounting equation, in, 215, 216, 227
  company and corporation, 215
  liability risks, 251
  limited liability corporation, 67, 72, 74, 76, 78
  limited liability partnership, 67, 70, 71
  long-term, 216–218
  personal, 69
  product, 34, 251, 256, 283
  short-term, 216–218
  tax, 214
License and licensing, 20, 30, 31, 56, 59, 63, 67, 83, 86, 161, 170, 273
Life-style business, 80, 86, 160
Limited partner, 69, 70
Line management, 87, 89, 94
Line of credit, 235, 245
Liquidation, 35
Liquidity, 216, 222, 223, 227
  ratio, 222, 227
Lobbyist, 21, 26, 283
Lockout, 126, 130
Logistics, 171
Long-range plan, 225

Long-term liabilities, 217, 218
Low-contact services, 139–141
  see also High-contact services

M
M-1, 233, 242
M-2, 233, 242
M-3, 233, 242
Magnuson-Moss Warranty-Federal Trade Commission Act (1975), *see* Trade, Magnuson-Moss Warranty-Federal Trade Commission Act (1975)
Mail-order retailing, 178
Major medical insurance, 257
Management, 4–6, 12, 16, 18, 27, 40, 43, 49, 60, 69, 70, 81, 87–92, 94–105, 108, 111–114, 116, 117, 119–121, 133–138, 140, 141, 144, 147, 159, 171, 191, 198, 199, 201–209, 212, 213, 223–225, 243, 273, 279–284, 286, 287, 290
  chain of command, 87, 89, 94, 96
  decision-making, 27, 60, 90–92, 94, 101, 104, 105, 108, 203, 205, 212
  development, 111, 113, 114, 119
  fundamentals, 95
  human resources, *see* Personnel, human resources management
  information, 201–209, 212, 282
    data, 202–205, 207, 212, 282
      external, 202, 212
      internal, 202, 212
      median, 208
      methods of collection, 202–204, 212
      mode, 208
      presenting, 205
      primary, 202, 212
      processing and analyzing, 204, 205, 207, 212, 282
      electronic, 282
      secondary, 202, 212
    decision-support systems, 205
    information management, 201
    management information system (MIS), 201, 203–205, 212
    statistical analysis, 206–208, 209, 212
      analyzing statistical data, 207
      correlation analysis, 209
      displaying statistical information, 206
      index numbers, 208
      time-series analysis, 209, 212
  leadership strategies for motivation, 95–97, 99, 101–103, 108
    aspects of, 97, 101–103, 108
      leadership styles, 97, 101–103, 108
        autocratic, 101, 108
        behavior, 101, 102
          employee-centered, 102
          job-centered, 102

laissez-faire, 101, 102, 108
motivation, 102, 103
  Maslow's Hierarchy of Needs, 102, 103
  Theory X and Theory Y, 103
participative, 101, 108
situational, 97, 101, 102, 108
controlling, 95, 96, 99, 101
levels of, 94, 97, 98, 100, 108, 273, 283
  authority versus responsibility, 97
  first-line management, 97, 98, 100, 108
  middle management, 97, 98, 100, 108
  top management, 94, 97, 98, 108, 273, 283
management by objectives (MBO), 103, 104
managerial accounting, 213
marketing, *see* Marketing, management
process, 6, 18, 60, 91, 95, 96, 99–101, 111, 112, 119, 133–137, 140, 144, 147, 171, 191, 198, 199, 203, 205, 212, 224, 225, 243, 283
  leading or directing, 100
  organizing, 100
  planning, 6, 18, 60, 91, 95, 96, 99–101, 111, 112, 119, 133–137, 140, 144, 147, 171, 191, 198, 199, 203, 205, 212, 224, 225, 243, 283
    goals, 99
    materials requirement planning (MRP), 136, 137
    mission, 99
    purpose, 99
    strategic, 100
    tactical, 100
    tools, 100, 101, 199, 203, 212, 283
      budgets, 100
      management, 101, 199, 203, 212, 283
      policies, 100
      rules, 100
resources, 4, 16, 40, 95, 97, 111–113, 117, 119, 134, 138, 159, 223, 224, 243, 279
  human resources, 111–113, 117, 279
  information resources, 4, 16, 40
skills, 4, 5, 12, 16, 43, 49, 69, 70, 81, 88, 95, 96, 98, 99, 103, 108, 111–114, 116, 119–121, 141, 280–282, 284, 286, 287, 290
  conceptual, 98, 99, 108
  human, 5, 12, 16, 43, 49, 69, 99, 108, 119, 282, 284
  management, 70, 95, 96, 98, 114, 119
semiskilled workers, 282

Index

specialized, 88
technical, 98, 99, 108, 114
unskilled workers, 121, 282
time-series analysis, 209
theories of, 89, 95–97, 108
   classical, 89, 96, 97
      behavioral school, 96, 97
      Fayol, Henri, 89, 96
      Weber, Max, 96
   contingency approach, 97
   management science, 97, 108
      operations research (OR), 97, 108
   scientific management, 95, 96, 108
   systems approach, 97
Margin requirement, 237
Market, 4–12, 16–20, 26, 27, 42, 43, 53–55, 58–60, 63, 73, 75, 79, 80, 91, 116, 127, 133, 134, 137, 138, 144, 148–153, 156, 158–161, 164–167, 170, 173–175, 177, 178, 185–187, 190, 191, 194, 195, 198, 202, 233, 237, 239, 242, 252, 262, 263, 267–269, 271–274, 276, 283, 285
   controlled-market system, 17
   coverage, 173
   free-market system, 8, 10, 17, 55, 60
   global market, 11, 53, 54, 59, 133, 134, 137
      see also Trade, international
   hypermarkets, 178, 185
   investor market, 16
   labor market, 11, 127, 285
   market economy, 5, 6
   market forces, 20
   market information and knowledge, 18, 59, 148, 156, 160, 165, 170, 174, 175, 185
      test-market, 160, 170
   market research, 148, 151–153, 194, 283
   market share, 164, 170, 191
   market value and market price, 7, 12, 116, 127
   money market or financial market, 233, 239, 242
   segmentation, 149, 150, 156, 177, 178, 267, 269, 271, 274
      consumer market, 149, 150, 156
      government market, 149, 156
      industrial market, 149, 150, 156
      institutional market, 149, 156, 267
      OTC market, 268, 269, 271, 274
      producer market, 149, 156
      reseller market, 150, 156
      retail market, 178
   specialized market, 79
   stock and securities market, 10, 116, 262, 263, 267, 272, 273, 276
      primary, 263, 276
      secondary, 263, 267, 276
   supermarkets, 138, 167, 177, 178, 185, 191, 195, 202
   see also Marketing
   see also Trade

Marketing, 3, 4, 7, 10, 11, 13, 16, 18, 19, 21, 22, 26, 30, 32, 40, 41, 43, 45, 47, 48, 54, 57, 59, 60, 63, 72, 79–81, 83, 84, 86, 89, 97, 111, 127, 131–135, 137, 138, 140, 145, 147–154, 156–168, 170–179, 181, 182, 185–189, 191–196, 198, 201, 202, 204, 205, 214, 220, 221, 231, 236, 237, 239, 242, 246, 251, 256, 262, 263, 266, 269, 270, 273, 276, 283
   buying, 13, 19, 59, 81, 84, 148, 150, 153, 154, 156, 168, 173, 175, 180, 185, 192, 194, 195, 221, 236, 237, 242, 246, 262, 263, 266, 269, 270, 276
      economic factors, 153
      industrial, 154
      on margin, 270, 276
      psychological factors, 154
         emotional motives, 154
         rational motives, 154
      social factors, 154
   concept, 147, 148, 151–153, 194, 283
   concept of utility, 147
      place, 147
      possession, 147
      time, 147
   market research, 148, 151–153, 194, 283
   marketing strategy, 152, 153
      place, 152
      price, 152
      product, 152
      promotion, 152
   development of marketing orientation, 149
   functions, 147, 148
      exchange, 148
      facilitation, 148
      physical distribution, 148
   management, 145, 153, 173, 179, 185, 283
   markets and market segmentation, see Market, segmentation
   mix, 153, 186, 194
   orientation (customer orientation), 149
   products, 3, 4, 7, 10, 11, 13, 16, 18, 21, 22, 30, 32, 40, 41, 43, 45, 47, 48, 54, 57, 59, 60, 63, 72, 79–81, 83, 86, 89, 97, 111, 127, 131–135, 137, 138, 140, 147–153, 156–164, 166–168, 170–179, 181, 182, 186–189, 191–195, 198, 201, 202, 204, 205, 220, 231, 239, 251, 256, 273
      consumer, 45, 47, 151, 162, 171, 173, 193
         convenience goods, 151, 162
         shopping goods, 151, 162
         specialty goods, 151, 162
      finished, 4, 131, 138, 147, 150, 156
      industrial, 150, 151, 171, 193
      life-cycle of, 159
      mix, 158, 162

      positioning, 187
      product line, 170
   pricing, 7, 19, 26, 57, 147, 157, 159, 160, 163–167, 170, 201, 214
      competition-based, 166
      cost-based, 165
      discount pricing, 167
      methods, 164, 166
      multiple-unit pricing, 167
      objectives, 163, 164, 167
      penetration pricing, 166
      policy, 164
      prestige pricing, 167
      price skimming, 166
      strategies, 166
      tactics, 167
      threshold pricing, 167
      unfair, 19, 26
   promotional strategies, 186, 187, 196
      see also Distribution, channels of,
      tools, 151
Markup, 165
Maslow's Hierarchy of Needs, see Management, leadership strategies for motivation, aspects of leadership styles, motivation, Maslow's Hierarchy of Needs
Mass production, see Production, mass production
Materials handling, 180, 181
Materials requirements planning (MRP), 136, 137, 144
McGregor, Douglas, see Management, leadership strategies for motivation, aspects of, leadership styles, motivation, Theory X and Theory Y
Mean, 207–209, 212
Mechanization, 10, 133, 137, 139, 282
Median, 207–209, 212
Media plan, 191, 198
Mediation, 127
Merchant wholesaler, 59, 175, 176, 185
Merger, 19, 26, 75, 78, 246
   horizontal, 75, 78
   vertical, 75, 78
Mission, 87, 99, 100
Missionary selling, 193, 194
Mixed economy, 5
Mode, 207–209, 212
Modem, 204
Money, 11, 13, 22, 34–36, 39, 42, 47, 48, 52, 54–56, 58, 60, 63, 69, 72, 76, 82, 90, 116, 139, 148, 153, 156, 168, 174, 175, 177, 178, 180, 185, 202, 214, 218, 223, 227, 231–239, 242, 244, 245, 247, 249, 254, 258, 259, 265, 273, 276, 283
   American banking system, 11, 13, 22, 34–36, 39, 42, 47, 48, 52, 69, 72, 76, 82, 47, 48, 69, 90, 116, 139, 148, 153, 156, 168, 174, 175, 177, 178, 180, 185, 202, 214, 218, 223, 227,

231–239, 242, 244, 245, 247, 249, 254, 258, 259, 265, 273, 276, 283
   commercial banks, 234, 236, 237, 239, 242, 245, 247, 259
   credit, 11, 13, 22, 34–36, 39, 47, 48, 52, 69, 76, 90, 116, 148, 153, 156, 168, 174, 175, 177, 178, 180, 185, 202, 214, 218, 223, 227, 231, 233–239, 242, 244, 245, 247, 249, 254, 259, 283
      agreements, 47, 245
      checking credit information, 239
      creditor, 34–36, 39, 69, 76, 202, 223, 245
      line of, 235, 242, 245, 249
      management, 238, 239
         Five Cs of Credit, 238, 239
      merchants, 48
      risk, 175, 185
      trade credit, 245
      transactions, 238
   credit unions, 116, 234, 235, 242, 254
   federal reserve system, 72, 233, 236, 237, 242, 254
      role of, 72, 236, 237, 242, 254
         banker's bank, 236, 242
         check-clearing, 237
         deposit insurance, 72, 237, 242, 254
         discount rate, 237, 242
         government's bank, 236, 242
         open-market operations, 237, 242
         reserve requirement, 237, 242
         selective credit controls, 237
      structure of, 236
   financial institutions, 42, 82, 232–234, 237, 239, 247, 273, 276
   mutual savings banks, 234, 235
   non-deposit institutions, 234, 235
   savings and loan associations (S&Ls), 234, 238, 239, 254
   services, 48, 139, 153, 156, 168, 178, 233, 235, 236, 239, 242, 258, 265
      automated teller machines (ATMs), 139, 178, 236
      credit cards, 48, 153, 156, 168, 233, 236
      deposit-side services, 233, 235, 239, 242, 258, 265
         checking accounts, 235, 239, 242
         NOW accounts, 233, 235, 242
         savings accounts, 233, 242, 258, 265
      lending-side services, 235
      trust services, 236

Money (Continued)
  changes in the money and banking system, 239
  characteristics of, 232, 242
  functions of, 231
  money-market fund, 233, 242
  supply, 233, 236, 237, 242
    M-1, 233, 242
    M-2, 233, 242
    M-3, 233, 242
  types of, 54–56, 58, 60, 63, 232–236, 242, 258, 265
    currency, 54–56, 58, 60, 63, 232–236, 242
    demand deposits, 232–235, 242
    money-market funds, 233, 242
    other checkable deposits, 233, 242
    plastic money, 233, 242
    savings accounts, 233, 242, 258, 265
    time deposits, 233–235, 242
Monopoly, 7, 16, 18–20, 26, 73, 78
  monopolistic competition, *see* Competition, monopolistic
  natural monopolies, 20, 26
  regulation of, 19
  rights, 78
  see also Economic systems, Government regulation, monopolies, regulation of,
  see also Economic systems, American, monopolies
Multinational firms, *see* Trade, international, levels of involvement, multinational firms
Mutual fund, 263, 267, 274, 276
Mutual insurance company, 254, 261
Myers-Briggs Type Indicator (MBTI), *see* Business careers, choosing, understanding self-assessment, personality characteristics, Myers-Briggs Type Indicator (MBTI)

N
National Association of Securities Dealers Automated Quotation (NASDAQ), *see* Securities, exchanges, National Association of Securities Dealers Automated Quotation (NASDAQ)
National bank, 234, 236
National Conference of Commissioners on Uniform State Laws, *see* Commercial law, uniform commercial code (UCC), National Conference of Commissioners on Uniform State Laws
Natural monopoly, *see* Monopoly, natural monopolies
Negotiable instrument, 32, 33
Net income, 218, 219, 221–223
Net profit margin, 223, 227
Network, 17, 18, 26, 81, 92, 94, 171, 175, 182, 185, 189, 190, 268, 285, 290
  of brokers, 268

computer, 18, 182, 268
of contacts (networking), 285, 290
information, 175, 185
of laws and regulations, 17, 26
supply chain network, 171
television, 189, 190
transmission and telecommunications, 81, 182
Networking, *see* Network, of contacts (networking)
New York Stock Exchange (NYSE), *see* Securities, exchanges, New York Stock Exchange (NYSE)
No-load fund, 267
Nonprofit or not-for-profit corporation, *see* Corporation, types of, private, nonprofit
North American Free Trade Agreement (NAFTA), *see* International economic communities, North American Free Trade Agreement (NAFTA)
Nuclear Regulatory Commission (NRC), *see* Economic systems, American, government regulation, federal regulatory agencies, Nuclear Regulatory Commission (NRC)

O
Objective, of organization, 95, 98–101, 103, 104, 147, 153, 159, 163, 164, 167, 170, 187, 191, 194, 198, 243, 244, 249
Oligopoly, 7, 8, 16
Operating expenses, 23, 219, 220, 224
Operations planning, 134, 144
Opportunity cost, 4, 5, 16
Order processing, 180, 193
Organization chart, 87, 88, 90, 92, 94
Organization of Petroleum Exporting Countries (OPEC), *see* International economic communities, Organization of Petroleum Exporting Countries (OPEC)
Organizational structure, *see* Structure, organizational
Orientation, 112, 113, 149
  customer, 149
  HRM, 113
  marketing, 149
  production, 149
  sales, 149
  staffing, 112
Over-the-counter (OTC) market, 268, 269, 271, 274
Owners' equity, 215–218, 223, 227

P
Partnership, 9, 59, 67, 69–74, 76, 78, 246, 259, 284
Patent, 28, 31, 39, 48, 160, 216, 217
Penetration pricing, 166
Performance appraisal, 103, 111, 114, 119
Personal property, *see* Property, personal
Personnel, 5, 6, 8, 13, 20, 21, 23, 26, 35, 42, 44, 49, 52, 69, 89, 91,

94–96, 98, 100, 102, 109, 111–117, 119–123, 125, 127, 130, 140, 165, 179, 195, 202, 206, 217, 219, 221, 238, 257, 261, 283, 284
cost, 140
human resources management, 5, 6, 8, 13, 21, 23, 26, 35, 42, 44, 49, 52, 91, 95, 96, 102, 111–117, 119–123, 125, 127, 130, 165, 202, 206, 217, 219, 221, 238, 257, 261, 283, 284
compensation, 5, 6, 8, 13, 21, 23, 26, 35, 42, 44, 49, 52, 91, 95, 96, 102, 115–117, 119–123, 125, 127, 130, 165, 202, 206, 217, 219, 221, 238, 257, 261, 283, 284
  comparable worth, 116
  employee benefits, 116, 119
  incentive, 35, 96, 119
    bonuses, 96, 115
    commissions, 35, 115
  salary, 5, 23, 35, 91, 115, 116, 119, 122, 125, 165, 202, 217, 219, 221, 238, 257, 261, 283, 284
  wages, 5, 6, 8, 13, 21, 23, 26, 35, 42, 44, 49, 52, 95, 102, 115–117, 119–123, 127, 130, 206, 261, 283
    level, 116
    individual, 116
    measuring, 116
    minimum wages, 44, 52, 117, 119, 123
    structure, 116
    federal legislation, impact on, 117
performance appraisal, 103, 111, 114, 115, 119
  layoff, 115
  reduction in force (RIF), 115
  resignation, 115
  retirement, 115
  separation, 114
  termination, 115
planning, 111
staffing, 112, 113
  hiring, 112
  orientation, 113
  recruiting, 112
  selection, 112, 113
  training and development, 113, 114
sales, 179
Physical distribution functions, 148
Place utility, 131
Planned economy, 5
Point-of-purchase (POP) displays, 195, 198
Popular industries, 81, 82
  manufacturing business, 82
  retail business, 81
  service business, 81
  wholesale business, 81
Positioning the product, 159, 187
Possession utility, 147, 148
Preferred stock, 249, 263, 266, 267, 271, 276

Price, 5–8, 12, 13, 16–20, 22, 26, 30–32, 42, 47, 48, 55, 56, 58, 59, 63, 75, 76, 104, 116, 127, 134, 141, 147, 151, 152, 153, 156–158, 160–168, 174, 177, 187, 193–196, 198, 208, 237, 252, 262–265, 267–272
  call price, 265
  conversion price, 267
  coupons, 195
  discrimination, 19, 26
  government price support, 7
  net price, 168
  price wars, 20
  skimming, 166
  strategies, 166
  tactics, 167
    discount, 167
    multiple-unit pricing, 167
    prestige, 167
    price lining, 167
    psychological, 167
    threshold, 167
  see also Marketing, product and pricing strategies
Primary data, 202, 212
Prime rate, 237, 247
Principal, 34
Private accountant, 213, 227
Private corporation, 73
Private law, 28
Producer market, 149, 156
Product, 3–8, 10–13, 16, 18, 19, 21, 22, 30–34, 39–41, 43, 45, 47, 48, 53, 54, 57, 59, 60, 63, 72, 79–81, 83, 84, 86, 88, 89, 91, 94, 97, 111, 127, 131–138, 140, 144, 147–168, 170–179, 181, 182, 185–189, 191–196, 198, 201–205, 220, 231, 244–246, 250–252, 256, 273, 283
  brands, 7, 31, 59, 147, 151, 154, 158–162, 164, 167, 170, 178, 188, 189, 193, 198, 202, 203, 283
  branding, 160
  loyalty, 158, 161, 162, 164, 170
  mark, 160
  name, 160, 161
  types of, 161
  commercialize, 160
  consumer, 47, 151, 172, 173, 193
  decision, 147
  development, 11, 159, 170, 246, 283
  differentiation, 8, 157, 166
  flow, 132
  gross domestic product (GDP), 12
  gross national product (GNP), 12
  industrial, 151, 172
  layout, 134
  liability, 34, 251, 283
  life-cycle, 158, 159, 166, 189
    declining stage, 159
    extending, 159
    growth stage, 158
    introductory stage, 158
    maturity stage, 158
  line, 157, 158, 170

mix, 158
new product strategies, 166
packaging and labeling, 162, 191
positioning, 187
quality, 84
warranty, 163
Production, 4, 5, 10, 12, 13, 40, 79, 95–97, 100, 103, 108, 114, 121, 131–141, 144, 149, 162, 205, 282
factors of, 4, 5, 40, 97, 100
goods, of, 5, 10, 12, 13, 95, 96, 100, 103, 108, 114, 131–137, 139, 140, 144, 162, 205, 282
production processes, 5, 10, 12, 13, 95, 96, 100, 103, 108, 114, 131–133, 134, 137, 139, 144, 205, 282
automation, 133, 137, 139, 282
methods used to effect the transformation, 132
production line and assembly line, 5, 100, 133, 134, 137, 139 144
productivity, 10, 12, 13, 95, 96, 103, 108, 114, 133, 137, 205, 282
rate, 12, 13
robotics and computerized production, 133, 139, 144
computer-aided design (CAD), 133, 139, 144
computer-aided manufacturing (CAM), 133, 144
types of production, 132, 144
types of transformation, 131
operations, 96, 134–137, 140, 144, 162
controlling production, 136, 137, 144, 162
inventory control, 137, 144, 162
Just-in-Time (JIT) inventory control, 137, 144
quality control, 136, 137
statistical, 137
Gantt Chart, 96, 135, 144
planning and scheduling, 134, 140
production facility planning, 134
Program Evaluation and Review Technique (PERT), 135, 136, 140
mass production, 79, 121
orientation, 149
production and operations management (POM), 131, 136, 138, 144
services, of, 138–141
characteristics of services, 139
customization, 139
customized services, 139
perishability, 139
controlling services production, 141
planning services operations, 140
quality control, 141
scheduling service operations, 140, 141
appointment scheduling, 140
fixed scheduling, 141
queuing theory, 140
routing, 141
service production processes, 138, 139
methods of transformation, 138
service flow, 138
types of service production, 139
types of transformation, 138
Productivity, see Production, goods, of, production processes, productivity
Profit, 3, 4, 6–9, 12, 16, 20, 22, 34, 35, 40–42, 44, 56, 59, 68–71, 73, 75, 76, 78, 80, 83, 84, 86, 99, 100, 116, 120, 126, 147, 149–153, 156–159, 163–165, 170, 187, 218, 219, 221, 223, 224, 227, 234, 235, 238, 242, 243, 245, 246, 250, 252–254, 257, 261–266, 270, 271
margin, 151, 165, 223, 227
profit-and-loss statement, 218
sharing, 116
short-term, 159
Profitability, 11, 42, 80, 158, 159, 221, 223, 227
ratio, 223, 227
Program Evaluation and Review Technique (PERT) chart, see Production, goods, of, operations, Program Evaluation and Review Technique (PERT)
Promissory note, 33, 218, 244, 245, 249
Promotion, 19, 83, 84, 87–89, 147, 149, 151–153, 160, 161, 163, 167, 180, 186–196, 198, 219, 221, 280, 282–285
methods, 19, 83, 84, 87–89, 147, 149, 151–153, 160, 161, 163, 167, 180, 186–192, 194, 195, 198, 219, 221, 280, 282–285
advertising, 19, 83, 84, 87–89, 147, 149, 151–153, 160, 161, 163, 167, 180, 186–192, 195, 198, 219, 221, 280, 282–285
advertising agencies, 192, 198, 284
advertising campaign, 191, 192, 198
advertising media, 151, 152, 186, 189–191, 198
direct mail, 189, 190, 198
interactive, 191
local, 151, 188
magazines, 189, 190, 198
national, 151
newspapers, 186, 189, 190, 198
online and internet, 191, 198
outdoor advertising, 189, 190, 198
billboard, 190
radio, 189, 190, 198
telemarketing, 198
television, 152, 186, 189, 190, 198
advertising platform, 191, 198
manager, 88
mass, 151, 187, 198
message, 191, 198
objectives, 191, 198
regulation of, 192
consumer action, 192
industry self-regulation, 192
types of, 188, 189, 198
advocacy, 188, 198
immediate response, 198
institutional, 188, 198
message, 188, 189
informative, 189
persuasive, 189
reminder, 189
primary demand, 188, 198
selective or brand, 188, 198
comparative, 188, 198
immediate response, 188
reminder, 188, 198
publicity and public relations, 186, 195, 198
sales promotion, 147, 152, 186, 194, 198, 219
objectives, 187, 191, 198
advertising, 191, 198
communicating information, 187
controlling sales volume, 187, 198
positioning products, 187
personal selling, 147, 151, 152, 167, 180, 186, 187, 193, 194, 198
creative selling, 193, 198
missionary selling, 193, 194
objectives, 194
order processing, 180, 193
promotional mix, 186, 194
sales, 152, 186, 195, 198
coupons, 152, 186, 195, 198
point-of-purchase displays, 195, 198
purchasing incentives, 195, 198
trade shows, 195, 198
strategies, 186, 187, 196, 198
pull, 187, 198
push, 187, 198
Property, 28, 30–32, 39, 48, 160, 216, 217, 239
personal property, 28, 30–32, 39, 48, 160, 216, 217, 239
intangible personal property, 31, 39
copyright, 28, 31, 39, 216
patents, 28, 31, 39, 48, 160, 216, 217
trademarks, 31, 39, 160, 216
transfer of, 31
tangible personal property, 30–32
transfer of, 31, 32
COD (collect on delivery), 32
FOB (free on board), 32
Destination Basis, 32
Point of Origin (or Shipping Point), 32
property law, 30
real property, 30, 31, 239
transfer of, 31
deeds, 31
leases, 31
Prospecting, 193, 194, 198
Protectionism, 55, 56, 63
Prototype, 160
Psychographics, 150, 156
Public accountant, 72, 213, 214, 227, 238
Public corporation, 72, 73, 78, 214, 221
quasi, 73, 78
Publicity, 127, 152, 153, 186, 195, 196, 198
Public law, 28, 162
Public relations, 45, 87, 152, 186, 195, 196, 198, 283
Pull strategy, 187, 198
Purchasing, 5, 13, 54, 63, 72, 73, 76, 83, 97, 133, 134, 137, 144, 153, 154, 156, 162, 168, 170, 195, 198, 233, 238, 246, 283
Pure competition, see Competition, pure
Pure Food and Drug Act (1906), see Social responsibilities, Pure Food and Drug Act (1906)
Pure risk, 250, 251, 261
Push strategy, 187, 198
Put, 271

Q

Quality circle, 137
Quality control, 83, 86, 136, 137, 141
Quantity discount, 167, 168
Quasi-public corporation, 73, 78

R

Random sample, 205
Real property, 30, 31, 239
Recruiting, 69, 111, 112, 119
external, 112
internal, 112, 119
Regulatory law, see Government regulation
Reserve requirement, 237, 242
Resources, 3–6, 8, 9, 12, 16, 40, 44, 45, 53, 56, 57, 59, 70, 80, 81, 87, 90, 95, 97, 111–113, 117, 119, 131–134, 137, 138, 144, 159, 163, 173, 223, 224, 231, 243, 279, 290
availability of, 4
Retailer, 11, 81, 148, 150, 151, 156, 161, 165–168, 172–176, 178, 179, 185, 187, 195, 198, 244

Return on investment, 164, 205, 223
Revaluation, 55
  see also Devaluation
Revenues, 3, 16, 18, 21–23, 26, 53, 55, 73, 100, 115, 157, 159, 163, 191, 214, 215, 218, 219, 227, 244
  government's, 18, 21, 26, 55, 214, 227
Right-to-work laws, 123
Risk, 3, 4, 8, 59, 60, 80, 81, 83, 148, 156, 159, 175, 185, 195, 205, 214, 233, 234, 238, 239, 244, 247, 250–252, 254–257, 261–265, 270, 276, 284, 290
  credit risk, 175, 185
  insurable risk, 252
  (Continued)
  nature of, 60, 250, 261
    economic, 60
    political, 60
    pure risk, 250, 261
    speculative risk, 250, 261
  risk management, 250, 251, 254, 256, 261
    techniques of, 251, 261
      risk assumption, 251, 261
      risk avoidance, 251, 261
      risk reduction, 251, 261
      risk transfer, 251, 261
  uninsurable risk, 252
  see also insurance
Robinson-Patman Act (1936), see Economic systems, American, government regulation, antitrust legislation, Robinson-Patman Act (1936)
Round lot, 269

S

Salary, 5, 23, 35, 91, 115, 116, 119, 122, 125, 165, 202, 217, 219, 221, 238, 257, 261, 283, 284
Sales, 3, 7, 11, 20, 21, 22, 31, 34, 42, 48, 52, 55, 59, 69, 70, 71, 80, 83, 86–88, 98, 100, 103, 113, 115, 147–149, 151, 152, 158, 159, 162–164, 167, 168, 172, 173, 175–180, 185–187, 191, 193, 194, 196, 198, 201–207, 209, 210, 214, 215, 218, 219, 221, 223, 224, 238, 244, 263, 267, 273, 280, 282–284
  agent, 176
  budget, 224
  consultant, 178
  industrial, 193
  office, 175, 176
  orientation, 149
  outlets, 152
  promotion, 147, 152, 186, 194, 198
  representative, 34, 88, 151, 194, 204, 205, 221
  retail, 193
  revenues, 3, 100, 115, 163, 214, 215, 244
  statistics, 11
  taxes, 21, 22
  techniques, 151
  volume, 3, 152, 159, 164, 187, 198, 284
  see also Promotion, sales

Sample, 137, 152, 186, 195, 198, 203, 205, 212, 285
Savings account, 233, 242, 258, 265
Savings and loan association (S&L), 234, 254
Savings Association Insurance Fund, see Insurance, public insurance, other, Savings Association Insurance Fund
Scrambled merchandising, 177, 178, 185
Seasonal discounts, 168
Secondary data, 202, 212
Securities, 8, 10, 13, 22, 31, 39, 71–74, 78, 161, 208, 213, 214, 216–218, 221, 227, 235, 236, 239, 242, 246, 247, 249, 250, 254, 255, 261–274, 276, 284, 287
  bonds, 13, 22, 31, 39, 74, 161, 216, 218, 235, 236, 239, 242, 246, 247, 249, 250, 255, 262–268, 271, 273, 276
    company's view, 262
    corporate securities, 71, 72, 217, 249, 254, 262–267, 271, 273, 274, 276
    types of, 71, 72, 217, 249, 263–267, 271, 273, 274, 276
      bonds, 264–267, 276
        callable bonds, 265, 276
        convertible bonds, 264, 265, 267, 276
        debenture, 264, 276
          subordinated, 264, 276
        income bonds, 264, 276
        industrial development bonds, 264, 276
        junk bonds, 265, 266, 276
        mortgage bonds, 264, 276
        ratings, 265
          bond-rating services, 265
        serial bonds, 265, 276
        sinking-fund bonds, 265, 276
        subordinated debentures, 264, 276
        zero-coupon bonds, 265, 276
      common stocks, 72, 217, 249, 263, 266, 267, 273, 276
      mutual funds, 263, 267, 274, 276
        closed-end funds, 267
        investment goals, 267
        load and no-load funds, 267
        open-end funds, 267
      preferred stocks, 71, 249, 263, 266, 267, 271, 276
    exchanges, 73, 208, 267–271, 273, 274, 276, 284, 287
      American Stock Exchange (AMEX), 267, 268, 273

National Association of Securities Dealers Automated Quotation (NASDAQ), 268–271, 274
National Market System (NMS), 268
OTC stocks, 268–271, 274
  buying and selling securities, 269
  commission broker's role, 269
  orders and lots, 269
  specialist's role, 269
  stockbroker's role, 269
  trading tactics, 270
    buying on margin, 270
    options, 270, 271
      calls, 271
      puts, 271
    selling short, 270
    typical transaction, 270
Small Capital (Small Caps) Market, 268
New York Stock Exchange (NYSE), 208, 267, 268, 273
regional exchanges, 268
financial news, reading, 208, 268, 271–273, 276
  American Stock Exchange Value Index, 273
  bond prices, 271
  Dow Jones Composite Average, 272
  Dow Jones Industrial Average, 208, 272, 276
  Dow Jones Transportation Average, 272
  Dow Jones Utility Average, 272
  listed stocks, 271
  NASDAQ Composite Index, 273
  New York Stock Exchange Composite Index (NYSE Composite), 273
  Standard & Poor's Index (S&P 500), 273, 276
  stock averages, 271, 272
investor's view, 262
role of, 262
Securities and Exchange Commission (SEC), 213, 214, 218, 221, 227, 274, 276, 284
securities market, 8, 10, 72, 74, 78, 218, 221, 246, 254, 261–263, 266, 272, 276
  capital gains, 262, 276
  dividends, 8, 72, 74, 78, 218, 221, 246, 254, 261, 262, 266, 272, 276
  interest, 276
  primary, 263, 276
  role of, 262
  secondary, 263, 276
  see also Financial management, securities market
stocks, 22, 31, 39, 73, 216, 235, 239, 246, 250, 262, 263, 265–269, 271–274
  listed, 271

trading, regulation of, 273, 274, 276
  federal regulation, 273, 274, 276
    Securities Act (1933), 273
    Securities Exchange Act (1934), 274, 276
    other federal regulations, 274
      Federal Securities Act (1964), 274
      Investment Company Act (1940), 274
      Maloney Act (1938), 274
      Securities Investors Protection Act (SIPC, 1970), 274
  state regulation, 273
Scarcity, 4, 5
Selection, 83, 112, 113, 116, 133, 134, 147, 167, 202, 285
  customers' selection process, 202
  HRM selection policy, 113
  job opportunities, of, 285
  location, 83
  marketing channels, 147
  site, 133, 134
  staff, 112, 113
Selective distribution, 174, 185
Selling expenses, 219–221
Selling price, 8, 151, 160, 164, 165, 237, 267, 269
Selling short, 270
Serial bonds, 265, 276
Services, 3–6, 8, 9, 11–13, 16, 17, 20–23, 26, 27, 30, 40–44, 47, 53–55, 59, 72, 73, 78–83, 86, 88, 89, 94, 97, 104, 115, 124, 130, 131, 133, 137–141, 144, 147–149, 151, 152, 154, 156, 157, 163, 165, 168, 171–177, 179–182, 185, 186, 188, 191–193, 195, 196, 198, 202, 208, 213, 214, 218, 221, 227, 231, 233–236, 238, 239, 242, 245, 254, 262, 265, 268, 269, 271, 273, 279, 281–283, 285, 290
  characteristics, 139
    customization, 139
    customized, 139
    perishability, 139
  controlling, 141
  flow, 138
  high-contact services, 139–141
  low-contact services, 140, 141
  organizations, 89
  planning, 140
  production of, 131, 137–139, 141, 282
  productivity, 133
  public utility service, 73
  routing, 141
  scheduling, 140, 141
    fixed, 141
  sector, 11, 43, 138
  service business, 81, 86
  types of, 139
    automation, 139
    computerization, 139
    mechanization, 139
  see also Goods
  see also Production, services, of

Sherman Antitrust Act (1890), *see* Economic systems, American, government regulation, antitrust legislation, Sherman Antitrust Act (1890)
Shopping goods, 151, 156
Shop steward, 125
Short-range plan, 225
Sinking-fund bond, 265, 276
Situational leadership, 101, 102, 108
Small business, 3, 79–83, 86, 90, 246, 254
   advantage, 80
   disadvantage, 80
   government, and, 80, 82, 83, 86
     small business administration (SBA), 80, 82, 83, 86
      SBA loans, 82, 86
       direct, 82, 86
       guaranteed loans, 82, 86
       participation loans, 82, 86
      Small Business Investment Corporation (SBIC) loans, 82, 86
      SBA programs, 82, 83, 86
       Small Business Development Centers (SBDCs), 83, 86
   types of, 80, 81, 86
     cottage business, 80, 81, 86
     high-growth venture business, 80
     lifestyle business, 80
     niche business, 80
Social responsibility, 8, 17, 20, 21, 23, 26, 29, 32, 44–49, 52, 102, 108, 114, 116, 117, 119–124, 130, 162, 163, 239, 250, 251, 283
   areas of, 46
     environmental issues, 46
      laws protecting the environment, 46
       Chemical Safety Information, Site Security, and Fuels Regulatory Relief Act (1999), 46
       Clean Air Amendment (1970), 46
       Clean Air Amendment (1977), 46
       Comprehensive Environmental Response, Compensation, and Liability Act (or Superfund, 1980), 46
       Emergency Planning & Community Right-to-Know Act (1986), 46
       Food Quality Protection Act (1996), 46
       National Environmental Policy Act (1970), 46
       Noise Control Act (1972), 46
       Oil Pollution Act (1990), 46
       Pollution Prevention Act (1990), 46
       Resource Conservation and Recovery Act (1984), 46
       Resource Recovery Act (1970), 46
       Superfund Amendments and Reauthorization Act (1986), 46
       Water Pollution Control Act (amendment, 1972), 46
       Water Quality Improvement Act (1970), 46
   Clayton Act (1914), *see* Economic systems, American, government regulation, antitrust legislation, Clayton Act (1914)
   consumer issues, 8, 17, 20, 21, 26, 29, 32, 44–49, 52, 102, 108, 114, 116, 117, 119–124, 130, 162, 163, 239, 250, 251, 283
     appeal, right to, 29
     choose, right to, 8, 47, 52
     file suit, right to, 47
     form unions, right to, 123
     heard, right to be, 47, 52
     information, right to be, 47, 52
     know, right to, 46
     laws protecting the consumer, 47–49, 52, 116, 117, 119, 123, 162, 163, 239
      Age Discrimination in Employment Act (1967), 49, 52, 117, 119
      Child Protection and Toy Act (1969), 48
      Cigarette Labeling Act (1956), 48
      Civil Rights Act (Title VII, 1964), 47, 49, 117, 119
      Color Additives Amendment (1962), 48
      Consumer Product Safety Commission Act (1972), 48
      Credit Card Liability Act (1970), 48
      Drug Price Competition and Patent Restoration Act (1984), 48
      Equal Credit Opportunity Act (1974), 48
      Equal Credit Opportunity Act (amendment, 1976), 48
      Equal Pay Act (1963), 49
      Equal Pay Act (1973), 116, 119
      Executive Order 11246 (1965), 49
      Fair Credit Billing Act (1974), 48
      Fair Credit Reporting Act (1970), 239
      Fair Credit Reporting Act (1971), 48
      Fair Credit Reporting Act (2001), 48
      Fair Debt Collection Practices Act (1977), 48
      Fair Labor Standards Act (FLSA, 1938), 49, 117, 119, 123
      Fair Packaging and Labeling Act (1966), 48, 162
      Federal Hazardous Substances Labeling Act (1960), 48
      Flammable Fabrics Act (1967), 48
      Kefauver-Harris Drug Amendments (1962), 48
      Land Sales Disclosure Act (1968), 48
      Magnuson-Moss Warranty-Federal Trade Commission Act (1975), 48, 163
      Motor Vehicle Safety Act (1966), 48
      Occupational Safety and Health Act (OSHA, 1970), 49, 117, 119
      Orphan Drug Act (1985), 48
      Trade Regulation Rule (1972), 48
      Truth in Lending Act (1968), 48
      Vocational Rehabilitation Act (1973), 49
      Wholesome Meat Act (1967), 48
     organize, right to, 121, 122, 124, 130
     safety, right to, 17, 20, 21, 26, 32, 44–49, 52, 102, 108, 114, 117, 119, 120, 162, 250, 251, 283
   work, right to, 123
   employee issues, 23, 26, 47
     Equal Employment Opportunity Act (1972), 47
     Equal Employment Opportunity Commission (EEOC), 47
   evolution of, 44
   Interstate Commerce Act (1887), 44
   Pure Food and Drug Act (1906), 44
   Sherman Antitrust Act (1890), *see* Economic systems, American, government regulation, antitrust legislation, Sherman Antitrust Act (1890)
   strategies, 45, 52
     accommodation, 45, 52
     defense, 45, 52
     denial, 45, 52
     proactive, 45, 52
     reaction, 45, 52
Social Security system, *see* Government, role of, social security system
Socialism, *see* Economic systems, socialism
Software, 18, 82, 191, 195, 273
Sole proprietorship, 9, 67–70, 72, 78, 218, 246
Specialist, 114, 159, 269, 270, 282, 283
Specialization, 9, 10, 41, 53, 55, 88
Specialty store, 177, 179
Speculative risk, 250, 251, 261
Staffing, 111, 112, 119
State bank, 234, 236
Statement of cash flows, 216, 221, 222, 227
Statistics, 11, 203, 205, 212, 222
Statutory law, 27, 28, 39
Stock average or stock index, 271, 272
Stockbroker, 239, 269, 283
Stock insurance company, 254, 261
Stock split, 266
Strategy, 7, 8, 31, 32, 39, 48, 59, 72, 76, 80, 111, 127, 141, 147, 148, 151, 152, 154, 157–168, 170, 173, 174, 176–178, 185, 188, 189, 193, 216, 218, 219, 237, 242, 245, 246, 250, 251, 265, 269
   pricing, 7, 76, 111, 127, 141, 152, 158, 159, 164–168, 170, 173, 177, 178, 185, 218, 219, 237, 242, 245, 246, 265, 269
     existing products, 111, 152, 158, 159, 166, 167
     market price, 7, 127, 166, 167
     new-product, 166
     methods, 165, 166
      competition-based, 166
      cost-based, 165
       breakeven point, calculation of, 165
       determining markup and gross profit margin, 165
       determining total cost, 165
   objectives, 164, 170
     company image, 164, 170
     loss-containment and survival, 164, 170
     market-share, 164, 170
     profit-making, 164, 170
     social and ethical concern, 164
   tactics, 76, 141, 164, 167, 168, 173, 177, 178, 185, 218, 219, 237, 242, 245, 246, 265, 269
     discount pricing, 76, 141, 164, 167, 168, 173, 177, 178, 185, 218, 219, 237, 242, 245, 246, 265, 269
     multiple-unit pricing, 167
     prestige pricing, 167
     price lining, 167
     psychological pricing, 167
     threshold pricing, 167

Index

Strategy (Continued)
  product, 7, 8, 31, 32, 39, 48, 59, 72, 80, 111, 147, 148, 151, 152, 154, 157–164, 166, 167, 170, 174, 176–178, 188, 189, 193, 216, 246, 250, 251
    brands and branding, 7, 31, 32, 39, 48, 59, 163, 147, 151, 154, 158–162, 164, 167, 170, 177, 178, 188, 189, 193, 198, 202, 203, 216, 283
      brand loyalty, 158, 161, 162, 164, 170, 189
      brand mark, 160, 161
      brand name, 7, 59, 160–162, 177, 178, 188
      manager, 283
    packaging and labeling, 48, 162
    strategies, 162
      family, 162
      individual, 162
    trademark, 31, 39, 160, 216
    types of, 161
      generic, 161
      licensed, 161
      manufacturer (or producer), 161
      store (or private), 161
    warranties, 32, 39, 48, 163
      full, 163
      express, 32, 163
      implied, 32
      limited, 163
  new product development, 72, 80, 111, 147, 148, 152, 157–159, 162, 164, 166, 174, 189, 193, 246, 250, 251
  product differentiation, 7, 8, 157, 163, 166
  product life cycle, 158, 159, 166, 170, 189
    decline stage, 159, 170, 189
    extending, 159
    growth stage, 158, 170, 189
    introductory stage, 158, 166, 170, 189
    maturity stage, 158, 170, 189
  product line, 111, 157–159, 162, 170, 176
  product mix, 158, 162
Strike, 121–124, 126, 127, 130, 255, 257
Structure, Organizational, 87–92, 94
  centralized versus decentralized, 90
  delegation, role of, 90
    accountability, 90
    authority, 90
    responsibility, 90
  Herzberg's Motivation–Hygiene Theory, 91
  line and staff management, 89
  matrix organization, 89
  organization chart, 87, 88, 90, 92, 94
  organization within organization, 92

  organizational height, 90, 94
  span of management, 90
  specialization and departmentalization within, 88
  see also Formation and Structure, of business
Subsidiary, 73, 98
Supermarket, 138, 167, 177, 178, 185, 191, 195, 202, 239
Supply, 4, 6, 7, 11, 16, 17, 21, 26, 31, 43, 54, 73, 75, 78, 83, 94, 111, 112, 119, 126, 134, 135, 148, 149, 163, 171, 174, 175, 177, 180, 181, 193, 214, 233, 234, 236, 237, 239, 242, 262, 269, 271, 276
  chains, 75, 78, 171
  money, 233, 234, 236, 237, 239, 242
Survey, 152, 201–203, 212, 281, 284
Sustainability, 3–8, 18, 19, 21,23, 26, 29, 32, 34, 36, 40–42, 44, 45, 47, 49, 52, 54, 55, 60, 67, 69–76, 78–80, 83, 86–92, 94–105, 108, 111–117, 119–125, 130, 134, 136, 137, 140, 141, 144, 153, 159, 160, 180, 183, 188–191, 198, 201–205, 209, 213, 214, 224, 225, 227, 235, 243–245, 251, 253–258, 262, 261, 262, 266–268, 276, 282, 283, 285, 290
  economic, 40
  environmental, 3–8, 18, 19, 21,23, 26, 29, 32, 34, 36, 40–42, 44, 45, 47, 49, 52, 54, 55, 60, 67, 69–76, 78–80, 83, 86–92, 94–105, 108, 111–117, 119–125, 130, 134, 136, 137, 140, 141, 144, 153, 159, 160, 180, 183, 188–191, 198, 201–205, 209, 213, 214, 224, 225, 227, 235, 243–245, 251, 253–258, 262, 261, 262, 266–268, 276, 282, 283, 285, 290
    balance, need for, 41
    elements of, 7, 29, 32, 36, 41, 42, 113, 114, 134, 137, 140, 144, 180, 183, 201, 202, 214, 227, 245
    external stakeholders, 7, 29, 32, 42, 52, 72, 79, 86, 113, 114, 134, 137, 140, 144, 180, 183, 201, 202, 214, 227, 245
      clients, 42
      competitors, 42
      customers, 42
      financial institutions, 42
      government, 42
      labor unions, 42
      the media, 42
      special interest groups, 42
      suppliers, 7, 29, 32, 36, 41, 42, 52, 72, 79, 86, 114, 134, 137, 140, 144, 180, 183, 201, 202, 214, 227, 245
      vendors, 42, 113, 114

    internal stakeholders, 3–6, 19, 21, 23, 26, 34, 36, 40–42, 44, 45, 47, 49, 52, 55, 67, 69–76, 78, 80, 83, 86–92, 94–105, 108, 111–117, 119–125, 130, 136, 137, 141, 159, 188, 189, 191, 198, 201–205, 209, 213, 214, 224, 225, 227, 235, 243, 244, 251, 253–258, 261, 262, 266–268, 276, 282, 283, 285, 290
      directors, 19, 26, 34, 41, 42, 71–73, 78, 100, 125, 189, 191, 198, 254, 266, 276
      employees, 3–5, 21, 23, 26, 34, 36, 41, 42, 44, 45, 47, 49, 67, 69–72, 74, 78, 80, 83, 86–92, 94, 96, 100–104, 108, 111–117, 119–125, 130, 137, 202, 213, 235, 251, 253–258, 261, 285, 290
      managers, 4, 6, 40–42, 52, 55, 71, 72, 80, 88–91, 94–105, 108, 112–117, 119, 136, 137, 141, 159, 188, 201–205, 209, 213, 214, 224, 225, 227, 243, 244, 251, 257, 267, 276, 282, 283
      shareholders, 42, 44, 52, 72–76, 78, 262, 266, 268, 276
    forces of change, 8, 18, 42–44, 54, 60, 153, 159, 160, 190, 191
      economic variables, 42
        cyclical changes, 42
        structural changes, 42
      political variables, 44
      social variables, 8, 18, 42, 43, 54, 153, 160, 190, 191
        demographics, 18, 42, 43, 153, 190, 191
        lifestyles, 8, 42, 43, 54, 160
        social values, 42, 43
      technological variables, 43, 60, 159
        research and development (R&D), 43, 60, 159
  open versus closed systems, 40, 41
    closed system, 40, 41
    open system, 41
    the Systems Theory, 40, 41
  social responsibilities, see social responsibilities
Supply, 4, 6, 7, 11, 16, 17, 21, 26, 31, 43, 54, 73, 75, 78, 83, 94, 111, 112, 119, 126, 134, 135, 148, 149, 163, 171, 174, 175, 177, 180, 193, 214, 233, 234, 236, 237, 239, 242, 262, 269, 271, 276

  money supply, 233, 234, 236, 237, 242
  supply chain, 11, 75, 78, 171
  see also Economic forces, supply
  see also Demand
Syndicate, 73

T

Tall organization, 90, 91, 94
Target market, 150, 186, 190, 191, 198
Tariff, 9, 18, 22, 55–57, 63
Taxation, 18, 21–23, 26, 74, 76, 153, 257
  major taxes, 21, 22, 76, 153
    corporate income tax, 21, 22
    customs duties, 21, 22
    excise tax, 21, 22
    personal income tax, 21, 76
    property tax, 22, 153
    sales tax, 22
    value-added tax (VAT), 21, 22
  other taxes, 23, 26, 257
    estate and gift tax,
    social security tax, 23, 26, 257
    unemployment tax, 23, 26
      Federal Unemployment Tax Act (FUTA), 23, 26
Telemarketing, 193, 194, 198
Theory X, 103
Theory Y, 103
Time deposit, 233–235, 242
Time-series analysis or trend analysis, 209, 212
Time utility, 147, 148
Tort, 28, 29, 32, 33, 34, 39
Tort Law, see Business law, tort law
Trade, 9, 11–13, 18–21, 26, 28, 31, 36, 43–45, 48, 53–60, 63, 67, 73, 114, 148, 151, 160, 167, 168, 188, 192, 194, 195, 198, 244, 245, 249, 268–270, 272, 273, 282, 284, 285, 290
  associations, 36, 45, 58, 114, 188
  balance of, 12, 13, 54, 55, 57, 63
    trade deficit, 13, 54, 55, 63
    trade surplus, 13, 54, 63
  colonial, 9
  credit, 244, 245, 249
  discounts, 167, 168
  domestic, 9, 20
    interstate, 20
      Interstate Trade Commission (ICC), 20
  fair trade, 43
  Federal Trade Commission (FTC), 19, 26, 28, 44, 192, 194, 198
  Federal Trade Commission Act (1914), 19, 26, 28, 44, 192, 194, 198
  free trade, 55, 58
  groups, 188
  international, 9, 11, 12, 13, 19, 22, 36, 53–60, 63
    agreements, 56
      General Agreement on Tariffs and Trade (GATT), 56, 57, 63
      Kennedy round, 56
      Tokyo round, 56
    balance of payments, 54, 55, 63

Index

balance of trade, 12, 13, 54, 55, 57, 63
currency, 54–56, 58, 60, 63, 232–234, 236, 242
  exchange rates, 54, 55
    devaluation, 55
    international currency fluctuations, 60
    revaluation, 55
  foreign exchange control, 56, 63
  U.S. Comptroller of the Currency, 234
disputes, 63
European Free Trade Association (EFTA), 58
export, 9, 13, 54–56, 58, 59, 63
foundation of, 53
import, 13, 22, 54–56, 59, 60, 63
  import duties, 60
  import quota, 56, 63
Latin American Free Trade Association, 58
levels of involvement, 53, 59, 60, 63, 90
  direct investment, 59, 60
  exporting, *see* Trade, export
  international firms, 59, 60, 63
  international joint venture, 59
  licensing, 59
  multinational firms, 53, 59, 60, 63, 90
North American Free Trade Agreement (NAFTA), 58
specialization, 53, 55, 56, 58, 71
  absolute advantage, 53
  comparative advantage, 53
restriction on, 9, 55, 56, 63
  bureaucratic red tape, 56
  embargoes, 9, 56, 63
  foreign-exchange control, 56, 63
  import quotas, 56, 63
  tariffs and customs duties, 9, 22, 55–57, 63
  protective, 55, 63
  revenue, 55

see also General Agreement on Tariffs and Trade (GATT)
trade barrier, 56, 58, 60, 63
United Nations agencies, role in financing international trade, 57
  International Monetary Fund (IMF), 57
  World Bank, 57
journals and publications, 151, 284, 285, 290
Magnuson-Moss Warranty-Federal Trade Commission Act (1975), 48
  restrictions on, 55, 56
stocks and share trading, 268–270, 272, 273
trade practice rules, 192
Trade Regulation Rule (1972), 48
U.S./Canada Free Trade Agreement, 58
Trademark, 31, 39, 160, 216
  U.S. Patent and Trademark Office, 160
Trade secrets, 31, 34
Trade show, 195, 198
Trade surplus, 13, 54, 63
Transportation, 6, 9, 10, 18, 20, 32, 44, 54, 73, 87, 134, 138, 139, 141, 144, 148, 150, 152, 153, 156, 157, 174, 180–183, 202, 255, 272, 273, 276, 282
  Department of Transportation, 202
  industries and companies, 20, 273, 276
  means of, 138, 182, 255
    airfreight, 182
    pipelines, 20, 73, 182
    railroad, 10, 20, 139, 180–182, 255
      Federal Railroad Commission (FRC), 20
    ships, 32, 54, 87, 138, 174, 180–182, 255
    telecommunications, 182
    trucks, 150, 180, 182, 255
    water transport, 182

Transportation Average (Dow Jones), 272
Transportation and Utility Average (Dow Jones), 272

U

Unemployment, 12, 16, 23, 26, 116, 125, 202, 205, 209, 253, 261
  cyclical, 12, 16
  frictional, 12, 16
  insurance, 116, 253, 261
  seasonal, 12, 16
  structural, 12, 16
  tax, 23, 26
    Federal Unemployment Tax Act (FUTA), 23, 26
Uninsurable risk, 252
Union shop, 123, 125, 130
Unsecured loan, 245
U.S./Canada Free Trade Agreement, *see* International economic communities, U.S./Canada Free Trade Agreement
U.S. Comptroller of the Currency, 234
Utility, 7, 19, 26, 31, 73, 78, 131, 147, 148, 209, 272
  concept of, 147
  costs, 209
  stocks, 272
  utility companies, 7, 19, 26, 31, 73, 78
  utility of form, 131
  utility of place, 131, 147, 148
  utility of possession, 131, 147
  utility of time, 131, 147, 148

V

Value-added tax (VAT), 21, 22
Variable, 42, 43, 44, 91, 96, 108, 206, 209, 210
  economic, 42
  political, 44
  psychological, 96, 108
  social, 42, 96, 108
  technological, 43
Variable costs, 165
Vertical marketing system (VMSs), 173, 185
Vertical merger, 75, 78

W

Wages, 5, 6, 8, 13, 21, 23, 26, 35, 42, 44, 49, 52, 95, 102, 115–117, 119–123, 125, 127, 130, 206, 261, 283
Warehouse store, 177
Warehousing, 138, 173, 175, 180, 181, 185, 245
  distribution centers, 180
  private, 180
  public, 180, 245
Warranty, 32, 39, 48, 163
  express, 32, 39, 163
  full, 163
  implied, 32, 39
  limited, 163
  Magnuson-Moss Warranty – Federal Trade Commission Act (1975), 48, 163
  see also Commercial law, warranties
Wholesaler, 13, 59, 80, 81, 86, 148, 150, 156, 161, 168, 172–176, 185, 187, 198, 203, 244
  financial aid, 174
  market information, 174
  promotion assistance, 174
  service to manufacturers, 175
  service to retailers, 174
  types of, 175, 176, 185
    commission merchants, agents, brokers, 176
    full-service wholesalers, 175, 185
    merchant wholesalers, 175, 185
Workers' compensation, 116
World Bank, *see* Trade, international, agreements, United National Agencies, World Bank

Y

Yellow dog contract, 122

Z

Zero-based budgeting, 224, 225, 227
Zero-coupon bond, 265, 276

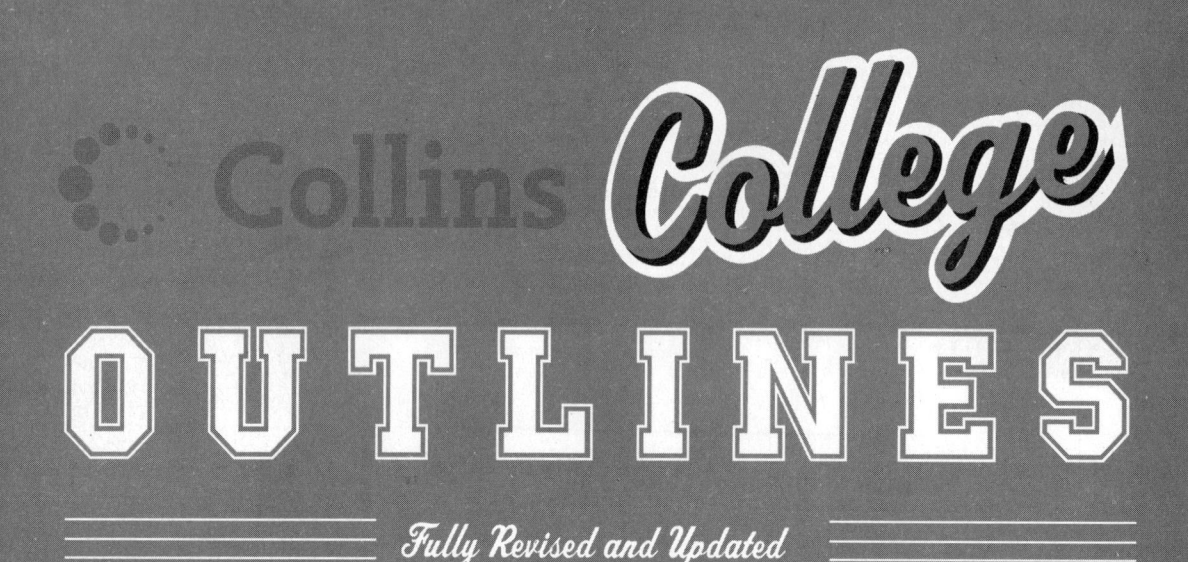

Collins College OUTLINES
Fully Revised and Updated

INTRODUCTION TO BUSINESS
H. James Williams
ISBN 978-0-06-088149-8 (paperback)

WESTERN CIVILIZATION FROM 1500
Ahmed Ibrahim and Walter Kirchner
ISBN: 978-0-06-088160-3 (paperback)

COLLEGE CHEMISTRY*
Drew H. Wolfe and Steven Boone
ISBN: 978-0-06-088147-4 (paperback)

COLLEGE BIOLOGY*
Marshall Sundberg
ISBN: 978-0-06-088161-0 (paperback)

BASIC MATHEMATICS
Lawrence A. Trivieri
ISBN 978-0-06-088146-7 (paperback)

INTRODUCTION TO CALCULUS
Joan Van Glabek
ISBN 978-0-06-088150-4 (paperback)

INTRODUCTION TO AMERICAN GOVERNMENT*
Larry Elowitz
ISBN 978-0-06-088151-1 (paperback)

INTRODUCTION TO PSYCHOLOGY*
Joseph Johnson and Ann L. Weber
ISBN 978-0-06-088152-8 (paperback)

MODERN EUROPEAN HISTORY
John R. Barber
ISBN 978-0-06-088153-5 (paperback)

ORGANIC CHEMISTRY
Michael Smith
ISBN 978-0-06-088154-2 (paperback)

UNITED STATES HISTORY TO 1877*
Light Cummins and Arnold M. Rice
ISBN 978-0-06-088159-7 (paperback)

WESTERN CIVILIZATION TO 1500
John Chuchiak and Walter Kirchner
ISBN 978-0-06-088162-7 (paperback)

ABNORMAL PSYCHOLOGY
Sarah Sifers
ISBN 978-0-06-088145-0 (paperback)

UNITED STATES HISTORY FROM 1865*
John Baick and Arnold M. Rice
ISBN 978-0-06-088158-0 (paperback)

ELEMENTARY ALGEBRA
Joan Van Glabek
ISBN 978-0-06-088148-1 (paperback)

SPANISH GRAMMAR
Ana Fairchild and Juan Mendez
ISBN 978-0-06-088157-3 (paperback)

***PERFECT FOR AP REVIEW**

Available wherever books are sold, or call 1-800-331-3761 to order.